A Natural Selection

A Natural Selection

WILDLIFE WRITINGS FROM THE CLEETHORPES CHRONICLE

BILL MEEK

To Sarah & Ross
Best wishes
Bill Meek

THE CHOIR PRESS

First published in the United Kingdom in 2018 by
The Choir Press

ISBN 978-1-911589-45-7

Contents

Introduction

This book brings together in one place all of the wildlife columns from the Cleethorpes Chronicle between April 2014 and the paper's demise in August 2017. In fact it does more than that – at the time of the Chronicle's final edition, several more pieces were finished but as yet unpublished. These are also included here, so even regular readers should find something new.

Right from the start I planned that these columns should build up into a portrait of the natural history of Cleethorpes and North East Lincolnshire, such that that if a layperson had any query about our local wildlife it would stand a fairly good chance of being answered somewhere among what I had written. In each column I set out to achieve three things: 1) to provide the reader with something he or she didn't already know, 2) to give examples from the local area, and 3) to encourage people to go out and get involved by doing something for themselves. Although I almost never achieved all three, I hope I never failed completely.

The natural history of Cleethorpes would seem a subject destined only for a small and specialised audience. Actually, I don't know why this should be so – the vast majority of natural history writing has a strong geographical element, and its appeal is scarcely lessened by the fact that one's own area isn't usually involved. Accounts of small and seemingly inconsequential places form much of the foundation of the natural sciences and environmental movement generally, and in any case, much of it is the same wherever you go.

It is a very interesting historical moment to be producing an account of our area's natural history. With the world's wildlife facing threats from climate change, habitat destruction and the movement of non-indigenous species around the globe, the forces for environmental good and evil are fascinatingly poised. Although the argument for the protection of the environment has been had and won, decision-makers still seem to treat the environment as a disposable luxury, or worse, an irritation, in the face of more immediate economic concerns. The environment is still all but invisible in election campaigns, and some politicians seem to get away with a level of disingenuousness and ignorance on the subject of the environment which on any other would almost certainly get them the sack.

Wildlife, of course, doesn't interest everybody. This is extraordinary really, as in geological terms we are animals only lifted from the wild in the last blink of an eye, whose connection with nature is tightly evolved into our every cell. Any attempt to improve the health and wellbeing of the nation without providing access to nature would seem destined to founder on this basic truth. Appreciation of what passes for the natural world these days is, of course, profoundly enhanced by a little knowledge, and the purpose of this book is to help with that in some small way.

One thing of which we can be certain is that the future of the natural world will not look like the present – things will change. There will always be some sort of wildlife to inspire, calm, heal and amaze people, but the species, numbers and ways of experiencing it will shift through time. This means that although much of the subject matter in this book is relatively well-prepared to survive posterity, some is very much 'of its time', and is certain to be quickly, if not already, superseded. In the end this may be the book's main legacy – to provide a brief and evocative snapshot of one small place's natural history in the context of changing times. I hope that if changes in our wildlife turn out to be predominantly for the worse, we note the irony, from this book and abundant other writings going back to the 1960s and beyond, that the problems were known all along, but not acted upon.

I tried as far as possible to make these short pieces relevant to the time of year in which they appeared in print. Odd subjects with no special seasonal relevance were scattered among the rest more or less at random. In order to impart some structure on this collection, I have decided not to place them in the order in which they were published, but to group them more logically by month of the year, irrespective of the year they first appeared.

At the time of publication, each of my columns was illustrated by a wonderful photograph which, as far as I could manage, would be donated from a local photographer. I need to extend thanks in particular to Don Davis, Colin Smale and Carole Crawford, who made contributions of really exceptional quality on a regular basis. I also need to thank Cleethorpes Chronicle owner Nigel Lowther who always gave me the freedom to write what I liked and, true to the forward-thinking and self-confident ethic of his paper, didn't seem too bothered about the odd strong opinion.

Bill Meek, September 2017

January

Our Town and its Wildlife. As a child I would look at picture books on wildlife and wonder why there were so many supposedly British creatures that didn't seem to be part of my everyday experience here in the fields and byways of Lincolnshire. Stag Beetles and fritillary butterflies, eagles, polecats and giant bush-crickets, sundews, Salmon and Strawberry Trees. Early on, I concluded that I must live in a relatively dull part of the country for nature, and living here I would have to be content with a much more mundane subset of Britain's flora and fauna. With the benefit of hindsight it is worth revisiting the question – as a county, how does North East Lincolnshire compare with other parts of Britain in terms of its wildlife?

The most basic division of the natural environment in Britain is into the hilly, wet, pastoral north and west, and the lowland, dry, arable south and east. The 'divide' between the two runs very approximately on a diagonal from the River Severn in the south to Flamborough Head in the north, placing us here in North East Lincolnshire near the northern tip of the 'southern' type. This southern region generally tends to be richer in warmth-loving creatures, including a generally good representation of insects and reptiles, although here, close to its northern limit, these groups tends to be a little less diverse.

As far as insects go, this situation is changing, as many charismatic species are extending their range northwards with increasing summer temperatures. We have gained many colourful insects in recent decades, including several dragonflies and butterflies, Britain's largest resident moth, and our first bush-crickets.

Special wildlife tends to live in special places. Here in North East Lincolnshire we have no mountains, bogs or heaths. Our small and recently-created county extends a short distance into the chalk Wolds, although little indigenous chalk habitat remains, and in any case the northern chalk is very much a poor relation to that in the south. Apart from that, we sit upon rich but unexceptional soils, which like everywhere, suffer from the ill-effects of agricultural fertilisation. Once fertilised, a piece of ground is rarely the same again, with any relaxation of management leading to domination by common, aggressive weeds and their ubiquitous attendant animals.

Ancient woodland is uncommon in northern Lincolnshire generally, although in Bradley and Dixon Woods we have a valuable fragment.

The jewel among North East Lincolnshire's wildlife habitats is undoubtedly its coastline. The diversity of life here is a result of two strong gradients: firstly from landward to seaward one passes in a very short distance from urban areas, sometimes built patchily on old, drained outmarsh fields, through old dunes and slacks, to saltmarsh, to newer dunes, to mudflat to the marine environment itself – all habitats with a strong degree of 'naturalness'. Along the other axis, we pass from docks and industrial land with their suite of exotic aliens, through the towns proper, through miles of sandy 'edgeland' to the beginnings of untamed estuarine wilderness. Along our coast we see probably the best area of similar size for plant species-richness in the whole of Lincolnshire, with many rarities.

The east coast generally has abundant marine life, including fish, seals, porpoises and other 'cetaceans'. 'Falls' of rare birds occur in autumn. For all of these things, however, our position slightly within the estuary mouth is a disadvantage. Not so for our migratory waterbirds, which gather in large numbers to take advantage of the phenomenal productivity of the Humber's sediments. These birds have international recognition and protection for both numbers and diversity. From a wildlife point of view, these coastal riches are definitely our area's 'claim to fame'.

Ducks. Everybody knows a duck when they see one. Having plenty of water, North East Lincolnshire is blessed with more than its fair share of sorts.

Ducks fall into several natural groupings which are not particularly closely-related. Some of the similarities are probably a result of 'convergent evolution' – that is to say, they have developed similar features owing to the fact that they share the same aquatic lifestyle.

The most obvious division among the ducks is between the so-called 'dabbling' ducks and the 'diving' ducks. Dabbling ducks are those which 'up-end' when they feed, so that their bottoms stick out of the water. For this behaviour they are equipped with slightly smaller, more centrally placed legs and feet than the diving ducks. They also have longer wings, enabling them to take off almost vertically in an emergency, albeit with a fair amount of splashing.

This group includes the common old Mallard, but also in our area wild birds such as Pintail, Wigeon, Shoveler, Teal and Garganey. The males of these species in breeding dress are some of the most stunningly-plumaged of all birds when seen well.

In contrast, diving ducks are those which dive completely beneath the surface and swim underwater for their food. This group can feed in much deeper water, and for this purpose they have larger webbed feet, placed much further back on the body. They tend to have shorter wings, so cannot become airborne without a run-up along the surface of the water. In our area the common Tufted Duck and ever-decreasing Pochard are in this category. Another, the Scaup, may be occasionally seen.

You would think that a duck swimming underwater in winter would find it impossible to stay warm. In fact, when these ducks dive they trap a thick layer of air within their feathers, and it is this that insulates them. But this in turn gives diving ducks the problem of extreme buoyancy, and while underwater they have to work furiously to keep themselves down there. When they rise back to the surface, which they do simply by ceasing to paddle, small diving ducks like Tufted Ducks must spread their feet near the surface to stop themselves shooting straight out of the water.

An additional problem is that the increased water pressure as a duck descends squeezes the layer of trapped air so it becomes thinner the deeper the duck dives. This means that diving too deep can make ducks lose body heat very rapidly. In addition, always a little air escapes from the feathers as bubbles. This is why, after a short series of deep dives, diving ducks will stay at the surface for a while to warm up again, occasionally standing up in the water and flapping their wings to replenish the lost insulating layer of air.

There is a third important sub-family of ducks: the 'sea ducks', although some are by no means exclusively maritime. These also dive for their food, and include such shy inhabitants of larger lakes and open sea as the Common and Velvet Scoters, Long-tailed Duck, Smew, Goldeneye and Eider. All of these may be seen in North East Lincolnshire at various times. Also included in this group are the two large 'sawbills', the Goosander and Red-breasted Merganser.

These two species may not be immediately recognisable as ducks, their bills being long, thin and serrated. This is an adaptation for catching and holding onto small fish during underwater dives. Goosander is a fairly regular visitor to the lake in Cleethorpes Country Park, while Merganser may occasionally be seen on the sea.

This just leaves a small, miscellaneous group of ducks within our British fauna which occupy branches of their own on the family tree. The large, mostly-white Shelduck, which is a common sight on the saltmarsh at Cleethorpes, is a kind of halfway house between ducks and geese. The small Ruddy Duck, which belongs to a grouping known as 'stiff-tails' is subject to an eradication programme in Britain at the moment and is now very unlikely to be seen. The evolutionary affiliations of the large, feral Muscovy Ducks we see on the Boating Lake, and the extravagantly-plumaged Mandarin and Wood Ducks which occasionally pop up in the wild, are obscure and still to be worked out with certainty.

First Flowers of the Year. Have you seen a flowering Snowdrop yet? Or Daffodil? Is spring early or late this year? The study of the timing of events in nature is known as 'phenology'. The commonest kind of phenological data collected are indeed 'firsts' in spring; Cuckoo, Swallow, Snowdrop, etc. For centuries this kind of information has been recorded as a curiosity by interested gardeners and naturalists. Nowadays however, it has an additional use – as a vital source of evidence as to how our wildlife is responding to climate change. Warmer springs are said to lead to earlier events. First flowering of Snowdrops, for example, is thought to advance an average of 3 days for every 1^0C increase.

Some organisms are more useful than others in this respect. Some plants, for example, can flower in any month, like Chickweed, Daisy or Gorse, so these are of limited use. Others, while in flower at the New Year, are merely hangers-on from last year's summer season, such as late-flowering Hogweed, Charlock or Yarrow.

A small number of genuine winter-flowering species are our own UK natives, such as Hazel (whose catkins are sometimes called 'lamb's-tails'), Lesser Celandine and Coltsfoot. However, among our winter flowers there is a strong bias towards non-natives, for the simple reason that such plants were purposely brought here to provide early colour in our dreary winters. Snowdrops, Winter Aconites, Crocuses, garden Daffodils and Cyclamen, for example, all have their ancestral homes in the hills and mountains of the Mediterranean and Middle East, but can now be used perfectly well in the UK to measure the timing of events in spring.

Locally, 2015 already looks like being the earliest spring in recent times. Snowdrop flowers are traditionally thought of as being the first botanical sign of spring, but actually this honour should go to the lesser-known Winter Heliotrope, which I saw blooming at the beginning of December in Covenham village. Its white flowers have a purple tinge and smell of vanilla, and the plant forms large clonal patches along roadsides. For an easily-located example, look opposite the Ice Cream Shop at Brigsley or along the entrance road to the new Par 3 development in Humberston. Snowdrop itself was extremely early this year, blooming even before the New Year in Tetney, and by 2nd January in Barnoldby-le-Beck and Grainsby. Similarly, Winter Aconite was in flower on an extremely advanced 1st January in Cleethorpes. The dangling lambs'-tails of Hazel were also shedding pollen before the New Year, and by January 3rd at least four Daffodils flowered by the roadside in Barnoldby-le-Beck. In some years these very same yellow flowers do not appear until mid-March.

Nothing, of course, can be read into the events of a single year – climate change is about trends over the long-term. While there have been some very warm years since the millennium, there is considered to be no recognised trend in the timing of spring events over this period. It remains to be seen whether the current extremely early year will affect this. When the whole twentieth century is included in the calculation, the trend towards earlier springs is readily apparent, and this has been widely cited by scientists as being among the most visible manifestations of global warming.

There is now a small army of volunteers recording spring 'firsts' and other phenological events in the UK, and anyone can get involved.

Winter Wagtail Roosts. There are rather few British wild birds which would preferentially head for the centres of our towns and cities. The Peregrine could be said to be one, with some nesting on city buildings and spending their lives above the streets, feeding mainly on pigeons. The familiar Starling can be another. Another is the Waxwing, whose winter flocks, in 'irruption' years, may appear anywhere there are ornamental berries in abundance – most often municipal plantings in towns. And there is another, which not only shares our population centres, but is also an exclusively British bird – the Pied Wagtail.

Once known, the explosive "chizzick" call of the Pied Wagtail is regularly heard overhead, and often alerts you to the presence of the species on the ground. When seen, Pied Wagtails may be immediately known by their black and white head pattern, characteristic jerky walk, and habit of constantly wagging their long tails. They have fine-tipped bills, and survive by taking insects which are too small for other ground-feeding birds to bother with – one of the secrets of their success.

Everywhere else in this wagtail's huge range, which stretches right across Eurasia to Alaska, other, paler subspecies are the norm, known collectively as 'White Wagtail'. The male of our own Pied Wagtail has a smart black back, and even the females are darker than their cousins abroad. I have heard of foreign delegates at an international bird conference rushing to the window to watch a male Pied Wagtail on the lawn outside; although entirely commonplace to us, it is something that can be seen only rarely on parts of the nearest Continent, or here in Britain.

During the daytime, Pied Wagtails can be found literally anywhere, but are especially likely to be seen on playing fields and lawns, in the vicinity of water, or around farmyards, where tiny insects are always plentiful.

They nest in almost any suitable cavity, from buildings and dry stone walls to drainpipes and farm machinery.

For some reason this characterful small bird has never captured the public imagination like the Robin, Blackbird or Magpie. This is strange because not only is it uniquely British, but it is hugely charismatic for its size, often quite tame, and ubiquitous in town and country alike.

The Pied Wagtail's most interesting habit is its tendency to form large winter roosts in public places in towns and cities. The reason for communal roosting is basically to share warmth and information. When birds leave in the morning, the best places to feed can be discovered simply by following those birds which leave purposefully and seem to be in the best condition.

Pied Wagtails roost in trees, but unusually seem to prefer places which are both well-lit and populated by people. There are probably two reasons for this – firstly for safety, as there is an unwillingness for their predators to enter such places. Also, town centres tend to be a degree or two warmer than the open countryside, which can mean life or death to such a small bird.

At around dusk in winter, Pied Wagtails may start to gather in ones, twos or small groups, in traditional stands of trees in town centres, or the car parks of places like supermarkets, filling stations, leisure centres and hospitals. As their numbers build, their distinctive calls will ring out, as they seem to call others to them. In some places, hundreds, or even thousands of wagtails can congregate by the time night falls.

Having been alerted by noisy incoming birds at dusk, an upward glance into trees in town car parks during the darkness of midwinter can sometimes reveal scores of roosting wagtails, adorning the branches like Christmas decorations or unseasonal fruit. This is a true winter wildlife spectacle in the heart of the town.

Urban Foxes. There have always been foxes in the Cleethorpes area. However, there can be no doubt at all that they have become both more numerous and bolder. Nowadays the sight of apparently fearless foxes sharing our streets and gardens is an everyday occurrence.

Foxes first started coming into cities in the late 1930s, when they became regular in Bristol and London. Other cities followed, and slowly the urban habit took hold across the country.

Although 'canids' and therefore relatives of dogs, foxes can seem strangely cat-like, with their elongate, vertical pupils and retractable claws. Foxes are omnivorous, and will eat almost anything, from beetles and berries, earthworms and spiders, to carrion and live prey. Their well-documented sprees of surplus killing when faced with captive animals may be an adaptation to an irregular supply of food, the intention being to cache the excess for leaner times. However, some have suggested that this behavior simply represents over-stimulation when a fox encounters multiple prey items which do not run away – a situation which would almost never occur in nature.

Although foxes have had to endure much cruelty at the hands of humans over the years – for sport, for the protection of domestic animals and for the fur trade – most people are broadly welcoming of foxes in towns. Although they may very occasionally take pets such as rabbits, guinea pigs and chickens which are not securely caged, or rummage through the odd bin bag, there are still plenty of people who welcome foxes into their gardens, taking pleasure from a meeting with a truly wild animal, and even feeding them kitchen scraps.

Foxes tend to shy away from humans and larger animals, only ever attacking out of fear. They tend to be nervous of domestic cats, and although cat fur has been periodically found in fox droppings, some think that cats are only eaten as carrion after a road kill. Really close encounters between foxes and humans tend to occur only where foxes are fed by people.

Town foxes are exactly the same as country foxes – indeed some animals may commute between one habitat and the other. Leafy suburbs are the preferred breeding places for urban foxes, as larger gardens provide hiding places during the day, and sheds and other outbuildings under which they can build their 'earths'.

Although they have become more apparent, we are very unlikely to become overrun with foxes, as their populations are thought to be strongly self-regulating. The last population estimate in the 1980s assessed the UK urban fox population at about 33,000 animals, some 10,000 of those in London. This is thought to have remained broadly stable ever since, although numbers can be periodically depleted by outbreaks of mange – an unpleasant disease, invariably fatal for the fox, caused by the same mite which causes scabies in humans.

Foxes breed once a year, usually producing a litter of four or five, but rarely up to thirteen cubs. They mate in deepest winter, and it is at this time that foxes most impinge on our consciousness with their nocturnal vocalisations. Foxes have a varied repertoire of calls, but the most commonly heard is a *"wow wow wow"* when animals approach each other. A characteristic midwinter sound is a repeated far-carrying scream given out by the vixen to indicate she is ready to mate.

You may hear some people suggest that a cull of urban foxes is needed, or that foxes should be trapped and returned to the countryside. In fact culls do not work, as foxes breed rapidly, and vacated territories are quickly re-occupied. Foxes returned to the countryside may suffer at the hands of foxes already there, or simply come straight back.

Fox. Photo: Don Davis

We ought to be inspired by encounters with wild animals. But if you really don't like foxes there are simple ways to discourage them from using your garden. Prickly plants or tall fences may deter them, and both sonic and smell-based fox deterrents are available. Prevent access under sheds, so they can't build an earth there. Keep rabbit and guinea pig hutches secured with welded mesh, not chicken wire. And most importantly, keep bins and composters tightly shut, and never leave dog bones or other potential food out overnight.

Starfish wrecks. In January 2013, Cleethorpes beach became the subject of national news as thousands of dead starfish washed up dead on the shore. The winding trail of dead animals stretched the length of the resort, sending bemused walkers out to examine the sad scene and take photographs for posterity.

In fact, this is not an uncommon occurrence – the same happens quite regularly on other parts of the British coastline – indeed the same thing occurred here at Cleethorpes just a year before that in 2012, and on numerous other occasions going back through the years. I remember seeing truly huge numbers – hundreds of thousands – of starfish piled up in a broad strip on Cleethorpes's main holiday sands twenty or more years ago, again in winter.

The obvious question is: why does this happen? Some catastrophe befalls the poor animals, but what? On such occasions it is common for news reports to try to create a story where there isn't one. Contrary to what you may sometimes read, scientists are not really "baffled". The starfish have not stranded *themselves* as whales sometimes do, although their unexplained tendency to roll up in a ball when buffeted by currents might leave them more susceptible to being washed up. No devastating starfish plague is the cause of death, although such plagues exist. The truth is they have simply been dislodged or washed from soft substrate or from their feeding grounds, and deposited up the shore by winter storms – there is probably no more to it than that. The clue to this is the abundant inanimate accompaniment of empty fish egg cases and shells, especially razor shells.

A single species makes up the overwhelming majority of the dead creatures – the Common Starfish *Asterias rubens*. Not only is this an extremely abundant creature which can occur in intertidal, as well as subtidal waters, but unusually it can tolerate slightly brackish water, and therefore finds a home within the mouth of our estuary. The colour in life varies from light brown or pinkish to a delicate violet, but dead animals may turn a striking orange. The species is identified by its rough upper surface and single row of short, white spines down the centre of each limb.

In life, Common Starfish are predators. Although feeding on a range of other sea creatures, their favourite food is bivalve molluscs, especially mussels. They will attach themselves to the mussel and use suction to prize a small opening between the animal's two shells – maybe as little as 0.1mm, then evert their stomachs through their mouths (like turning a pocket inside out) and into the gap between the valves, and begin digesting the mussel inside.

Radial symmetry, while common in the world of plants and fungi, in the animal kingdom is only found among the creatures of the sea; basically jellyfish relatives and starfish relatives (although starfish are evolved from bilaterally-symmetrical ancestors – a trait still apparent in their larvae). This unusual body form makes starfish one of the earliest animals that children learn to recognise. It is amazing that they strike such a chord when you consider most children's lack of regular access to the sea. But here in Cleethorpes we may see literally millions of starfish in our lifetime if we walk the beach after storms often enough.

A good search of our beach's starfish wrecks may turn up other, related echinoderms – I have found the many-rayed Common Sun-star, *Crossaster papposus* and smooth, purple *Henricia* among the heaps of dead *Asterias rubens*, and reports from elsewhere suggest that Brittle-stars and Heart Urchins may also turn up. In the past I have been guilty of not looking hard enough for other marine creatures in these strandings, but as the phenomenon will undoubtedly reoccur, I'm sure I will get my chance.

Ravens. Ravens are one of those birds you can never get tired of watching. They are Europe's largest perching birds, highly intelligent and resourceful, easily tamed, and superb fliers. They have an enormous world range, occupying almost the whole of the northern hemisphere from the deserts of the Middle East to the Arctic, from below sea level to the tops of high mountains, occupying almost any habitat. So why do we not see them here in North East Lincolnshire?

In fact they were widespread all over Britain, including Lincolnshire, until the early 1800s, often performing a valuable service by consuming human waste in cities and towns. After this the Raven underwent a catastrophic decline due to persecution by gamekeepers and farmers, not helped by the popularity of egg-collecting and a demand for Raven chicks for domestication as pets. The Raven's range in Britain quickly retreated to the remoter uplands of the north and west, and the last breeding attempt in Lincolnshire before they were lost was in about 1860.

However, with a relaxation in persecution and a degree of protection now afforded the species by EU law, the Raven is again on the march eastwards back into its old strongholds. Ravens are now relatively common again throughout the midlands of England, being absent only from a strip of land broadly equating to the counties of the English east coast. In fact there has been a single breeding site for Raven in Lincolnshire for several years now, near Grantham – but that is all we have.

Ravens have a very varied, but mostly animal diet. They are well able to catch and kill small animals for themselves, but they would much rather feed on carrion, their main food source. They nest early in the year in inaccessible spots in trees, on buildings, quarries, cliffs and sometimes pylons, favouring hilly districts. For this reason, it may transpire that Ravens never fully reoccupy North East Lincolnshire, with its flat, manicured and almost exclusively arable landscape. Ravens however would seem likely to become much more frequent as a casual visitor to our area in the future. None has been seen yet, but already this winter Ravens have been spotted close by at North Thoresby and Louth, and a few sightings have also been made in the Wolds. In Cambridgeshire to the south, Ravens are already relatively frequent non-breeding visitors in much the same kind of country as we have in Lincolnshire.

A Raven is likely to be heard before it is seen. Its loud, harsh croaking call is much deeper than that of other crows, and should immediately elicit a glance to the skies. Ravens are large, being longer in all their parts even than a Buzzard, so if there is any doubt as to whether a bird is a Raven based on size, it probably isn't. They are rangier in shape than other crows, with a thick bill, shaggy throat feathers and a slightly wedge-shaped tail. Their flight can be very varied – on hot days Ravens can soar much like raptors, but more usually their direct flight contains noticeable playfulness, and occasionally a Raven will do a full sideways roll in the air.

So who will be the first person to see a Raven in North East Lincolnshire? The day can't be far away.

Update:
In 2017 a pair of Ravens bred in the Lincolnshire Wolds. So getting closer!

Tides. Last week's flood warnings in Cleethorpes made us more aware of the tides and their direction of travel down the east coast of England. Even when not threatening us with inundation, here in North East Lincolnshire the tides are part of our daily life. They dictate the entry and departure of shipping from our ports, and cause drastic and continuous changes to the appearance of our coastline. They create great swathes of habitat for both our estuary wildlife and our holidaymakers.

Almost nothing about the study of tides turns out to be simple, but one thing we all know is that they are caused primarily by the gravitational pull of the moon. In fact, this should probably be more accurately described as water being squeezed towards an imaginary Earth-moon line, which has the effect of creating tidal bulges simultaneously on *both* sides of the Earth; that is, on the side facing, *and* the side facing away from, the moon. So if the moon was fixed in the sky, there would be a permanent bulge of water on the side of the Earth facing the moon, and another on the exact opposite side of the globe. The areas in between, at right angles to the moon's pull, would have permanent troughs.

But the Earth is of course spinning, once every twenty-four hours. The moon orbits the Earth in the same direction that the Earth spins, but much more slowly – once every twenty-eight days. So it actually takes twenty-four hours and fifty minutes for the moon to come back to the same place overhead, and half that, twelve hours and twenty-five minutes, for one high tide to be replaced by the next (remembering the bulge on the opposite side). That extra twenty-five minutes means that high tide on any one day is an average of fifty minutes later than the equivalent one the day before.

All this assumes an idealised spherical planet entirely covered by water of equal depth. In reality, of course, there are land-masses in the way with irregular coastlines, as well as dramatic sea-floor topography – oceanic ridges, shelves, trenches and the like. In addition, the Coriolis effect acts to throw moving water to one side, which makes tidal water move around the Earth in sweeping curves rather than straight lines, sometimes leading to gyre-like swirls called 'amphidromic points'. These swirls experience minimal tidal rise and fall at their centres, but effects become more dramatic as you pass outwards.

It is not just the moon that exerts a gravitational pull on the Earth, but also the sun. Although much larger, the sun is also much further away, and its pulling power is a little under half that of the moon. When the sun and moon are in alignment, at new moon and full moon, the two forces reinforce each other, and tides are higher. These are known as spring tides, although they have nothing to do with spring, the season. The highest spring tides occur when the moon is closest to the Earth in its orbit.

Similarly when the pull of moon and sun are at right angles to one another, the tides are less high. These are neap tides. On top of all this, further variations in tide height are caused by factors like air pressure, winds and natural currents.

When tides hit shallow water and convoluted coastlines such as we have here in the British Isles, all sorts of complexity arises. The shape of our coastlines, especially narrow channels, can considerably increase the vertical range of the tide.

Suffice it to say that here in the UK, our twice-daily tidal bulge arrives with us from out in the Atlantic to the south-west. The first land it hits is the coast of south-west Ireland. Here the waterbody splits in two, with half travelling northwards, up and around Scotland, with a minor sub-branch entering the northern part of the Irish Sea. The other travels eastwards, where it is soon split again by Land's End, from there travelling both northwards up the Irish Sea, and further south along the English Channel coast. High tide hits Dover about the same time as the tides entering the Irish Sea from north and south meet at Liverpool.

Meanwhile, the tidal bulge which travelled northwards has now rounded the top of Scotland and is starting to make its way back down the North Sea and towards the east coast of England. This bulge of water, travelling basically anti-clockwise around the shallow basin of the North Sea, gives us our high tide here in Lincolnshire, arriving here more than twelve hours after it first hit southern Ireland. Indeed it takes *another* six hours after that to reach Dover (via the complication of a small amphidromic point in the southern North Sea), where it is by now so late that it mixes with the southern half of the *next* high tide.

Some ports have tidal idiosyncrasies that work in their favour. For example at Southampton, water travelling one side of the Isle of Wight gets there quicker than that travelling the other way round, giving it a sort of double high tide. This allows shipping to use the port for more hours in a day than other places. Similarly, Weymouth has a double low tide.

For beach safety, it is worth remembering that the highest tides are also those which go out the furthest, meaning that the tide may come in extremely quickly if it has been out a long way. The period exactly in between low and high tides is when it is moving the fastest.

As a general rule, it is always best to go out on the beach on a falling tide.

New Year Plant Hunt. The fieldwork is now over for the Botanical Society of Britain and Ireland's fifth annual 'New Year Plant Hunt'. For the second year in a row, results have defied expectations and made national news.

The New Year Plant Hunt is another one of those bits of 'citizen science', in which anyone can take part. The idea was simply to set aside up to three hours on any day between the 1st and 4th of January 2016, and see how many wild plants you could find *in flower* in your local area. Only native and naturalised species count, so nothing in gardens or municipal plantings could be included.

According to the books, in the UK there should be about twenty or thirty species of plant flowering at New Year. A few of these will be the earliest plants of the coming spring – naturalised garden bulbs, Hazel catkins and the like. Others will be annuals of waste ground – opportunist flowerers, capable of blooming and seeding at any time of year, such as Chickweed and Shepherd's Purse. But there will also be some of last summer's meadow and wayside plants clinging on to their final blooms before they're killed off by the frosts of winter. This means that if the first half of the winter is very mild, the number of plants in flower should be higher. This climatic element is where the science comes in.

Last year, New Year 2015, followed one of the warmest early winters on record, and the results astounded everyone, with no fewer than 368 species of plant found in flower nationwide. This is a whopping 15% of our entire British flora. A year later, the last months of 2015 were again extremely mild, with no more than the odd touch of frost leading up to the New Year. Once more the numbers of species in flower at the start of 2016 were amazingly high, with no less than 612 recorded across the country.

As you might expect, the warm, damp south-west of Britain produced many of the highest scores. By contrast, in Scotland, just a handful of species was the norm, although the warmer, weedier city centres scored a little higher. Here in cold, dry Lincolnshire we tended to fall somewhere between the two extremes. The most-recorded flowers nationwide are always similar from year to year, with Daisy, Dandelion and Groundsel consistently comprising the 'top three'.

My own efforts this year centered on the Meridian Showground in Cleethorpes on the morning of New Year's Day. Only wild or naturalised plants counted, so I couldn't include the planted Snowberry or Laurustinus provided by the council, or the ornamental Wallflower blooming alongside the mini-railway.

After a couple of hours I clocked up a respectable 26 flowering species, with a further two, Henbit Deadnettle and Clustered Mouse-ear, showing some colour in their buds, but not strictly 'out'. Three species, Mexican Fleabane, Greater Periwinkle and Spanish Broom were only dubiously wild, but certainly naturalised, so they went on the list. The rest were either opportunist annuals of waste ground, or perennials clinging on from the previous summer.

The 'best' species were Hare's-foot Clover found growing on the sand dunes – a charismatic little plant with 'furry'-looking flowerheads, great to see at any time of year – and the yellow Hoary Mustard, also on the dunes. The latter is an uncommon alien species spreading strongly in the wild, which has been present at Cleethorpes now for several years.

Although it has a serious side, the count's main aim is really to recruit people to nature, conservation and the environmental cause. It brings beginners and experts together, inspiring and educating people on the subject of our wild flora, and it is great PR for the Society. Most of all, it's a bit of fun, getting people to think and learn about flowers at this darkest and most colour-starved time of year.

So don't miss the next New Year Plant Hunt – it's a great excuse to get some fresh air after the excesses of Christmas. In the meantime there's more citizen science coming up at the end of January, as we see the return of the RSPB's Big Garden Birdwatch. If you want to take part, visit the RSPB online to request details.

Wildlife and Roads. Nowadays we have become inured to the slaughter of wildlife on our roads. It is not nice to see, but we just think it can't be helped.

There are many reasons why wildlife may actually be attracted to roads. Where roads pass through woodland, larger animals may treat them like rides. Bats may use them as feeding corridors, and insects may take advantage of the well lit 'edge habitat' they create.

Where roads cross open countryside, vehicles kill astronomical numbers of insects, which are then scavenged from the tarmac by insect-eaters such as Hedgehogs and small birds. Birds may also use the road surface for dust-bathing, drinking from puddles, feeding on spilt grain, or simply warming up, in the process putting themselves at risk. Pheasants and Rabbits living on the grass verges may stray out onto the tarmac and be killed. These in turn all provide food for crows, Magpies, Foxes, Stoats and Badgers which, when hit by cars, become the largest and most obvious animal casualties.

The number of animals killed on roads is many times higher than the visible 'corpse count' would suggest. Fast-moving cars may launch animals into the verge where they are never found. Injured animals may be able to drag themselves off to the nearest cover before dying. Many dead animals are just too small to be noticed, or may be scavenged so quickly by birds of prey (which may also use roadside poles as lookout perches), that they are hardly ever seen. So rich are roads as a source of fresh carrion that the spread of Buzzards and Red Kites into new areas has undoubtedly been facilitated by the supply of roadkill.

Roadkill is the only way most of us have of seeing many mammals which are otherwise very shy. The only Otters I have seen in England were dead on roads. The spread of the Polecat eastwards out of its stronghold in the Welsh borders, and also that of the Muntjac from south-east to north-west in the UK, are best measured by recording their occurrence as roadkill. Ironically, if a species seems to be being killed more often than usual, it can actually indicate that local populations are doing well. Otters and Badgers provide a good example of this.

For some animals, roads pose a different kind of problem: by acting as barriers to dispersal. Some species show a marked reluctance to cross roads, and others, such as amphibians returning to their breeding ponds, may do so, but are too slow to avoid traffic and are frequently run over. As a result, the countryside for these species is effectively divided up into a patchwork of separate 'cells' with little exchange of individuals between them. Luckily, just a little mixing will stop this from causing problems with inbreeding, but an inability to disperse may be catastrophic when changes to habitats make them unsuitable.

No-one knows how many birds are killed on Britain's roads each year, but an estimate has been made of 60 million – an extraordinary number. The noise, activity and light from a busy road may affect breeding birds for hundreds of metres either side, and where hedges occur on both sides of a road, mortality among small birds from collisions may be extremely high. Birds such as Barn Owls may actively use roadside verges for hunting, and so often become road casualties.

It is difficult to know how to address this problem. We do not seem about to reorganise society in a way which reduces the need for motor transport.

Road design has a role to play, especially strategically-placed underpasses or 'green bridges'. On new roads, hedges could be placed well away from the tarmac, or grown sufficiently tall that a bird or bat passing over them will also pass over the top of speeding vehicles. Wire gantries designed to draw bats to a height out of reach of passing traffic have been shown to be ineffective, and for this group we must return to the drawing board.

Interestingly, there seems to be a threshold traffic speed, said to be about 50mph, below which bird strikes decrease sharply. This is thought to be because this is about the maximum speed of an approaching predator such as a Sparrowhawk, so birds are evolved to cope with evasion of an object moving at this speed.

Some have suggested that flashing headlights at approaching animals gives them an extra split second to see you and react. Ultimately, however, the only real answer is to drive a little more carefully through the countryside which, let's face it, might be a good idea anyway.

Cypresses. That statuesque group of evergreen trees the cypresses, with their flattened, fern-like sprays of scaly leaves, occupy a strange position in the natural history of Britain. They are abundant, but as they are not really considered 'wild', they are often completely ignored by county floras and plant registers.

Naturalists seem generally not to like them. Gardeners, on the other hand, love them, unless their gardens lie on the shady side of someone else's fast-growing Leylandii hedge. From an ecological point of view, we are always taught that cypresses are very poor for wildlife, but this is to ignore the evidence of our eyes. Even if it were true, the landscape value of cypresses could be said to more than make up for any deficiency in the habitats they create.

Everywhere you go, gardens, parks, cemeteries and other public places will contain cypresses. The classic Mediterranean landscape tree, the tree of Renaissance paintings with it's dark, slightly gothic, columnar form, is the Italian Cypress. It is easy to overlook where it occurs here in our greener and wetter climate, but identification is helped by its large cones, up to 4 cm across.

Also with large cones is the Monterey Cypress, which can be identified by its horizontally-held outer sprays, giving it a characteristic spreading shape. Our town has many large specimens, and a fine group, comprising a yellowish cultivar, occurs as the centrepiece of Humberston Cemetery.

The Sawara Cypress has small cones, resembling dried-up peas, while the Nootka Cypress has cones which are also small, but whose scales usually have pointed projections. I know of only one of the latter locally, in the grounds of the Linkage Trust (formerly Weelsby Hall), although I'm sure there are others.

But the two commonest cypresses, by a very long way, are the Lawson's Cypress and the dreaded Leylandii. Lawson's Cypress can be found in almost all formal tree planting situations as well as in numerous gardens. There are several hundred cultivars, resulting in trees with a remarkable variety of shapes, foliage textures and colours, ranging from almost yellow through to almost blue. Certain features, however, can help to identify Lawson's Cypress. The leading shoot at the top of a tree tends to droop. The cones, which are small (and never flask shaped as in the quite similar Thujas, which in any case have foliage which smells like pineapple or bubblegum), have modest projections on their scales. The tiny leaves have a translucent gland in the centre, seen when held up to the light.

Less common in parks and cemeteries, but almost ubiquitous where there are gardens, farmsteads or other properties requiring to be screened, is the notorious Leylandii. This controversial but abundant tree first arose accidentally in 1888 in a tree collection in Powys, as a hybrid between Monterey and Nootka Cypresses. This was a remarkable union between two relatively distantly-related trees, although the hybridisation event has been repeated many times since, and there are now many common cultivars. Leylandii foliage is dense, and the tree fast-growing. Slightly worryingly, no British Leylandii tree has come anywhere near to reaching its full potential height to date.

The leading shoot of Leylandii tends not to droop, but be conspicuously upright. The leaves do not have a central translucent gland, and some varieties can be recognised by the endmost couple of divisions of the leaves growing at right-angles to the rest of the spray.

Leylandii can be a desperate nuisance where people live close together, and it causes many thousands of costly disputes between neighbours. These are folks who, ironically, probably grew Leylandii in the first place to keep themselves and their neighbours apart.

Naturalists tend to be very sniffy about this tree too. But dense cover of Leylandii provides nesting habitat for a range of birds, including Woodpigeons, Collared Doves, thrushes and finches, as well as secluded roosting places for other birds. Greenfinches, in particular, while not exclusively associated with evergreens are evidently commoner where they occur. Other small birds such as Coal Tit and the tiny Goldcrest show a marked association with all conifers, including cypresses.

Nor is it true to say that nothing eats the foliage of cypresses. A small number of moths have colonised Britain with imported cypresses and are currently munching their way across the country, the most prominent being the Blair's Shoulder Knot, first seen in 1951 and now common in North East Lincolnshire. The Freyer's Pug, a resident cypress-feeding moth, is also present here, and the tiny, ginger micro-moth *Argyresthia cupressella* is heading this way, having been first recorded in Britain in 1997. The caterpillar of the Fan-foot moth will take the withered leaves of Leylandii, although the books won't tell you so. A few other generalist-feeding moths will also accept cypress as a foodplant, and cypress may also host Cypress Aphids and scale insects, providing food for birds hunting among the foliage.

Cypresses, despite their abundance, somehow seem to escape the naturalist's radar. This is strange, because you could hardly see a more handsome tree than a large Monterey Cypress, and all the cypresses would seem to have a clear role in the ecosystems of all kinds of man-made environments.

Capital Letters. I have been picked up on my grammar this week, specifically my use of capital letters for the English, or vernacular, names of species.

In fact this is a debate which has raged, without conclusion, ever since I have had anything to do with natural history. Both sides have strong advocates and detractors, and there is still no settled 'right way'.

With Latin names the situation is simple: the generic name has a capital but the specific name doesn't. Italics are generally used. So our own species is *Homo sapiens*.

By the normal rules of grammar, names of species in English should not have capital letters. Proper nouns begin with capital letters; common nouns don't. Although some consider the names of species a kind of 'honorary' proper noun, rightly they are not. So most scientific journals, National Geographic, Scientific American and the magazines of the Royal Society for the Protection of Birds and Royal Horticultural Society, do not use capitals for names of species. They argue that species names are not 'special' – if they were you would have to give capitals to 'cauliflower' and 'lion'.

The trouble is that this leads to all sorts of problems. Even if you don't capitalise names, proper nouns *within* names must still have capitals, so this means you have to know the origin of every name. For example, 'Norway spruce' must still have a capital 'N'. But what about Sitka spruce? Well yes, actually, because Sitka is a town in Alaska, but you would need to know that. So what about Lodgepole pine? No, I don't know either. What about 'mandarin duck', or 'ragged robin'? It is all asking too much.

The next problem comes when you get a species name which contains an adjective or qualifier, as a great many do. Without capitals, for example, what separates a little egret (the species) from merely any egret of limited size?

There are four common species of 'white' butterfly in North East Lincolnshire. One of them is large: the Large White. The other three are small: the Small White, the Green-veined White and the Orange Tip. If you don't capitalise you can get horrors like: 'two of my three small whites were small whites but one of them may have been a small large white'. Here in North East Lincolnshire we also have three common terns, one of which is the Common Tern, and five common gulls, one of which is the Common Gull, to which the same problem applies.

Capitals solve this, and for this reason, capitals are used for species names by the Audubon Society, International Ornithologists' Union, British Birds, British Wildlife Magazine, and the magazines of Butterfly Conservation, the Wildflower Society and the Botanical Society of Britain and Ireland.

And me.

Another interesting grammatical issue is the use of the 'hunting plural'. Why with some bird species is the plural the same as the singular (e.g. a flock of Mallard) but in others not (a flock of Chaffinches)? This distinction is intuitively understood by bird enthusiasts, but what is the basis for it?

The most popular theory is that animal species which were traditionally hunted, herded or occurred in uncountable numbers, have their plurals 'unmarked' – so you get 'deer', 'sheep' and 'fish'. This usage also applies, by extension, to birds which are hunted. There is a suggestion that because of their relevance to people's everyday lives these words tend to be older than their fully pluralised equivalents, and take their rules from older, Germanic forms of English, where the 's' is not used.

In fact this is a very inexact science – we say 'cows', of course, and birdwatchers will often say 'Curlews', or, even more contrarily, 'Pheasants'. It can sometimes feel right to use the unmarked form for species which are related to, or flock *like* species which are hunted. One would always refer to 'a flock of Dunlin', for example, although there isn't much meat on one.

Big Garden Birdwatch. There is no simpler way of bringing nature close to the home than encouraging birds into the garden. The easiest way to attract birds and other wildlife is basically to do very little. Abandoning slug pellets and insecticides and leaving a decent vegetation cover to develop will help birds, especially if you have trees or shrubs bearing fruit, seeds or berries, or native species which harbour a rich variety of insect life in spring and summer. Any garden with at least some vegetation should be visited by birds.

These days more of us than ever are actively feeding birds. This cheap and recession-proof form of entertainment rarely fails to repay the effort, although it can take a few days at the beginning for birds to 'find' the food you have put out for them. As well as helping the birds survive difficult times of year, feeding the birds is an invaluable way of fostering an appreciation of nature, especially in children.

There is a much wider choice of bird foods available to buy these days than ever before, with the traditional peanuts commonly joined by niger, sunflower, millet and other seeds in various mixtures, suet or fat balls, and mealworms. Household waste and fruit can be valuable too – try the crumbs from the bottom of cereal packets, halved apples, cooked rice, leftover grated cheese or crushed biscuits. These days it is generally advised that birds should be fed all year round, but with certain rules attached. For example, in summer it is important to only feed peanuts through a fine mesh cage so that adults don't try to feed them whole to their young. Also it is essential when continuous-feeding to maintain good hygiene around feeders to prevent bird diseases such as trichomonosis.

The types of birds visiting gardens has changed over the years. Some of these changes are in line with general trends in UK abundance, while others represent changes of feeding habits among our native species. Climate change may also have had an effect, with, for instance, fewer thrushes visiting gardens in milder winters, when they have little difficulty finding food in the wider countryside.

Much of the data for the types of bird visiting gardens comes from so-called 'broad-and-shallow' recording schemes, foremost among which is the RSPB's 'Big Garden Birdwatch'. This is the largest bird survey in the world, and takes place for the 36th consecutive year this weekend, the 24th and

25th of January 2015. Last year nearly half-a-million people took part, helped by a methodology which is simplicity itself. All you need to do is choose an hour, any hour, at any time during the weekend, and record a maximum number for each species you see. If you have a good enough view of the garden, it can be done from the window with a cup of tea.

The RSPB would also like to know about other wildlife seen, such as deer, squirrels, Badgers, Hedgehogs, frogs and toads.

Although House Sparrow and Starling have consistently occupied first and second spots in the list over the life of the survey, overall numbers recorded have declined substantially, with 62% and 84% declines respectively since 1979. In fact Starling was pushed into third place in 2014 by Blue Tit. Song Thrush has also undergone a similar decline, but Goldfinch and Woodpigeon are now much commoner than they used to be. In 2014 for the first time, Great Spotted Woodpecker entered the top 20.

Remember to register to take part.

Sand, pebbles and Plastic. The beach here at Cleethorpes is the resort's main asset. The sand which forms our golden beaches is just one of the sediments, including silts, muds, shingles, gravels and cobbles, which coat the bottom of the North Sea and shape our east coast. Almost all of these sediments were deposited by retreating glaciers at the end of the Ice Age. Apart from a very modest supply of new soil and rock from the erosion of some coastlines to the north, and a small amount of material transported down the major rivers, little new material is now being added. Most of the sediment we are going to get is out there now, being sifted, sorted, worked and re-worked by the sea.

All beach materials originate to the north – this is because both the glaciers which brought the material in the first place and the longshore drift which moves it along the coast both travel, or do their work, from north to south.

David Robinson, in his 'Book of the Lincolnshire Seaside', lists some of the fascinating variety of pebbles carried southwards onto the open coasts of Lincolnshire by the glaciers: "igneous rocks like pink granites from near Aberdeen, basalts, gabbros, syenites and volcanic ashes from the Central Lowlands of Scotland, dolerite 'bluestones' from the Cheviot Hills, and rhomb porphyry from Norway (with its distinctive pale cuboid or diamond-shaped crystals set in a dark matrix); metamorphic rocks such as garnet schists, Lewisian gneiss and quartzites from the Northern Highlands of

Scotland; and sedimentary rocks like dark red sandstones from Central Scotland, millstone grit and grey limestone from the northern Pennines (on which ice scratches are best seen), carbonaceous siltstones from the Durham coalfield and calcareous mudstones from Robin Hood's Bay, together with chalk and flints, the latter of every conceivable shape, including flakes which show clear signs of having been fashioned by man".

Fossils, he goes on, include "sea urchins, crinoid (sea lily) stems, bivalve shells, bullet-shaped belemnites, sponges, corals, coiled ammonites, and the 'devil's toenail' (Gryphaea), the bark impressions of coal-age trees, and even the occasional dinosaur vertebra".

Here within the estuary mouth we may have to try a little harder to find such variety, and some of these rocks – especially some of the sedimentary types – are difficult to tell apart. But there are semi-precious stones to be hunted down by the determined beachcomber – jasper is very common, and the translucent orange carnelian, banded agate and amber are also probably out there somewhere.

While we take the golden sand on our Lincolnshire beaches for granted, we rarely stop to think what it is made of. As we have seen, all manner of miscellaneous rocks can occur on our beaches, all with a helping of shell fragments and a little coal. But our finest flowing sand is generally made up of only the most resistant stuff – mostly particles of hard, insoluble quartz.

Since the 1960s our sand has had a worrying new component – plastic. While it has revolutionised life for humans, plastic is very slow to degrade, and finds its way into the marine environment in large quantities. There is now not a beach in the world which does not have plastic particles as a component of its sand. Up to 3% by weight of plastic has been recorded in beach sand.

Particles of plastic smaller than 5mm have been called 'microplastics'. Many particles are very much smaller than this, and are sifted by the action of the sea to be the same size as the sediments of which they form a part. This makes them as good as invisible among sand.

Much of this plastic comes from the gradual weathering and chemical breakdown of larger plastic items such as bags and bottles – essentially litter – strewn around our beaches or dumped from ships. More problematically, much of the plastic flushed down the drain by people is already in the form of tiny particles, and these also finish up in the sea. These particles originate in cosmetics such as defoliators and scrubs, toothpastes, laundered nylon clothing, and abrasives added to 'sand-blasting' equipment.

Because they are the same size as the sand, plastic particles are consumed by creatures living in sediment, as well as by plankton-feeders in the open sea. This may not have mattered all that much, except for the fact that toxins such as pesticides and endocrine-disrupting chemicals such as BPA, as well as dyes, flame-retardants and detergents can adhere to, and accumulate in plastics, making the particles poisonous. These substances leach out of the plastic when it is consumed by animals. Because these chemicals are so persistent, a process known as 'bio-accumulation' can act to concentrate the toxins as they pass upwards through the food chain, so that larger animals, including humans, could get especially large doses.

Microplastics have been shown conclusively to damage the health of lugworms. They are also taken in by creatures such as mussels, scallops, starfish, amphipods and crabs. This also means that animals which feed on these prey items such as flatfish and wading birds could be accumulating persistent toxins in their tissues.

The situation can only get worse, unless we learn to prevent the accumulation of plastic and microplastic debris in marine habitats. This can only be done by better waste-handling practices, and replacement of plastic micro-beads in everyday products by alternative, organic substances.

If you paddle, sail, surf, swim, or just walk near the sea, you can help with this problem by taking part in a worldwide research project: the Worldwide Plastics Project. By contributing you can help researchers to understand the distribution of microplastics in the oceans.

In summer 2017, the UK committed to introducing a ban on plastic microbeads in 'rinse-off' products. Plastic in the marine environment, however, still remains an enormous problem.

Where Do Insects Go in Winter? The summer months are alive with insects, but where do they all go in the depths of winter? Their life cycle cannot be broken, so they have to be out there somewhere.

Some warmth-loving species invade Britain from the south every summer, either retreating back southwards or simply dying off when the weather turns cold. These species' continued presence in Britain relies on annual invasion from warmer parts. The Painted Lady Butterfly, the Hummingbird Hawkmoth and the abundant garden hoverfly the Marmalade Fly, are good examples.

Honeybees form clusters in the hive, and use the energy from stored honey to generate their own heat. By contrast, in bumblebees and colony-living wasps, all workers and males die off in the autumn, leaving just impregnated queens to sit out the winter, ready to start new colonies in the spring.

These queens, like the adults of many other insects, must find secluded, frost-free places in which to endure the colder months. Most such species enter a kind of dormancy, called *diapause,* at this time. These insects' body fluids may also become more concentrated, increasing their antifreeze properties, so that they can survive periods when the temperature falls below zero.

Sometimes clusters of overwintering adult ladybirds may be found under bark or in cracks in rocks or buildings, and if a grassland 'turf' is cut in winter and artificially warmed up, all manner of beetles and other creatures will become active and emerge from the tangled mass of litter and soil.

Stable-temperatured cellars, outhouses and tunnels may harbour the orange-splashed Herald Moth, which is easier to find at this time than ever it is in summer. It may be joined there by Small Tortoiseshell and Peacock Butterflies, which may sometimes find their way indoors and become prematurely active in midwinter. An advantage of overwintering as an adult is that activity can be resumed quickly at the first signs of spring.

Other species overwinter as eggs, larvae or pupae, with each strategy having its advantages and drawbacks. In winter, eggs are in the least danger of being killed by the cold, but overwintering as an egg is still a relatively uncommon strategy. Many more species overwinter as larvae; that is to say grubs or caterpillars. Larvae living in the soil simply burrow deeper in winter, while plant-feeding larvae retreat deep down into the frost-free recesses of their foodplant or the leaf litter below. Overwintering as a larva has the advantage that dormancy can be put on hold to resume feeding on warmer winter days.

A gardener digging beneath a tree in winter may turn up the huge shiny brown chrysalises of various members of the hawkmoth tribe. These are an example of insects spending the winter in the pupal stage.

Lastly, there are a few insects for which winter is the proper active season. Some occupy relatively stable environments such as the bottoms of ponds or indoors alongside humans, and these can carry on their lives all year without interruption.

Outside, sometimes crowds of those dancing flies the winter gnats can be seen performing in shafts of low midwinter sunshine. Some moths are on the wing in winter and at no other time, and a country drive on milder winter nights will catch a few moths in headlight beams. Classic among the winter species is the common, grey-brown Winter Moth. Like those of several winter-flying species, the female Winter Moth is wingless. While males must fly to find mates, for females wings are too metabolically costly and conspicuous for creatures living on the edge of what is biologically possible, without the protective cover of leaves.

February

Tawny Owls. Sometimes the appearance of a ground predator in woodland, or a cat in a well-wooded garden, may start off a cacophony of bird alarm calls. However, when such a commotion is heard for any length of time above the ground, every birdwatcher knows to look upwards for the roosting Tawny Owl which is inevitably somewhere close. With a bit of diligence the owl can almost always be found, usually close to the trunk of a tree, often partly obscured by Ivy or other foliage. The owl is invariably unmoved by the din, and may simply sit there with its eyes closed, indifferent to the mobbing.

The Tawny Owl is pretty much ubiquitous in England wherever there are trees, and is common in our area. Although nocturnal and so not usually seen, Tawny Owls are very vocal, especially in winter, and if you spend any time outside at night you will almost certainly have heard them.

The Tawny Owl is the stockiest of our owls, and it is well able to displace other owls from its woodland home. The owl's flight contains long glides on rounded wings, characteristically less undulating than other species, and with fewer wingbeats. The flight is silent, owing to the soft upper surfaces of the wings, and a sound-deadening fringe along the leading edge of the outer wing feathers. This helps the owl to approach its prey undetected.

Tawny Owls have rather better vision than humans, although the retinal resolution of both owl and human has evolved to the limit of what is possible for land vertebrates. The superior vision of owls is down to optical factors: the large eye, its tubular shape and the large number of tightly-packed retinal rods. Cone cells, with which humans see colour, are absent in owls – they are quite unnecessary at night.

The owl's hearing is very much better than ours. Ears which are placed asymmetrically on the head (the left is higher, smaller and downward-facing), make the owl particularly good at distance perception. The hearing is also very sensitive, although this ability is hampered when the sounds of the night are obscured by the patter of rain. As a consequence, owls may become very short of food during extended periods of wet weather.

It is by their nocturnal calls that Tawny Owls are best known to most people. It is the Tawny Owl which produces the iconic "tu-whit, tu-whoo" which has somehow become associated in the popular perception with all owls. In fact, these calls are unique to this species.

It was Shakespeare who first made the characterisation in "Love's Labour's Lost", Act 5 Scene 2:

> *When blood is nipped, and ways be foul,*
> *Then nightly sings the staring owl,*
> *   To-whoo;*
> *To-whit, to-whoo, a merry note,*
> *While greasy Joan doth keel the pot.*

Representations of this sort are, of course, rarely completely accurate. In fact, Tawny owls are capable of a wide range of calls including various yelps, and a strange purring or mechanical repeated note, uttered, it is thought, when the owl is under stress. But two types of call are much commoner than the rest, and are those most likely to be heard by people at night. The first of these is the long, wavering hoot of the male, so easy to mimic by blowing into cupped hands through slightly-parted thumbs. The owl can't tell the difference, and will nearly always respond if the mimic is persistent. 'Calling up' owls in this way is yet another schoolchild's pastime now seemingly on the wane. This call, at least, accounts for Shakespeare's "to-whoo".

The second call is that of the larger female – often written as "kewick" (or "tu-whit"), but actually, at close range, more like "u-wee".

"Tu-whit, tu-whoo", then, is not a call uttered by a single owl, but by a male and a female together. Abundant references to male and female owls 'duetting' make a distinctly unscientific leap – the most we can say is that the two owls may be calling at more or less the same time.

Tawny Owls often mate for life, are quite sedentary, and have well-defended territories which alter little from year to year. Winter is a good time to hear your own resident owls, as breeding time – late winter or early spring – approaches. If you find a Tawny Owl's nest later in the year, leave it alone – the adults will defend it vigorously, and have very sharp talons.

Disappearing Farmland Birds. In the UK, bird numbers overall are declining. But not all habitats have suffered equally, the birds of farmland having been especially badly hit. There were thought to be less than half as many farmland birds in 2014 as in 1970, with four species, Turtle Dove, Grey

Partridge, Tree Sparrow and Corn Bunting, having declined by more than 90%. Skylark, Lapwing, Starling and Yellow Wagtail are not far behind, and several others are still on a downward spiral.

The reason is a profound change in farming practices since the Second World War. Larger machinery has meant larger fields. A change from spring to winter sowing means that crops are now too high in the spring for some birds of open spaces to nest. Crops are 'cleaner' now, with land effectively sterilised over huge areas by modern herbicides. Gone are the small, untidy spring-sown fields and the tangled, neglected corners. A grossly simplified countryside has made food and nesting places for birds hard to find, and life easy for their predators.

These days, society demands environmental protection as well as food production from Britain's farmers. The EU insists on compliance to a set of basic environmental standards. Beyond these, the main mechanism for reversing the downward trend in farm wildlife has been so-called 'agri-environment schemes'. In these schemes, farmers commit themselves to measures to help wildlife on their land in return for payments for 'profits forgone'.

Generally speaking the thrust of agri-environment schemes has not been to make the cropped area more wildlife friendly. Rather, the preferred option has been to set aside a proportion of land to be 'managed' specifically for wildlife, separate from areas of intensive food production. The edges of fields and awkward corners are especially favoured for this, both for practicality, and by extending existing field margin outwards to create larger and more varied habitat patches. Provision for farmland birds can be seen here and there in our area, although I would like to see much more.

After much research and many incarnations of the schemes, it seems now that the most productive things you can do with areas set aside for wildlife are not to let them simply go wild, but sow them with either wild flowers or 'bird seed mixes'. The latter may contain plant species producing copious amounts of seed in winter such as Fodder Radish, Quinoa, Linseed, Millet or Kale. The numbers of birds feeding on these patches in early winter can be spectacular. In spring and summer, widened field margins containing a varied mix of native flowers and grasses may provide invertebrates for breeding birds to feed to their young, as well as resources for vital pollinating insects.

But despite the schemes, farmland birds are *still* declining. One problem is the so-called 'hungry gap', when sown seed-bearing plants are depleted. It is no use feeding birds in winter only for them to starve in the spring. Some form of supplementary feeding may prove to be the answer for this critical period.

After the success of the RSPB's Big Garden Birdwatch, there is now another 'broad and shallow' survey – so-called 'citizen science' – for farmers and landowners. They are being encouraged to take part in the largest survey of Britain's farmland birds in a few days time. Organised by the Game and Wildlife Conservation Trust, the third Big Farmland Bird Count takes place between February 6–14, 2016.

The survey only takes half an hour, and landowners are encouraged to stand somewhere where they can see a couple of hectares of farmland, preferably close to some newly-created winter bird habitat, and simply record what they see.

Last year, 950 farmers recorded 127 species of bird. Woodpigeon, Starling, Rook and Fieldfare were numerically the commonest species, with Blackbird, Robin, Blue Tit, Chaffinch, Carrion Crow and Pheasant also recorded on more than 70% of sites. While early days, there is hope that this survey will eventually build up to create a useful long-term dataset.

Most of Britain's suite of declining farmland birds can still be found in North East Lincolnshire. Woodpigeons, Jackdaws and Goldfinches have actually increased. Tree Sparrows, while they have become scarce, seem to be rallying a little. Most, however, are much less common than they used to be. Make the most of our fantastic Skylarks, Grey Partridges, Yellow Wagtails and Lapwings – their future is uncertain. Try South Sea Lane for Yellowhammer and possibly Linnet. Turtle Dove has become very rare here now, and if you see a Corn Bunting in our area, please tell me straight away.

Warming of the North Sea. Among the most obvious effects of climate change are the northwards expansion of warmth-loving creatures, and the earlier timing of natural events in spring. Indeed, these phenomena are often cited as evidence for a warming climate. On land, such effects are relatively straightforward to measure. But our town has traditionally turned its attention outwards to the marine environment – to the North Sea and beyond – and changes beneath the waves have possibly been even more pronounced. Eventually, global warming may lead to changes in our marine fauna that could affect our economy and even our diet, as traditionally-caught fish are lost from British waters.

Strangely, the sea actually mitigates global temperature rise by absorbing up to a third of the harmful carbon dioxide released into the atmosphere by humankind. However, the effect of this absorption is to make the water more acidic. Ocean acidification is now occurring faster than at any time in the last 300 million years, and is expected to continue through the 21st Century leading to a drop of 0.3 to 0.4 pH units.

The acidification of shallow waters will disadvantage creatures with calcium shells such as some algae, corals, sea urchins and molluscs, affecting the food chain. It is even thought that more acidic water may affect the growth, reproduction and behaviour of fish.

And all this is without an increase in temperature. In fact, water is a great retainer of heat, and the shelf seas surrounding the British Isles have warmed four times faster than the global average over the last 30 years, and are warmer now than at any time in the last 20,000 years. This is already leading to changes in North Sea ecosystems.

The effects of global warming on marine environments are easiest to observe around our coastlines. Numbers of some Arctic-breeding seabirds have decreased in Britain, although this may not reflect an actual decline, but merely a tendency for birds not to need to move so far southwards and westwards in winter. The breeding birds of sea cliffs and rocky islands have struggled recently, as their co-evolved relationships with their prey have been disrupted. If current trends continue, some birds, such as Great and Arctic Skuas, may not be able to breed in Britain for much longer. Others, such as Black Guillemot, Common Gull and Arctic Tern, may have to retreat to Britain's very northernmost outposts. Further south, it is thought that our valuable coastal habitats will be squeezed against immoveable sea defences by sea level rise (one of the consequences of warming), reducing their total area.

Here in Grimsby and Cleethorpes, it tends to be fish that have traditionally interested us, not to mention made our town its fortune. Populations of some of our North Sea fish have already been substantially depressed by trawling, even before we start to consider global warming. Individual fish nowadays tend to be smaller: because of both the direct and 'natural selection' effects of the harvesting of the larger animals over many years, but also by temperature change – warmer water can hold less oxygen, and can support only smaller individual fish.

As the climate warms, fish species tend to shift their distributions polewards or into deeper water. Northwards shifts have been shown for a whole range of cold-adapted species, including Cod, Haddock, Whiting and Mackerel. Substantial Mackerel shoals have now passed from British waters northwards into Icelandic and Faroe Islands waters, with consequences for quotas and management of stocks. A recent shift to deeper water has been shown for Cod, Cuckoo Ray, Dab and Plaice, among others. It is a worry that such species may eventually be forced by temperature rise into seas which are not the ideal depth for them, and so leave them with little available habitat.

In the sea, just as on land, species diversity is greatest at warmer, tropical latitudes. Climate change has led to the northwards spread of a rich, southern marine fauna into British waters. In the North Sea, eight times as many species have increased as decreased, these tending to be small, warmth-loving species from the south. While populations of cold-adapted species have halved, southern, so-called Lusitanian species, have increased by 250%. While they have always occurred here, Anchovy and Sardine, for example, are now thought to be permanently breeding in the southern North Sea, and these could conceivably form the staple of North Sea fisheries in the future.

In the end, we may have to forget our preferences for fish such as Haddock and Plaice, and start to look to southern Europe for our gastronomic inspiration. Global warming would seem set to alter fish communities in the North Sea for decades to come, and it doesn't help at all that those setting fishing quotas repeatedly refuse to follow scientific advice – something which could make the change messier and more rapid.

Wintering Warblers. One of the defining characteristics of that group of small, insect-eating birds the warblers is that they are migrants, our British birds visiting us only in the spring and summer months. In fact, one's chances of seeing a warbler in the middle of winter is nowadays many times greater than in the not so distant past, with four species now regularly present in the UK, three of those in our area.

Two of these four are actually sedentary species – that is to say they do not really migrate at all. The first, the Dartford Warbler is an uncommon but long-standing UK resident, present on southern heaths and coasts. Wandering birds in winter have reached south Lincolnshire, but they essentially spend the summer and winter on the same ground.

The other non-migrant is the Cetti's Warbler, a bird of tangled scrub near water, which first bred in the UK in 1972. Although a 'little brown job' which usually keeps itself to itself in a very impenetrable habitat, it has an explosive song which gives its presence away. Its tentative note or two then loud, clanging repeated figure is a classic 'holiday' sound, reminiscent of the reedy wetlands and wastelands of the Mediterranean. Brief snatches of this song can sometimes be heard throughout the year. Cetti's Warblers are undergoing a rapid expansion within the UK, and winter birds have recently been seen (or heard) at Town's Holt, Tetney Blow Wells, Newton Marsh Sewage Works, and Cleethorpes Country Park.

The other two winter warblers, the Blackcap and the Chiffchaff are two of our commonest migrants during the warmer months, when they can be heard singing wherever there are trees and dense ground cover for breeding. They are much less common here in the winter, but have been seen more and more regularly over recent decades, possibly helped by a warming climate.

The wintering habits of the two are quite different. The plain olive-brown Chiffchaff is usually to be found somewhere near water. Chiffchaffs are particularly fond of sewage or water treatment works, where a couple of degrees of extra heat are invaluable and ensure a supply of insects and other invertebrates throughout the cold season. Some of our wintering Chiffchaffs are our own breeding birds, but they can also visit us from any part of their European breeding range. Birds from Siberia can sometimes turn up here in winter, and these can be identified by their paler colour.

The Blackcap is the commonest of the winter warblers, and unlike the Chiffchaff, the vast majority of winter records come from gardens. The increased tendency to put food out for birds in winter and the slightly warmer temperatures, especially around habitation, are thought to have led to an increase in sightings in recent years. Blackcaps seen in the UK in winter are not the same birds we have here in summer, which all migrate to the Mediterranean and North Africa. Our winter birds originate from central Europe, which means they have travelled in an unusual north-westerly direction to reach their wintering grounds. Interestingly, it has been shown that in central Europe, UK-wintering Blackcaps and Mediterranean-wintering ones do not interbreed, which means that the two populations are distinct, despite occupying the same summer haunts. Scientists think that this could possibly represent the beginnings of separation into two distinct species. This is a fascinating example of human behavior – i.e. feeding birds in UK gardens – influencing evolution.

This winter (2014-15), Chiffchaff has been seen in Cleethorpes Country Park, and Blackcaps have been occasional garden visitors in North East

Lincolnshire. Male and female Blackaps can be told apart easily – the female's cap is not black but reddish-brown.

Grebes. The lake in Cleethorpes Country Park became the centre of attention among birdwatchers recently as it witnessed a mini-invasion of uncommon grebes.

The grebes are an ancient family. In all species, males and females look alike – indeed grebes go so far back that they are thought to pre-date the evolution of 'sexual dimorphism' in birds, with both sexes taking an equal role in display. While these may be thought of as primitive birds, this longevity should more properly be looked upon as a sign of highly successful and enduring design.

Grebes are specialised waterbirds which feed by diving for fish and other aquatic animals. In breeding plumage, they have been perfectly described by bird artist Eric Ennion, who said that grebes "are like Queen Anne furniture, splendid in front but not so fine behind. Nature spent her ingenuity on their ruffs and tippits – she had none left to provide them with proper tails". Unfortunately the extravagant colours and plumes of their front ends are lost in winter, which is when we tend to see the less common species here.

Five of the six British grebe species have been seen in our Country Park at some time. Only the extremely rare Pied-billed Grebe has not visited Cleethorpes since the Park's lake was created.

Two species of grebe are resident in our area. The largest, the Great Crested Grebe, can sometimes seen on the Country Park lake, where it has been known to breed. Even in years when breeding does not occur, a pair may sometimes be seen in the spring, engaging in their elaborate display. The birds, spreading their ruff-like chestnut and black ear-plumes, may face each other in the water, undertaking various head shaking and neck stretching movements, sometimes diving and rising right out of the water, all in superbly choreographed symmetry. At the climax of their display, two birds may tread water, necks craned, their bills draped with waterweed. In good light with reflections on the water, this can be one of the most engaging spectacles in the whole of nature.

The diminutive Little Grebe is the dumpiest and least charismatic of the family in Britain. Although it has attractive chestnut cheeks and yellow gape flanges in the breeding season, for most of the year its plumage comprises merely shades of brown. This is the commonest grebe in our area, and several may often be seen together on the lagoon by the Humber Mouth Yacht Club, as well as other places. The excited trill of the Little Grebe at breeding time is one of those subconsciously evocative sounds of watery places in summer.

In mid-January 2016, a report came of a rare Red-necked Grebe in Cleethorpes Country Park. This species breeds over much of northern Europe and the Baltic countries, but not in Britain, where it remains an uncommon visitor, with sightings peaking in winter. Although the proliferation of new waterbodies due to sand and gravel extraction has made its breeding habitat common in Britain, very few nesting attempts by Red-necked Grebe have been made here, and none has been successful.

On 28 January this grebe, which had by now become a very confiding long-stayer, was joined by not one but two similarly-uncommon Slavonian Grebes (pictured). These are somewhat more northerly breeders in Europe than the last species, with a tiny and vulnerable breeding population hanging on in northern Scotland. A small grebe, the Slavonian's clean black and white head pattern is set off, with good close views, by a startling red eye.

Slavonian Grebes winter in Britain every year in small numbers, with a few traditional sites along the east and south coast strongly favoured.

Slavonian Grebes – Cleethorpes Country Park.
Photo: Dave Bradbeer

Wherever there is water close to the east coast, there is always the chance that rare birds will drop in. The Cleethorpes Country Park lake's list of rarities is becoming quite respectable, and the water is always worth checking for unusual visitors. Sadly, in 2016 the fifth grebe, the small and smokier-cheeked Black-necked Grebe, didn't drop in to make a full house for the year.

Sturgeon. In 1324, Edward II decreed the Sturgeon to be a 'Royal Fish'. This meant that all Sturgeon caught or found in the waters of the Kingdom were to be considered, along with Mute Swans and whales, the property of the monarch. In those times Sturgeon would almost certainly have made their way up all the larger rivers of the British Isles to breed, including the Humber. Outside the breeding season Sturgeon were marine fish, being found in shallow continental seas over most of Europe.

These bottom-feeding fish are known for their elongate shape and wedge-shaped head, lack of scales and occasional great size, with some individuals growing to 20 feet long. Species closely related to our own Common or Atlantic Sturgeon living in Russia and the Middle East are the source of caviar. Sturgeon belong to one of the most ancient families of fish, having changed remarkably little since the time of the dinosaurs. This is thought to be a result of their long life, including taking many years to reach breeding age, and abundant prey. Also, they have few or no predators due to their large size, and the presence of bony armoured plates along their backs and sides.

Unfortunately, the Sturgeon has become one of Europe's most endangered animals, having been unable to survive the prolonged depredations of overfishing and the modification and pollution of its breeding rivers. Nowadays the only breeding population left in Europe is in the Garonne river in south-west France, a tributary of the Gironde, where the last spawning took place in 1994. The Sturgeon is now considered critically endangered; it is functionally extinct over much of Europe including the UK, and in real danger of total extinction. Very occasionally, wandering individual Sturgeon are still caught in UK waters, but because of their rarity these occurrences tend to make a paragraph or two in the national news.

Through the heyday of the Grimsby fishing industry Sturgeon were by no means commonly landed, although they were commercially valuable fish. This may have been through difficulty of capture rather than rarity. However, the exploits of one skipper defied the odds; in the early years of the twentieth century, Skipper Newson of Grimsby became known as the 'Sturgeon hunter'. Between 1906 and 1908 Newson landed nearly 1000 Sturgeon, netting him a small fortune. Newson would not tell anybody where his secret Sturgeon fishing grounds were located, although strenuous efforts have been made to work this out in retrospect. It is now thought that he may have fished close to the estuary of the German River Elbe, although to this day nobody is really sure.

In recent times there have been attempts to reintroduce Sturgeon to the wild in France and Germany. Although female Sturgeon take 16-18 years to attain breeding age (males take slightly less), French scientists have said that they hope adolescent Sturgeon from these reintroduction programmes will start appearing in UK waters, especially estuaries, in the next few years. Nowadays Sturgeon enjoy complete protection, although hazards such as river engineering and bycatch would still seem to threaten recovery.

Reinstating these leviathans of the deep will be a long business, but would seem worth the effort. However, for Sturgeon as for much other wildlife, we will need strong international co-operation, and to have a much more enlightened and 'joined up' attitude to the conservation of the seas than we have shown for most of our history.

National Nest Box Week. February 14 sees the beginning of the British Trust for Ornithology's National Nest Box Week. Valentine's Day is chosen as it is said to be the time of year when birds pair up and think about breeding. That birds pair up on Valentine's Day is of course tongue-in-cheek, but in fact, mid-late winter is as good a time as any to start thinking about providing artificial nest sites for birds in the coming season.

Natural holes in trees are not as common as they used to be, as a result of the modern habit of clearing away rotten branches or whole trees in towns, gardens and woodland. Similarly, modern buildings do not contain the nooks and crannies in which birds would once have nested. As a consequence, many species of common hole-nesting bird have declined, with shortage of nest sites being a main driver. This is where nestboxes come in.

One of the great things about making artificial nestboxes is the scope for creativity and improvisation. Birds prefer to nest in sheltered, safe locations, but in the wild they have to take what they can get, so there is no 'perfect' design for an artificial nest site. You can help the birds, however, by getting the size of the entrance hole exactly right; it must be just big enough to let them in, without being big enough to admit their predators. The ideal hole diameter is 25mm for Blue and Coal Tit, 28mm for Great Tit and Tree Sparrow, 32mm for House Sparrow and 45mm for Starling. Boxes are best placed out of reach of cats and other predators, out of full afternoon sun, and not where water will stream over them when it rains. Apart from that, anything is worth a try. Sparrows are colonial breeders, and will even nest in bird 'hotels', with multiple entrances.

Small, open-fronted boxes may be used by Robins, or if you are very lucky, by the much-declined Spotted Flycatcher. In more rural locations, much larger boxes can be used to attract owls or Kestrels, although these boxes are often taken over by Jackdaws or Stock Doves. I have seen Barn Owls nest in receptacles as varied as crates, chests and barrels, so long as the position is favourable.

One hole-nesting bird which really needs our help is the Swift. Suitable cavities in walls and roofs are hard to find these days, and Swifts have declined as a consequence. In fact, Swifts will nest fairly readily in artificial spaces, and special Swift boxes are available. There are even hollow 'Swift bricks' which can be incorporated into new buildings, which really ought to be more widely-used than they are. I know of two specially-built 'Swift towers' with no other purpose but to provide nesting places for Swifts, one in Cambridge and one in Belfast – there may be others.

Specialised boxes can these days also be bought for other animals such as bats and insects. But there is one insect which will commonly take over boxes

meant for birds – this is a relative newcomer to Britain, the Tree Bumblebee (pictured). This furry ginger, black and white bee first turned up in Wiltshire in 2001, but has since colonised the whole country. It is now one of the commonest bumblebees in North East Lincolnshire gardens, where it is particularly fond of *Cotoneaster* and *Ceanothus* flowers. There is no reason to be alarmed if these insects take over a bird box – the colony is 'annual', and will be gone by the autumn, and in the meantime the bees will help with pollination in the garden.

Information on National Nest Box Week can be found online.

The recently-arrived Tree Bumblebee.
Photo: Andre Karwath CC BY-SA 2.5
Wikimedia Commons

Stoats and Weasels. The nineteenth and early twentieth centuries were the great age of gamekeeping. Any wild predator would be routinely 'removed' from country estates, and among landowners a predator-free environment would have been considered a matter of pride, and a source of peer-pressure. In this way, many predator species, including some which posed little threat to game, were eliminated from large tracts of countryside. Even now, it is still possible to find 'gibbets' on which dangle the dead remains of numerous perceived pests.

By and large, the largest predators fared the worst. So, for example, among that familiar group the 'mustelids', the Pine Marten and Polecat are still rare even now, but the smaller Stoat and Weasel have remained among us and tolerably frequent, probably because they can breed so prolifically. We should say that the largest mustelid, the Otter, probably survived as a result of its aquatic habits, and because its status as a creature hunted for sport afforded it a degree of protection.

Nowadays, thankfully, we live in less bloodthirsty times, and Weasels and Stoats are both common, although Stoats are probably more likely to be seen on account of their larger size. The two are relatively easy to tell apart – Stoats are larger, have an arched back and bounding gait, and a black tip to the tail. Weasels are smaller, about the size of a 'stretched-out mouse' and keep lower to the ground when they run. Their tails are shorter in relation to the body, and have no black tips.

Both animals are voracious predators, with an essentially similar diet. Because of their size, Weasels tend to primarily take smaller prey such as mice and voles, although they will also take birds and their eggs, and amphibians. Like Stoats, on occasions they may attack and kill creatures very much larger than themselves. Stoats tend on average to take larger prey, with a distinct liking for Rabbits.

Both Stoats and Weasels will occasionally perform a kind of erratic 'dance' in the presence of their prey, which seems to confuse or hypnotise them, bringing them into striking distance for capture. Both species will kill a prey animal with a bite to the neck or throat if they can, but if they can only grasp the prey by another part of the body they may simply hang on to the poor creature for as long as it takes for it to die. A Stoat killing a Rabbit in this way can be a drawn out and very unpleasant ordeal.

Young Stoats are reproductively mature from three weeks old, and so female Stoats may already be pregnant when they leave the nest. Because they have delayed implantation, fertilised eggs don't start to develop until up to ten months after mating. Weasels will have two litters a year – Stoats only one, in spring, but that single litter may contain up to thirteen kits, although the average is closer to nine.

One difference between the two species is that in Britain, only the Stoat will ever turn white in winter – a state known as 'ermine'. However, most Stoats here do not turn white, and Stoats in ermine are relatively scarce. The white coat can occur when the weather during the autumn moult is very cold, growing underneath the summer brown one, so that when the brown coat is shed, the white one is revealed. This explains why a Stoat's coat may seem to turn from brown to white very quickly – sometimes within as little as three days. Occasionally, a Stoat's coat will turn only partially white – the areas most likely to stay brown are the crown, a stripe along the back, and rings around the eyes. Sometimes part of a Stoat's fur may not change completely to white, but appear a kind of yellowish.

If a Stoat has turned white one winter, it is more likely to also turn white the next, even if the weather is mild. When there is no snow, a white Stoat will stand out a mile, and this may explain the odd fact that Stoats in ermine are reported more often in mild winters than snowy ones.

Even when a Stoat has turned otherwise completely white, the tip of its tail will always remain black. In the ermine garments of historic royals, judges and peers, each black spot is the tip of a white Stoat's tail.

If you know where a Stoat in ermine can be seen this, or any winter, please get in touch.

Blooming Gorse. Winter and early spring can be a drab time of year. Any flowers daring to brave late frosts tend to belong to introduced species specifically brought here for their unseasonal colour. An honourable exception is the common, native Gorse, whose cheery yellow pea-flowers are on show throughout the winter – indeed throughout the year.

"When gorse is in bloom, kissing is in season" goes the old saying, which is a way of saying that Gorse never really goes out of flower. Some may tell you that this stems from the theory that the flowers of our Common Gorse are generally associated with the first half of the year, with the other two British species (neither of which we have in North East Lincolnshire) with the second, leading to a near-continuous display. In fact, even in our area, at least a little Common Gorse can be found blooming almost any time.

Gorse is an abundant species throughout Britain, but less so on heavy, calcareous soils such as ours. It prefers acidic or nutritionally-poor, well-drained soils, and becomes visibly more dominant as a roadside plant once you hit the sandier soils on the far (western) side of the Wolds.

The massed yellow flowers of Gorse can be a spectacular landscape feature, completely transforming some habitats such as coastal heaths. Gorse reaches peak flowering in spring, and when occurring *en masse*, Gorse flowers give off a powerful, and slightly unexpected, smell of coconut.

But none of this explains why Gorse produces flowers throughout the year.

The first thing to note is that the colourful, scented flowers of Gorse are obviously designed to attract flying insects, and these are in very short supply during winter. In fact, Gorse is partly self-fertile, but produces more seed when pollinating insects are present.

The real reason that Gorse produces flowers out of season is to try to escape a small insect which eats its developing seeds – the Gorse Seed Weevil.

In fact there are two sorts of Gorse plant, thought to be genetically distinct, with different strategies for avoiding the depredations of the weevil. First are those which produce flowers throughout the winter and into early spring. These go unmolested by weevils, which cannot tolerate the cold. However, they also find pollinators harder to come by, and must flower for longer to take advantage of the rare mild days when flying insects are about. When these more congenial interludes occur, this kind of Gorse finds itself with very little competition for pollinators, but such a strategy can easily backfire.

The second type produces flowers only in the spring, but for a shorter time and in much greater profusion. While coming under attack from the weevil, such plants have abundant pollinators, and produce enough seed to overwhelm the ability of the weevil to eat them all, leaving some to ripen successfully.

For reasons to do with the fact that their flowering periods overlap, the two types of Gorse manage to persist together in a finely-balanced equilibrium.

Reports of flowering Gorse in North Lincolnshire are currently being collated, with records stretching from the 1890s right up to the present day. As expected, Gorse flowers have been recorded in every month of the year except, interestingly, July and August – otherwise our floweriest months. March is the month with the most records of Gorse in flower, although April has nearly as many.

Gorse flowers in February

The results clearly reflect the two flowering strategies, with records consistently high through the winter, a strong spring peak, and a summer lull.

If you inspect the seed pods of Gorse you may find tiny holes made by the weevils. The adult insect, should you find one, is tiny but charismatic on close inspection, with a long, snout-like projection on its head, called a rostrum. On a warm, dry day you may hear Gorse pods popping open with an audible crackling sound. This is the moment when the adult Gorse Seed Weevils find themselves released into the world.

Seashells. I was always taught that the seashell fauna of the Humber estuary was a species-poor one. For this reason I have scarcely given the shells on Cleethorpes beach a second look, lazily 'clumping' them into about six categories – broadly cockles, mussels, oysters, razors, whelks, and the small fragile pink or apricot-coloured tellins. Previously I had always have left it at that, and concentrated on birds and plants instead.

This winter I decided to go out to the strandline and put this right. Out on the beach behind Pleasure Island are some banks of shells so thick that you can see them from the sea wall, so I thought this would be a good place to start.

To my surprise, in a couple of hours I had collected a good selection which turned out, after some help with identification from gurus David Feld and Helgi Gudmundsson to contain no fewer than 32 species. The actual number ever recorded at Cleethorpes, including fossil shells, is between fifty and sixty.

Seashells are of course just the dead remains of sediment-living molluscs, washed up by the tide. The selection of shells on the beach does not really reflect the abundance of live animals under the water or sediment, being more a result of the sifting and sorting action of the sea.

The common Cockle was the commonest shell to be found. Oysters actually comprised two species, as did both mussels and periwinkles, and there were three kinds of whelk. Absolutely distinctive were Slipper Limpet, American Piddock and the large, square-ended Blunt Gaper. A hint of the exotic was provided by the little purple-spotted Painted Topshell. Sadly I did not find a very rare 'left-handed' Whelk, or the little 'murex' *Boreotrophon truncatus,* a collector's favourite also known as the Ribbed Spindle Shell or Bobtail Trophon, which although not common, certainly turns up here in small numbers.

But my search did come up with a couple of surprises. The first was among the thin wavy strandline of black coal dust occupying the gentle mud slope to the seaward side of the outer dunes. Examination of this strip of coal on hands and knees revealed hundreds or thousands of tiny 'turret' shells just a few millimetres in size, which would normally go completely unnoticed by a casual passer-by. Even more surprising is that many of these shells were fresh or brackish water species, whose empty shells had presumably been washed out of inland waterways onto the beach. The little Laver Spire Shell, an estuary specialist and an important food for wading birds, was also common.

The other surprise involved some of the largest shells on the beach, the 'razor shells'. There are traditionally three species of razor on our beach, which may all be abundant after storms. The easiest to identify is also the largest, the Pod Razor Shell, a handsome shell told by its absolutely straight, parallel sides. This was still common on the beach when I looked. Amazingly, most or all of the other razor shells found, that is to say the slightly curved ones, turned out to be neither of the two other common species, but the very similar alien invader, the American Jack-knife Clam.

As its name suggests this large mollusc is native to America. Its free-swimming larvae were brought to Europe in the ballast water of cargo ships. It was first recorded in Europe from the German Waddensee in 1979 and soon became common there. The first record in Britain was from Holme on the north Norfolk coast in 1989, and from there it has spread, eventually becoming abundant in the Thames estuary and The Wash. It has now, as my search confirms, become the dominant razor shell species on the Humber too.

Invasive, non-native organisms are one of the biggest threats to natural ecosystems worldwide. It is telling that such a profound change can occur on our own beach, and what's more, go unnoticed by almost everybody.

Shells on Cleethorpes beach

Kingfishers. Here in Cleethorpes we may occasionally gain a glimpse of what is surely Britain's most exotic-looking bird, the Kingfisher. This is the most northerly and widespread member of a mainly tropical family, and a bird instantly recognised by everybody. The image of a perched Kingfisher is a staple design on crockery, tea towels, calendars, and anything else on which British birds are used as a design. Yet the most astonishing flash of colour is reserved for when the bird takes to the wing – especially in flight away from the watcher. Ironically, this is the view one usually gets, as one flushes a previously unseen bird from a waterside perch. So bright is the blue of a Kingfisher's back that it may almost seem luminous – unfeasibly so on a dull day. One can sometimes be aware of the flash of blue but not the bird which makes it.

In birds in the hand, the blue feathers of a Kingfisher's back are slightly disappointing, for it is not the pigment that creates the effect, but feathers whose surface is micro-sculpted for iridescence. In the wild, the brilliant blue streak along a waterway is often accompanied by an explosive squeaking call, which once known, is just as distinctive a sign that this bird is around.

Kingfishers are seldom seen away from water. They prefer still or slow-flowing waterbodies and need a supply of small fish, less than about 9cm long, on which to feed. They will frequent coarse fish nurseries, but will also take minnows and sticklebacks from smaller streams and ponds, catching well over 100 such fish a day when feeding young. Their technique, to sit motionless on a regular waterside vantage point and make sudden, short dives into the water below, is a habit which endears them to photographers, as it is not only action-packed, but to an extent, predictable.

Kingfishers require a vertical or overhanging mud bank in which to make a nest hole, usually, but not always, adjacent to water. Outside the breeding season they prefer to stay around the same area if they can, but will move away if conditions become unsuitable. Young birds tend to be the most adventurous in this respect.

While I know of no Kingfisher nesting site immediately around Cleethorpes, they do not breed far away, and spreading away from their natal areas brings them frequently onto our local area. If we are lucky we may see them on any substantial enough ditch or pond; Buck Beck and Cleethorpes Country Park are as good as anywhere. When the weather is exceptionally cold, Kingfishers may take to marine habitats to find food, and I have seen them fishing in our saltmarsh creeks in the very worst winters.

Kingfishers have had to put up with a lot from humans over the years. They have been persecuted by Trout and Salmon fisheries, and their blue feathers have been used as fashion accessories. Their good looks once made them a taxidermists' favourite. Pollution and the engineering of waterways has destroyed much Kingfisher habitat during the last century, and more recently, water abstraction has been a problem, leaving smaller streams to run dry in summer.

Kingfisher. Photo: Don Davis

But the Kingfisher's biggest enemy is a hard winter, and if it is cold enough for long enough, the great majority of British birds may be killed off. Luckily, they can breed relatively quickly, producing an average of two broods of six chicks a year, so numbers tend to recover faster than most.

Mermaids' purses. There can be few people who ever walked along a British beach who haven't at some point found one of those black or brown, four-horned cases colloquially known as 'mermaid's purses'. Made of collagen and keratin, the same proteins contained in human hair and fingernails, a mermaid's purse is the empty egg-case of a marine, cartilaginous fish – a shark, skate or ray.

Some cartilaginous fish don't produce egg-cases at all, instead giving birth to live young. But there are more than ten species of skates and rays in British waters, and a few species of shark, which do produce them. Once hatched, the empty cases often wash ashore, where it is relatively easy to collect and identify them. This process can yield valuable information on the distribution and status of the various species, some of which are in decline.

The female fish will lay eggs in pairs (one from each ovary), and anchor them, in their cases, to the seabed using mucus filaments. Each developing embryo feeds on a yolk-sac within its case, with an incubation time from about five months to over a year depending on species. Small slits open up along the horns of the case through which oxygenated water is pumped by movements of the developing fish's tail. When the yolk is all gone, the young fish emerges from the case, looking like a miniature version of the adult. The empty case is then at the mercy of the currents.

Sharks, skates and rays produce eggs throughout the year, so egg-cases can be found at any time. Obviously, after a storm is best, when a lot of debris has been thrown up the beach, and a substantial strandline has developed. Egg-cases may be tangled up in seaweed and other material, and it is important not to thrust your hand in to litter too enthusiastically as the strandline can contain some nasty surprises. A stick, or a good old kick might be the best first option.

When an egg-case is found, it should be soaked to make it easier to identify. Fresh water in a bucket is fine, and the case may take several hours to re-hydrate to its original, pliable state. It is important to squeeze the air out of the case so it sinks, to help it along.

There are only two sharks whose egg-cases could realistically be found on our beach. Much the commonest of these is the Small-spotted Catshark, also known as the Lesser-spotted Dogfish, which can grow to just over half a metre long. The egg-case is about 4cm × 2cm, not including the long, curly tendrils at each corner. In old specimens, some of these projections may be broken off. The case is usually brownish, but the colour is unreliable in identification. A case similar but very much larger may belong to the Nursehound – another related catshark. The adult can attain more than a metre and a half when full-grown. Another species, the Blackmouth Catshark is a deeper water species whose capsules rarely wash ashore.

Skates and rays are those flattened, roughly diamond-shaped fish which lie on the seabed at rest. Their eyes sit on the top (dorsal) side, while their mouths, nostrils and gills are on the lower (ventral) side. Skates differ from rays in numerous small ways, but the whole group suffers from historical mis-naming. Technically, all rays give birth to live young, with only skates producing egg-cases. Thus Blonde, Small-eyed, Thornback, Undulate, Spotted and Cuckoo Rays are all actually skates, but it is probably wise not to interfere with the names everyone is used to.

Thornback and Spotted Rays are probably the two species whose egg-cases are most likely to be found on our Lincolnshire beaches, but Blonde and Starry Rays are not out of the question. The things to look for are the length, width and texture of the case (not including any projections), the relative lengths of the horns, and presence or absence of a distinct 'keel' along the sides.

The Shark Trust wants to know about any egg-case you find, to help them build up a picture of the conservation status of our sharks and skates. Although the sea can carry empty egg-cases some distance, locations of washed up material can give valuable clues to the position of nurseries at sea. Please take a photo of cases if you can, and record the time and place you found them.

Visit The Shark Trust's 'Great Eggcase Hunt Project' website, which contains lots of information including identification keys, and details of how to submit records.

Birds Surviving Winter. I have always been amazed at how birds manage to survive outdoors even through the coldest winters. Their metabolism is faster than ours, and the body temperature they have to maintain is higher – on average about 40 degrees, which makes it even more impressive.

In fact, keeping warm requires energy, and birds will generally be ok in the cold as long as they can find enough to eat. Feathers provide superb insulation, and they may grow more densely in winter, the extra padding cutting energy expenditure by up to 15%. Birds can control blood flow to their legs and feet, helping to conserve heat, although long-legged birds may still be seen with one leg tucked up in their feathers, or even sitting down so both are covered. They may also tuck their bills into their backs while roosting.

Birds may lay down extra fat reserves ready for winter, and stick out their feathers more to create a thicker layer of trapped air on cold days. Plump-looking birds in winter may not necessarily be well-fed, but merely fluffed up.

The very smallest birds are those which should, in theory, lose heat most rapidly. Like all perching birds, they need to find somewhere sheltered to roost at night, as heat loss increases by about 10% for every metre per second rise in wind speed. As a consequence, conifers and other evergreens may be preferred to leafless branches, and some birds may find various kinds of hole or cavity in which to spend the night. Wherever you see Wellingtonia trees, those huge ornamental conifers with the soft, reddish, spongy bark, look on the trunk for the little cup-like indentations made by Treecreepers for roosting.

Very small birds may roost communally to keep warm. It is said that two Long-tailed Tits huddling together may save 27% of their energy expenditure each, while three together may save an amazing 39%. On occasions, dozens of birds such as Wrens may be seen emerging from nestboxes or other cavities on a winter's morning, having huddled together overnight. Birds roosting singly may choose a place which has some residual heat from the day's sunlight, such as against a south facing tree trunk or wall.

Of course the wading birds out on the Humber can have no shelter at all. Having already moved to our estuaries to escape intolerable cold on their breeding grounds, they may move on again if icy conditions make feeding difficult, generally travelling southwards or westwards each time. Because of the carrying capacity of the various feeding areas, by the end of the winter, waders may be strung out across the estuaries of western Europe and west Africa. There is a trade-off at play here between the need to find warmer conditions and the need to remain as close to the breeding grounds as possible, to lessen the hazards and stresses of the return migration.

Nevertheless, very cold weather may still cause mortality in waders. Food availability in estuary mud tends to vary greatly from year to year, and in a good year birds are usually ok unless there is prolonged covering of ice and snow. In a bad year, icy conditions can make an already bad situation catastrophic. Prey species bury deeper in cold weather, and mass die-offs of common prey species such as cockles, may occur. When you start to see Oystercatchers feeding on inland grassy roadsides and roundabouts, as you do occasionally in Cleethorpes in winter, you know conditions out on the estuary are not too good.

There are things you can do to help garden birds survive the winter. First among these is to provide good quality food, remembering of course to keep surfaces and feeders clean to avoid disease.

Out on the beach, please do not flush flocks of birds unnecessarily in cold weather. The wasted time and energy in repeatedly escaping walkers, jet-skiers and dogs can actually, in the worst cases, kill them.

Offshore Windfarms. The UK has set a target to produce 15% of its energy from renewable sources by 2020. As we all know, the Humber is to be at the heart of the UK's renewable energy industry, primarily because of our convenient port facilities ready and waiting to service huge new offshore windfarms in the North Sea.

Some of the proposed turbine arrays are so vast they defy the imagination. Millions of birds migrating between Scandinavia and Lincolnshire in autumn will eventually have to pick their way through two giant 'arrays", the so-called Dogger Bank Array and the Hornsea Array, as well as many smaller coastal operations. The latter, from tip to tip, is bigger than the distance from Cleethorpes to the Mersey estuary, and the former is 3.5 times the size of East Yorkshire; so there is no chance whatsoever of simple avoidance. And what of life beneath the sea? The North Sea is not a sterile wasteland, but contains a diversity of marine life, which will doubtless be affected by the installation of a forest of pillars on the sea floor.

It is thought that the disturbance and noise from pile-driving during the construction phase of wind farms will prove intolerable to marine mammals such as porpoises and seals, but when complete, the footings of the towers could develop into artificial reefs around which wildlife can flourish. Also, although fishing within windfarms will not be officially outlawed, it will probably not occur for safety reasons, and the arrays will become 'accidental' nature reserves. While much of what will happen to undersea life is conjecture there are likely to be winners and losers, although it seems to be agreed that the changes may not be all bad once the arrays are up and running.

There are two main ways in which offshore windfarms will impact birds: collisions with pillars or spinning turbine blades, and displacement from feeding habitat. It is calculated that 99% of individual seabirds will be able to simply avoid the turbines, with some such as Gannet avoiding the array altogether. Studies of the heights at which seabirds fly have indicated that Cormorants, the larger gulls and Common Tern will be at the greatest risk of being mown out of the air by giant rotating blades, although at least some mortality is predicted for almost all species considered. Other seabirds and larger terrestrial birds migrating over the sea, it is said, tend to fly somewhat too low for mortality to seriously impact on populations, although evidence is scant and the thresholds used are entirely arbitrary.

Much less is said about the many millions of small to medium-sized passerine birds which migrate across the North Sea from Scandinavia to the UK in autumn each year, to take advantage of our habitable winters. The same birds must also make the return journey in the spring. The degree of mortality among these birds is unknowable, at least until they fail to turn up. Maintenance platforms at the bases of columns might even give exhausted passerines somewhere to land, in the same way that they sometimes land on ships in the North Sea. But it seems entirely plausible (and was predicted back in 2006) that high bird mortality will occur in darkness or periods of poor visibility, as terrestrial birds making dangerous sea crossings collide with pillars and blades, to which they may even be attracted by lights.

As any birdwatcher will tell you, the nights of the year during which mass migration of birds will occur is to an extent predictable. Turning off turbines at these times, or lighting them such that they are highly visible could help, although one can't see any enthusiasm for such measures at the present time.

It seems that the prospects for birds of these huge wind farms is not great, but the move to offshore wind power now has unstoppable momentum. One must, of course, weigh the problems against the effects on our climate of continuing to burn fossil fuels, which will also have a profound negative effect on wildlife.

March

Leucism. Over the years I have seen countless birds that one would describe as 'partial albino', and some individuals which were completely white. The sight of a flying white Blackbird bouncing away through a winter woodland is one not quickly forgotten, and I have seen a completely white Jackdaw, and once an all-white Black-headed Gull. Birds with white patches are relatively common, and although albino and partial albino birds are supposed to suffer reduced breeding success, I have seen a Blackbird with a completely white head raise a brood of chicks.

From time to time I have also seen birds which are much paler than they should normally be, but not white – a sandy-coloured Starling at Humberston immediately springs to mind – and these birds are usually described by birdwatchers as 'leucistic'.

In fact, the terminology is confused. True 'albinos' are rarely, if ever, seen in the wild. They have a genetic disorder which means they cannot make tyrosinine, an enzyme necessary for the formation of melanin, the pigment which makes all dark colours. True albinos have uncoloured (pink) legs and bill, and their eyes also look pink or red, because in the absence of pigment the blood vessels can be seen. Birds which are true albinos have poor eyesight and sometimes hearing, and brittle feathers, and along with their extreme obviousness to predators, they almost never last more than a day or two in the wild.

Technically, a bird is either an albino or it is not, so 'partial albino' is actually a term with no meaning. However, it is a useful way of describing partially white birds, and birdwatchers are not quite ready to stop using the term just yet.

When laypeople describe mysterious birds they have seen, if the description includes white patches one immediately suspects the bird was a partial albino version of something common. The way that white feathers often occur along well-defined feather tracts can easily make one think that the white is part of the bird's normal plumage.

All birds which are either wholly, or partly white or pale when they are not supposed to be (so long as they are not rare true albinos) are correctly described as 'leucistic'. There are very many reasons why leucism may occur, and it is often not possible to work out the cause of the aberration in the field.

The colours of birds are created by three groups of chemicals – two different kinds of melanin, and carotenoids. Carotenoids make some reds and oranges, and this is why some birds which are otherwise white still have their red bits normally coloured.

One of the types of melanin produces blacks and greys, and the other red-browns and buffs. Normally, they work together to produce a bird's camouflaged plumage. Either, or both, can be missing. When looked at in these terms, many strange colour variations in birds can be explained in terms of one missing pigment or the other. However, there are many other ways that the production of melanin can be interrupted, diluted, or perhaps not deposited or oxidised properly, leading to all manner of bizarre pale colour schemes.

When normal colour patterns of birds are missing it can be amazing how a species' visual 'jizz' can be altered, making identification more difficult. In a strange optical illusion, white birds tend to look larger than the 'same bird but dark', and a lack of distinctive markings can make a bird's shape look quite untypical. My white Black-headed Gull looked surprisingly pigeon-like, despite standing alongside others of its kind.

EU vote. On Thursday June 23 2016, the nation will vote in a referendum on whether to remain in, or leave, the European Union. While the effects on wildlife may not come top of many people's concerns, the stakes for the UK's natural history and environmental standards are nevertheless high.

It is often stated that nature knows no international boundaries. Of course essentially it does not, although if your nation is an island, this can never be completely true. Nevertheless, initiatives rolled out over large areas will tend to work from a wider overview – be more 'joined-up' – than parochial ones. Issues like global warming can only be tackled internationally, and by setting Europe-wide directives, the EU makes sure that one country doesn't steal an economic march on its neighbours by trashing its own environment.

Over eighty percent of our environmental legislation – the laws that protect our wildlife – come from Europe. First among these are the Birds Directive and the Habitats Directive (known together as the Nature Directives). These are the cornerstone of nature conservation in Europe, and require all 28 member states to identify and care for a network of special places for nature. Nine hundred of these are in the UK, including the Humber Estuary. Overall, the Nature Directives protect over a thousand vulnerable species of animal and plant, in over 200 types of habitat. When you see huge flocks of Knot, godwits and plovers wheeling over the sands at Cleethorpes, you are seeing the Directives in action.

The current government *[2016]* is known to dislike the burden that environmental legislation places on business. However, the rules are not there to impede development, but to guide *sustainable* development by establishing tests: if a proposal causes an adverse impact on wildlife, developers are obliged to explore alternative options. If this is not possible and there are overriding reasons of public interest for the proposal to go ahead, developers are obliged to compensate for the damage caused.

The legislation enjoys widespread support, with over 75% of EU citizens saying they think environmental law is worthwhile. Developers here in the UK have had plenty of time to get used to it, having worked within EU rules now for some 35 years.

You will hear some people complain that European decision-makers are unaccountable to the UK electorate. Indeed they are, but when it comes to the environment, in a strange way this may be one of their strengths. It frees them up to make unpopular decisions for the good of the whole, and for posterity.

It should be said at this point that neither are transnational corporations elected, and their power over the fate of the environment in the countries in which they operate is arguably greater. So a government that cedes too much power to big business also takes control away from the voter, but in a different way. Of all the international forces which we cannot un-elect, the EU scores fairly highly in any test of benevolence.

The UK does have a little of its own wildlife legislation – the Wildlife and Countryside Act (1981) springs immediately to mind. This would of course be unaffected by exiting the EU.

It is not up to me to tell you how to vote on Europe. The EU is far from perfect, and recently it has shown a very worrying tendency to introduce initiatives releasing business from democracy, which to me are the very opposite of its purpose.

But if you care about wildlife, you must decide whether you trust our own government, among whose immediate concerns may be to appease the huge building, farming and landowning lobbies as well as the business community, to replace the lost EU environmental legislation with versions of its own which come up to the same high standards.

This piece was published on 3 March 2016. On 23 June 2016, the UK voted to leave the EU.

The Irreplaceable Flowers of spring. Much is made these days of the need to put back – to re-create – quality habitats in a countryside simplified and homogenised by modern agriculture. By far the most efficient mechanism for doing this is agri-environment schemes, whereby farmers are paid to give over a proportion of their land to wildlife. But just taking land out of cropping and leaving it to regenerate naturally often gives very disappointing results, especially on heavy, fertile soils like ours. At worst, it creates nothing more than a monoculture of pernicious weeds – Blackgrass or Barren Brome are common problems; or thistles perhaps, which although temporarily fabulous for a few specialised creatures, can never really be the answer.

An approach particularly favoured these days is the use of so-called 'wildflower mixes' whereby the farmer is paid to sow an authentic-looking suite of native wild flowers and fine-leaved grasses on field corners or margins, managing the resulting vegetation to provide an extravaganza of colour at the height of summer when pollinating insects are at their peak. There are specialist flower mixes to match various soils and climatic conditions, with the aim usually being to provide a relatively convincing substitute for indigenous meadow vegetation so much of which has been lost. Although pollinating insects and other invertebrates are supposed to be the immediate beneficiaries, the unspoken hope is that over the long term, a kind of 'naturalness' will gradually be conferred upon such vegetation by gradual ecological change, natural selection and cultural acclimatisation, all helped along by a traditional meadow-type cutting regime.

But one flowery situation which the seed companies have never been able to properly recreate is that which pertains in the early spring. This, arguably, is the time of greatest need for many of our most important pollinating insects. Queen bumblebees coming out of hibernation need pollen and nectar sources to begin new colonies. Many early-appearing flies need nectar sources from February or March onwards. A good number of moths and solitary bees have a single annual generation whose flight season is the early spring. And those butterflies which have spent the winter as adults also need sources of early nectar.

In hedgerows and woodland edges everywhere, shrubs provide much of the early floral resource. Sallow blossom, by which we mean pussy willow – the flowers of the Goat and Grey Willows – is an invaluable pollen and nectar source at this time of year. Sallows are simple to propagate, and plugging gaps in hedgerows with this valuable tree instead of the usual, and already abundant hawthorn, might improve the resource available to the earliest flying insects. The large, yellow male catkins (the greener female catkins occur on separate trees) are a magnet for early bees, flies and butterflies on sunny days from February and March onwards. After dark, moths take over, and species including a number of characteristic early-season 'quakers' and 'drabs', as well as the boldly-marked Hebrew Character, can be seen by torchlight, taking the nectar.

On the ground, look in early spring sunshine for the charismatic Bee-fly on wayside flowers of Ground Ivy and Primrose, and for the earliest solitary bees on Dandelions. A good clump of flowering White Deadnettle will seldom be without attendant ginger Common Carder Bees.

These blooms, along with Coltsfoot, the red deadnettles, Green Alkanet, Speedwells and the like, are not the sort of flowers you would ever realistically sow. Cowslip may be sown, but seed of Primrose, its close relative and another early species, is expensive. Other sowable plants which could perhaps afford early nectar such as autumn-sown Phacelia or Crimson Clover, would create a very clumsy substitute for a wild habitat.

There is a constant danger that we come to see habitat recreation as a substitute for protecting the wildlife habitats we already have. It would be all too easy to unthinkingly use the setting aside of new land for wildlife as a convenient excuse, or sop, for the destruction of unappreciated ancient features. We should use the essential flowers of early spring as a lesson, for there can be no replacement for these – no sown seed mixtures has so far managed to mitigate losses of the indigenous flowers of this vital time.

The first priority is to protect the habitats we have, and to a much greater extent these days, we are doing this. Then we can add to this basic stock by the creation of new habitats, and the principles and methods we need to do so are being refined with every passing year. Methods of reversing biodiversity loss on farmland by habitat creation are to an extent now known and proven, and just need a political will to roll out.

However, that there is still no way of providing a substitute for the indispensable wayside flowers of early spring is telling us something – that habitat creation isn't enough on its own. The only way of retaining our regular farmland in good order is by an attitude of judicious neglect; to value our countryside's 'infrastructure' of tangled hedgerows, field margins and scruffy corners, and to battle general obsessions with tidiness.

Little Egrets. Walk the beaches at the south end of our resort these days and you will undoubtedly see a small elegant white heron or two among the marshes and creeks. At rest they stand motionless with their heads tucked into their shoulders, but when feeding they may strut frantically to and fro, constantly half-opening their wings so as to retain their balance, and striking out at fish or crustaceans in the shallows. In flight, they stand out beautifully against the dull greens and browns of the marsh, and their characteristic black legs with large yellow feet can be seen trailing behind.

These most noticeable inhabitants of the marsh are Little Egrets, and their rapid spread into our area is one of the most profound changes to North East Lincolnshire's bird life in the last fifteen years.

Little Egret has a huge world range, being found across the warmer parts of the Old World from Europe to South Africa and Australia. On the other side of the Atlantic, the species is replaced by the very similar and closely-related Snowy Egret.

Through the 1950s, Little Egrets in France started to spread northwards, possibly as a result of a subtle warming of the climate, finally reaching the coast of Brittany in 1960. After consolidating its numbers there, the species used these new colonies as a springboard to invade south-west England.

Before 1989, Little Egret was a very scarce visitor to the British Isles. However this year saw the first of several influxes, this time of about 50 birds, centred on the estuaries of the south-west, just a short hop from Brittany. Further influxes followed, with some 200 birds in 1993, 650 in 1995 and over 1000 in 1999, again strongly concentrated on the south coast.

By the millennium, Little Egret was still a very rare bird in Lincolnshire, with only eight birds having ever been recorded. My own first was one fishing the brackish pools of the Saltfleetby-Theddlethorpe Nature Reserve in April 1995 – a great rarity at the time and a novel sight, which I had travelled to see.

Breeding was recorded for the first time in Britain in 1996 at Brownsea Island in Dorset, and in southern Ireland the following year.

Following this first breeding attempt this species has seen an extraordinary expansion around the coasts of the southern half of the British Isles, and to a more limited extent inland. Many breeding colonies now occur, including a small handful along the Lincolnshire coast. Little Egrets usually nest in trees, associating with colonies of their larger relatives the Grey Heron. In the breeding season the Little Egret's plumage includes long, trailing head and body plumes, which were once much in demand for the fashion industry.

After breeding there is a dispersal of young birds, and in the UK this leads to a strong peak in Little Egret numbers in late summer and early autumn. Although populations may be knocked back by hard winters, small numbers can still be seen at Cleethorpes throughout the year. At times it has been possible to see thirty or more together on the marsh; an amazing spectacle, inconceivable not so long ago.

Little Egret. Photo: Colin Smale
www.fotolincs.com

Egrets are among the most beautiful of all birds. Their colonisation has been natural, and as far as anybody knows, they are completely ecologically benign. They are a most welcome new addition to our county's avifauna.

Sticklebacks. Sticklebacks are the archetypal 'tiddlers'. They bring back sunny childhood memories of pond dipping and jam jars, and are the first fish that most people catch for themselves. Although far too small to be taken seriously by anglers, they must have started innumerable people on a lifelong interest in natural history and the countryside.

In the UK we have three species of stickleback. All three can live in marine environments, but only one, the Fifteen-spined Stickleback, is confined to salt water. The other two are now more often to be found in brackish and fresh water, inhabiting all manner of ponds, lakes, streams and dykes, where they should be familiar to everyone.

Evolutionarily, all sticklebacks started off as sea fish. Sticklebacks have no scales, and predation by other fish in the marine environment has caused them to develop numerous defensive adaptations. These include a series of armoured lateral plates, including a strengthened 'girdle' around the centre of the fish. Then, of course, there are the spines which give them their name – not only along the back, where they can be raised or lowered, but also two more on the underside at about the mid-point. By raising the spines, sticklebacks may cause predators to spit them out, allowing them to live another day.

Sticklebacks living in the sea tend to be large and well-armoured, and look more or less the same throughout their extensive world range. However, at the end of the ice age some 8,000 – 10,000 years ago, some marine sticklebacks started to move inland and colonise newly-created fresh waterbodies. Once inland, populations of sticklebacks became separated from each other, and started to evolve independently. So freshwater sticklebacks, unlike their marine cousins, are extremely variable from place to place, and provide some of the very best subject matter for studies of evolution in action. Sticklebacks are also easy to keep and breed in the laboratory – Three-spined Stickleback is one of the few species to have its whole genome sequenced.

One thing freshwater sticklebacks tend to have in common is a lessening of the armour they needed when they lived in the sea. Most have a reduced numbers of protective plates, and some populations of stickleback in Scotland now have no spines at all. This is probably a response to different kinds of predator pressure in fresh water, reflecting a preference for manoeuvrability over bodily defences in this environment.

In the UK as a whole, the commonest species is the Three-spined Stickleback. The male in breeding dress is known as a 'red doctor', with bright blue eyes as well as variable amounts of red colouration on its underside.

Although this species is common enough here, interestingly it is not the stickleback that one encounters most often in ponds and ditches around Cleethorpes. This honour goes to the fish we now know as Nine-spined Stickleback. As children we used to call them Ten-spined Sticklebacks, although the number of dorsal spines hasn't gone down – it has always been variable, between 7 and 12.

The Nine-spined Stickleback is a slightly smaller fish – indeed it is the smallest freshwater fish in Britain. It is slightly more streamlined than its three-spined relative, and is usually silvery-brown in colour. Males in the breeding season do not turn red, but black. The amount of black is variable, and occasionally we would catch fish which were almost completely black.

Sticklebacks eat almost anything, and almost anything eats them. This means that they are integral to the functioning of the ecosystems in which they live. Unusually among fish, the male stickleback builds a nest – a kind of tunnel – out of vegetable matter. It tries to persuade a female to lay her eggs inside through an elaborate courtship ritual. If successful, the male will guard the nest, occasionally fanning the eggs with oxygenated water. The male will attend to the newly-hatched fry until they move away to fend for themselves.

The Speed of Spring. In Britain we are very fond of our changing seasons. Our mild winters and cool summers make spring and autumn in particular very drawn-out, so there is always something happening in the natural world.

For example, for some, spring comes with the first Snowdrops just after Christmas, but could still be said to be going on when the last Spotted Flycatcher arrives from Africa in mid to late May. Similarly, the autumn migration of birds begins, arguably, in June or July, although richly-coloured autumn leaves may still be seen on the trees in December.

Now, as we approach the middle of March, signs of spring are starting to trickle along. The timing of spring is not the same from year to year, with some springs clearly earlier than others. In fact, there has been a very strong tendency towards early springs in recent times – taken to be evidence for global warming.

Spring comes earlier in the south than the north. Last year, a collaboration between the Woodland Trust, British Science Association and BBC Springwatch set out to measure the 'speed of spring' as it travelled northwards across the British Isles. They found that on average, spring travelled at 1.9mph, or 45 miles a day, taking nearly three weeks to travel the length of the country. Interestingly, the gradient was not directly south-north, but orientated south-west to north-east.

As you might expect, not all signs of spring travelled at the same speed – for example:

Ladybird – 6.5mph
Hawthorn leafing – 6.3mph
Swallows arriving – 2.4mph
Hawthorn flowering – 1.9mph
Orange tip butterfly – 1.4mph
Oak first leafing – 1.3mph
Frogspawn – 1mph

Spring nowadays appears to move northwards faster than it used to. Data from 1891-1947 showed spring managing only a relatively ponderous 1.2mph south to north, or 28 miles a day. The increase in speed in recent times can obviously store up problems for the life-cycles of species in closely-knit ecosystems, especially the further north you go.

While the vast majority of spring events occur earlier than they used to, this cannot be said of all. For example, the arrival of Cuckoo and Swallow in spring does not seem to have advanced at all. If this is also true of other migrant birds, they may increasingly find that on their breeding grounds the peak in abundance of their food has already passed by their time of maximum need, when they have chicks in the nest.

The most intriguing result of all concerns a common wild flower which is very characteristic of this time of year – a cheerful yellow bloom of waste places and ditch-sides and a true harbinger of spring – the Coltsfoot. Although the data show that Coltsfoot comes into flower earlier in warmer springs, the date of first flowering has moved substantially backwards right across its range, now coming into bloom an average of 13 days later than a century ago. This goes strongly against the majority trend, and the reasons are completely unknown. This just goes to show that sometimes the effects of global warming, if indeed this is the reason, may be far from straightforward.

Coltsfoot is unusual in that its flowers appear before its leaves. The groups of yellow flowers sitting on scaly stems are one of the most evocative sign of spring, but at this time there is no foliage in sight. This comes later on, the leaf forming roughly the shape of a splayed hoof, hence the plant's name.

Cleethorpes Country Park is a good place to see Coltsfoot, especially by the bridge at the western end of the lake. Once this most evocative flower is seen, you know spring proper is not far away.

The Mystery of Star Jelly. A couple of times over the last ten or so years I have been asked to confirm the identity of blobs of mysterious clear or whitish jelly which have appeared as though by magic on lawns in our area. I have found the same thing myself just once or twice over the years, always in grassland. This jelly seems to belong to the natural world, although nothing else about it is obvious.

In fact, this phenomenon constitutes one of the most enduring mysteries in nature. No problem in the whole of natural history, including the Loch Ness

Monster, seems to have been tackled with as much imagination as this: the problem of 'star jelly'.

Other names for this substance include 'star-slime', 'star-shoot', 'star-slough' and 'star-slutch'. According to Robert Burton it is *Sternenrotz* (star snot) in German, and to National Geographic, *pwdre ser* (rot of the stars) in Welsh. The first description of star jelly seems to have been made in the fourteenth century, and detailed accounts of the same unmistakable phenomenon have been made with regularity ever since. It is a relatively common occurrence.

There are a multitude of paranormal explanations for the origins of this substance. The 'star' reference, which implies extra-terrestrial, if not supernatural origin, seems to be present everywhere the stuff has been given a name. It has been announced confidently by the magazine *Fate* to originate in space, as "cellular organic matter" which exists as "prestellar molecular clouds". There are many references to it having been deposited on Earth during meteor showers, and indeed, the randomness of the locations in which it is found do seem to confirm that it has been deposited from the sky.

Trying to be more rational, an obvious explanation is that it must be some sort of fungus. Microscopic examination often finds fungus filaments contained within the jelly, but these are thought to be merely growing in it, rather than responsible for it. DNA tests tend to prove inconclusive because of contamination.

No slime mould precisely fits the description, although certain other fungi may resemble blobs of white or clear jelly – notably the 'White Brain' (*Exidia thuretiana*) and 'Crystal Brain' (*Myxarium nucleatum*), both found commonly enough. But these should, by rights, always be seen growing on dead wood, and not on lawns or in other random places. No-one should really mistake this substance for the cyanobacterium which bears the actual English name 'Star Jelly' – *Nostoc commune* – which looks like a succulent, slimy, khaki-coloured seaweed.

The actual explanation – that is the one on which most experts settle – is extremely gruesome, so if you're currently eating, please stop now and read on later.

The substance is amphibian in origin. It is thought to be the jelly from the oviducts of female frogs and toads, with which the little black eggs have not yet been combined to make frog- or toadspawn. The unfortunate animal has been preyed upon – eaten – possibly by a Heron or some other carnivore, and either the jelly-like material ejected before swallowing, or the whole creature swallowed and the nasty bits regurgitated. Once on the ground, the substance tends to swell on contact with water (from wet grass or rain) becoming hugely expanded and unrecognisable. Eventually it starts to decompose, making it even more so.

Clues as to the true identity are sometimes found alongside or within the jelly, in the form of the remains of the oviducts or ovaries of the unfortunate amphibian, or little bundles of black eggs, looking like caviar, beside the jelly. The latter are probably eaten preferentially by any passing scavenger, explaining why they're not seen more often.

While asteroid gloop, angel hair and jellyfish UFOs constitute superficially more attractive explanations, the real answer is more mundane. Indeed, what was already a revolting phenomenon becomes even worse when you know the cause. It just goes to show that the things predators have to do to survive aren't always pretty, but that human imagination is boundless.

Cherry Plum. The cherries are among our most extravagantly-blossomed trees, and March is the month when the earliest of our common species, the Cherry Plum *Prunus cerasifera* bursts copiously into flower, transforming urban and rural landscapes alike, and ushering in the spring.

Cherry Plum is not native to Britain, coming originally from south-east Europe, south-west and central Asia. It was first recorded here in the sixteenth century, but most of our trees were planted after about 1930. It has found its way into many wild situations, and conspicuous patches of white blossom in hedgerows and the edges of woodlands from late February onwards will undoubtedly be this species. In such rural locations, it can be told from the ubiquitous native Blackthorn by its larger flowers, first-year twigs which are green not black, and much earlier leaf-burst, as well as its consistently earlier flowering time.

But it is in villages and towns where the transformation is most complete, with the 'wild', white-flowered type being joined by cultivars with pink flowers and purple foliage. It is very common in larger gardens, and is also planted as a street tree for early spring interest. The cultivated variety 'pissardii', with blackish twigs, deep pink buds and nearly-white flowers, creates arguably the greatest spectacle, especially in full spring sunshine. Another common variety, 'nigra', has deeper pink flowers and still darker foliage.

When in full flower, this species is difficult to miss along Grimsby's leafier thoroughfares, such as Weelsby Road, Bargate, and in the People's Park area, although it is found almost everywhere in smaller quantities. In Cleethorpes there is a particularly floriferous group of trees on Oxford Street near the junction with Highgate. Along Buck Beck as it passes down the side of Pleasure Island, both white and pink varieties grow in great profusion as though wild, with the two flowering at slightly different times.

Producing flowers at such an early season poses problems for an insect-pollinated tree. If the weather at flowering time is good the blossoms may be alive with insects, including early hoverflies, solitary bees, honeybees and queen bumblebees, and even early butterflies such as Small Tortoiseshell, Peacock and Comma. This should lead to successful pollination, and in such a year cropping can be very heavy. However if the weather is bad, which in March it frequently is, fruiting can be poor or missed completely.

The great genus *Prunus* to which Cherry Plum belongs contains all the cherries, plums, damsons and gages, as well as Sloe, Peach, Apricot and Almond. The evergreen Laurel, with its leaves containing poisonous prussic acid, is also a *Prunus*. The young leaves of Laurel were once used for making killing bottles in the days when taking insects for collections was more widespread.

The fruits of the Cherry Plum vary greatly in both colour and taste, differing with variety, ripeness, and even from tree to tree. They are described as inedible by some texts, although this is harsh. In fact they can be used in all the same recipes as plums – jams and jellies, liqueurs, cakes puddings and pies. The yellow ones are particularly good.

After flowering, Cherry Plum becomes an unprepossessing small tree, whose leaves do not produce the extravagant autumn reds and yellows of its relative the larger Wild Cherry, which flowers in May. Wild Cherry is a native tree, although nowadays deciding whether an individual tree is naturally occurring or planted is often difficult. The smaller Bird Cherry, with its conical racemes of white flowers, is also technically native in Britain, but never in our area, where it occurs in odd places but is always sown.

For me, Cherry Plum is the star of this charismatic genus, simply because it flowers right at the end of winter when you need it most.

Submerged forest. If you walk out onto the beach opposite Cleethorpes's Wonderland at very low tide, you may see the remains of tree stumps or fallen trees sticking out of the mud – a peculiar phenomenon, known here for over 200 years. The stumps look like they belong to the remains of an ancient forest. So where did they come from? Did woodland ever grow on the beach?

At the end of the Ice Age, Lincolnshire and the continent of Europe were connected by land. When the climate wasn't too cold, woodland may have stretched between England and Denmark with scarcely a break. There is plenty of evidence for this – lumps of wood and the remains of extinct fauna have regularly been hauled from the floor of the North Sea by trawlers, and more recently by windfarm construction.

Massive sea level rise caused by the melting of the ice finally cut Britain off from the near continent about 6,000 years ago, turning us into an island. The Dogger Bank was the last large piece of land to be covered by water, and even now sits only 20 metres or so below the surface of the middle of the North Sea.

Sea level still continued to rise after that, albeit more slowly and with periodic temporary reversals. For the last 3,500 years it has probably fluctuated no more than 2 metres from today's levels.

Our Cleethorpes foreshore tree stumps – comprising familiar species – Oaks, Birches and Alders among others – have been carbon dated at about 4,000 years old, or just a little older. Such ancient remains would never have survived on the surface of the land, although some may still be buried beneath coastal sediments. Beneath the North Sea, forest remains can survive encased in anaerobic mud, but they are inaccessible and out of human sight. Only in the dynamic inter-tidal zone of our seashores are they revealed to us, although once this ancient wood is exposed its days are numbered, as the depredations of the weather, the waves and human activity all set about wearing it away. For this reason it is important to map and document our ancient forest while we can.

Other patches of inter-tidal submerged forest can be found in various places both up and down the coast from Cleethorpes, although much must have been lost to coastal engineering, beach replenishment and natural coastal processes, as well as historical collection by people for fuel.

In 1979, Shane Johnson of Scartho, while out bait-digging among Cleethorpes's submerged forest, made the extraordinary find of a large hand-axe with a shaft of Poplar wood, which has since been dated at about 3,300 years old. It was already known that late Neolithic humans had roamed this ancient landscape, from numerous finds of flint blades and scrapers, antler picks and the like, both here and further along our coast. This age marks approximately the time that humankind was starting to swap a hunter-gatherer existence for a more settled agricultural lifestyle. Interestingly, although still ancient, this hand-axe proved to be some 700 years younger than the peaty layer in which was embedded, highlighting the pitfalls of ageing implements and artefacts from the substrate in which they end up.

Even more amazingly, in 2015, the remains of what is believed to be an ancient trackway were found out on our Wonderland beach, looking like a wide ladder laid out on the ground, formed of unworked Oak. This feature, running towards the sea, would perhaps indicate the need of Neolithic people need to cross marshy or boggy ground.

That such an important archaeological site exists so close to our promenade remains unknown to many. Our submerged forest and its man-made relics are now technically protected, although much has already been taken or destroyed. Some is reported to have been damaged by fishing. Souvenirs abound – in 1954, the Civic leaders of Sheffield and Cleethorpes met up and sawed off chunks to take away. One may come across numerous wooden objects supposedly fashioned from our ancient forest around the town, many never catalogued. It is said that a trinket box made from our beach's wood was given to the Queen on her first visit to Grimsby and Cleethorpes.

Cleethorpes's 'submerged forest'.
Copyright CITiZAN, photograph by Megan Clement

The underlying trend in sea level is still upwards, and this will be exacerbated by human-induced climate change. Problematically, many of our population centres, including large parts of our own town, are built at sea level, and even now it is a devil of a job to dissuade people from building in flood risk areas. One tends to forgive the builders of the past, although seeing trees apparently growing under the sea should at least have given them pause for thought.

Early butterflies. If you've been out and about in North East Lincolnshire in the last few weeks you should have seen a butterfly or two by now. The first one I heard about this year was on 9th February 2015 – a fine Peacock nectaring on spring flowers near Cleethorpes Boating Lake, spotted by Carole

Crawford. This was the first genuinely warm day after a run of cold weather, which is very often the time when the first butterfly appears.

While Peacock is generally the most likely species to be seen first in our area, there are others which could conceivably take the prize, and these fall into three groups.

Firstly, there are the migrants – for us, this means Red Admiral and Painted Lady. In the UK as a whole, the Red Admiral is the butterfly most likely to be seen early in the year, although records are strongly biased towards the south of England. In most years, a Red Admiral is seen somewhere on New Year's Day. Red Admirals and Painted Ladies are not usually able to overwinter in Britain, but can migrate northwards from warmer climes at pretty much any time. While migration is commoner later in the year, odd individuals do reach us in winter.

The second group contains those species which hibernate as adult butterflies. Doing this allows them to burst into action as soon as the temperature reaches about 13 degrees, taking advantage of spring flowers and getting on with breeding. There are four of these: Peacock, Small Tortoiseshell, Brimstone and Comma. Further south or in more wooded districts, the pale yellow Brimstone is usually the first to appear, often in February. This species usually hibernates among evergreens such as Holly or Ivy where its closed wings are beautifully camouflaged. Once on the wing, it can be seen powering purposefully across country in search of its larval foodplants, Buckthorn or Alder Buckthorn.

The other three in this group seek to lay their eggs on nettles. In our area, Peacock is usually run close by Small Tortoiseshell for the first spring sighting, while the Comma is usually slightly more reluctant to appear. The Comma is a relatively new colonist with us, having arrived here in the mid-1990s in response to global warming. In flight, the Peacock will usually look large and black, whereas the chestnut-orange colouration of the two slightly smaller species should be visible with half a good view.

The third group contains the species which overwinter as chrysalises. These species have metamorphosis which is nearly complete by the time the warm weather comes along, and do not need much of a push to emerge and get onto the wing in the spring. Although these butterflies are not usually the ones seen first, they are certainly out and about in April, and if the other species have somehow eluded you thus far, one of this group could be the first you see. They include the three common 'whites', although for some reason it is usually the Small White which is the earliest to appear. The plain butter-coloured underside of the Small White differentiates it from the similarly-sized Green-veined White, with Large White usually identifiable by size.

The Holly Blue is also out in April – it will be the only blue butterfly seen at this time, and nearly always associated with evergreen shrubs. The last of this group is the Speckled Wood, which is another global warming-related colonist in our area. Although it arrived in North East Lincolnshire somewhat later than the Comma, it is now one of the commonest butterflies here in late summer gardens and woodland. This butterfly is brown, patterned with beige spots, and invariably inhabits places with dappled shade from trees. The first to be seen is usually a few days into April.

Frogspawn. We are coming up to that time of year when people start to report frogspawn in their garden ponds or local waterbodies. There cannot be anybody above a certain age who didn't, as a child, go through the ritual of collecting frogspawn and rearing tadpoles, at least at school. This means that the early life stages of the Common Frog are possibly the best-known of any British wild animal.

A very mild winter can encourage early spawning by frogs, with some, somewhere, usually reported in December, although February or March are more usual. Early spawning may be ok if the weather remains fairly mild for the remainder of the winter. But if a cold snap follows and a layer of ice forms over floating frogspawn it can be fatal, although a little spawn lying deeper in the water may survive.

To try to save frogspawn, I have known people place a cover over a pond to protect it from hard frost, or even remove the spawn into a bucket and place it somewhere less exposed, such as an outbuilding, before returning it to the water afterwards. This amount of effort is probably not necessary – in the end, numbers are self-regulating, with frost at the spawn stage only the first of many catastrophes which will decimate tadpole numbers through the course of the spring.

The amount of frogspawn in a pond can sometimes be extreme, and I have seen largish ponds whose entire surface was covered in mats of spawn. This can eventually lead to an extraordinary black mass of young tadpoles in the warm shallows. This seeming excess is entirely natural, and there is no such thing as too much spawn, nor too many tadpoles. It is a breeding strategy typical of amphibians the world over, and with the wide range of predators and diseases that tadpoles face, not to mention competition between the tadpoles themselves, only a very tiny proportion will ever survive to become froglets. Similarly, only a tiny proportion of those froglets will become adult frogs.

At the other extreme, you may be wondering why your pond doesn't seem to have any frogs or frogspawn in it. A new pond might take a couple of years to be colonised. Perhaps your pond is simply not suitable – accessible ponds whose water is warmed by the sun, are best.

We are told that what we must *not* do is move spawn from one pond to another. To do this risks transferring fungal diseases, or highly invasive water plants, to places where they were previously absent. However, frogs are generally adept at finding breeding places by themselves, and if you have a long-standing pond and frogs are not there already, there is probably a good reason.

Sadly, frogs are much less common these days than they used to be, and an absence of frogs in a particular pond may reflect local population decline. Perhaps other, nearby breeding ponds from which frogs could disperse have been lost, or 'corridors' of terrestrial vegetation through which frogs can travel overland has deteriorated. Hostile intervening developments such as roads may prevent migrating frogs from reaching an isolated pond.

But frogspawn is still relatively easy to find in many of its old traditional places; the dykes of Cleethorpes Country Park still usually hold a little.

The principles involved in raising froglets from frogspawn are for most of us so familiar as not to need describing. If you know any modern children who have somehow avoided this rite of passage, please do introduce them to the miracle of amphibian metamorphosis. It may be an important step in gaining an appreciation of the natural world which will never leave them.

Plants of Walls. Plants have a variety of different survival strategies. Those able to thrive only in the most perfect conditions – stable, damp, fertile places – must be able to aggressively outcompete other species to hold their own in such an agreeable environment.

Other, less competitive species effectively avoid the competition by being able to grow in places where the others can't. Plants, for example, which can survive regular destruction of their habitat by being able to grow, flower and set seed very quickly, are known as ruderals. This category includes many annuals, including most of our cornfield weeds – poppies and the like.

A final group of plants is able to compete by being able to tolerate stress – to grow on the very limits of what is biologically possible. This may mean extreme heat or cold, parched, bone-dry places, extreme soil types, or where there is very little soil.

Man-made, town-centre habitats very often favour the latter group of plants. Old buildings and walls have their characteristic suite of plant species, often those which can tolerate extremely dry conditions, and the most rudimentary of soils.

Three kinds of urban habitat tend to provide much of the opportunity for stone- and wall-dwelling plants in towns – derelict sites, churchyards, and railways. In our own area we must add docks to this list, and garden walls are also very important.

The very commonest plants on walls are probably those which can grow anywhere dry and stony. First among these is probably Buddleia, which can germinate and grow almost anywhere. After this probably come plants of waste ground like Canadian Fleabane and Oxford Ragwort.

But some are almost exclusively wall specialists. That relative of Nettles and Hop, the Pellitory of the Wall, is seldom seen anywhere except on walls. Like its relatives, its flowers are fairly inconspicuous, and apart from the sticky, red stems, the plant is rather uncharismatic. Much more colourful is the climbing Ivy-leaved Toadflax, present in Britain since the early seventeenth century, and now common on walls everywhere. When in flower, the small lilac and yellow snapdragon-like flowers bend towards the light, but after flowering, the stems bend back the other way, to increase the chance of depositing the seeds back into the wall. Look for it, for example, on the front garden walls of Frederick Street, opposite Bursar Street School. On Grimsby docks, another toadflax, the Purple Toadflax, is a common wall plant – a pink variety is almost as common as the more usual purple sort.

Possibly even more colourful is another alien, the Yellow Corydalis. Although much commoner in the damper west of the country, it can be seen here and there on walls in our area, usually associated with gardens.

Wallflower, as its name suggests, can live on robust old walls, where it is often joined by Red Valerian, and sometimes Snapdragon – all, of course, garden escapes, but able to grow in stony places in their homelands.

No list of classic wall plants can ignore the ferns. In the dry east of England, ferns are rather poorly represented, and unlike those species already mentioned, wall-dwelling ferns are likely to seek out the darker, damper spots. Overhangs on railway platforms and north-facing garden walls are the classic places to find them.

Four species are overwhelmingly dominant on walls in our area – firstly the Male Fern, which very seldom achieves anything like its full size on our walls. The same could be said of the Hartstongue fern, which is nevertheless identified easily by its strap-like, undivided fronds. Two small ferns in the genus *Asplenium* finish off the quartet – the little Wall Rue, our smallest native fern, and the delicate Maidenhair Spleenwort, with its two ranks of tiny leaflets along a dark central stalk. It is possible that other ferns lie undiscovered on our area's walls – I always think that the Black Spleenwort is one which may be lurking somewhere, and both Hard Shield Fern and the distinctive Polypody are recorded.

People have an unfortunate habit of removing ferns and other plants from garden walls – I can't imagine why – I think any garden wall looks better with them than without them. In Cleethorpes, ferns can be seen on garden walls along many of the older streets; also in cracks on the sea-facing side of the Natwest Bank on Sea View Street, if they haven't been removed. Welholme Galleries has a good crop of ferns of three species, but these are also periodically removed. On Grimsby Docks, look for ferns on old derelict buildings, such as the old brick railway station. There is a nice Hartstongue on the vertical side of the Riverhead near The Barge.

The Last Willow Tit? It is very common for two species which look almost exactly the same to differ in their ecological and habitat requirements. Indeed it has to be this way – if they were too similar, so the theory goes, one would be slightly better adapted to its environment than the other, and exclude it by competition.

Two such species are the Marsh Tit and the Willow Tit, a pair of tiny, black-capped woodland birds which were only identified as separate species about a hundred years ago. The first of these, the Marsh Tit, is an inhabitant of larger blocks of woodland with a well-developed shrub layer. Because this habitat is scarce in North East Lincolnshire, this bird has never lived here.

The second of this pair of lookalikes, the Willow Tit, tends to inhabit smaller, damper and scrubbier woodlands. Unlike the Marsh Tit, which needs to find ready-made holes in which to nest, the Willow Tit excavates its own hole in rotten wood, which may explain its preference for damper places. In an extremely short space of time, the Willow Tit has undergone a catastrophic decline over many parts of its range. Indeed it is the fastest-disappearing British bird, with a fall of 80% registered in just 15 years.

This decline would have been inconceivable forty years ago. On any winter woodland walk around North East Lincolnshire an encounter with a mixed flock of roving tits and Goldcrests would often include Willow Tits. They would be given away by their metallic, nasal calls – you wouldn't have to see them to know they were there. If you were lucky, you may find a Willow Tit's nest in the springtime, as I remember doing, aged eleven, in a little patch of wet, scrubby, woodland on land now lost beneath the Cleethorpes Country Park housing estate.

The reasons for the decline of Willow Tit are still essentially unknown – there are only weak correlations between their decline and either numbers of predators or catastrophic habitat loss, as happened when the Country Park was built. The degradation in *quality* of habitat by drying out, the removal of dead wood, or grazing of the all-important shrub layer by increasing numbers of deer, may be a cause. It is rather more likely that Willow Tits are out-competed in woodlands by the more adaptable Blue Tit and Great Tit, the latter two being given a considerable boost by the provision of garden food and nestboxes by humans. So we may be partly to blame.

Willow Tits are now almost completely absent from the south-east quarter of England, except for a few small outlying populations in rural Lincolnshire, Norfolk and Suffolk. In our area, I saw a Willow Tit at Tetney Blow Wells and heard of another at Newton Marsh, Tetney in 2007. Another (my last) was at Killingholme in the early part of 2009, and one was also seen at the same time near the Humber bank west of Grimsby. A lone Willow Tit was seen along Newton Marsh Lane, Tetney on 10th November 2010 with another three weeks later at Tetney Blow Wells on 3 December 2010.

For a long time we assumed that this sighting would be the last, but intriguingly, a Willow Tit was seen by Justin Carr on North Moss Lane, Stallingborough, on March 11th 2016.

If you can contribute any more recent Willow Tit sightings in North East Lincolnshire please do tell me – they are very rare here now, and any record from now on could be the genuine last for this tiny, unassuming bird which was once so common.

Many thanks to Ian Shepherd, Steve Meek, Dave Bradbeer, Chris Atkin and Justin Carr for their records.

Update: a single Willow Tit was reported on 27 August 2017 at Tetney Blow Wells.

Rookeries. No other land bird in Britain places its nest in such open view as the Rook. Rooks have no need for concealment, finding protection in numbers, and nesting in the flimsy upper branches of the tallest trees. Rooks' nests are made all the more conspicuous by the fact that they start to build in late winter when there are no leaves to hide them, and there are few other signs of spring.

Rooks have paired up by January, and are already starting to compete for the coveted central locations within the rookery by this time. By March, the breeding season is well underway. Contrary to an age-old myth, Rooks do not use the same nests from year to year. In fact, Rooks' nests are not held together so firmly by a mud lining as those of their close relatives the Carrion Crow and the Magpie and so tend to disintegrate, especially during winter storms. Rooks may sometimes build a new nest on top of an old platform if it has survived the winter, but will usually dismantle the remains of old nests for materials, as well as stealing twigs from each others' nests, in order to build new structures.

Groups of mature elms traditionally provided the classic location for rookeries, although since Dutch elm disease took hold in the 1970s such sites have no longer been available. Rooks will nest in any available group of tall trees, although proximity to farmland makes a site more attractive. They will avoid both the centres of cities and the interiors of dense woodland.

The end of March is usually the last opportunity to see and count Rooks' nests unhindered by new growth of leaves, although some nest building continues into April. From the second half of March a female Rook may start her clutch, with less experienced birds breeding slightly later. Four to six mottled, blue-green eggs are laid, which hatch after 16-18 days. The young fledge after about 32 days, and by the beginning of June, rookeries are as good as deserted.

Rooks' sociability – their tendency to occur in close flocks – is a strong characteristic of the species outside the breeding season as well as at nesting time. It is said that Rooks can always be told from Carrion Crows by this tendency to flock, with crows, by contrast, only occurring in ones and twos. In our area this is not quite true, as large groups of Carrion Crows can occur on the strandline of the beach if food there is plentiful; at Saltfleetby I once saw more than 200 Carrion Crows together on the beach in winter. But inland, this rule is a good one. Rooks can be further told from crows by their 'shaggier', more reflective plumage; also, adults have a white patch of bare skin around the base of the bill.

All of the rookeries close to where I live are smaller than the national average, which is said to be about 24 pairs. Having said that, they are more or less stable in numbers from year to year, and some have been there a very long time – I can remember the rookery by the mini-roundabout in Humberston being present nearly fifty years ago, and I'm sure it is much older still. This longevity has led to many places being defined by their rookeries, and more towns and villages in the UK are named after the Rook than any other bird.

Rooks' social interactions make them wonderful to watch. Immense, noisy flights to roost at dusk by Rooks and Jackdaws in winter, as well as frantic chases and towering aerobatics above a rookery in the spring, are more entertaining than anything you'll see from a common old crow.

Doggerland. The county of Lincolnshire is one of the easier ones to pick out on a map, as it is defined by its coastline. But what we today know as Lincolnshire was, not so long ago, landlocked within the extensive continent of Europe. The current coastline – the 'shape' of our county, was created by sea level rise.

The last glacial maximum occurred between approximately 26,000 and 20,000 years ago. Ice spread down as far as Lincolnshire, then receded northwards again. Even when the ice was not present, 'Lincolnshire' would have had an inhospitable cold climate, like the tundra today. The land would have been roamed by giant, cold-tolerant creatures such as Woolly Mammoth and Woolly Rhinoceros.

The ice kept huge quantities of water locked up, so sea levels were much lower, at one time about 127m below those of today. What is now the North Sea was dry land – a region we now call 'Doggerland'.

About 12,000 years ago a period of warming began. Low-lying areas were inundated by water released from retreating ice sheets, and the land became richly vegetated, with swamps and forests grazed by herds of deer, Elk, Wild Boar, Beaver and Aurochs (wild cattle). These would have been hunted by Mesolithic people, who would also have had to live alongside bears, Lynx and Wolves.

By 9,000 years ago, sea level rise was continuing apace, and only a large island was left in the middle of what is now the North Sea. About 7,000 years ago this island was finally submerged. To this day, trawlers still drag up the bones of land mammals and chunks of wood from the bed of the North Sea, and marine life such as coral, hydroids, starfish and crustaceans make a home on ancient submerged tree stumps.

That island is still essentially there, submerged beneath the North Sea – it is the Dogger Bank. Despite being between 78 and 180 miles from the coast of England, in places it sits only 17 metres below the surface of the sea. It is now a huge sandbank, occupying British, Dutch and German waters, supporting a great wealth of sand-dwelling marine life. This provides a huge food source for a variety of fish, many of which also spawn here. Seabirds from the breeding colonies of eastern Britain will travel to the Dogger Bank for the rich pickings, and the fish-rich waters attract numerous underwater predators as well as cetaceans up to the size of Minke Whale.

Three points need to be made. Firstly, of the huge herds of grazing 'megafauna' and their predators which once roamed Lincolnshire and adjacent lands, only a few deer and domestic farm animals remain. Although the giant beasts are gone, our wildlife habitats are still essentially co-adapted with them. Examples include the way that large trees can regenerate when extensively damaged, the toughness of the roots of Holly and Yew, and disruptive black and white colouration of birch bark, not to mention the fearsome armour of Blackthorn. These are all responses to extinct herbivores – huge elephants, rhinoceroses and the like. These animals' absence is one of the main reasons why wildlife habitats must these days be managed by humans to keep them in balance, and in favourable condition.

Secondly, the Dogger Bank, with its wildlife riches, although it now has a fisheries management plan in place, still receives grossly inadequate conservation priority and insufficient practical protection – from beam trawling, from oil and gas extraction, and from giant wind farms. This situation could be radically improved.

Thirdly, sea level rise has not stopped. Although still going on in the background, it is being accelerated by human-induced climate change. Tackling global warming entails a lot of painful changes to our lifestyles, and nobody suggesting such changes does so to make friends. The more than 97% of climate scientists who are telling us that the problem is real and are asking us to do something about it, are therefore probably worth paying attention to.

April

Muntjac. Most of the UK's larger animals are very familiar to us, being easily recognisable even by children. One's first sighting of a Muntjac in Britain can therefore come as a bit of a surprise. Muntjac is a tiny deer, no more than 20 inches tall, with only rudimentary antlers or no antlers at all, and large scent glands below its eyes. The male has prominent tusks and black markings on its head, as well as 'pedicels' or antler bosses, which give rise to an alternative name of 'Rib-faced Deer'. When startled, a Muntjac will skulk away quickly with its short tail held aloft, revealing a white underside, often uttering a loud bark as it goes. In its reddish summer coat, a Muntjac could be mistaken for a fox as it quickly disappears into the undergrowth. But with a decent view, it looks like nothing you've ever seen before.

Muntjac, like all deer currently living in England, descend from introduced animals and escapes from captivity. Muntjac have been kept in collections since the 19th Century and early escapes no doubt occurred. In 1947–9, the 11th Duke of Bedford famously released Muntjac at several sites in the southern half of England, from which they slowly spread, and they have now become very common across much of the south.

The first Muntjac seen in Lincolnshire were in the 1960s. Rather than an expansion of southern populations, these are more likely to have been the result of more recent, local releases, with a rather patchy distribution suggesting several sites of origin in mid- and south Lincolnshire, and possibly along the coast.

Muntjac differ from all other British deer in that they have no pronounced breeding season. Females, or does, reach puberty at about seven months old and start breeding regardless of the time of year. Pregnancy lasts about 210 days, at the end of which a single kid is born. They will mate again as little as 2–3 days later, and so will spend most of their adult lives pregnant. Males, or bucks, use their tusks for fighting as well as feeding, generally defending a territory until their tusks break, which usually marks the end of that animal's reproductive life.

Muntjac are not yet a familiar sight in North East Lincolnshire, as we have so little of their favoured dense woodland habitat. However, a few have been

Muntjac. Photo: Colin Smale www.fotolincs.com

reported in some of the larger woodlands and wilder gardens. They are quite secretive, so there are probably more around than you think, and despite laws introduced in the 1990s prohibiting further releases into the wild, they seem certain to become commoner in the future. This is not great news for gardeners as they are herbivores with a liking for a variety of low-growing plants and flowers. However, some people will no doubt welcome them as an interesting addition to the garden fauna.

Inbreeding in Plants. Now is the time when many of our spring flowers burst forth, making us look forward to the better weather ahead. Three of the most characteristic of these which you will see everywhere in spring – Primrose, Lungwort and Forsythia – although unrelated, have something fascinating in common.

Take a mass of yellow wild Primroses on a woodland floor or along an old hedge-bank. Take a close look at the flowers – the petals are fused at their bases into a tube. In some of the flowers, the tip of the female organ, the stigma, looking like the greenish head of a pin, sits right in the mouth of the tube, flush with the extended petals. Pulling the flower apart will reveal the male parts, the anthers, hidden much further down the tube, well concealed.

But in other Primrose flowers the reverse will be true, with the pollen-covered anthers, held in place by radial 'spokes', in the mouth of the tube, and the pin-like head of the stigma hidden deep below. So although the plants are all one species, there are two versions of the flower which have a kind of reciprocal configuration – the first known as 'pin', and the second 'thrum'. Lungwort and Forsythia also have 'pin' and 'thrum' flowers.

Charles Darwin was the first to suggest a reason for this. Insects fertilise flowers by carrying the pollen from the anthers of one plant to the stigma of another. He concluded that the pin/thrum dichotomy was designed not only to prevent a flower from pollinating itself, but to make sure that pollination only occurred among plants that were unlike each other, to eliminate the adverse effects of inbreeding. Pollen collected from anthers in a given position would be more likely to be wiped off on stigmas in the same position on another plant, he thought.

There are some plants, however, for which inbreeding is actually desirable. These can often pollinate themselves, or even produce seeds without fertilisation – effectively by cloning. Examples of the latter include some dandelions, hawkweeds and brambles. This can be a good strategy in an emergency – say where pollination would not otherwise occur, or if the plant is perfectly suited to its environment. But these plants are not particularly good at coping with change, and must remain well-adapted to their surroundings if they are not to become evolutionary dead-ends. As with animals, outbreeding, with the genetic variability it creates, tends to be best.

There are other mechanisms apart from 'pin' and 'thrum' flowers to prevent inbreeding. Some are to do with non-synchronised maturing of the male and female parts. Some are chemical, and therefore invisible to the eye. Others concern the sculpturing of the surfaces of pollen and stigma, allowing only un-alike plants to physically fertilise each other. In fact, it is now known that incompatibility at the genetic level always evolves first, and the physical adaptations, such as 'pin' and 'thrum' flowers, evolve later, simply to make an existing system less wasteful.

The proportions of 'pin' and 'thrum' flowers in Primroses tend to be about 50:50. But the ratios in other flowers such as those already mentioned, as well as pin and thrum species appearing later in the summer such as Sea Lavender, are much less well-known. This is a gap in our knowledge to which anybody can easily contribute, given a little bit of time and an interest.

A fascinating variation on the 'pin' and 'thrum' situation can be seen in the common Purple Loosestrife, which also flowers later in the summer. This is a plant whose handsome spikes of flowers can be found fairly easily alongside ponds and waterways in North East Lincolnshire. In a Purple Loosestrife flower, there are not two but three different configurations of anthers and stigmas. The stigma always occupies one of three different positions – low, middle or high – with male anthers always occurring in the two where the stigma is not. A similar three-way arrangement occurs in our non-native pink-

and yellow-sorrels of the genus Oxalis. We have them naturalised on the dunes at Humberston Fitties, although no-one has yet looked to see which form they are.

The very best way of avoiding inbreeding, of course, is to have male and female parts on completely separate plants. These so-called 'dioecious' species include Holly, willows, Red and White Campions, Juniper, Nettle and Dog's Mercury.

A dioecious flower to look for in April on roadsides and riverbanks is the native Butterbur. It forms extensive patches, with large, heart-shaped leaves and flowers like dirty-pink bottlebrushes. Each colony is either wholly male or wholly female, with the difference often discernible from a moving car. If you find a colony and sex it, especially if it is male, please tell me where you saw it.

Bullfinches. The beautiful Bullfinch is encountered far less often than you would expect for a relatively common bird. Inhabitants of thick, woody cover, they reveal themselves much more often once the simple call is learned. Bullfinches have many unusual features which separate them from their relatives, and have a long-standing relationship with humans, both as friend and foe.

A male Bullfinch is one of the most handsome of birds, with its smart black cap, glossy rose-pink underparts, and the stout 'bull neck' that gives it its name. Females are similarly patterned, but the underparts are a more subdued brownish grey. As they fly away from the observer, both sexes can be identified by their striking white rump and black tail.

Bullfinches are difficult birds to survey in spring, as they favour such densely-vegetated places and have no obvious, well-known song. The contact call, which is heard much more often, is a single, slightly downslurred note sounding rather like a short, mournful human whistle. The call would be easy not to notice, but is completely distinctive once known. In fact Bullfinches do have a song of sorts – a simple series of blunt, creaking and piping sounds – but it is quiet and seldom heard, and when encountered unexpectedly may catch out even experienced birdwatchers.

This reluctance to vocalise strongly is odd, because at one time Bullfinches were very much in demand for the cage bird trade owing to their powers of mimicry. Much gentler-natured than parrots, in captivity Bullfinches will learn a variety of short tunes if they are repeated to them enough, and occasionally will also mimic human speech. Large numbers were once imported from

Germany for this purpose, but they were taken from the wild in this country too.

Bullfinches are herbivores, feeding on a variety of wild seeds. Foremost among these are the 'keys' of Ash, but they are also partial to the seeds of docks, nettles, brambles and birch, among others. In the spring, a Bullfinch's diet widens to include the buds of trees such as Hawthorn, Blackthorn and Sallow, and especially the flower buds of fruit trees.

When it comes to cultivated fruit, Bullfinches are very picky in the buds they choose to consume. It is said that they especially favour the flower buds of Morello Cherry, and prefer Conference and Williams Pears to Comice. They are also partial to the buds of most apples (although they are said to prefer 'eaters'), gooseberries and currants, and have been recorded consuming more than 30 fruit buds per minute.

Inevitably, this has brought Bullfinches into conflict with fruit growers, who until relatively recently used to trap and kill Bullfinches by the thousand.

In fact, this slaughter was pretty futile, as it has been calculated that a fruit tree can lose up to 50% of its flower buds without any loss of yield, and that killing even large numbers of Bullfinches makes almost no impact whatsoever on populations in the long-term. Nowadays, the fashionable way to discourage Bullfinches is by the removal of dense vegetation from the vicinity of orchards so that they have no nearby cover.

Bullfinches avoid the most treeless landscapes and the centres of cities, but may be seen almost anywhere else. They are fairly sedentary, although they will spread away from breeding areas in winter in search of food. Numbers are now stable to increasing, but still thought to be about 40% down on the late 1960s, and for this reason Bullfinches are now protected from trapping or killing.

Unusually, Bullfinches tend to remain in pairs throughout the year, although pairs may join together into small flocks in winter. Bright blue eggs are laid in a nest which, unlike that of any other common small bird, is made of twigs.

Watch out for the charismatic Bullfinch – it is fairly shy, but once you are familiar with its simple but characteristic whistling note, you will seem to encounter it much more often.

'Naturalness' and Feral Daffodils. I once knew someone who was on his way to an ancient woodland having been promised a chance to see his first ever Dormice, but turned round and went home when he found out the

Dormice in question were part of a reintroduction programme. The hand of humankind was too great for him to keep his interest – he wanted his first experience of Dormice to be "natural – the real thing", he said. He didn't want to see special wildlife in a place where it had been merely "put by people" – for that, he said he can "go to the zoo".

Although 'naturalness' is actually quite a complex concept, naturalists seem to understand it and seek it as a matter of intuition. Someone who by definition likes things that are 'natural' must struggle daily with the philosophical complexities of trying to record, enjoy and protect a countryside containing many introduced species, almost every aspect of which is modified by human use. Introduced species can seem somehow less respectable than natives, although interestingly, attitudes to unnaturalness can soften if a species is here long enough – poppies for example, Fallow Deer, and Little Owls, none of which are indigenous to Britain.

When the concept is applied to habitats, 'naturalness' may be used as a way of judging sites in terms of their conservation priority, or worthiness for protection. This means that the word has had to acquire a working definition. In fact, when deconstructed, it turns out that a place with high naturalness has no implicit wildlife value at all, but tends usually to gain protection incidentally by virtue of having scored highly on other measures, such as species diversity, rarity, fragility or 'intrinsic appeal'. Although its meaning is relatively easy to understand, naturalness in practice may be used as nothing more than a synonym for other things which are not all that natural at all.

Having said that, here on the Lincolnshire coast we have some genuine naturalness, in the estuarine wilderness we see when we look south from Cleethorpes, with its shifting sediments, glittering creeks, bird-filled marshes and unobstructed sweeping tides. Despite no longer being able to wander unchecked across the landscape in line with global processes, and with the large grazing animals of pre-history now gone, this is still probably as close to a natural habitat as you'll now find in lowland Britain. Being in close proximity to such a genuine wilderness is a health-giving privilege that is one of the joys of living here, and which we should never take for granted.

Arguments about 'naturalness' find an absurd extreme in the discussion about 'feral Daffodils'. This is a conversation which any two botanists must inevitably come round to if they spend long enough together, for it is something on which they all have an opinion. Why it should be – when on a country drive one passes hedgerows full of wild plum, fields of poppies, flattened Grey Squirrels, Harlequin Ladybirds on the windscreen and any number of half-tame Pheasants running all over the place – that one should pick on Daffodils as the most controversial and ire-inspiring alien, is rather odd. But people do.

It is not a coincidence that many of our most colourful early flowers are introductions, for they were introduced specifically for this reason – to break up the colourlessness of late winter and sometimes agonisingly ponderous onset of spring. Planting Daffodils out on middle-of-nowhere roadsides has obviously been a method of alleviating this seasonal endurance test for many people over many years, for it happens almost everywhere you go. Daffodils in the countryside can sometimes indicate sites of former habitation, where only the garden flowers now remain. But usually they do not.

It is something about Daffodils that gets people worked up – they are such a cheerful colour; they occur incongruously down the centre of verges in well-spaced clumps or strips, their unnaturalness compounded by the fact that you know they cannot possibly have spread there on their own. They are the gaudiest thing for miles, and the bright yellow, which appears exactly when you need it most, cannot fail to do you good. But they are, and look, wholly unnatural, and for some purists this can be too much of a conceptual clash.

Among botanists I think I have found something of a north-south split on the subject. Folks from the south, and the south-west even more so, can passionately detest remote roadside Daffodils, for the rudeness of the intrusion they make into both the psychology of the seasons and the indigenous vegetation of roadsides. And the less like our very rare, native daffodil the cultivar involved looks, the more they dislike them.

They should try a northern Lincolnshire spring, I tell them, especially a late one. The overdose of khaki dreariness, and the sometimes tormenting reluctance of winter cold to relent right through April and beyond, can be altogether too great for the human spirit. You can't deny people a few Daffodils on roadsides under those circumstances.

If you're one of those people who has an opinion either way about feral roadside daffs, the country roads around Rothwell in the Wolds, as well as the Peaks Parkway and the A16 out of Grimsby, are particularly good/bad for them.

Barn Owls. It is almost impossible to imagine any aspect of natural history which could give more pleasure than watching Barn Owls on a summer's evening. Their silent, stuttering, moth-like flight along dykesides and above grassy pastures at dusk, their ghostly whiteness, and their 'almost human', heart-shaped face with its forward-facing eyes, make this bird well-loved by pretty much everyone.

Barn Owls have had an eventful couple of years. The exceptionally cold April and May of 2013 made that year one of the worst ever for breeding Barn Owls. However, in 2014 Barn Owls bounced back in style, with the most productive year on record, in terms of fledglings reared per breeding attempt. This must have been helped by a natural surge in numbers of prey in the wild.

The Barn Owl declined steadily throughout the twentieth century in the UK, and by the latter years was not at all common, although Lincolnshire was not the worst affected and always kept its fair share. Profound changes in the countryside over that time proved disadvantageous to the Barn Owl: the disappearance of corn-ricks, always alive with mice, took away a source of easy food. Organochlorine pesticides in the 1950s and 60s, which accumulated in the food chain, also took their toll. Increases in traffic on country roads led to more collisions with cars, and this is still a major cause of mortality today.

It has been said that the huge decrease in rough grassland during the twentieth century took away much of the Barn Owls' feeding habitat, making its main food, Field Voles, harder to find. This theory is now thought to be overstated, as studies of their feeding habits have shown that Barn Owls can simply switch food items from Field Voles to the more ubiquitous Wood Mouse, or other opportunist catches, in more arable environments.

Nowadays it is a shortage of nest sites which is the limiting factor in the expansion of Barn Owl populations. Barn Owls will often nest in holes in trees, but are more often associated with outbuildings, especially, as their name suggest, barns. The demolition of old, rural buildings and the conversion of barns to new dwellings has led to a dearth of suitable breeding places for owls.

This situation can be easily reversed, as Barn Owls are one of the simplest species to provide nesting habitat for, and they will take readily to man-made nest sites in rural locations. They will nest in almost any kind of receptacle which is the right sort of size, either placed in a tree, or preferably inside an undisturbed interior space like a barn or outbuilding. As one drives round the countryside one can sometimes see Barn Owl boxes placed on poles along field edges, and these will also be readily used, although Barn Owls may be 'pushed out' by smaller but more aggressive species such as Jackdaws and Stock Doves. Barn Owls can breed at very high densities if the nest sites are there to be used.

Barn Owl. Photo: Don Davis

Barn Owls produce a variety of shrieking, hissing and snoring calls, which can be very disarming at night, or when entering a building where breeding is taking place. These calls have led to one of its old country names of 'screech owl'. Barn Owls' presence is further given away by pellets on the ground below nest and roost sites, which in well-used places can be very numerous indeed.

The soaking and dissection of owl pellets used to be a staple activity for schoolchildren, but is much less often practiced these days. This is a great shame, as it teaches much about an area's small mammal fauna as well as about its owls, and always constitutes an inspiring and educational piece of ecological detective work.

Web-forming caterpillars. You may have noticed that all through the winter, the bare twigs of the Sea Buckthorn on the dunes at the south end of our resort have been littered with thousands of patches of unsightly white webbing. These are the protective silk tents of the caterpillars of the Brown-tail Moth, which are spending the winter communally inside. In fact, these caterpillars are doubly protected, not only by the silk tents, which deter attacks from birds, but by brown, irritating hairs which cover both the caterpillars themselves and their webs. These hairs can cause a skin reaction in humans when touched, and may sometimes even cause problems when carried on the wind. Every now and again, we see a brief burst of media hysteria about supposed infestations of these dangerous caterpillars, but in fact they are with us all the time, and mostly cause little trouble.

The adult Brown-tail moth flies in July and August. It is middle-sized, stocky with a hairy body, and is pure white except for the tip of the tail which is brown – hence the name. The irritating brown hairs on the tail are transferred onto the eggs when they are laid, and give the offspring their first bit of protection from predators.

As the caterpillars hatch and start to grow in the autumn, the silk tents become very conspicuous for a time, until winter kicks in and the caterpillars become more or less dormant inside.

In the spring, the caterpillars resume feeding within their tents, and may even bask on the outside in spring sunshine. Again the silk webs become very conspicuous. Although common on our Sea Buckthorn, Brown-tail webs can also be found inland on many types of shrub, particularly Hawthorn and Blackthorn. There are usually a few webs to be found in the scrubbier parts of Cleethorpes Country Park.

In late spring the caterpillars outgrow their webs and strike out, becoming free-living. At this point they can be identified by their blackish bodies with two white stripes down the sides, and two raised, orange tubercles on the upperside towards the rear end.

While hysteria isn't necessary, it is a good idea not to touch these caterpillars or their webs. Their hairs can cause an unpleasant rash, and would be extremely painful if they got into your eyes or mouth. While grown-ups might instinctively leave them alone, it might be worth reminding children to do the same.

The Brown-tail is by no means the only type of caterpillar to create silk tents. Between April and June, along our coastline and occasionally elsewhere, you may also come across the tents of Lackey Moth caterpillars. In sunny weather, Lackey caterpillars may also gather on the outside of their tents to bask, where their distinctive colouration – longitudinal stripes of orange, blue and white on a dark background, and blue heads, may identify them. These caterpillars will also leave the tent and become free-living as they get older. Their hairs are moderately irritating to people, but not nearly as bad as those of the Brown-tail.

A close relative of the Lackey is the Small Eggar, whose silk larval tents may be the size of a small football. If you find this species, whose caterpillars are dark with deep ginger back markings edged with white, please tell me, as they're now extremely rare.

Occasionally in early summer, one will see whole lengths of hedgerow which have been completely defoliated, and appear shrouded in a ghostly, continuous covering of silk. This is the work of thousands of caterpillars of an Ermine Moth, one of a group of closely-related species of the genus

Yponomeuta. The vegetation usually recovers when the caterpillars, which are not hairy and completely harmless, pupate in late summer. The adult moths are small and fairly inconspicuous – long and thin at rest, white or silvery in colour with black spots, hence 'ermine'.

Finally, further south in Europe, two conspicuous, related, web-forming moths, the Oak Processionary and the Pine Processionary, are very serious forestry pests, which not only defoliate valuable timber trees, but their caterpillars also have irritating hairs. The former has become established in London and parts of the Home Counties during 2016, and seems set to spread. The latter is not really a British species yet, and one hopes it will be kept at bay. If you see either of these species in the UK, you are obliged to report the sighting so that attempts to control them may take place.

Brown-tail Moth larval webs on Sea Buckthorn at Cleethorpes

Alien plants. The older field guides to British wild flowers contain a major weakness which can sometimes make them quite difficult to use. The problem is that they generally cover only native species, or at least include only the oldest and most thoroughly naturalised introductions – a situation which does not reflect the reality of the vegetation around us. Nowadays, introduced plants occur abundantly in many wild and semi-wild situations, and many are essential parts of British landscape and culture.

The situation with field guides these days is much improved, and one now has a reasonable chance of identifying any plant found in the wild. The modern 'bible' for the identification of British wild plants, a weighty, technical and mostly pictureless tome called *The New Flora of the British Isles* by Clive Stace, now contains native and alien species in about equal numbers. In fact, there are many more uncommon alien species not even mentioned, but to show that the bias is still with us, natives which are equally rare are always included.

Nowadays, botanists place introduced plants into two basic groups. Firstly, there are those which have been here a very long time indeed – more than 500 years – and have become thoroughly integrated into our flora. These plants, which botanists call 'archaeophytes', have now pretty much attained the same conservation status as indigenous plants. The list of archaeophytes is relatively short, but includes a host of familiar weeds of farmland, which is not surprising as the transportation of seed for agriculture is how they got here. Poppies are included here; also Shepherd's Purse and deadnettles, Cut-leaved Cranesbill, some speedwells, spurges and mayweeds. Also included here are anciently-introduced food- and medicinal plants such as Apple, Garlic, Horseradish, Feverfew and Opium Poppy.

More recent arrivals among our plants are known as 'neophytes', and are typified by garden escapes. Although they haven't been here long, some neophytes have quickly become important parts of our everyday lives.

Two trees – Horse Chestnut and Sycamore – fall into this category. Horse Chestnut is mostly an ornamental, growing mainly where it is planted. Nevertheless, it is sown so widely and is so charismatic when leafing, flowering, and later in the production of conkers, that it is hard to imagine our suburbs and villages without it. Even the winter twigs have acquired a vernacular name – 'sticky buds'.

Sycamore, by contrast, behaves much more like a native tree. Large specimens abound in all sorts of places and it regenerates extremely freely, the strap-like double cotyledons popping up abundantly in flowerbeds and natural woodlands anywhere the species occurs. Indeed so prodigiously can it reproduce that the flora of many valuable woodlands find themselves under threat from its abundant offspring, and the species may need to be thinned or removed.

Sycamore is also quite salt-tolerant, and is nearly always the last broadleaved tree one encounters as one moves towards the sea in Lincolnshire, forming much-needed shelter for many coastal farmsteads and the first landing place for incoming migrant birds.

Buddleia (first wild record 1922) is another recent introduction which it is now hard to imagine being without. Grown abundantly in gardens as 'Butterfly Bush', it will escape and grow in almost any urban setting, requiring only the most rudimentary soil in which to grow. Derelict industrial sites may sometimes contain forests of Buddleia.

Two smallish woody neophytes, Snowberry and Flowering Currant, have also become almost ubiquitous in Britain. The former is sown equally as both landscaping in towns and game cover in the countryside, where its white berries are absolutely distinctive. Sadly, almost nothing eats them, and the berries often just rot on the bush. Look for it on the small road past the pumping station near the Cleethorpes light railway station.

Also to be seen there are the deep pink flowers of Flowering Currant – an invaluable resource for bees in early spring. This species' name indicates ornamental origin, rather than being valued for its fruits. It is also very abundant along the verges of the Peaks Parkway to the south of the Weelsby Road crossing, and in many places elsewhere.

To think of our larger gardens, roadside woodlands or churchyards in winter without carpets of white Snowdrops is inconceivable, and the species is now a firmly established favourite in Britain, and icon of late winter. Despite this, the species was first recorded here only at the end of the sixteenth century, and wasn't recorded in the wild until 1778.

Sand dunes are a habitat which always seems susceptible to invasion by neophytes. Two such recent introductions now very abundant along our sandy seawall at Humberston Fitties are the intensely-scented Japanese Rose and the white-flowered Snow-in-Summer, the latter looking for all the world like it has always been there.

Officially the commonest neophyte in the UK – the one recorded over the widest area and in the greatest abundance – is also one of the most unprepossessing of all our everyday plants. First recorded here only in 1869, Pineappleweed is now present everywhere there is bare soil along trampled tracks and roadsides and in muddy field gateways. So widespread and abundant is it now, that the recentness of its introduction seems quite extraordinary. Despite being so unassuming in appearance, I find it almost impossible to pass by without giving its greenish-yellow, domed, rayless flowerheads a squeeze, for the distinctive and unique smell of pineapple which gives this plant its special appeal.

Solitary bees. There are nearly three hundred species of bee in the UK, of which the well-known, domestic Honeybee is just one. Less than thirty are bumblebees; all the rest are so-called 'solitary bees'.

April is the time of year when solitary bees begin to attract attention. There are four species in particular which I am often asked about by gardeners and householders. They are all present in our area, and three of them may make an appearance around about now.

Solitary bees do not form large, co-operative colonies in a single nest, with queen and worker castes, as do Honeybees and bumblebees. Although solitary bee nests may often be found in close proximity, or even loose colonies, each individual nest is technically an independent entity. Solitary bee adults are just plain male or female, although different sexes of the same species often look very different.

One of the most common ways in which solitary bees attract attention is when a number of little soil 'volcanoes' appear in lawns and the edges of garden paths and tracks. Each mound of earth contains a single hole in the centre, about half a centimetre wide. These are the work of the Tawny Mining Bee. With patience you will see the bright ginger-orange females entering and leaving, to provision the nest. Each burrow contains several sealed underground 'cells', each one of which contains an egg and enough food (pollen) to sustain the emerging larva to adulthood.

The main question I am asked is whether the little volcanoes will be a permanent fixture in lawns, which need to be mown. In fact the mound of earth will disappear within a couple of weeks, with the developing bees safely secreted below the ground. Mowing is probably harmless at any time, but certainly after this point. In the meantime, slightly longer grass would seem a small price to pay to keep populations of these fascinating, beneficial insects safe and well.

Occasionally I am told by a householder in spring that they have a colony of bumblebees nesting in the soft mortar of an old wall or chimney. In fact there is one species of bumblebee which will nest above ground in a suitable cavity, but its colonies don't really get going until later in the summer. More often than not the culprit is another solitary bee, whose female looks very much like an all-black bumblebee, except for reddish hairs on its hind legs. This is the Hairy-footed Flower bee. The nests don't constitute a colony as such, but a loose aggregation of separate nests. Colonies may last a long time in the same place if the habitat remains suitable – one Northamptonshire colony was known in the same place for 200 years. Dead bees in a fireplace are sometimes the first sign of occupation.

These days it is common to see so-called 'bee hotels' for sale, or placed outside in flowery places. These look something like bird boxes or sometimes bigger structures, filled with hollow stems or other tubes (there is one

particularly extravagant one on a roadside at Humberston Fitties – pictured). These can provide artificial nest sites for several aerial-nesting solitary bee species, but the commonest, and the one which will use these most readily, is the Red Mason Bee. This is a chestnut-brown species – two small 'horns' on the face identify the female with certainty.

The last solitary bee to deserve a special mention flies slightly later in the year, and is the insect responsible for those half-moon cut-outs from leaves that irritate rose-growers so much. These are the work of one of a small handful of closely-related species, the Leaf-cutter Bees. These are also aerial-nesters, which fashion their nursery cells out of the collected sections of leaf, with roses a favourite. Like the last species, they will also use bee hotels.

All of these solitary bees have their brood parasites, or 'cuckoo' species. If the wrong species of bee appears to be entering a nest, this will almost certainly be the explanation.

A final word – if you grow the white-woolly Lamb's Ear *Stachys byzantina* in your garden, do watch out for the large, very handsome and very territorial Wool Carder Bee. Records of it in Lincolnshire are few, but we have it here in North East Lincolnshire, and I'm sure it is very under-recorded.

A 'hotel' for bees and other insects at Humberston Fitties

Scarce Tortoiseshell. For wildlife watchers in North East Lincolnshire there is a new sign of spring to look out for this year *[2015]*. Now the warm weather has arrived, eyes are peeled for the first sighting of a completely new butterfly for our county fauna: the Scarce Tortoiseshell. So recent is its arrival in the UK that you won't find this species in any British butterfly book published before 2015.

The first sighting of a Scarce Tortoiseshell in Britain was a female at

Shipbourne near Sevenoaks in west Kent on 2 July 1953. It was considered an extremely rare vagrant, and nobody could be really sure that it hadn't originated from a deliberate release into the wild. The species wasn't seen again in the UK for 61 years, reappearing in 2014. The butterfly's normal range extends from central and eastern Europe right across to China and Japan, but last year an unprecedented wave of migration occurred across Europe from east to west, resulting in sightings throughout western Europe. After unprecedented numbers built up in the Netherlands, eventually more than 30 butterflies crossed the water to the UK. These were distributed widely, from Devon northwards to Tyne and Wear, but were mainly centered around East Anglia. There was a single Lincolnshire record, from Chambers Farm Wood (between Lincoln and Horncastle) on 17 July, although many arrivals must have been missed.

All Tortoiseshell butterflies go into hibernation in late summer, and as the 2014 butterfly season drew to a close, so sightings of Scarce Tortoiseshell tailed off. The Scarce Tortoiseshell usually experiences much colder winters than its British relatives, and nobody was quite sure whether they would survive our relatively mild winter climate. But sure enough this spring, sightings started to come in from far-flung locations from March onwards, proving that the species could overwinter here successfully.

This year it is hoped that breeding will be recorded from the UK for the first time ever. While our common Small Tortoiseshell caterpillars are nettle-feeders, Scarce Tortoiseshell adults are said to feed at sap runs on birch trees, with females laying their eggs on willows.

The Scarce Tortoiseshell is very similar to our own common or garden Small Tortoiseshell, but is a slightly larger and plainer butterfly. It has a less striking black and yellow pattern along the leading edges of its wings, and less developed blue 'lunules' around the edges. It has pale legs, which give it the alternative name of 'Yellow-legged Tortoiseshell'. Perhaps the most helpful distinguishing feature is the hindwings, where the orange colouration extends much further in towards the body than it does in a Small Tortoiseshell.

Rather confusingly, there is a third tortoiseshell to consider – the Large Tortoiseshell. This was once widespread in Britain but has been functionally extinct for 40 or so years, appearing from time to time only as a very rare vagrant or when released from captivity. It is very similar to a Scarce Tortoiseshell but has yellow, not white marks just in from the corner of its wings, and a narrower black border to the forewings.

So this spring, it is important to scrutinise every tortoiseshell butterfly you see. If you suspect you have a Scarce Tortoiseshell it is extremely important to take a photograph if you possibly can – something much easier to do than in the past, with modern camera phones always at the ready.

Nobody knows whether the population of Scarce Tortoiseshells in Britain will persist – perhaps it will not. Up to the time of writing, no-one has yet seen one in North East Lincolnshire, although a 'possible' was seen briefly by Chris Heaton among the flowers in Grimsby Cemetery on 8th April. Keep looking – somebody may well be lucky and get the first confirmed record. Recording a new species from a group so charismatic, few in number and well-studied as butterflies would be a real red letter day.

This article appeared in April 2015. The predicted local sightings of Scarce Tortoiseshell did not materialise, but it is surely only a matter of time before another invasion occurs.

Speedwells. Anyone attempting to better acquaint themselves with our area's wild flowers must sooner or later get to grips with that attractive and diverse group, the speedwells. As many as twelve species may be seen here, with most open habitats containing one species or another. As a group, speedwells are easily recognised – no other kind of flower has the same combination of four rounded, blue petals joined at the base, and two stamens. However, it is rarely necessary to examine them so closely – the 'look' of a speedwell is distinctive enough. Even after flowering, the flattened, double fruit also make speedwells easy to recognise.

Four of our speedwells are only found in or near water. Three of these are uncommon in our area – the Pink-flowered Water, Blue-flowered Water and Marsh Speedwells. The fourth however, Brooklime, is very common near all kinds of water including quite insubstantial ditches; even waterlogged woodland tracks. Its fleshy, short-stalked leaves are easily recognised even without the flowers, which when present are royal blue and borne in paired, opposite spikes from the bases of the leaves.

Back on dry land, our two tiniest speedwells both bear their flowers on simple upright spikes. Thyme-leaved speedwell has whitish flowers with blue veins, looking very pale blue from a distance, while Wall Speedwell has even tinier, deep royal blue flowers. Both are found in all kinds of grassy and waste places, the latter especially common anywhere there is bare soil, such as field edges, allotments, anthills, garden plant pots and all kinds of urban waste ground. There is usually a little in the short turf surrounding the Boating Lake car park.

Much larger-flowered is the most handsome of all the native speedwells, Germander Speedwell. Its deep blue flowers with an obvious white centre give it the alternative name of 'Bird's-eye'. This is thought to be the plant which gave the whole group its name 'speed-well', probably because of its commonness on road- and waysides. The flowers occur in loose heads, or racemes, borne from the leaf-bases. The plant may be found on grasslands, field or woodland edges anywhere.

This brings to us those similar, rather straggly-looking pale blue-flowered speedwells whose flowers are borne singly on stalks from the bases of the upper leaves – the classic light blue weeds of field edges and bare ground. In fact, none of the group is native to this country, but the one which has been with us the longest is the Ivy-leaved Speedwell. This is a relatively small and pale-flowered, mostly spring-blooming plant, which can be recognised by the pronounced side-lobes to its leaves – hence the name. It is a common weed of gardens and cultivated land, and can be seen in abundance in the wildlife area of Pier Gardens, in places around the Cleethorpes 'Old Dunes' near the Boating Lake, and in many of the promenade's flowerbeds.

The other four species in this group comprise an interesting quartet of introduced weeds. The first two are very similar, much-declined plants of arable land, the Green-field and Grey-field Speedwells. The former was first recorded in Britain in the sixteenth century, and the latter in the eighteenth, both becoming common field weeds for a time, with the second gradually replacing the first in abundance. Both are very much rarer these days, being themselves replaced by the similar but larger Common Field Speedwell, first recorded in 1826 and now by far the most abundant speedwell in Britain. It has the same sky blue flowers, although the slightly splayed valves of its fruit separate it from the two older introductions. It can be found flowering in any month of the year and occurs almost anywhere there is bare soil, including all sorts of rural and urban situations. Among many other places, it occurs around the bases of the trees along the road behind the Meridian Showground.

When a light blue speedwell occurs in the closed turf of lawns, it is likely to be the last of this group, the Slender Speedwell. First imported as a rockery plant, Slender Speedwell first escaped into the wild in 1838, but was not recorded wild again until 1927. It was not until the 1950s or even later that the species really took off, soon becoming a pest of lawns the length and breadth of the country.

Interestingly, while the other speedwells in this group are highly self-fertile, Slender Speedwell is not, and must reproduce by fragments of cut material being transported from one place to another, which being a plant of mown lawns, it does very readily. Slender Speedwell may be found anywhere there is short grass, and for a few days in spring may make large areas of mown grassland shimmer silvery-blue. I have seen this phenomenon in Weelsby Woods and in the Ravendale Valley among other places, although the species has the strange habit of disappearing as suddenly as it came. Being a relative newcomer, the fortunes of this landscape-transforming plant in the future remain to be seen.

Skylarks. References to British birdsong in culture and the arts are dominated by two species: the Nightingale and the Skylark. Both are exceptional singers. Here in North East Lincolnshire we have no Nightingales, although one doesn't have to travel all that far to find them. Apart from the exceptional quality and tone of the sounds they produce, the evocative power of the Nightingale's song is enhanced by the fact that they sing after dark, when sound travels further and other birds have fallen silent.

The Skylark, however, remains one of the commonest farmland birds in Europe, and is readily heard, and seen, in our area. Its unbroken cascades of glittering trills falling from the sky on a sunny day are the very epitome of the British springtime, and some might say an essential component of the farmed landscape itself.

Skylarks are birds of open places; you will never see a Skylark in, or even under, a tree, and even on farmland they tend to avoid anything 'sticking up' like hedgerows. This means that they were probably unknown in Britain until Bronze Age and early Iron Age people cleared the wildwood and created grasslands for them to colonise, but since then they have been ever-present where humans have worked the land. Skylarks need no song perch, rising almost vertically into the sky as they sing until almost invisible, their song seeming to drift in waves in and out of conscious thought.

In winter, Skylarks tend to congregate wherever there is food, but again, always in open situations. Our own saltmarsh at Cleethorpes always holds many Skylarks in winter, and they remain a component of the 'little brown' bird fauna of farmland throughout the year. Outside the breeding season they may occasionally be given away by their harsh chirruping call, white outer tail feathers and white trailing edges to the wings when flushed, or during the little quarrels and chases which anticipate pairing at the end of winter.

Skylarks were once so common that sacksful would arrive at London's markets daily, and they would be eaten dozens at a time. However, like many other birds of farmland, the Skylark has suffered a huge decline in numbers since the end of the Second World War, due to 'cleaner' crops, the switch from spring to winter cropping, and the loss of weedy stubbles and untended, insect rich corners. Despite its drab, brown appearance, the Skylark's exceptional and well-loved song has made it something of a flagship for the plight of the whole suite of declining farmland birds.

The Skylark's song is celebrated with innumerable references in the arts. Chaucer, William Blake, Coleridge, Wordsworth, Elizabeth Barrett Browning, Shelley and Ted Hughes all wrote about the Skylark and its song. Most famously perhaps, it inspired Ralph Vaughan Williams's orchestral piece 'The Lark Ascending', a now essential, almost definitive, part of the English pastoral tradition. That piece was itself inspired by a poem of the same name by George Meredith, in which Meredith described the Skylark's song as a 'silver chain of sound'.

In an attempt to impart a flavour of home for emigrants, Skylarks were exported for release into the wild wherever English people tended to settle. They are now an established part of the bird fauna of Australia and New Zealand, but in the Americas, attempts to introduce them have almost universally failed. The Skylark finally disappeared from one of its last two North American haunts, San Juan Island in Washington State, around the year 2000, and now hangs on precariously at a single location, in the south of Vancouver Island, where Skylarks are something of a wildlife tourist attraction. There is nothing else like the song of the Skylark among the birdlife of America.

So here in its authentic homeland we should appreciate the song of the Skylark, and never let its numbers get too low.

Bee-flies. Because they're warmth-loving and highly mobile, insects tend to be very good indicators of climate change, and many species have recently expanded their ranges northwards in line with increased summer temperatures. As global warming has kicked in, several species have colonised

North East Lincolnshire from the south. Now is exactly the time of year to see one such species, the splendid and charismatic little Bee-fly. Plump, ginger and with a proboscis almost as long as its body, the Bee-fly is an agile flier, hovering at flowers rather like a hummingbird, using its long 'beak' to extract nectar. At rest, the Bee-fly's attractively black-patterned wings are swept back like a fighter aircraft. At this time of year Bee-flies can be seen hovering around Primroses, Violets or Ground-ivy in the wild, and species such as Aubretia, Wallflowers and Lungwort in gardens. Although it resembles a bee (to deter predators), the Bee-fly is completely harmless to humans. Bee-flies are far from harmless to other insects, which they parasitise – females can be watched hovering over areas of bare earth, laying their eggs close to the burrows of solitary bees, wasps and beetles during April and early May. The hatched fly larvae enter the host insect's nest and eat the larva of the host.

Always frequent in the south of England and recorded as far north as Scotland, Bee-flies have become much commoner in the Midlands and north in recent years, and have only become really conspicuous in North East Lincolnshire gardens in the last couple of springs.

The Bee-fly isn't the only insect to have colonised this area in response to global warming. Three species of butterfly have all done the same in recent times: the Comma about twenty years ago, the Speckled Wood some fifteen years ago, and the Essex Skipper in very recent times. One of the commonest bumblebees in Cleethorpes gardens, the ginger, black and white Tree Bumblebee, is another recent colonist. First recorded in Britain in 2001 in Wiltshire, this species took a mere ten years to spread northwards and become abundant in North East Lincolnshire. Lastly, Britain's largest resident moth, the magnificent Privet Hawkmoth, has also been seen much more commonly in Cleethorpes gardens in the last couple of years, and would seem set to cause a few more shocks at lighted kitchen windows before the end of the summer.

This article was the very first, appearing in April 2014.

The Blackbird's Nest. There are almost as many kinds of birds' nest as there are kinds of birds. All manner of cups, platforms, domes, scrapes, mounds and cavities are used – Cuckoos lay their eggs in other birds' nests, and some birds make no nest at all.

But because of its familiarity, the archetypal bird's nest in peoples' minds in probably that of the common Blackbird. This is one of the first wild breeding birds most people encounter as a child. Many gardens have, somewhere in them, a bush, hedge or climber thick enough to hold a breeding Blackbird, and its robust, grassy cup with its speckled blue eggs must be known by everybody.

Scientists have pulled Blackbird's nests apart and tested the contained materials for their mechanical properties. They found a strong outer wall of interwoven twigs, roots and leaves, inside which is built an inner cup of weaker and less rigid materials such as dried grass. Inside all of this is a cup of mud, into which plant material is incorporated. The base of the nest contains heavier and more rigid materials than the sides.

All in all, a Blackbird's nest is a remarkable piece of engineering for an animal guided only by instinct and the memory of its own nest, and using only its bill as a tool.

As every schoolchild would once have known, a similar nest but with a smooth mud lining belongs not to a Blackbird, but a Song Thrush. This, and the Song Thrush's clearer blue eggs, is how the two nests are told apart if the adult is not seen. Forty years ago these two thrushes were about as common as each other, but while Blackbirds are still fairly plentiful, Song Thrushes are now much less so.

Having made the effort to hide or disguise its nest, blue seems an illogical colour for a Blackbird's eggs, given the high visibility. In fact, the reasons for this colouration remain essentially unknown. Blue eggs can be remarkably cryptic in the dappled light inside dense vegetation, and predators may not see colours the same as we do. Pigmented eggs are said to be stronger than unpigmented ones. But the real reason may be that the colour has evolved in response to a brood parasite, such as our modern Cuckoo, which is no longer with us.

When camouflage isn't an issue, such as in hole-nesting birds, eggs tend to be white. Many cup-nesting species have eggs which are camouflaged, perhaps an earth colour, or speckled with brown. But if a Cuckoo-type brood parasite gets too good at passing off its own eggs as those of the host, this triggers an evolutionary response in the host which sees its eggs evolve to look less and less like the parasite's, and so it goes on in a kind of evolutionary 'arms race'. There are very few pigments involved in egg colouration, and blue is one of the few available colours an egg can turn. Modern Cuckoos do not parasitise Blackbirds, so we can only guess as to the historical culprit.

When the nest is finished, a female Blackbird will lay one egg per day, usually in the morning, until the clutch of between two and five eggs is complete. Only then will she start incubating them all together, so that the brood will hatch all at the same time. Up until this point, the eggs are cold. This means that if you find a nest with cold eggs, they may not be deserted, but just part of an incomplete clutch.

In Blackbirds, incubation takes two weeks, and fledging another two weeks after that. A Blackbird may have three, or even four broods in a season.

Beyond a certain point, maturing chicks are capable of scattering away from the nest even though they are not quite ready. This anti-predator response is called 'exploding', and may lead to the adult birds tending to the chicks outside the nest for a few extra days.

If you find a chick which seems abandoned, leave it alone – its parents will almost certainly be close by, waiting to come and feed it.

It remains for me to repeat, as I do every year, that all birds' nests are protected by law while they are in use. It cannot be the bird's job to tell you its nest is there, so by clipping a hedge in spring or summer without knowing whether it contains a bird's nest, you may be inadvertently breaking the law.

White Butterflies. The almost perpetual presence of white butterflies, especially when the sun is shining, is one of the things that defines the British summer. The 'whites' can be found the length and breadth of the UK and in almost any open habitat. They are regular visitors to gardens, where they all seem to get lumped together as 'cabbage whites'.

We have four rather similar species of white butterfly in our area, all of which overwinter as chrysalises, and all of which use members of the great family of crucifers (Brassicaceae) as their larval foodplants. Three of the four species are double-brooded, and can be seen on the wing from April right through until early autumn, with perhaps a lull in late June between the two generations. The fourth species is single brooded, and a spring speciality, flying from late April through to about the third week in May – occasionally later. This means that around now, and for the next few weeks, is the only time of year when all four 'whites' fly together.

'Cabbage White' is a term generally used by gardeners, and has a derogatory overtone. It describes these butterflies' annoying tendency to decimate cruciferous garden vegetables such cabbage, kale, broccoli, Brussels sprouts, radishes and mustard. Netting is the answer, of course, not harmful chemicals, but the net must not touch the leaves, or the butterflies will simply lay their eggs through it.

In fact, what gardeners describe as Cabbage White is actually two species – the Large White and the Small White. The Large White generally does the most damage in the garden or allotment, the voracious, hairy, black-and-yellow patterned caterpillars suddenly appearing in numbers and reducing edible crucifers to a skeleton. Nasturtiums are another favourite, which may take a hammering. Small White caterpillars, in contrast, are a much more subdued and better-camouflaged green colour, and tend to occur in smaller numbers. The caterpillars of both species may also be found on wild crucifers, such as Charlock, Garlic Mustard, Wild Radish and Hedge Mustard.

The adult Large White Butterfly is significantly bigger than the other whites – a step difference which can often identify the species even in flight. Occasional smaller individuals occur, which require examination of the markings to identify. Large whites have a strong black 'boomerang' mark on the outer corner of the forewing, while Small White's wingtip markings are greyer, and more of a horizontal 'bullet' shape. Males of both species are plainer in their general markings than females, but the same rules apply.

Following the same pattern of timing and general abundance is a third species, the Green-veined White. Its caterpillars are also green, and tend to be slightly less of a problem in the garden, and more restricted to the wild crucifers. The adult is easily identified by its underside, which is not plain like the two Cabbage Whites, but has its venation picked out in what looks like green – actually on close inspection an intimate mixture of black and yellow scales.

It is much harder to separate Green-veined and Small Whites from the upperside, although the dark wing-corner markings of Green-veined White stretch much further down the side of the wing. In flight, these two species are extremely difficult to tell apart.

The spring specialist of the four – the 'white' that only flies around now – is the Orange Tip. The male is unmistakable, and one of Britain's more striking butterflies. However, the female does not have the bright orange wingtips, and in flight looks very much like a Small or Green-veined White. At rest, the underside is again the clue, with black and yellow scales making a green-looking mottled pattern, quite unlike the net-like wing venation of the Green-veined White. The upperside is also reasonably distinctive with a good view, the wingtips being rounder than the other species, with extensive greyish tips and a single dark 'comma' mark near the centre of the forewing.

Male Orange Tip. Photo: Charles J Sharp CC BY-SA 4.0 Wikimedia Commons

Male Orange Tips are probably more likely to be seen than females, as they quarter any kind of open habitat looking for a mate. The females are usually found in the vicinity of their foodplants, Cuckoo Flower, Garlic Mustard and Hedge Mustard. The eggs are laid on the flower stalks, and so are some of the easiest to find of all the butterflies. The caterpillars avoid competing with those of other whites by eating the developing seedpods, although they will also take leaves and flowers.

Try to obtain a close encounter with the beautiful male Orange Tip – there are only a few weeks when you can do so, before they are gone for another year.

Spanish Bluebell. There are several things which make botany one of the more difficult of natural history's disciplines. There are a lot of species of plants, and many look very similar to each other. Plants can exhibit a variety of growth forms so they don't necessarily look like the pictures in the book. And botanists are also expected to be able to identify the majority of species when not in flower.

There are a manageable 1500 or so native plants in the British Isles. However, if you also consider species brought here by people but now growing commonly in the wild, the number is double this, and there are tens of thousands more species and cultivars in gardens and collections.

Garden escapes provide one of the commonest problems for the beginner. Many garden plants have native relatives, and it is easy to mistakenly ascribe plants originating in cultivation to the nearest wild species.

Trees and shrubs pose a particular problem, as they are so often sown by people. Over 80% of our trees and shrubs are of undisclosed Continental origin, and there are many lookalikes – what have been called 'false natives'. Similarly, plants sown in wildflower seed mixtures may not be as described on the packet, or at least may not turn out to be quite the same as local forms. Some perfectly legitimate native species may also be grown in gardens but escape, leaving no clue as to their origin.

One such problem even affects Britain's most popular and celebrated wild flower, the Bluebell. Despite being common almost throughout Britain, our native Bluebell has a very restricted world range, which encompasses only the Atlantic fringe of western Europe from the Netherlands down to northern Portugal. The brilliant sight of an ancient woodland carpeted with a mass of flowering Bluebells is a peculiarly British one. If you have ever tried to photograph a Bluebell wood you will know that the colour is nearly impossible to capture.

But our native plant is not the one traditionally sown in gardens, this distinction being held by the Spanish Bluebell. This is a native of Spain, Portugal and north Africa, introduced here about 300 years ago, whose world range is even more restricted than that of our own. Nobody familiar with the native species should really confuse the two – Spanish Bluebells have paler and much more openly-spreading flowers, which do not all nod to one side like the native plant.

The problem is that in the UK the two species hybridise freely, and nowadays the vast majority of alien Bluebells found in the wild are hybrids. These are usually, but not always, to be found in the vicinity of habitation or where garden plants have been dumped. Hybrids, and especially their backcrosses, can look very like either parent, but usually something in between.

Hybrid Bluebells usually have wider leaves than native ones. Generally, their flowers are slightly bell-shaped rather than tubular, and the contained anthers may be bluish, not cream. Usually the flowerheads do not strongly nod to one side. The scent of our own Bluebell is sweeter and more complex than its European relatives or the hybrid.

Because of the propensity for interbreeding, much has been made of the threat to our spectacular native Bluebell woods from the rampaging hybrid. Although the hybrid is strongly increasing in Britain, so far there is no evidence of dilution of our woodland populations – maybe it is just a slow process.

You can see a good show of native Bluebells in Dixon Wood, although the hybrid also occurs there. Other good local native Bluebell woods include those at Irby Dales and in the Beesby Valley between North Thoresby and Wold Newton. Both Bluebells are recorded in Weelsby Woods, although I can only find hybrids there now. Hybrid Bluebells have now unfortunately appeared on the 'Old Dunes' Site of Special Scientific Interest situated behind the Boating

Lake next to the Jungle Zoo, where will be in flower for the next couple of weeks.

Tardigrades. Did you know there are bears in your garden? If you have so much as a window box, you are playing host to one of the most astonishing animals living on Earth. You may have thousands, or even millions of them, for they can be found anywhere damp, from among mosses and lichens to leaf litter and soil, as well as both marine and freshwater environments. They live everywhere on the planet, from deep ocean sediments to the tops of the Himalayas, to the canopy of rainforest trees.

These are tardigrades, or 'water bears'. Once described as the cutest of all invertebrates, tardigrades are slow moving, plump, and have been likened to eight-legged pandas, each leg with a small set of claws. Their tubular mouthparts contain stylets, which they use to feed on plant cells, algae and small invertebrates.

Tardigrades occupy their own phylum in the tree of life, which means that they aren't insects, or arachnids, or crustaceans – they are just tardigrades. They are one of the oldest living creatures on Earth, first appearing during the mid-Cambrian period some 530 million years ago, close to the origins of complex life.

The most amazing thing about tardigrades is their ability to survive almost anything you can throw at them. When faced with extremely cold or dry conditions, a tardigrade's moisture content can fall from about 85% to about 3% to protect its cells. The animal shrivels to a dried state about a third of its normal volume, called a 'tun'. In this state, the metabolic processes are brought to an almost complete, or absolute standstill, and this is what gets them through. They will readily pop back to life, however, when rehydrated.

Tardigrades have been heated to 151 degrees Celsius for several minutes and survived. They have been cooled to a whisker above absolute zero (-272.95 degrees Celsius); three times as cold as anything ever recorded in the natural environment, and come back to life. They can easily survive several days at minus 200 degrees.

Tardigrades can easily withstand being placed in a vacuum, but can also survive pressures six times that at the bottom of the deepest ocean trench. They can survive in a bone dry state for nearly ten years, and once a movement was detected in a 120-year-old specimen from dried moss, although whether this constitutes 'survival' is arguable.

Tardigrades can also withstand radiation up to 1000 times that which would kill other animals, including humans, as they also have exceptional ability to repair their own damaged DNA.

So far, tardigrades are the first known animals to survive unprotected in outer space. More than two thirds of individuals sent into orbit were revived within half an hour of being rehydrated back on Earth, and a few individuals also survived intense UV radiation from the sun while they were up there. While it is often suggested that cockroaches will outlive humankind on Earth, tardigrades would out-survive cockroaches by a mile.

If you're wondering why you've never seen the ubiquitous tardigrade, it is, of course, because they are very small. Having said that, the largest is over 1mm in length, so well visible to the naked eye. They can certainly be seen easily with a relatively low-power microscope, or high-power hand lens, making them a perfect subject for students or beginners in microscopy. They are most easily collected by squeezing trapped water out of wet moss.

May

Hirundines. While driving round town this week I have seen two or three people trimming their garden hedges. We are now comfortably into the bird breeding season so this activity is potentially illegal if there are birds actively nesting inside the vegetation. In this situation it is the gardener's responsibility to be certain that no nest is being disturbed, and ignorance is no defence. However, if you're one of the 'trimmers', you're not alone, as this must be one of the most widely-flouted laws in the book.

This is the time of year when we see a host of summer visitors returning to our shores, including that delightful trio of aerial specialists, the 'hirundines', otherwise known as swallows and martins. The first to arrive, sometimes in March, is the little brown Sand Martin, which is purely a passage bird in North East Lincolnshire, gathering near water en route to breeding colonies in sandy cliff faces – there are many such colonies in Lincolnshire as a whole. Next to arrive is the familiar Swallow, and lastly the House Martin, readily identified in flight by its shorter tail and white rump. The harsh chirrup of House Martins above towns and villages is in many ways the sound of a summer's day.

Until the nineteenth century it was widely believed that Swallows hibernated in the mud at the bottom of ponds. Fittingly, the Swallow was one of the first birds to have its migratory pattern worked out, when in 1912 a bird fitted with a leg ring in Britain was recovered in Natal, South Africa the following mid-winter. In stark contrast, to this day nobody really knows where House Martins spend the winter – surely one of the most glaring gaps in our knowledge of British birds. Next year for the first time the British Trust for Ornithology intends to fit tiny tracking devices to British House Martins so this conundrum can finally be settled.

House Martins will nest under the eaves of even quite new houses around the Cleethorpes area. Before humankind and houses came along, this was a cliff-nesting species, and House Martins can still be seen nesting on sea cliffs in a few places along the west coast of Britain. Most people privileged enough to have their houses chosen for building by House Martins welcome them as fascinating temporary guests. Having said this, they can make a mess of the windows and patio below, so are not received so enthusiastically by everybody.

Again though, the law requires that House martins, like all wild birds, must be left to complete their breeding cycle undisturbed.

Three White Flowers of the Spring. With spring bursting forth on Lincolnshire's roadsides, three special white flowers deserve a mention.

Anybody travelling the major roads of Britain over the last few weeks may have noticed large drifts of a tiny white flower with a slight hint of pink, on central reservations. This is the fascinating little Danish Scurvygrass *Cochlearia danica*. Danish Scurvygrass was originally an exclusively seaside plant, growing on saltmarshes, dunes and sea walls round the coasts of Britain, but since the 1980s it has left its maritime home and spread along salted roads the length and breadth of the country. At one time there was a suggestion that it preferred to 'travel' along dual carriageways as, it was thought, slugs couldn't cross the road to central reservations to eat it, but this theory has lost credibility in recent times. Strangely, although Danish Scurvygrass has never been recorded on the Cleethorpes seafront, it is now fast approaching the resort 'the back way' along winter-salted roads, this year (2014) reaching nearly as far as Hewitt's Circus.

The second white flower is the ubiquitous Cow Parsley *Anthriscus sylvestris*, noteworthy for its sheer visual dominance in the landscape. Indeed it is hard to imagine Lincolnshire roadsides and woodland edges in spring without this flower. Alternative names include 'Queen Anne's lace' and 'Keck', the latter almost certainly something to do with the sound made when walking through the dead stems in winter. Loss of old meadows since World War II has meant that the vast majority of Lincolnshire's diverse flower-rich grassland now occurs on roadsides. However, an abundance of Cow Parsley is a sign of degradation – that at some time in the past the ground has received a damaging dose of fertiliser, and in terms of diversity its value is now partly or wholly lost.

Last of the three is the Hoary Cress *Lepidium draba*, which I mention simply because every year without fail someone asks me to name this plant, whose flowers suddenly become conspicuous in April and May. Standing about a foot tall with bright green foliage topped with foamy, cream-coloured umbels of flowers, this plant is common in our area on road- and ditch-sides, especially on light soils near the sea. Although now widespread this plant is in fact an alien first recorded in Britain in the early 1800s, when it was thought to have been introduced to Britain in the straw mattresses of typhus- and malaria-stricken soldiers returning from the Napoleonic Wars. Look for it, among other places, by Pleasure Island or along the A180 by the docks.

Swifts. Each year, the first few Swifts are seen in Britain in April, often powering northwards along obvious migration routes, or near water where they can reliably find early-season insects. However it isn't until a few days into May – so any time now – that our own summering Swifts settle in and reoccupy the skies above our homes. From this time onwards there is not a spot in the country where Swifts can't be seen overhead – their dark, sickle-winged outlines are an essential part of our midsummer skies.

But by early August each year, Swifts are gone. They spend only a quarter of the year with us, arriving significantly later, and leaving earlier, than those other fork-tailed aerial specialists, the 'hirundines' – swallows and martins – to which they are superficially similar. In fact, Swifts are not particularly closely-related to hirundines (the nearest relatives to swifts and swiftlets are hummingbirds), and they are ecologically distinct in many important ways.

The long, thin, swept-back wings of the Swift are ideal for fast flight, but don't allow great manoeuvrability. For this reason, Swifts habitually fly higher than swallows and martins, and require a more unobstructed route to the nest.

Even in the breeding season, Swifts may travel large distances to find food. They will take advantage of any place where aerial prey accumulates, congregating especially in situations where warm air is undercut by cold air and forced to rise. Sea breeze fronts, or squall lines ahead of thunderstorms are classic situations where Swifts may gather.

Despite having trouble feeding in wet weather, large numbers of Swifts have been seen making co-ordinated movements straight into an approaching frontal system. This movement, although counter-intuitive, takes the Swifts through the worst of the rain as quickly as possible, into unstable air behind, where feeding conditions are ideal. Having flown against the wind, all the Swifts need to do is follow the track of the weather system back to where they started.

Occasionally in very poor weather, or when low-level air suddenly becomes calm at the end of the day, Swift flocks may follow their prey almost to ground level, feeding especially near water. To be surrounded by a mass of Swifts powering past at eye level or below is an unforgettable experience.

Frantic 'screaming parties' of Swifts usually indicate breeding nearby, and occur mostly in the evenings. After sunset, Swifts will fall silent and suddenly all rise to a great height, sometimes, where possible, moving out over the sea first. This was always seen as an essential prerequisite to a night sleeping on the wing, but it is now known that Swifts will ascend like this again at dawn, casting doubt on this theory. Gaining height at this time is probably a way of taking advantage of multiple environmental cues which only occur together at twilight – visible landmarks, stars and polarisation patterns, the latter used to calibrate the birds' magnetic compass. These cues are used both for navigation, and to assess the progress of weather systems. Compared with Swifts, humans seem hopelessly oblivious to such things.

Despite nesting almost exclusively in the roof-spaces of human dwellings, very few people have ever seen a Swift's nest, and they remain mysterious and enigmatic birds. Once the young bird makes its first flight, it may not touch land again for four years, and then only when it needs, itself, to breed. Swifts do almost everything on the wing, including sleep, mate, drink, bathe and collect nesting material. They feed on airborne insects and spiders, and have been recorded feeding on more species of animal than any other bird – 312 kinds of prey are recorded, and this is certainly an underestimate.

Swifts are long-lived for birds their size, reaching an average of between five and six years. The oldest recorded individual was at least 18, and thought to have travelled 4 million miles or more in its lifetime. Despite this, Swifts have seriously declined in the UK, with a third disappearing in the last 20 years. The reasons may be partly due to the widespread use of pesticides in agriculture leading to a dearth of insects, but is almost certainly to do with the unsuitability of modern buildings for nesting. Older buildings with accessible cavities and roof-spaces are increasingly being either demolished or refurbished, and even when buildings are suitable for Swifts, steps are often taken to exclude them, although why you would want to do this is anybody's guess.

Swifts will use DIY or commercially available nest boxes, integrated nest bricks or trays, which can be installed into the upper parts of old or new buildings alike. Recordings of Swifts' calls may be used to attract birds from the skies to these new nest sites for the first time. There is really no downside to having breeding Swifts, and personally I think we should insist that architects and builders provide measures to help this icon of summer at every opportunity, and make provision for them on our own home wherever we can.

Oilseed Rape. April and May is the time of year when the landscape of lowland England turns into a patchwork of green and brilliant yellow, as the Oilseed Rape comes into flower.

Oilseed Rape is lowland Britain's commonest flower by a mile. Some enjoy the brilliant masses of springtime colour, and some even the far-carrying mustard-like smell of some of its varieties. Others, however, yearn for a time when the spring lowlands were a more sober patchwork of subtler greens and browns. These days Rape is a profitable crop, often sown in extremely simple rotations with cereals. In the Rape years the farmer is able to spray off pernicious grass weeds such as Blackgrass and Barren Brome which reside in the soil.

Oilseed Rape is one of those large yellow 'crucifers' which often cause problems of identification when found in the wild. Confusion over the scientific naming of both Rape and its relatives has not helped. *Brassica rapa,* for example, is Turnip, not Rape. Rape is *Brassica napus* subspecies *oleifera,* but subspecies *rapifera* is not Rape but Swede. To add to all of this, in some parts of the UK people call a swede (the vegetable) a turnip. The only properly wild plant in this group is the Wild Turnip *Brassica rapa* subspecies *campestris,* which inhabits the banks of streams and rivers, often adjacent to Oilseed Rape fields, where the two occasionally hybridise. The above-ground parts of all these plants look very similar to each other, and to several other brassicas, and they require practice to separate.

Oilseed Rape in a monoculture tends to be better for wildlife than the winter wheat or barley with which it is alternated, especially with the tendency these days to spray out all the broad-leaved weeds, which are so important for farmland wildlife, from cereal crops. Although as a crop, winter Oilseed Rape is too tall in the spring for some classic, declining farmland birds such as Skylark or Lapwing to nest in, some birds will breed in it, such as Reed Bunting, Sedge Warbler, Whitethroat and Yellow Wagtail, as well as partridges and Pheasant.

Also, Oilseed Rape yield is substantially increased by the presence of pollinating insects, which means that at least a little wildlife is desirable within the crop. While domestic honeybees were once thought to be the main pollinators (although Rape honey isn't said to be all that great), it is now known that the crop is pollinated more or less equally by honeybees, bumblebees and a host of wild solitary bees, which may also make their nests in the soil beneath the crop. Other insects, such as hoverflies and pollen beetles, may also be common among Rape flowers.

Oilseed Rape has occupied a central place in the debate about genetically-modified (GM) crops. GM Rape allows much freer use of pesticides, eliminating weeds and other biodiversity from the crop. Another fear is that Rape will hybridise with its close relatives, naturalised or in the wild, passing altered genes into wild ecosystems. This could hypothetically lead to wild plants resistant to attack by insects, or which cannot be controlled using common herbicides. Because they are pollinated by flying insects, the degree of isolation which would be needed to prevent contact between GM Rape and its wild relatives would have to be huge – unrealistically so.

A side-effect of the abundance of Rape fields in lowland Britain is that Oilseed Rape has now become one of our commonest wild plants on road- and ditch-sides, where it originates from seed spilt during harvest or transportation. It is quite common now to see natural waysides almost as solidly yellow as the field itself. In fact Rape, as a species, is a poor competitor in the wild (as are most crops), and if Rape seems to be persisting on road and dyke-sides for many years it is very likely that it does so by regular replenishment from new spilt seed.

Lords and Ladies. Late April and May is the time when one of North East Lincolnshire's, indeed Britain's, most extraordinary wild plants comes into flower. The delightfully weird Lords and Ladies or Cuckoo Pint (*Arum maculatum*), once described as 'a crafty and malignant antediluvian vegetable', is in a category of its own among the native British flora in terms of its distinctive appearance and combination of bizarre characters.

Patches of the dark green, arrow-shaped leaves of Lords and Ladies start to appear about February. The leaves can sometimes sport black patches, which give the plant its specific epithet 'maculatum', meaning 'spotted'. In our area it is common in woodlands, hedgerows, and along many of the older boundaries and roadsides.

Lords and Ladies is poisonous, the bright red berries, which appear on conspicuous spikes in late summer, especially so – they are worth avoiding. The ground-up roots were once made into a starch for stiffening ruffs and mens' beards, although prolonged use was said to cause blistering to the launderer. Lords and Ladies' commonness in the wild, and unique and somewhat suggestive appearance, has led to this species having the highest number of recorded English names of any plant (many of them rude), including the longest: 'Kitty-come-down-the-lane-jump-up-and-kiss-me'.

Lords and Ladies' extraordinary pollination mechanism deserves special mention. As soon as the distinctive green hoods, or 'spathes' open in the spring, the contained purple 'spadix' gives off an unpleasant smell, vaguely like manure. It disperses this scent far and wide by becoming warm at its tip, often 15 degrees above the surrounding air. The purpose of the smell is to attract tiny flies called Moth Flies, or Owl Midges. These flies, with stubby, brown scaly wings, are usually attracted to wet, rotting organic matter and dung, and can be very abundant where such things occur, including in the drains of houses. They find the smell of the Lords and Ladies' spadix irresistible, although peculiarly, only female flies seem to be involved.

Moth Flies, once deceived by the smell, cannot grip the smooth, oily purple spadix and fall, or climb, down through a ring of downward-directed bristles into the swollen chamber at the base of the spathe, where they are trapped. Inside this chamber are receptive female flowers, which are duly pollinated by the struggling flies.

Male flowers, occurring just above the female flowers, ripen about a day later when the female flowers have become unreceptive (so that self-pollination is avoided), and proceed to dust the captive flies with pollen. Finally, the bristles in the neck of the swelling wither so that they are no longer an obstruction, unblocking the neck and allowing the little pollen-laden flies to escape back into the wild. The flies are then free to be re-trapped by another Lords and Ladies flower, and the process is repeated.

As if this was not all strange enough, Lords and Ladies, or to be precise its pollen, has been said to give off light, supposedly making the flowers glow in the dark. This explains several of its multifarious vernacular names including 'fairy lamps' and 'shiners'. However, much about this peculiar suggestion does not ring true. It seems that myths of glowing Lords and Ladies arose on the riverbanks of ancient Fenland, and have been variously passed on and reinforced in that district up into modern times. In fact, Lords and Ladies is far from common in the Fens proper, and is not really a plant of riverbanks. I believe that the glowing pollen theory is pure nonsense; I have never seen it, and I cannot find anybody who has. It is much more likely that the similarity of the flower to a lamp containing a candle, and the visibility of the pale green spathes in moonlight or at dusk, is the explanation.

If you have ever seen Lords and Ladies glow in the dark, please get in touch!

Gardening for Wildlife. Traditionally, a garden was somewhere where nature would have been tamed and manipulated – a place for growing regimented exotic ornamentals, vegetables and herbs free from weeds and hungry pests. With wildlife plentiful just the other side of the garden fence, there was no need to invite it into one's own backyard.

But with the intensification of farming leading to a deterioration in the quality of the wider countryside, the concept of gardens as refuges for wildlife has come to the fore. Nowadays it is understood by everybody that gardens have a vital role to play in the conservation of the nation's wildlife. Books and TV advice on wildlife gardening are everywhere.

Although the average garden is fairly small, gardens in total occupy about 3% of the land area of England and Wales. Gardens differ from proper countryside in several important ways – they are extremely structurally diverse over a small area, usually with an unnaturally high plant diversity including many exotics and non-natives. They are also relatively disturbed environments – mainly by people, but also by pets. Flowers are usually abundant – indeed, they occur at a level matched only by the very most floriferous natural habitats.

Even the most conventional gardens – those with the usual manicured lawn and well-weeded herbaceous borders – can be managed with wildlife in mind. Firstly, it is important not to negate all the good work by using peat-based compost or rocks taken from natural limestone pavements. The use of weedkillers and pesticides could be relaxed or avoided completely. Cats should be prevented from killing birds and small mammals, and features such as hedgerows and compost heaps left alone in the breeding season. Such a garden, however neat, will be legitimately doing its bit for the nation's wildlife.

Even within a formal garden situation, additional measures can be taken to help animals, such as planting berry-bearing shrubs and other cover, or providing bird feeders and nestboxes.

The next level of wildlife gardening is to try to recreate semi-natural habitats in the garden itself – meadows, ponds, hedgerows and the like. This isn't the same as letting nature take over, and requires some skill to do well. But the rewards are worth it.

Information on how to manage a garden for wildlife is abundantly available – but it is worth stating some important principles right at the start, and busting some myths. Firstly, although country gardens are likely to be better, town gardens may be very rich in wildlife indeed, and the effect of positive management for wildlife tends to trump the effect of location.

Secondly, although larger gardens tend to be technically richer in species, wildlife doesn't distinguish between the end of your property and the start of your neighbour's. This means that the concept of a small garden is an illusion. It is the green space created by all the gardens together that matters, and every small part of that is important.

Even if an effort is made to garden specifically for wildlife, if everybody did so in the same way, the resulting garden resource would be less diverse than if gardeners each did something slightly different. The only attempt to date at getting adjacent gardeners to co-operate for wildlife in this way – a recent project in Sheffield – failed. Nevertheless, a little originality, doing something unusual, can go a long way to making a large area of adjacent gardens as varied as possible.

Gardens, even ones managed for wildlife, can never be miniature versions of the countryside. For example, long grass and dead wood are hugely under-represented in gardens, compared with the wild. These habitats might look scruffy, but if you can bear to, providing them would be extremely useful in balancing things up.

It is a deeply-ingrained generalisation that native plant species are always better for wildlife than non-natives. You usually can't go wrong with natives, of course. But herbivorous creatures can often find a good substitute – often a related species – among a garden's non-native flora. The vast majority of garden animals are, in any case, predators, parasites, detritivores or pollinators, which either don't care about the species of plant they find themselves on, or may even find a higher quality resource among the garden's non-natives.

The single best way to make a garden better for wildlife is by providing three-dimensional complexity – i.e. a mixture of trees, shrubs, flowers, grasses, barish ground and (very importantly) water, in close proximity. This increases the number of niches available for different species.

Three species of animal in particular epitomise the importance of gardens for wildlife – Song Thrush, Hedgehog and Common Frog. Provide habitat for these three, and countless other species will also be helped. We could add to this list the pollinating insects which have declined so steeply in the wider countryside, and for which gardens are now so important. But most gardeners don't need encouragement to provide flowers – it is already what they do best.

Gulls on Roofs. There has been a remarkable change in the behavior of two of our large gull species in the last half a century, which can be seen clearly in our area. Before that time, both the Herring Gull and its close relative the Lesser Black-backed Gull were almost exclusively coastal breeders, with the highest densities in the rocky west of the country.

Herring Gulls would spread out in the winter to wherever they could find food, but they remained mostly coastal. Nearly all Lesser Black-backed Gulls would leave the UK in the winter, spending this period to the south, in France, Portugal or Morocco.

The Herring Gull is the archetypal 'seagull' with the raucous, laughing call, a pale grey back, yellow bill and pink legs. Lesser Black-backed Gull is identical in size, but a rather smarter bird, with a dark grey back and yellow legs.

Both species are opportunist feeders. Their traditional feeding habitat is at sea or in the intertidal zone. But both have learned to take advantage of the activities of humans, finding abundant food in cities, at fish docks, and especially at landfill sites. This has brought them inland in large numbers.

Lesser Black-backed Gulls are now hugely increased as a wintering species in the UK, and both species have adopted the roofs of urban, industrial sites and residential housing for nesting. This change in habit has now brought these gulls far inland, with breeding colonies now as distant from the sea as Birmingham. On urban rooftops, as in the rural colonies of the west coast, these two species may nest in mixed colonies.

In North East Lincolnshire the roof-nesting habit started about ten years ago, and is increasing sharply, as it is across the UK as a whole. The rise in roof-nesting Herring Gulls stands in stark contrast to the species' general fortunes, which tend strongly downwards. Many domestic dwellings and flat-roofed industrial buildings in both Grimsby and Cleethorpes now hold breeding Herring Gulls or Lesser Black-backed Gulls, especially near the docks or along the coastal strip. Look, for an example, along the flat rooftops along Victoria Street South in Grimsby.

During May, most pairs of gulls have eggs, and this is the stage of the breeding cycle when the colony is at its quietest. Chicks may finally fledge in August.

Being bold and opportunistic, gulls are birds to which some people take a strong dislike – this is especially so when they nest in towns. Breeding gulls are noisy, and may foul or damage flat roofs. Their nests may occasionally block gutters and flues, or hold moisture against the building structure. Additional problems may occur when they have chicks, especially when these are accidentally displaced from the nest. Adult gulls will defend them vigorously, causing them to dive and swoop on both people and pets.

Despite the potential nuisance, it is illegal to capture, injure or destroy any wild bird or interfere with its nest or eggs. Only when there is a need to preserve public health or public safety may an authorised person take such actions. Noise, or damage to property, are not considered legitimate excused for harming gulls.

There are various measures which can be deployed to deter gulls from nesting on buildings. However, all such work should be carried out by an authorised person, as inexpertly undertaken work risks harming the birds and breaking the law.

Personally I see no need to bother them unless there is a pressing reason. If you have a chance to witness the full breeding cycle from a discrete standpoint, you may enjoy a masterclass in animal behavior, as well as enjoying an encounter with truly wild creatures during the most important part of their year.

Hawthorn. There is a small group of plants whose contribution to our Lincolnshire landscape can scarcely be overstated. Among our woodland and farmland trees, we must mention the ubiquitous Ash. Closer to the ground, there is the smothering white Cow Parsley of May and June roadsides, and of course the ubiquitous Oilseed Rape, which turns the countryside bright yellow in spring. There remains a single dominating landscape plant to mention – the ubiquitous shrub of hedgerows – the Hawthorn, or May.

Hawthorn was always a common tree, whose foam-like masses of white flowers would have graced woodlands, downland and neglected rural corners everywhere. Hawthorn gained even more prominence during the Enclosure Acts of the eighteenth and nineteenth centuries, when an estimated 200,000 miles of it were sown as hedgerows to mark the boundaries of newly-privatised land. Today there is scarcely a hedgerow anywhere which doesn't contain Hawthorn, and many are composed entirely of it.

Hawthorn makes the perfect hedgerow shrub – fast-growing, fiendishly thorny and readily-trained, it can quickly form a barrier impenetrable to humans and livestock alike. Regular management, sometimes by the old practice of 'laying', keeps it nicely dense at the base. Nowadays, one encounters much less livestock in the fields of eastern England, but the widespread removal of redundant hedgerows has thankfully come to a stop. Far too many, however, are still flailed into a dwarfed, gappy, pointless strip, serving little purpose to either people or wildlife.

British hedgerows undergo a succession of flushes of blossom as the spring progresses. The introduced Cherry Plum is the first to flower in the leafless surroundings of February or March, although the blossoms tends to form no more than small white patches here and there. Next, in early April, comes Blackthorn, whose more extensive masses of white flowers appear before the leaves, creating an attractive contrast between the blooms and the dark twigs on which they're borne.

The timing of the first Hawthorn blossom is variable from year to year, but usually occurs here in late April, with peak flowering in the second half of May. The flowers in no small part make the season what it is, and this is the only British plant named after the month in which it blooms.

Not only do creamy masses of Hawthorn flowers dominate the lowland landscape at this time, but the smell of Hawthorn blossom is also highly characteristic of the season. It is a complex scent: heavy, more evocative than sweet, and not enjoyed by everyone. Although associated with one of the most uplifting seasons of the year, the smell is said by those with experience of such things to have a hint of dead bodies or gangrene; indeed one of the chemicals involved – triethylamine – is the same.

Hawthorn is the subject of more folklore than any other British plant. In particular, there is widespread misgiving about bringing the flowers into the house. Apart from the smell, there is something about the colour scheme of white flowers and red berries which is subconsciously disconcerting, again probably because of the reminder of death. Red and white flowers together are still, today, unpopular in hospitals.

On a happier note, Hawthorn hedges are great for wildlife, providing abundant, well-protected nest sites for birds and foodplant for countless insects. The autumn berries, or haws, provide an invaluable feast for winter thrushes.

The flesh of haws may be made into jams and jellies but are not great raw. The fresh green leaves of Hawthorn are also edible, and known across the country as 'bread and cheese'. I have tried them once, and once was enough.

Occasionally, you may find a strip of Hawthorn hedgerow which consistently sprouts its fresh spring foliage earlier in the year than Hawthorns elsewhere. While this may indicate a warm or sheltered microclimate, it is more likely to give away plants of continental origin, imported from abroad especially for hedge-planting.

Very rarely, Hawthorns occur which flower at entirely the wrong time of year, in December. Many of these trees are known to be descendants – usually from cuttings – of the most famous such tree, the Holy Thorn at Glastonbury, although winter-flowering 'sports' have been known to arise afresh. I have found a Hawthorn flowering in December at Blakeney in Norfolk, but have never seen the phenomenon in Lincolnshire.

There is a second species of Hawthorn which is very much rarer – the so-called Midland Hawthorn. Earlier-flowering and more of a woodland plant, its leaves are simpler in shape – mainly three-lobed – and shinier. The flowers have two stigmas instead of one, and the haws, two contained seeds. Where the two grow together, an array of hybrids may arise with intermediate, or mixed, characters. We have what is probably native Midland Hawthorn in Bradley Woods and Healing Covert, and planted specimens elsewhere, including the Carr Plantation of Weelsby Woods, and Pier Gardens.

If you know of a winter-flowering, or a Midland Hawthorn, please get in touch.

Great Crested Newts. These days, major planning applications usually have to be accompanied by an ecological survey so that no protected habitats or species are harmed during the construction process. Without specialist advice it is all too easy to break wildlife laws by accident.

The animals which frustrate and hold up developers most often are bats and Great Crested Newts, as both are common, especially in man-made environments, but nevertheless comprehensively protected.

The legal situation regarding the protection of Great Crested Newts is currently a mess, satisfying neither developers nor conservationists. So firstly, why are Great Crested Newts so highly protected when they are so common?

On a worldwide scale, the Great Crested Newt is not threatened. Indeed, it is one of the most widely-distributed 'tailed' amphibians in the world, occurring from Britain and France eastwards right across Europe to central Asia, inhabiting tens of thousands of breeding ponds. It was given an international conservation priority in 1979, later enshrined in UK law in 1981, due to a decline across its European range which has continued to this day. On balance, given the steepness of the decline and the susceptibility of the species to loss of its pond habitat, protection seems justified.

Great Crested Newt surveying is a complex business, involving cold-searching for eggs, 'lamping' waterbodies at night, and extensive bottle-trapping. Up to four complete surveys are necessary before it can be concluded with any certainty that newts are *not* present. Surveyors are usually paid professionals, and need to be licensed to carry out their work.

The relevant government agency spends a fortune administering the licensing process, and the surveyors then need to be paid at specialists' rates for what can be a big job. All this money has to be found from somewhere. What is more, the need for a licence means that a child cannot so much as dip a net into a pond with Great Crested Newts in it without breaking the law.

What is worse, developers, having often become hostile to both newts and their surveyors during the process, are almost never stopped from proceeding based on the presence of Great Crested Newts. They must often provide extremely expensive 'mitigation' (usually translocation of newts) at their own expense. This almost never works, and when it fails, there are no consequences.

Lost in all of these political failings is the fact that the Great Crested Newt is a beautiful animal. It is large, dwarfing other British newts, and a male in breeding dress is one of the most, I would say *the* most, charismatic and extravagant creatures to be seen in the whole of the British fauna. With its streamlined shape, silver tail-stripe, huge ragged crest running the length of its body and tail, and brilliant orange and yellow, black spotted underbelly, it seems designed for high fantasy – almost needlessly exotic. You need to see one in real life, in water, to appreciate that this is nothing less than a real-life dragon. Also, the ponds where they live are often bursting with life, and protection of newts always has the knock-on effect of protecting a whole lot of other wildlife too.

The answer must surely be to identify the very best places for Great Crested Newts, which will usually be complexes of ponds set within well-structured semi-natural surroundings, and protect them *properly*, using existing high-level designations. In such places, there will be no argument that planning applications will fail. The survey licence needs to be removed – interest in wildlife is hardly served by preventing people from looking for it, especially in habitats as rewarding as ponds.

Where developers really *must* pay for and provide mitigation, this should be in the form of the reinstatement of dilapidated ponds or the provision of new ones, strategically placed to strengthen or extend existing populations.

We are privileged to have Great Crested Newts in several of North East Lincolnshire's ponds. This would be the time of year to go and see them at their best, if it were not, quite ludicrously, illegal.

Birdsong. With the dawn chorus now at its tumultuous best, I often wonder why so few people seem to know their common bird songs. Some of course may not have the slightest interest in such things, but many more I suspect just think the effort required to learn them is too great. This is a shame, as being able to recognise twenty-five or so bird songs can transform a spring walk to the point that a whole new aural understanding emerges, and fifty would see you right in just about any British habitat. Yet many of the same people who think it is too hard can easily name pop songs by the hundred, or the voices of countless celebrities, based on the briefest snatches of sound. In comparison, learning a few bird songs is not so hard.

It is almost always male birds which sing, and the purpose of course is to establish territories and attract mates, with the strongest and most skillful singers displaying superior 'fitness' to breed. The bird's sound-producing organ is called the syrinx – a double structure, each half of which can be manipulated independently to create the more complex songs. Efficient use of air passing through the syrinx ensures power, and some birds can sing while inhaling as well as exhaling.

Although birdsong would seem an essential ingredient in any portrayal of the country idyll, in fact the period of the year during which all birds sing together is relatively short. Our resident species might start in earnest in March, joined on arrival in April by the migrant summer visitors, but by July all is mostly quiet again except for the wistful Robin, the only species which habitually sings throughout the year.

Many bird songs are simple and immutable – they never alter. Others are more varied and musical, and have to be identified by a combination of pitch, timbre and pace, which, apart from a couple of tricky species pairs, is not as hard as it sounds. Robin and Blackbird are two such species, which are so common that once learned they account for a large slab of the soundscapes of town and country alike. Once these two are known, songs that are different tend to stand out.

There are now innumerable websites and phone 'apps' for identifying British birdsongs, so it is easier than ever to get to grips with the commoner species. For the fastest start, learn Blackbird, Robin and Chaffinch. For sheer power from a tiny bird, try Wren. For nostalgia try Song Thrush, and for sheer fluid brilliance, try Garden Warbler. If you hear a singing Turtle Dove this spring, do tell me – they have become extremely uncommon in recent years.

Waders from the Far North. By now the vast majority of the Humber's wading birds have started their long journey back north to their breeding grounds. It is those species which breed furthest north which have to plan their journeys the most carefully, as the Arctic summer is very short, and they only have a very brief window in which to lay their eggs and fledge young before they have to make their way back south again.

So which of our waders travels the furthest north – closest to the Pole – to breed?

No wader can breed on Arctic pack ice – all require snow-free terra firma. The closest point of actual land to the North Pole is the north coast of Greenland; a region called Peary Land. Only slightly further from the Pole is Ellesmere Island, technically part of Canada, to the west.

This northernmost land is so inhospitable that breeding by birds is not even possible in some summers, and so remote that very few people have ever set foot there, especially to look for birds. It is known however that our own Turnstone breeds there. Outside the breeding season this characterful, short-billed bird has an almost worldwide distribution, including Cleethorpes beach, where it is common. We know through bird ringing that Turnstones from these most northerly lands occur on British coastlines.

Turnstones will eat almost anything, and are often so tame that they will run around the feet of holidaymakers on the promenade, scavenging for scraps. Out on the beach they tend to inhabit breakwaters or places where there are rocks or seaweed, although they can also be seen on the open beach with other waders.

But there are three other species which challenge the Turnstone for the title of 'most northerly', and all three are also common on our beach here in Cleethorpes. These are the Sanderling, the Ringed Plover and the Knot. Interestingly the Sanderling, like the Turnstone, is habitually quite tame – these are the small white sandpipers which scuttle like clockwork toys ahead of walkers on the tideline wherever the beach is sandy. Like Turnstone, Sanderling also has a worldwide distribution in winter, with British beaches sometimes hosting birds from far-northern Greenland and Canada. On our beach, numbers of northbound migrants peak in May.

The next species, the handsomely-marked Ringed Plover, has a much wider breeding range, including the UK. Disturbance usually prevents successful breeding on Cleethorpes's outer sand dunes, and peak numbers tend to occur here on passage. Ringed Plovers have a so-called 'leapfrog' migration, in which the birds breeding the furthest north travel the furthest south for the winter, with birds from more central parts of the range being much more sedentary. Some far northerly-breeding Ringed Plovers may pass through the Humber, with a spring peak in May, although most tend to take a more westerly route.

Lastly, the Knot is the most numerous wader on the Humber Estuary, and any huge swirling mass of waders seen at high tide at Cleethorpes is likely to comprise this species. Just like Turnstone and Sanderling, it is known that our British birds come from the high Arctic Greenland/Canada breeding population, some of the most northerly-breeding on Earth. All three species will use Iceland as a staging post on their way to and from the UK.

Several other of our wader species travel very far north to breed, but do not quite reach the northerly limits of dry land as do these four. To gain a firm answer to the question 'which wader is the planet's most northerly breeder' is possibly asking too much, but you can see all of the candidates on our own beach for much of the year.

A single Sanderling, two Ringed Plover and four Turnstone mingle with Dunlin on Cleethorpes Beach

Some Local Orchids. Many people harbour a desire to know more about our wild plants, but to embark on such a study is no small undertaking, requiring a long apprenticeship. For this reason, many dip their toe by concentrating on one group at a time.

The family with which most people acquaint themselves first are the orchids. As a result, orchids almost certainly have more devotees than all of the other plant families put together.

So what is the special appeal of the orchids? Firstly, the British wild orchid flora is manageably small. Most are highly exotic-looking, and some are very rare – an ideal formula for the collector. With a little imagination the forms of the flowers of some species can be likened to humans or other animals, so have added appeal. Being an evolutionarily recent group, they are still throwing up new hybrids and forms, and some pose a formidable identification challenge. They have sophisticated breeding systems, and they are very photogenic.

It is a common myth that *all* orchids are rare – in fact, quite a few are moderately common. Another myth is that they are highly-sensitive denizens of rich and ancient habitats. Again, some are. But similarly, many may be found in the most ephemeral of places – dunes, quarries, spoil tips, roundabouts, rail- and runways, or newly-created grasslands – or at least in otherwise quite dull, recently-created woodland.

In Cleethorpes our huge population of Southern Marsh Orchids on the dunes behind the Boating Lake became something of a tourist attraction for a time, although this relatively recent spectacle is now much reduced after the habitat was spoiled by a very high tide. Other populations occur on ditchsides, docks and other miscellaneous grassland locations around our area.

Another opportunist is the beautiful Bee Orchid. Surely the most exotic-looking wild flower on the Lincolnshire list, its extraordinary blooms stand in stark contrast to some of the varied and often scruffy places the plant tends to turn up.

Many people are surprised to discover that Bee Orchids enjoy no statutory protection at all – although they look amazing, they are simply too common. In our area you may see them along the coast at Cleethorpes, on Waltham aerodrome, on railways, tracksides and woodland rides or if you are very lucky, almost any kind of grassland situation.

The first orchid of the year to flower locally is the Early Purple Orchid. This handsome purple flower is more confined to stable habitats than the last two, inhabiting older woodlands, banks and ditchsides. It can be found in Dixon/Bradley Woods, Roxton Wood, Irby Dale, the woodlands of the Brocklesby Estate and occasionally elsewhere, flowering at the same time as the Bluebells.

The white or pale pink Common Spotted Orchid is the most frequently-occurring orchid here, inhabiting open woodlands, grassland and scrub, as well as more ephemeral habitats such as spoil tips and quarries. There are plenty in Cleethorpes Country Park if you know where to look, growing among Southern Marsh Orchids. A few also grow on the coastal dunes where they may hybridise with the Marsh Orchids.

Another of our orchids, the Broad-leaved Helleborine, is tied to shady woodlands, but apart from that is not particularly choosy, growing in some quite unimpressive habitat in the Carr Plantation, part of Weelsby Woods. It also occurs in Roxton Woods, in some years in large numbers. It is one of the later-flowering species – July and August are best.

The lime-green-flowered Twayblade, with its distinctive pair of rounded leaves at the base, is another mainly woodland species found in higher quality habitats here and there, and the handsome Pyramidal Orchid becomes visible on a few grassy roadsides and coastal dunes when its heads of magenta-pink flowers are in full bloom in June – look on the slopes of Covenham Reservoir, or if you're lucky on the Laceby Bypass.

The most astonishing local orchid find in recent years was made by Chris Heaton, who discovered a large population of White Helleborines in Grimsby Cemetery. This is a rare, May-flowering orchid, whose nearest wild station is way to the south in the Chilterns, where it inhabits shady Beechwoods. One is tempted to conclude that our own plants were introduced here on boots which had previously trodden its chalky southern haunts – an extraordinary coincidence, but the kind of event which explains many of our odder plant distributions. Tantalisingly, there is an old 1950s record of what were conceivably native White Helleborines from Brough on the Humber's north bank, so the truth is that nobody actually knows where they came from – it is a fascinating enigma.

Blue Butterflies. Last week a friend told me she had seen a blue butterfly in her small Cleethorpes garden and asked me what I thought it could be.

Here in North East Lincolnshire we are poorly off for members of the 'blue' family of butterflies, and seven of Britain's nine blues can be immediately discounted – four only occur in the south, one is a habitat specialist on heathland and limestone grassland neither of which we have, and the remaining two are brown in colour, not blue. This leaves only two species available to us here in North East Lincolnshire, the Common Blue and the Holly Blue.

The temptation at this point is always to say "well mine will be the 'common' one", but vernacular names can be misleading and, of course, the 'other' one must occur somewhere.

In fact, this is a good example of a situation where two species which look similar have completely different habitats and behaviour to help us with an identification. Common Blue (its name is not misleading this time) is indeed Britain's most widely-distributed blue butterfly, occurring in open habitats where it flies low over the ground, always near its foodplant, Bird's-foot Trefoil. By contrast, Holly Blue occurs only in more enclosed, sheltered places such as gardens and churchyards, where is it almost always associated with evergreens. Because of this difference in habitat, Holly Blue tends to quarter vegetation 'up and down', rather than along the ground. It also flies a little earlier in the year than the Common Blue. So my friend's Butterfly is a Holly Blue.

Holly Blue is a fascinating butterfly. It is the only British species whose two annual generations require different foodplants, with the first (spring) brood of caterpillars feeding on Holly, and the second (autumn) brood feeding on Ivy or other shrubs. The adult butterflies are also noted for extreme variations in abundance from year to year, with fluctuations occurring on a regular cycle. This is caused by a classic 'density-dependent' relationship with a species of parasitic wasp – when butterflies increase, their parasites increase too; this causes butterfly numbers to crash so the parasite crashes too, and the cycle starts again.

Look for the Holly Blue around now in gardens and other sheltered places with evergreens. With a good view its underside will be seen to be white. The other 'blue, the Common Blue, can be seen on waste ground or short, open, flowery grassland – it is particularly conspicuous on the dunes at Cleethorpes at 'orchid time'. If you can get one to sit still, its underside is the colour of milky tea.

The Three Pipistrelles. When one sees a small bat foraging at dusk around North East Lincolnshire's towns and gardens, it is all too easy just to dismiss it as a Pipistrelle, although this is *probably* what it is – Pipistrelles are by far the commonest bats in Britain, and indeed Europe.

For many years until quite recently, it was thought that British Pipistrelles all belonged to a single species. Then gradually bat workers started to notice that the frequency of Pipistrelles' echolocation calls tended to fall into two distinct camps, with one sort having its peak frequency at about 45 kHz and the other at about 55 kHz. It was even suggested that there were other slight physical differences between the two sorts. One worker went so far as to give the two sorts names – 'bandits' and 'browns'. A landmark scientific paper in 1992 asked the question 'could they be completely separate species?'

A good deal of work followed to make sure that the two sorts of Pipistrelle weren't actually the same – that the differences couldn't just be accounted for by males and females, young or old bats, or even bats avoiding certain frequencies when foraging in the same place, to prevent 'jamming' each others' signals. It was soon found that roosts always contained either one sort or the other, and that calls were consistent within a type. The two were finally declared to be separate species in 1999, initially known as '45' and '55' Pipistrelles. Nowadays we know them as Common and Soprano Pipistrelles, the lower/larger of the two species keeping the original name. Both live commonly among us here in North East Lincolnshire.

So before about 2000, descriptions of Common Pipistrelle in books actually refer to two species. DNA studies have shown that the two Pipistrelles aren't even particularly closely related, having diverged somewhere between 5 and 10 million years ago – longer than some other pairs of British species which have always been known to be distinct.

Now that we know there are two sorts, and bat detectors which can separate the echolocation frequencies have become better and cheaper, it seems slightly odd that we ever thought they were the same. Soprano Pipistrelles are slightly smaller, with paler fur and a pinker nose. Their roosts may be larger, and give off a stronger musty smell than those of the Common Pipistrelle. They are said to be more likely to forage near water. Soprano Pipistrelle, although living alongside Common Pipistrelle in the UK, has a more northerly-centered distribution in Europe. However, not a single one of these features, including the frequency of the call, is absolutely diagnostic – there is overlap – and one still occasionally encounters a Pipistrelle which one cannot name with certainty.

There was always another species of Pipistrelle in the UK, which nobody really expected to see because it was a great rarity, the Nathusius's Pipistrelle. First recorded from Shetland in 1940, further records of this slightly larger species were very few and far between, and the species was for many years considered to be nothing more than a very rare vagrant. Gradually, more records emerged, and its status was upgraded to migrant winter visitor. In the

1990s, discoveries of males exhibiting courtship behavior and mating in the UK led to the realisation that this was also a British breeding species. Excitingly, the first maternity roost of Nathusius's Pipistrelle to be discovered in the UK was in Lincolnshire – at Skegness – in the late 1990s, with two more found soon afterwards in Northern Ireland. More have since been discovered.

Unusually, Nathusius's Pipistrelles are known to be migratory, with populations breeding in Eastern Europe travelling to west central Europe and Iberia for the winter. Between the two is a zone where both resident and migratory bats occur, and Britain is now thought to be within this zone. The species evidently breeds here, but bats caught in the UK have also been picked up on the Continent, and Nathusius's Pipstrelles are sometimes grounded on rigs and boats in the North Sea. Nathusius's Pipistrelle is now known to be much more widely-distributed here than was ever thought, with our resident bats joined by migratory bats in winter. It seems unlikely that the species was overlooked all this time, and we are fairly certain that it is spreading and becoming much commoner.

Nathusius's Pipistrelle is recorded from North East Lincolnshire, and is particularly frequent along the drains of the Lincolnshire outmarsh. Having said that, there is still a huge amount to learn about its distribution and movements. On a bat detector, its echolocation calls peak fairly consistently at 40 kHz, significantly lower than the other two.

So what was thought to be one species is now three, which modern technology makes it very much easier to separate. So little is still known about them, however, that every piece of information on these, or any bat, is still extremely valuable.

If you know where there is a bat roost, please get in touch – either with me, or the Lincolnshire Bat Group.

BioBlitz. Nature conservation can't work without information on what lives where, and a running theme of this column has always been to encourage people to submit records of the wildlife they see. Well now you can do it in style, as Cleethorpes hosts an all-day 'BioBlitz' event on Saturday June 4th 2016.

BioBlitz is an attempt to identify as many species as possible in a given area in twenty-four hours. This one marks a co-operation between North East Lincolnshire Council, the Lincolnshire Naturalists' Union and the Greater Lincolnshire Nature Partnership. Experts will be on hand, and although they will engage in some serious recording themselves, the austere atmosphere of a Naturalists' Union field excursion will be forgotten for the day and replaced by an emphasis on mass-participation, education and fun. BioBlitz is all about the public – there will be activities for kids, adults, beginners and experts alike. At its best, BioBlitz should feel like a 'festival of wildlife'.

The Discovery Centre will act as base for the collection of records throughout the day, and although there will be a meet-up there at 10 a.m., no formalities are necessary and people can come and go as they please. In addition to the daytime searches, moth-trapping and bat walks will take place in both the Country Park and around the Discovery Centre from 9pm, with the Centre remaining open for toilets and coffee until midnight.

During BioBlitz events, many people are surprised by the wealth of wildlife living on their doorstep. Something unexpected almost always turns up, and light is often thrown on areas needing further study. First-timers may often make valuable discoveries by looking in places that the experts don't. But it's not all about new finds; up-to-date records for common species are also extremely welcome, and every record collected during the day will be added to local and national biodiversity databases.

There have been previous BioBlitz events in Lincolnshire – the one at Chambers Farm Wood near Wragby turned up several new species for the county, as well as a nationally rare spider. BioBlitz took place at the Horncastle headquarters of the Lincolnshire Wildlife Trust annually for five consecutive years, and the total number of species recorded topped 1000.

The precise area to be blitzed this time is Cleethorpes Country Park, the Boating Lake grounds, and over onto the dunes and foreshore.

This diverse tract of land should provide rich pickings. The Country Park contains remnants of old Lincolnshire outmarsh fields with their wildlife-rich hedgerows and dykes, as well as new wetlands and newly-planted woodland. The short turf and sandy soils surrounding the Boating Lake are already known to contain a host of rare plants, but there are undoubtedly discoveries to be made. The Cleethorpes foreshore is one of the richest couple of miles in Lincolnshire for plant and animal life, with its combination of natural and human-influenced habitats, and zonation from terrestrial habitats right through to dune, marsh and fully marine environments, all within a short distance. Apart from charismatic groups such as butterflies, the invertebrate fauna of this area has received little attention, and this is where the real discoveries could be made.

While looking for new records, don't forget to pay your respects to the rarities which are already known. See if you can pick out the rare native subspecies of Black Poplar close to the entrance to Oriental Express. The extremely rare Smooth Rupturewort is quite cryptic but its bright green foliage stands out among the close-grazed grassland at the southern end of the Boating Lake. Easier to see is the pink-flowered Shining Cranesbill in the Old Dunes near the Jungle Zoo; look for the Lesser Meadow Rue there too. See if you can find the last few magenta flowers of Salsify in the country Park. Three species of orchid are technically possible. Watch out for the Common Blue butterfly and the last of the Orange Tips, as well as the Boating Lake's single summering Pink-footed Goose.

If you can re-find either of two quite uncharismatic plants on the dunes, the Dense Silky-bent or the Saltmarsh Flat-sedge, not seen there for many years, you will be the star of the day.

Do ask me if you would like help with the identification of any species found locally. Sometimes identifications are possible with just a good photo taken on a smartphone.

Ash Dieback. Between the late 1960s and early 1980s, Dutch Elm disease wiped out almost every mature elm tree from the English landscape. In fact, elms are still there, but they cannot grow very tall without becoming re-infected, so they are now restricted to scrubby undergrowth along wood edges and in hedgerows. Although not the first such historical outbreak, the disease caused a classic English landscape feature much loved by Constable, Wordsworth and country people everywhere, to be lost. We do not seem to miss them now – we have already re-adjusted to a poorer world.

A landscape without Ash trees is even more inconceivable, but now, owing to a newly-arrived disease, 'Ash dieback' (caused by a fungus, *Hymenoscyphus fraxineus*), this is what we could be facing.

Ash is ubiquitous in the British Isles as a native plant, and the commonest tree in Lincolnshire. It is abundant as a 'standard' along roadsides, hedgerows and in fields, and also constitutes a large proportion of many Lincolnshire woodlands and plantations, including our own Weelsby Woods. It is very late to come into leaf; always – despite the proverb – after Oak. This allows woodland flowers a good opportunity to flower without shade.

Although it has no showy blossoms or colourful, edible fruits, its strong, grey, simply divided trunks and stout, upswept twigs are an essential component of the local landscape. Ash leaves turn a subdued, smoky green in autumn, becoming flushed with olive-yellow just before falling, creating in large part the characteristic colour palette of Lincolnshire waysides and woodlands at the start of winter.

Ash is the obligatory foodplant of 29 species of invertebrate, and is exceptionally good for hole-nesting birds such as woodpeckers, Starlings and tits, and locally until recently, Ring-necked Parakeets. Bats will also use holes in Ash for maternity roosts. The common little round, black fungi known as 'King Alfred's Cakes' occur only on Ash.

Nobody knows exactly when Ash dieback first arrived in the UK. Outbreaks in East Anglia are thought to be natural occurrences, spores having been blown across the sea from infected parts of the near Continent. Elsewhere in Britain the blame can be well and truly laid at the door of new plantings of young trees imported from infected areas abroad. That Ash should be imported at all is ridiculous – it is extremely common as a sapling in the wild, and these need only to be pulled up and stuck somewhere else to grow perfectly well.

One does not come across Ash dieback every day, although there are now records from all parts of Britain. It would seem destined to become much commoner in future years. Look for dead, stiff, drooping leaves, and sunken black marks where twig meets branch. In more advanced cases a strong canker can develop on branches, and trees trying to fight off the disease can grow twigs and leaves in unsightly 'knots' and bunches.

Nobody knows what proportion of our Ashes will be killed by this disease – indeed not all infected trees actually die – but we hope that the total elimination we saw in Elm is not repeated. Remedial measures have been attempted, but all seem likely to fail.

The best way to proceed would be to immediately stop unnecessary international trade in trees, and instead of worrying about pests and diseases already out of control, concentrate on stopping ones not yet arrived from reaching our shores.

First among these must be Emerald Ash Borer, said to be 'the most feared beetle on Earth', which has now reached Europe on its westward march. If it arrives here this insect will, if Ash dieback hasn't done it already, undoubtedly kill every Ash tree stone dead. Without Ash, Lincolnshire would, or will, look a very different place.

Hairstreaks. Behaviourally, the butterflies of Britain fall into two groups. Firstly there are those which range far and wide across country to find new habitat in which to lay eggs and breed. These are said to have an 'open' population structure, and include the 'whites', Brimstone, Peacock, Small Tortoiseshell, and all migrant species.

Three quarters of Britain's butterfly species, however, do not share this strategy. These are said to have 'closed' population structures, and tend never to move far from where they were born, forming discrete colonies in suitable habitat. These include the 'browns', the 'skippers', and the Small Copper.

Butterflies falling into the latter category include the 'hairstreaks', of which we in Lincolnshire have three of the five British species. As butterflies go they are small and relatively inconspicuous, and their elusive behavior make them even more so. Their flight period is quite short, with each having only a single annual brood. Any sighting of a hairstreak in North East Lincolnshire is a special occasion, although all three are undoubtedly under-recorded.

First in the year to take to the wing is the Green Hairstreak. This is Britain's only truly green butterfly. In fact it is only its underside which is green, although this is the side it shows to the observer at rest, when it can be effectively camouflaged against leaves. The upperside, which is rarely seen, is plain brown.

Green Hairstreaks are found in coarse or dune grassland, scrub or clearings in woodland, where they lay their eggs on a variety of herbs and shrubs. This is the only one of the three hairstreaks never to have been recorded in North East Lincolnshire proper, although there is a colony just over the border at Tetney, and several along the coast from Grainthorpe southwards. You may see them on the wing now.

The other two species are very strongly associated with trees. The male Purple Hairstreak is one of Britain's more striking butterflies, having an upperside which is entirely a beautiful iridescent purple. Despite this, it is a very difficult species to see, and easily overlooked. It is usually associated with Oak, its sole foodplant, and the best way to locate it is to train binoculars towards the top of a prominent Oak tree during July. Purple Hairstreaks, which look grey in flight, may be seen flitting erratically around the uppermost branches, especially towards the end of a hot day. Although views may be poor, any butterfly conforming exactly to this description can scarcely be anything else. On rare occasions they do come down from the treetops, and then it can be seen what handsome butterflies they really are.

Lastly, the White-letter Hairstreak is the 'original' hairstreak – that is to say, it the species for which the name was coined. All hairstreaks have a fine white 'hair' line on their undersides, but in this species it describes a neat 'W' shape near the tip of the hindwing. White-letter Hairstreak is an Elm specialist, and when Dutch elm disease struck in the 1970s, conservationists feared for the butterfly's future in Britain. However, the species seems to have survived on the scrubby regrowth of Elm which can still be found in hedgerows and around the edges of woodland today. This is another small, brown species whose erratic flight around upper branches makes it relatively difficult to see. It is however somewhat more ready to come down to take nectar from flowers such as bramble and thistles than its Purple relative. If you know of a good stand of Elms, do have a careful look for this butterfly in mid-July.

Both Purple and White-letter Hairstreak have known colonies in North East Lincolnshire, although they are few, and all records are valuable. All three species are easily missed, and one feels certain that there are still local discoveries to be made.

Spring Migration, 2014. With the bird migration now drawing to a close, it's becoming clear that spring of 2014 hasn't been a classic for rarities. Although there are still a few days left to find a 'mega', I'm going to tempt fate by trying to sum up the best of the season in North East Lincolnshire.

Spring movements kicked off with a Black Redstart in Grimsby on 24th March. Wheatears were next, being seen throughout the spring on permanent grasslands and along the coast on their way to their breeding grounds in stony upland districts in Britain and Scandinavia. Birds passing through in May tend to be slightly more colourful and longer-winged and are probably heading for Iceland or Greenland.

On 10th April a splendid Osprey soared majestically over Cleethorpes and Humberston against a clear blue sky, accompanied by mobbing gulls, with another over Grimsby four days later. A female Ring Ouzel, the so-called 'mountain blackbird', was at Gooseman's Field by the Peaks Parkway on its way to its upland summer haunts.

There was a high count of eight Common Sandpipers at Cleethorpes Country Park on 4th May this year, this date probably indicating birds en route to Scandinavia rather than British birds which should be on their breeding grounds by that time. This small wader has a characteristic flight, whirring low over water and gliding on bowed wings when flushed, and a 'bobbing' motion on land. A single Wood Sandpiper flew over Cleethorpes Coast Local Nature Reserve on 10th May, identified by its call.

In most springs the unusual 'reeling' song of the Grasshopper Warbler can be heard somewhere in our area, although these days they tend to move on rather than staying here to breed. One was singing in Cleethorpes Country Park on 18th April.

Slightly out-of-area, the fields behind the sea wall at Tetney/North Cotes are a good place to look for migrating Dotterel in May (preferring those fields sown to peas). This year the peak count of these enigmatic mountain waders was 25.

A Spoonbill at Humberston Fitties on 8th May may have been the same bird seen on and off there since last autumn. But for star quality the highlight of the season was a smart summer-plumaged Black-necked Grebe at the Humber Mouth Yacht Club pools on 24th April. This bird gave close views on the main lagoon, diving for food and posing for photographers. There is a small breeding population of these grebes in Britain – less than 50 pairs – although this individual probably originated from continental Europe.

A week or so into June all birds should be on their breeding grounds and the chance of finding a rarity drops off, and we settle down into the calmer days of summer.

Good work as always by Dave Bradbeer, John Nelson, Ian Shepherd, Chris Heaton, Derick Evans and James Smith for finding birds locally and making their records available.

June

Churchyards. As our countryside becomes gradually more simplified and impoverished by larger scale, cleaner and more efficient farming, the little islands of neglect, untended corners and tangled backwaters that remain become more and more important for the survival of our wildlife. In upland districts, these places may be found on hillsides too steep to farm. Where landscapes are flatter, as in our own area, important scraps of habitat may exist on roadsides, around the industrial fringes of towns and villages, on brownfield land, or on sites waiting to be developed. Even gardens themselves tend now to be much richer than the countryside from which they are carved.

One old habitat common to all population centres, from villages to the largest cities, is churchyards. These often survive as relics of an older countryside – islands of old, little-disturbed meadow-type grasslands, ancient, spreading hedgerows and mature trees. Walls and gravestones act as surrogates for rock outcrops and cliffs, and may hold ferns and mosses, as well as providing a warm microclimate for animals when heated by the sun.

A tendency for churchyards to be either ultra-manicured or the opposite, completely overgrown, wastes the opportunity they afford for wildlife, although this can be improved by more enlightened management. Even where churchyard grasslands are kept constantly short by the mower, a rich meadow-type perennial flora may persist, ready to flower when there is a change of regime. Edges of churchyards may escape the mower altogether, and some uncommon plants may survive – look for Goldilocks Buttercup at Bradley and Great Coates, and Woodruff at Humberston. Many churchyards have cheering displays of Snowdrops and sometimes Aconites in late winter.

Churchyards are usually very attractive to birds, although the species present are not particularly 'special', mainly comprising denizens of hedgerows, woodland edge and man-made environments which find it increasingly hard to survive in today's arable monocultures and secure, modern buildings. Churchyards may slightly favour birds which prefer conifers such as Goldcrest, Coal Tit and possibly Greenfinch. Rural churchyards very often hold rookeries, as they may provide the groups of tall trees close to pasture grassland that they require. If the stonework or roofs of churches are not particularly sound, they may provide breeding sites for cavity-nesting birds. Church towers sometimes hold breeding Jackdaws, Kestrels or Stock Doves, and these species may also use cavities in churchyard trees.

It is thought that about 80% of our churches are used by bats. The belfry is actually the part of the church in which they are least likely to occur – in the breeding season bats, like us, prefer somewhere warm and free from draughts, and these areas usually occur much lower in the building. Messy droppings (although dry and crumbly) and urine staining on wall hangings can make bats inside churches unpopular with churchgoers, although bats are of course protected, and these days an accommodation is usually reached between the needs of bats and people. Lincolnshire's Tattershall Church is one of the best in the country for bats, and the Lincolnshire Bat Group works closely with the church users there, conducting an annual, voluntary summer clean-up alongside the usual surveys.

The presence of so much bare stone makes churchyards of special interest to those interested in lichens. Certainly, the great variety of colours among our churchyard lichens adds considerably to such places' aesthetic appeal. Gravestones are handily provided with dates, so that the rate of growth and speed of colonisation of the various species can be easily measured.

When it comes to management for wildlife, churchyards have the advantage of being largely free from economic pressures, and many of the factors which have so impoverished much of our other land, such as excessive fertility and chemical sprays. That an amount of greenery is seen to be desirable in a churchyard is also a good starting point. Ideal management of churchyard grasslands should acknowledge the need for heterogeneity, with a variety of simultaneous cutting regimes. Some rough areas should always be left to flower and set seed in peace.

In North East Lincolnshire our churchyards tend to be the manicured type, and in many there is much scope for a bit of judicious neglect. For this to occur, a culture change may be necessary among those with an unhelpful zeal for tidiness. Such churchyards are mainly of interest only for their trees, such as the Walnuts at Great Coates, Wellingtonia at Grainsby, cedars at Old Clee, and countless Yews.

Out in the villages, a richer variety of churchyard types can be found. I always think that Marshchapel church provides the model to follow, with the villagers contributing to an overt presumption in favour of wildlife in their management of the churchyard. A rich tapestry of vegetation types always includes some which is 'let go'. Nestboxes are provided, and the trees hold a respectable rookery. In summer, look out for the much declined Spotted Flycatcher, which breeds there.

Ring-necked Parakeet, and other hole-nesters. Any visitor to London's western suburbs these days cannot fail to notice the screeching calls and long-tailed flight silhouettes of Britain's naturalised parrot, the Ring-necked Parakeet. The raucous call of parakeets is now the commonest wild sound over much of the capital, their numbers having exploded since they first bred in about 1971. This increase is probably a result of food provided for them on Londoners' bird tables in winter. For many years, Esher Rugby Club in Surrey was the place to go and see their largest gatherings, with several thousand birds flying in to roost there from all parts of London.

Although London is still the overwhelming stronghold for this bird, very gradually it has colonised other English cities. A glance at the distribution map for the species shows breeding pairs in isolated locations, but seldom far from human population centres.

But there is an odd outlier bang on Grimsby, and this is the tiny breeding population in Weelsby Woods. For a time, this small group of parrots, beautiful grass-green except for a single blue-phase bird, was very nearly the most northerly wild parrot population in the world. They would nest very early in the year, before most people were paying attention, in old woodpecker holes in the Woods' Ash trees.

Ring-necked Parakeets would visit bird feeders in nearby gardens, and on their travels could be seen regularly as far away as Humberston Fitties. Sadly, as we speak *[2016]*, nobody has seen a Parakeet in the town for a year or two, and it seems that this fascinating population, so far from any other of its kind, is no more. The reasons for its demise are unknown.

This at least frees up some tree holes, which are always in limited supply, for our own native hole-dwelling birds. Although holes in trees occur naturally, any very neat, round hole towards the top of a tree has probably been originally excavated by the Great Spotted Woodpecker – the only one of Britain's three woodpeckers which is at all common in our area. In late winter and spring, the 'drumming' of the male Great Spotted Woodpecker may be heard. The rest of the time the species can easily be located by its explosive "chick" call. Once this call is learned, woodpeckers suddenly seem a lot more common than they did before.

Despite being pictured on the information panel at the entrance to Weelsby Woods, it is many years since the much-declined Lesser Spotted Woodpecker, little bigger than a sparrow, bred there. To see one anywhere in our area these days would make a red letter day.

The Green Woodpecker, our largest woodpecker, is common over much of Britain, but much less so here. Occasionally one will take up residence for a time, but they never seem to stay around and breed. Again, it is the call that attracts attention – a far-carrying laughing sound which gives this bird the alternative country name of 'yaffle'.

The little Nuthatch is the only bird which can traverse the vertical trunks of trees downwards as well as upwards. Always present as a breeder in Bradley and Dixon Woods, it only colonised Weelsby Woods in the 1990s, where it has been quite easy to see ever since. Nuthatches have a habit of constructing an inner ring, made of mud, into existing woodpecker holes, to make the entrance exactly the right size to admit their own species but not their predators. Once again, it is the call that gives the Nuthatch away – always loud, repeated or trilling notes, which tend to cut through the other bird sounds resounding among the treetops.

Much larger tree holes may be occupied by owls, Kestrels, Jackdaws or Stock Doves, and much smaller cavities by Blue or Great Tits. Treecreepers may nest in narrow fissures or behind peeling bark. The last hole-nester we must mention is the ubiquitous Starling, whose nest site may be given away in May or Early June by the noisy, persistent, high-pitched begging trills of the young birds.

If you have seen a Ring-necked Parakeet or Lesser Spotted Woodpecker in our area recently, please get in touch.

Ring-necked Parakeet in Weelsby Woods

Herbivory. When we sit in a woodland glade or grassy meadow in summer, we are aware of an incomprehensible diversity of life flying, flowering, crawling and chirping around us. While we can see only a fraction of these abundant life forms at one time, and identify fewer still, somehow the diversity in itself has an appeal – an aesthetic independent from its constituent parts. We assume, and we are generally right, that diversity in an ecosystem indicates health and stability. When it comes to it, we like to be surrounded by diversity, and our intuition tells us that it is a good thing.

But how has this explosion of life arisen? Why do there need to be quite so many species? In fact, much of the diversity can be accounted for by plants and insects – these are groups where proliferation has been especially rich – and the reasons are connected.

One of the reasons that plants have diversified so strongly is because they have had to find more and more novel ways of avoiding being eaten. For each new physical or chemical defence that plants evolve, insects evolve to cope and specialise in turn. So now, there is an enormous variety of specific, co-evolved relationships between insects and plants.

When you sit in a woodland, the insects which eat the Oak above your head will be a different lot than those which eat the nearby Hawthorn, and different again from those which eat the Bramble. This kind of specificity explains the narrow food choices of red Lily Beetles, Solomon's Seal Sawflies and Cabbage White caterpillars in your garden. Every child knows you have to feed caterpillars on the foodplant you found them on.

Generally, trees host many more species of herbivore than shrubs, and shrubs than wild flowers. Commoner plant species have more dependent herbivores than rare ones and recent introductions. The thousands of plant species introduced into Britain by people have created new opportunities but made things more complicated, with so many of them being related to plants already here.

In Britain, the species of plant on which you can find the greatest number of insects is Oak, followed by Willow, then Birch, Hawthorn, Blackthorn and Hazel. Rose, Apple and Poplar come next. When whole plant families are taken together, the daisies and thistles (Asteraceae) come out top, then the Rosaceae, then the grasses.

But there is another diversifying force to mention in the co-evolution of insects and plants – pollination. This of course means flowers, with plants this time trying to attract, rather than discourage, visits from insects. Although the resulting evolutionary pressure to split up into new, diverse forms is weaker, flowers must still evolve specific relationships with particular insects for pollination to occur reliably. Different flowers clearly attract very different types of insects.

There is a national database of insects and their foodplants (http://www.brc.ac.uk/dbif/homepage.aspx), which is constantly being updated and refined. Interestingly, some quite common species of plant have no recorded herbivores – for example the Short-fruited Willowherb, a common weed of waste ground everywhere, and the Southern Marsh and Common Spotted Orchids, such a speciality of our dunes at Cleethorpes.

Occasionally we witness a little step change in the relationships between insects and the plants they eat. A hundred years ago, the caterpillars of the Comma Butterfly fed only on Hop, and the species was very uncommon, being confined mostly to the Welsh borders. A switch to eating the much commoner Stinging Nettle was accompanied by an explosion in numbers and range, and the butterfly is now one of our commonest here in North East Lincolnshire.

Similarly, another butterfly, the Brown Argus, has switched foodplant from Rockrose – a beautiful yellow flower of chalk and limestone grassland – to any of a number of abundant wayside cranesbills, and so has also colonised our area in recent years. This small, quite inconspicuous butterfly looks like a very neat version of a female Common Blue with its brown wings bordered by orange markings and no hint of blue colouration on its upperside.

If you have found any insect eating our Cleethorpes dunes Orchids, please get in touch.

Feral Geese. It's that time of year again when Cleethorpes Boating Lake's feral geese can be seen carefully shepherding the year's goslings.

First to appear are the fluffy golden chicks of Greylag Geese. While extremely cute in the first few days of life, already by now some of the chicks will have moulted to become much less prepossessing animals – real 'ugly ducklings'. Following along slightly later are the smaller and greyer chicks of the lake's Barnacle Geese.

Seeing flocks of wild geese in their natural habitat is one of the finest spectacles in the whole of nature. In their wild state, Barnacle Geese breed much further north than Greylags. In historic times, Greylags would have bred throughout the flatter and wetter parts of England, but nowadays there are only about a thousand pairs of wild Greylag in Britain, all in northern and western Scotland. Numbers there are considerably swelled in winter by immigrants escaping the cold further north.

Barnacle Geese in the wild are exclusively Arctic breeders, with all the world's birds nesting in Novaya Zemlya, Svalbard and Greenland. Each breeding population is faithful to a particular wintering ground, with Caerlaverock on the Solway being a classic UK site to see large numbers in winter.

Despite migratory geese being the very epitome of wildness, geese tend to be easy to bring into domestication, and there has traditionally been good reason to do so, as they are both good to look at, and to eat. Indeed, most ordinary farmyard geese are Greylags or their descendants. The recolonisation of lowland England by wild-type Greylags occurred mainly during the twentieth century, largely as reintroductions by wildfowlers for sport, but also as a result of escaped domestic birds. In the years since, Greylags have found various kinds of man-made waterbody very much to their liking, and have increased dramatically as non-migratory, sometimes tame, feral birds.

There are far fewer of the smaller and more handsome Barnacle Geese naturalised in the UK; indeed, our Boating Lake population is noteworthy in this respect. But these too are increasing year on year, and seem set to become more familiar in lowland Britain. Very occasionally truly wild Barnacle Geese will turn up on the Lincolnshire coast in autumn – usually Dutch wintering birds which have 'overshot' on their migration from Russia.

In natural habitats, feral geese tend to be broadly tolerated, but not particularly well-liked. They can be too numerous, noisy, and feed on nearby crops. Their copious droppings can pollute smaller waterbodies and spoil the amenity value of lakeside grasslands. Feral geese are not taken particularly seriously by birdwatchers, who treat them as 'not properly wild', which indeed they are not, compared with their migratory cousins. When they are introduced, something of these species' association with northern wildernesses and great feats of natural navigation is lost.

On the other hand, they offer an opportunity for people to get closer to nature than they normally would. Encounters with animals, especially wild ones, can improve psychological health, and are an essential part of any child's education.

When we see our Barnacle Goose chicks being closely watched by their parents around the Boating Lake, we should consider their wild relatives –

identical creatures to these – in the Arctic. There, Barnacle Geese have to contend with a short summer and sometimes atrocious weather conditions. They nest on high cliffs to avoid the attentions of predators like Arctic Foxes. A chick's first journey when it leaves the nest is to leap from its ledge and plummet to the ground, where hopefully, if it has avoided injury on the way down, its parents will be present to save it from immediate death.

If it were not for naturalised birds such as ours, a newly-hatched Barnacle Goose chick would be something you would have to travel to some of the remotest and inhospitable places on Earth to see.

Barnacle Goose and chicks - Cleethorpes Boating Lake. Photo: Carole Crawford

Orchids on the Dunes. Cleethorpes has taken over from sites further down the Lincolnshire coast as the place to see the uncommon Southern Marsh Orchid *Dactylorhiza praetermissa*. In recent years tens of thousands of these exquisite flowers have graced the dune slacks of the Cleethorpes Local Nature Reserve, turning large areas of dune grassland magenta each June and creating one of Lincolnshire's major wildlife spectacles.

'Orchid time' is here again, but it seems like the display will be much reduced this year, owing to a winter tide which came 'over the top' this year, slightly changing the habitat. Having said this, there are still orchids there to see.

Here in North East Lincolnshire the Southern Marsh Orchid is close to the limit of its British range, being replaced in the wetter and hillier north-west by the smaller and darker Northern Marsh Orchid. As well as growing on sand dunes, Southern Marsh Orchids can be found in marshy habitats and on light, alkaline industrial soils such as colliery and fly waste. Another largish colony on Grimsby Docks was destroyed some years ago by the creation of hard standing for imported cars. Smaller numbers still occur elsewhere in our area with, for example, a few coming up annually on ditch-sides and in scrub in Cleethorpes Country Park.

Another closely-related orchid, the much paler pink Common Spotted Orchid *Dactylorhiza fuchsii* can also be found on the dunes at Cleethorpes, although in much smaller numbers. Occasionally the two species will hybridise, forming clumps of distinctive plants known as '*Dactylorhiza × grandis*' which are larger and more robust than either parent, a phenomenon known as heterosis, or 'hybrid vigour'. Southern Marsh Orchids with strong barring or 'leopard spots' on the leaves were once suspected to be hybrids or even a separate species. Nowadays they are considered no more than a variety of the parent plant.

This year's subdued orchid display indicates perfectly the fragility of rare wildlife habitat. Vegetation succession, pollution, untimely mowing, trampling, spread of invasive species and alterations to soil or water table are all factors which can lead to deterioration in isolated fragments of habitat. To complicate matters, most of these effects are potentially exacerbated by climate change. Coastal habitats tend to be particularly susceptible to change as they are naturally dynamic and often subject to forces outside human control.

One hopes that orchid numbers will recover in the short term, but clearly we need to enjoy this spectacle while we can. Choose a sunny day and do take a look, but remember to mind where you put your feet.

Southern Marsh Orchids on the dunes at Cleethorpes

Ticks. Some people's dislike of anything that crawls or flies is absolute and undiscriminating, and for me slightly sad, for they miss so much. At the other end of the scale there are those who may find wonder in the complex social organisation of wasps, or the miracle of evolution which is a horsefly or a flea. But there are some creepy crawlies which seem to have no redeeming qualities at all – their extinction would cause celebration across the board. First among these in our everyday countryside – at least those big enough to see – must be those blood-feeding parasites, the ticks.

The problem is that ticks are more than just an irritation – they can spread nasty diseases. Most worrying of these is Lyme disease, which can lead to viral-like meningitis, nerve damage and arthritis. It is a problem of which country people are constantly aware, but hysteria isn't necessary. I have been attacked by them dozens of times in the course of my work, and no serious illness has resulted, although I'm sure this is scant consolation for those not so lucky. For me, avoiding the countryside altogether would be the greater hardship.

We have 21 species of tick in Britain, which can be divided into 'soft' and 'hard' species. The former are a mainly tropical group and can only survive our climate by living in the nests of birds or mammals, where their hosts provide a captive feast. The lack of hard parts allows them to swell easily when imbibing the host's blood.

The 'hard' ticks have to take their chances in the outside world, where they spend their time alternating between sitting on the tips of grasses and other vegetation waiting for a potential host to come by, and rehydrating down among the wet litter layer.

Hard ticks' lifecycles comprise four stages – egg, larva, nymph and adult. Often, each of the active life stages will feed on a different host. Most of our ticks are specialists on birds or wild mammals, although some of these species may also attack humans. The species that gives us the most trouble, and which is the primary vector for Lyme disease, is variously known as the Deer, Sheep, or Castor-bean tick.

Once aboard a passing human, a tick will find a likely patch of bare skin, use cutting limbs to slice the top layer of flesh, and insert a sucking tube or 'hypostome', which has backwardly pointed barbs to keep it in place. Two hooked limbs called 'chelicerae' are used to do a kind of gruesome breaststroke, to bury the hypostome further. The tick lubricates the whole process with saliva, which is anaesthetic and anticoagulant, dissolving tissues and causing haemorrhaging, so that the tick has a pool of blood from which to feed. In some species the saliva also acts like a glue, to keep the tick in place. A rocking motion creates a pit, in which the tick becomes firmly embedded.

In the countryside, ticks may be found almost anywhere, but are much more likely to be encountered where there are large mammal hosts such a sheep and deer. In such places, pushing through vegetation such as Bracken or long grass may result in attachment.

There are precautions you can take to avoid the attentions of ticks. Insect repellents generally work, but should be applied after – that is, on top of – sunscreen. I have learned to cover up with light clothing even on hot days. Ticks sitting undetected on clothes can be killed by drying the clothes out thoroughly.

It is a ritual of people working in vegetated areas in summer to inspect themselves – or each other – for ticks after a day in the field. Ticks found quickly may not even be attached yet, and those caught within 24 hours of attachment are very much less likely to spread disease. Typical places to find attached ticks are armpits and the backs of knees, or under waistbands.

If you do find a tick half-buried in your skin, it isn't necessarily a cause for alarm, although of course it must be removed. This must be done with care – panicking and scratching at it with a fingernail is not the way. There are two things to avoid – squashing the body of the tick so it regurgitates its stomach contents back into your blood, and breaking off its mouthparts – which are usually quite well attached – so they remain in the wound. Even this isn't the end of the world – the mouthparts come out eventually, but may cause itching or secondary infection in the meantime.

There are various myths that ticks may be successfully removed with cigarette smoke, Vaseline or alcohol – don't try these. Tick-removal tools are available which look like a tiny claw from a claw-hammer, which grasp the tick very close to the skin without squashing it. A gentle twisting motion removes the tick, although no particular direction is best – the mouthparts are not screw-threaded, as some believe. Pointed-tipped tweezers can be used with care, if the tick is grasped as close to the skin as possible, or a piece of cotton wrapped round the mouthparts close to the skin, and pulled gently away, can work. Dispose of ticks by squashing inside tissue paper, or you could keep them for evidence in the unlikely event that you get ill.

If the site of the attachment develops a red 'bulls-eye' rash or you develop symptoms such as serious tiredness, fever, memory problems or muscle or joint pain, see a doctor – antibiotics may be needed.

Wild Roses. June is the time when our hedgerows, woodland edges and scrubby field corners are adorned with the abundant flowers of wild roses.

We have fourteen native species in the UK, which may hybridise in almost any combination. Some of these natives have a modest role in the development of our cultivated roses, although as you would expect, the wild plants tend to be much less extravagant. The flowers of our authentic wild roses are all white or pink, and their rose scent characteristic but often weak and fleeting. Four species deserve a mention in our area.

By far the commonest is the Dog Rose. This is the largest-flowered and most variable of the common native wild roses, with petals ranging from white to mid-pink. It is usually to be found clinging to some other plant for support, and is very common clambering up hedgerows or in scrub. In woodland situations it can be found flowering profusely way above the ground.

The Field Rose tends to be shorter, with smaller flowers which are always white. The styles – the female parts of the flower – are fused into a column, and the branches sometimes have a lovely greyish tint with a wine-red flush, especially on the side facing the light.

My personal favourite is the Sweetbriar – the 'eglantine' of Shakespeare. The flowers tend to be darker pink than those of Dog Rose, although the petals are paler at the bases. The flowers have the characteristic rose smell, but in this species the foliage is also scented, not of roses, but apples. This apple smell comes from a myriad little glands on the leaf's surface, which also make it slightly sticky to touch. On a damp, still day, the smell of apples can be detected several feet away from the plant. It tends to prefer the more calcareous soils, and in our area can be found in a few places including along the sea wall at Humberston Fitties, where it hybridises with Dog Rose.

The last of the four is actually not a native but an introduced alien, the Japanese Rose. This is a very robust plant much used in council plantings – roadside landscaping and roundabouts – which has a strong, and sometimes problematic, tendency to spread away from where it was first sown. It can become naturalised and run rampant, especially on sand dunes, a habitat in which it is very common at Cleethorpes. It is bushy with large, deep pink, intensely-scented flowers, and huge, rounded fruits, or hips. Unusually among the roses, the flowers and hips may often be found on the plant at the same time, making it a very fine-looking ornamental plant.

Although the fragrant petals of Japanese Rose may be collected and used for Turkish delight or rose jelly, it is the fruits of roses – rosehips – which are the parts generally collected for human consumption. In this, Japanese Rose is not so good as our less showy native species. Children of my generation and earlier would scrape out the hairy seed from the insides of rosehips and use them as 'itching powder' – yet another once-ubiquitous custom now all but disappeared, although perhaps that is a good thing. The red flesh which remains is the ingredient for rosehip syrup, which, similarly, is a taste etched into the memory of anyone above a certain age, but not so well-known now.

Rosehip syrup is made by boiling down the red outer flesh of rosehips with sugar, and sieving to remove any stray seeds. Rosehips contain more vitamin C than any other common fruit or vegetable, and in wartime they were systematically collected to supplement the diets of children. This syrup is the ingredient in all rosehip recipes.

All wild rose species are under-recorded in our area, because the presence of so many hard-to-identify hybrids makes many records unreliable. There is much work to do, and there are certainly discoveries to be made.

Cuckoos. Despite being one of the classic signs of spring, I have only seen two Cuckoos so far this year in North East Lincolnshire, and those rather later than I would have expected. I suppose this is not surprising, as according to the British Trust for Ornithology, Cuckoos have declined 65% in the UK since the early 1980s. The reasons are not known, but may be related to shortage of food, deterioration of conditions along migration routes, or declines in populations of host species.

Every child knows that Cuckoos lay their eggs in the nests of other birds. In the UK, four host species are used, and although we have all four breeding here in North East Lincolnshire personally I have only ever known local Cuckoos lay in the nests of Meadow Pipit and Dunnock.

A Cuckoo's egg laid in the nest of a Meadow Pipit is speckled brown to mimic those of the host, while one laid in the nest of a Dunnock is white, contrasting strongly with the clear bright blue of the Dunnock eggs. This raises several questions, such as how does a Cuckoo 'know' what colour egg to lay in what nest and how does it alter the colour? And why such close mimicry in one host, but not the other?

In fact, female Cuckoos are divided up into 'host races', which act almost like separate species, with each one specialising on a single host. A female Cuckoo round here is therefore most likely to be either a dedicated 'Meadow

Pipit Cuckoo' or a dedicated 'Dunnock Cuckoo'. Male Cuckoos can mate with any female, so at the end of the day Cuckoos still remain all the same species.

The excellent mimicry of the Cuckoo's egg laid in the Meadow Pipit's nest tells us that Meadow Pipits are very good at spotting fake eggs. A poorly-matched egg would be quickly thrown out. It is highly probable that Meadow Pipits' eggs have evolved their colouration over a very long period of time to be both camouflaged and *unlike* the eggs of Cuckoos, to make recognition easier. Cuckoos similarly have 'caught up' by evolving eggs more and more like those of the pipit so as not to be detected; a kind of evolutionary 'arms race'.

The lack of mimicry in eggs laid in Dunnock's nests tells us that Dunnock is a relatively new target in evolutionary terms. Its powers of discrimination are still poor, so there is no need for mimicry.

Cuckoos are with us only for a short time, and some will even start to return to their African winter quarters before the end of June, well before their own chicks are out of the nest. This means that the young birds have to find their own way to Africa without their parents to guide them – an incredible feat which defies human intuition. You can still see the browner young birds until about September.

Buttercups. We take buttercups for granted. Throughout the summer, they adorn roadsides and all kinds of grassy places, as well as turning our most brilliant meadows yellow, their colour often eclipsing all the other riches contained within the sward. They can be found almost everywhere, and are one of the first flowers children learn to recognise.

The origin of the name is quite straightforward – the flowers form cups and are associated with cow pastures. With a little imagination, the flowers may also be said to be the colour of butter.

Every country child knows the tradition of holding a buttercup under someone's chin to 'see if they like butter'. This works because of the extreme shininess and reflectance of the flower, and is a bit of an old joke, as it never fails to reflect yellow onto skin.

Buttercups are poisonous, especially so at flowering time. Horses and cows will avoid them unless forced to consume them by near-starvation. This partly explains buttercups' tendency to become abundant in fields where animals are kept. The toxins, however, rapidly degrade when the plant is picked or dried so that buttercups cause little trouble in hay. The sap of buttercups can cause skin irritation in humans, and there is a suggestion that in the past, beggars would use buttercups to blister their own skin to engender sympathy.

There are several species of buttercup in our area. Two, Celery-leaved Buttercup and Lesser Spearwort, are plants of ditches, ponds, and other watery places. Another, the Goldilocks Buttercup is an uncommon plant of woodlands, with the peculiar feature of having a flower which may lack some or all of its petals. It stands relatively erect for a buttercup, with upper leaves very different from its lower ones. Look for it along the central rides of Dixon and Bradley Woods.

'Ordinary' buttercups in our area actually comprise four species, two of which are extremely common, and one very nearly as frequent. The last is rare, but probably under-recorded.

Of the commonest two, the Meadow Buttercup has basal leaves whose five or seven lobes seem to spread out from a central point. In contrast, Creeping Buttercup, which often spreads by creeping runners to form patches, has leaves which are divided into three distinct parts, on short stalks.

Bulbous Buttercup has its 'sepals' (the bits directly underneath the flower) folded downwards so they sit appressed to the stem. The leaves are also in three sections but are altogether daintier than those of Creeping Buttercup. This species has a swollen stem base or 'bulb', if you can bear to dig it up. It is quite common, and a good place to see it is on the grassy slopes of the High Cliff in Cleethorpes, if you can get there before the mower!

The last of the four buttercups is much rarer, and was feared lost from our area when a small colony was destroyed by the building of the Kingsway Station for the Cleethorpes Coast Light Railway. This is the rare Hairy Buttercup. It looks very like a Bulbous Buttercup, but can be a leggier plant with more robust and shinier leaves. It is technically an annual, and therefore likely to grow in more disturbed situations than the other species, although personally I think it can also persist as a short-lived perennial. The sepals, which are bent downwards like those of Bulbous Buttercup, do not grip the stalk anything like as tightly, and there are other technical differences for which a good hand lens is required.

To see an example of the rare Hairy Buttercup, try along the passage linking Midfield Road and Church Lane in Humberston, along the side of the C of E School (although watch out for Creeping Buttercup which also grows there). Hairy Buttercup has also been found recently growing as a weed in the vicinity of Bradley Road in Grimsby.

If you find Hairy Buttercup in a new location, please get in touch.

Hawkmoths. Among our local wildlife, there are few creatures so awe-inspiring as the large hawkmoths. Hawkmoths are guaranteed to impress people across the board, and may turn children on to the pleasures of natural history in one go. Despite being utterly harmless, their sheer size often causes alarm, and I have shown them to landowners who had difficulty believing that such beasts roamed their land in the dead of night. In a moth trap, they may dwarf everything else in the catch, and even seasoned enthusiasts never get tired of seeing them.

Hawkmoths are not only very large, but fast and expert fliers. Happily, their extreme mobility means that even the very rarest migrant may make an unexpected appearance almost anywhere, lending even more appeal to the group.

The caterpillars are, if anything, even more unexpectedly huge than the adult moths, and are among the creatures people most regularly rush to tell me about or bring me when they find them. A Privet Hawkmoth caterpillar may be nearly four inches long and as thick as your thumb. A final extravagance is a horn on the end of the tail – a characteristic of all hawkmoth caterpillars.

A small number of hawkmoths are relatively common resident species and may come quite readily to gardens or lighted windows. The Poplar Hawkmoth has greyish, slightly ragged-looking wings, often sitting with the hindwings positioned in advance of the forewings. A reddish patch on the base of the hindwings is diagnostic. Children love to pick them up, although their clawed feet make them amazingly grippy, and if the moth doesn't want to be dislodged it is almost impossible to shift it.

Closely related is the slimmer, browner, Eyed Hawkmoth, whose camouflaged forewings hide a surprise when the moth is disturbed – large blue and black eye-spots on pink hindwings, designed to deter predators. I was once shown one resting up on willow in the garden of Cleethorpes Library – it was amazingly cryptic despite its size, and it took my two-year-old, for whom it was at eye level, to find it and point it out.

Almost as common and an urban specialist, is the Lime Hawkmoth. Olive and pinkish beige with a broken cross-band, this moth's caterpillars feed on Lime, a common street tree, and may be seen descending from their foodpant on to paths and pavements in late summer, looking for somewhere to pupate.

The most extravagant colour scheme belongs to the common Elephant Hawkmoth, whose deep cerise-pink and olive markings, despite being garish when taken out of its habitat, disguise it amazingly well among the foliage and flowers of its favourite foodplant, Rosebay Willowherb. It has a smaller and less common relative, the Small Elephant Hawkmoth, which can occasionally be seen feeding, hummingbird-style, at flowers such as Viper's Bugloss after dark.

A hawkmoth extending its range dramatically and now starting to appear in our area is the Pine Hawkmoth. While not particularly colourful, this is still a handsome moth with grainy grey brown forewings with dark streaks, and dark hindwings. I have seen one in our area so far, at Tetney.

A large bumblebee mimic, complete with clear wings, is the Broad-bordered Bee Hawkmoth, whose caterpillars may be first located by searching for characteristic 'bullet holes' in Honeysuckle leaves in summer.

The Privet Hawkmoth is the true giant among our resident species. This is a relative newcomer to our area, it is thought as a result of a warming climate. Its size alone should identify it, with a wingspan getting on for five inches, although the blackish thorax may be useful in separating it from the similar migrant Convolvulus Hawkmoth.

All the other hawkmoths are migrants, but may nevertheless try to breed here if conditions are right. The relatively common Hummingbird Hawkmoth has been dealt with by this column before. One of the most prized targets of naturalists everywhere is the truly enormous, yellow-banded Death's Head Hawkmoth, which has the infamous 'Silence of the Lambs' skull marking on its thorax. This moth, or its caterpillars, would once have turned up relatively frequently in English potato fields, but modern pesticides now make this very unlikely unless organic, allotment or garden potatoes are involved, and the species is now very rare. The adult moth can make a squeaking noise when disturbed, and having a relatively short proboscis for feeding at flowers, this moth may enter less well-defended beehives in search of sweet food. It is thought that its sound, chemical emissions and colouration all help it to avoid being attacked by bees.

A final species, although not as bulky, has an even greater wing-span than the Death's Head Hawkmoth. This is the migrant Convolvulus Hawkmoth, which visits our east coast in small numbers each year. The best chance of seeing it is by growing Tobacco Plant (*Nicotiana*) in the garden, and going out nightly in late summer and early autumn to inspect the flowers for feeding moths. The moth has a proboscis longer than the whole rest of its body put together, which it uses to feed on nectar during agile, hovering flight. I have seen one at Humberston, and it is an annual visitor at Spurn Point, where caterpillars have also been found.

Other hawkmoths may also be found here under exceptional circumstances, although all are very rare. With any sighting of one of the less common hawkmoths, please get in touch.

Cuckoo Spit. We are entering that time of year when grasslands, waysides and the wilder parts of gardens become festooned with those white blobs of froth known as 'cuckoo spit'. While one understands that they are not actually spit, it is still hard not to treat them with slight disgust.

A blob of cuckoo spit always contains a small green or yellow bug – readily uncovered when the froth is wiped away. The name 'cuckoo spit' is of ancient origin, coming from a time when it was suggested that the contained bug was a baby cuckoo – a ridiculous notion now, but borne of the fact that no-one had ever seen a cuckoo build a nest. The cuckoo reference may have persisted, like many other 'cuckoo' names in the natural world, because the spit appears in spring, the same season in which the Cuckoo arrives.

The bug is the immature stage, or nymph, of an insect called a froghopper. The nymph is soft and defenceless, and usually has two small coloured spots near the front end which look like eyes, but which are actually the buds from which the adult's wings will develop.

Froghopper nymphs feed by piercing plant stems and sucking up the juices, generally taking up much more than they need. They exude the excess out of the back end, at the same time blowing air into it from a special cavity under the abdomen, to create the froth. A small gland also incorporates a substance into the froth which help it keep its consistency.

The froth performs multiple functions, protecting the bug from temperature extremes and drying out, hiding it from view, and deterring predators with its unpleasant taste. There is really no need to treat it with disgust – it is made from little more than plant sap.

Eventually the nymph will metamorphose into an adult froghopper which does not live within froth, but is free-living among the vegetation. It looks rather similar to the nymph, but is sturdier and better-armoured, more camouflaged, and with wings which it folds over its back, tent-wise. The 'frog' reference comes from the wide and rather flattened head, and the tendency to jump to escape trouble with specially-developed back legs.

There are several species of froghopper which are difficult to tell apart, not helped by the fact that the commonest species, *Philaenus spumarius*, comes in a variety of colour forms. This species has the fact that the nymph lives within 'spit' recorded in the second part of its latin name.

Froghoppers are extremely common in grasslands and scrub in summer. If you try to pick one up you will notice that it will jump to escape – often an amazing distance for its size – and with an audible click.

In fact, froghoppers can jump about 70cm – the same as fleas but they weigh up to 60 times as much as fleas, making them the true jumping champions of the animal world. Their back legs are so specialised for jumping that they are useless in normal locomotion, being merely dragged along the ground when the insect walks. The back legs have a kind of 'locking' mechanism, and in order to jump, two large muscles, one for each leg, are contracted to the point that the legs snap open and all the force is released at once. Once airborne, the insect's wings help to carry it a little further. At the point of jumping, a froghopper subjects itself to about 400G. Humans can be in trouble at anything more than about 5G.

Although almost all froghoppers are cryptic in colouration, there is one notable exception. This is also one of our larger froghoppers: the Red-and-black Froghopper, with its bold, chequerboard pattern. The nymphs of this species do not live among the vegetation, but communally underground where they feed on roots, protected by a casing of solidified 'spit'.

Poppies. Red is an extremely unusual colour for a British wild flower. Traditional haymeadows, ancient woodlands and well-established grassy waysides will contain plenty of blue, purple-pink, yellow and white flowers, but no red blooms. The reason is simple – flowers have evolved in response to pollinating insects, not human aesthetics, and the vast majority of insects cannot see red.

So, I hear you say, what about poppies? Firstly, poppies are not native to Britain. They have been here a very long time, probably as long as agriculture itself, but they are nevertheless aliens. So successfully have they colonised Europe that no-one really knows when, or from where, they started out.

One has only to watch a clump of poppies for a few minutes on a sunny day to see that they are visited by bees. This is because their flowers reflect strongly in the ultraviolet part of the spectrum which insects *can* see, but we cannot. To a bee, a flower which was just red, without ultraviolet, would look black.

Because of its blood-red flowers and tendency to appear wherever earth is disturbed, the poppy has always been a potent symbol of remembrance, fertility and death. This goes back at least as far as the Egyptians, millennia before John McCrae made the same association in his poem 'In Flanders Fields', and the Royal British Legion adopted the poppy for its annual autumn appeal.

There are actually four species of wild red poppy in Britain. The rarest, Rough Poppy, has never occurred in North East Lincolnshire, and the next rarest, Prickly Poppy, is long lost from the county. The Common Poppy *Papaver rhoeas* is the abundant plant of cornfields. The last of the four, the Long-headed Poppy *Papaver dubium*, is still tolerably common on roadsides and waste places in North East Lincolnshire. It is never quite as intense red as the reddest Common Poppies, and never has black spots at the base of the petals. It can be most easily identified by the seed heads which are tall and thin rather than short and plump like those of the commoner species.

Long-headed Poppy can be further separated into two subspecies, which can be told apart by the colour of their sap. If you can bear to, snip through a fresh flower stalk and latex will ooze out; if it is pure white, it is the commoner subspecies '*dubium*'. If it is bright yellow, it is the more exacting subspecies '*lecoqii*' which usually inhabits heavier or chalkier soils. Every one I have checked in North East Lincolnshire so far has had white sap, but one feels that the other one is out there somewhere.

Sparrows. No wild bird is more closely associated with the activities of humankind than the common House Sparrow. Indeed it is virtually dependent on us, and its friendly chirping is a sound known to everybody in town and country alike.

The House Sparrow was once phenomenally abundant. From the era of 'high farming' in the eighteenth century well into the twentieth, they were perceived as pests, consuming our grain and upsetting livestock. Parishes would form 'clubs' dedicated to slaughtering as many sparrows as possible, with a bounty paid for dead birds or eggs.

The first natural decline in House Sparrow numbers was thought to coincide with the replacement of horses by the automobile in the early decades of the twentieth century. Spilled oats from nosebags and undigested seeds in horse droppings suddenly became unavailable, and faster-moving vehicles caused mortality in naïve young birds. But Sparrows remained common, and with the increasing domination of the planet by humans, the sparrow's future still looked bright.

Sparrow numbers did stay roughly stable until the 1970s. I remember at that time they seemed ubiquitous – our commonest bird. Their slightly scruffy nests could even be found away from buildings – I remember a loose colony in aerial epicormic growth of Lime trees in Weelsby Woods. Sparrows were particularly noticeable at harvest time, when huge flocks would gather in fields or wherever there was ripe grain.

But soon after that their numbers went into free-fall, and for every ten sparrows in the 1970s, we now have less than three – indeed in urban areas, less than one.

The decline in farmland sparrows is relatively easy to explain, as most birds in this habitat have shown a similar decrease over the same period. The intensification of agriculture – larger fields and machinery, loss of hedgerows and wild corners, shortage of weed seeds in winter and spring, and pesticide use leading to a drastic reduction in insects to feed their young, are the accepted mechanisms. For sparrows, we must add to this the removal of old farm buildings for nesting, and the improved sealing of grain stores after harvest.

The drop in urban House Sparrow numbers started a little later, but was more dramatic. Sparrows have now as good as disappeared from the centres of some European cities (e.g. London, Edinburgh, Glasgow, Dublin), while remaining fairly common in others (e.g. Manchester, Berlin, Paris) – a discrepancy which may yet provide important clues to their decline. Nevertheless, as we speak, we have no complete explanation.

Pollution doesn't seem to be the cause – at least not on its own. Studies into predation by Sparrowhawks and domestic cats have proved inconclusive. No disease has been found which could explain the decline. More dead sparrows are found where traffic is heavier, but this, again, is not enough to explain the losses on its own.

House Sparrow nest mainly in buildings – under tiles, in holes in soffits and fascias, and in other miscellaneous cavities. Old farm building are good for them, but in residential properties, modern tile designs tend not to have gaps, and re-roofing may block traditional nest sites.

The presence of decent-sized gardens has a strong positive effect, although adjacent wasteland, allotments, parks, schools, arable land or other green spaces may be just as good. Gardens where bird food is provided all year are preferred, and shrubs where sparrows can escape immediate danger also seem to be an essential prerequisite.

Despite the causes of the decline being so hard to pin down, after a while it is possible to get a 'feel' for good sparrow habitat. It includes human habitation of course, with buildings containing spaces for nesting. The proportion of an area containing un-manicured vegetation, including shrubs for refuge, must exceed a certain threshold. It is probably as simple as that.

In our area, some older, greener, more well-spaced housing estates are clearly sparrow-rich, while adjacent areas comprising newer buildings have almost none. Humberston Fitties probably provides the epitome of a good place for sparrows in our area. Indeed, sparrows are still very common there, and have always been so.

It is difficult to know what the individual can do to help sparrows, apart from provide feeders. Today's well-sealed houses built much too close together, and graveled or concreted gardens, are the enemy of sparrows, so anything that reverses these trends is good. Cavities for nesting, and proximity to unkempt green spaces including shrubs, are what is required.

Sparrows may indicate the health of the ecosystem in which they live, and in the end, if we stop hearing the cheery chirping of House Sparrows, we may well have to conclude, sadly, that our idea of modern living simply leaves no real room for wildlife.

We should mention our only other species of sparrow, the Tree Sparrow. It has also strongly declined, but can still be found here and there. It tends to inhabit slightly more rural locations, where the two species may occur together. Unlike the House Sparrow, the male and female look alike – the brown crown and black cheek-spots are diagnostic.

Elder. There are not many trees or shrubs whose foliage can be identified by their smell, but the Elder is one. It is an indescribable, slightly unpleasant but very evocative smell – the smell of childhood dens and flailed hedgerows, this being one of the very commonest of our wild woody plants, especially where the soil in enriched.

Elder is a species of contradictions. It is too small to be described as a tree, but too large for a shrub. On the positive side, Elder gives us two separate crops in a season: firstly in the early summer it produce the huge, well-known cymes of creamy flowers – the most extravagant of all the hedgerow blooms. The flowers' uses are many, but most common nowadays are elderflower cordial or champagne, or fritters made from the whole, deep fried umbel. The flowers have a rich scent, too intense for many tastes; it is said to be like honey, but this requires a good imagination.

The flowers are replaced later on by the huge, plate-like masses of black berries, beloved of wine-makers and autumn birds alike. The berries have a host of other culinary uses, but should always be cooked – they are slightly poisonous raw.

But equally, the smell of the foliage is not so appealing. The ground beneath Elder is dark and often devoid of all but the simplest vegetation. Elder often grows in places where soil is disturbed or damp, including on sites of old human habitation which have become derelict. It is a weedy plant from which any scrap of green twig will grow into a new tree, and can be very hard to eradicate completely. It is said to be the plant on which Judas hanged himself.

These mixed properties have led to a wealth of old superstitions. In old Lincolnshire folklore the roots of Elder were believed to be the home of a female spirit whose permission you had to seek before the branches were cut. But because of her presence, you would be also protected from lightning when sheltering in a storm beneath an Elder.

The contradictions do not stop there. Although the wood and roots of Elder are extremely hard, the twigs and branches have a centre filled with a light pith which must be one of the least dense solid substances to be found commonly in the natural world. I have heard of it used for holding tiny insect and plant specimens in place for dissection. When this pith is scraped away, the twigs become tubular, making them good for peashooters, whistles and bellows, among other things. Modern children seem to know nothing of these uses, being long separated these days from nature and the tricks of the woods.

Despite its commonness and native status in Britain, few insects will feed on Elder leaves. A species of tiny fly will make blotch mines in the leaves, and the caterpillar of one of Britain's most uncharismatic brown moths, the White-spotted Pug, will feed on the flowers. Elder twigs will sometimes be seen to be infested with waxy-looking dark grey aphids, which are able to sequester the same chemicals from the plant that give it the unpleasant smell, making them unpalatable to predators such as ladybirds.

Despite its lack of interest to insect enthusiasts, those interested in mosses and liverworts will head straight for Elder. Its fissured, corky, and more importantly, alkaline, bark makes it host to a number of uncommon species seldom found on other trees.

Dying Elder branches will often be host to a very characteristic fungus, known in the past as 'Jew's-ear' – a historical shortening of 'Judas's ear'. Nowadays, Jelly Ear or Wood Ear are considered more politically correct, although the scientific name retains the old meaning. These orangish or sometimes blackish fungi do indeed have the curious texture and flexibility of a human ear. They can technically be used in cooking, but apparently don't taste of much.

Colouration and Markings in Animals. Not long after taking an interest in natural history, one must start to wonder why the extraordinary range of colours and shapes found in the animal world have evolved, particularly among the birds and insects. Each has arisen by natural selection, without the hand of design or any consideration of human aesthetics, so why have organisms come to acquire such an astonishing array of wonderful patterns?

In some cases the markings are meant to be seen – they are signals. In others, they are meant *not* to be seen – they are camouflage. These are incompatible, and a creature must evolve either one or the other, or develop them somehow in combination. Both principles have a fascinating body of theory behind them.

Bright colours, especially black, yellow and red in combination, may be used to indicate that a creature is unpalatable to predators. This, of course, relies on predators learning the dangers associated with this colour scheme, but it plainly works, as it is so commonly encountered. Hornets, or the black and yellow caterpillars of the Cinnabar Moth that we see so often on Ragwort, are probably the best examples. Indeed, such colouration may be mimicked by other creatures for self-defence, even sneaky ones which are not actually poisonous, such as our many yellow and black striped garden hoverflies.

Sometimes bright colours may be used as a distraction rather than an indication of unpalatability. The coloured underwings of some moths and eyespots of butterflies come into this category. This phenomenon can be seen in five species of Yellow Underwing, which are among the commonest moths in our area. Occasionally one may come across the much larger Red Underwing, perhaps flying in the day when it may look larger even than our largest butterflies. These moths can be all but invisible at rest, but reveal their startling underwing colours when disturbed.

Flashes, bands or zigzags of white or other colours on otherwise camouflaged creatures can similarly distract a predator for long enough to escape, or, it is thought, make a moving animal harder to follow.

Finally among the markings that are meant to be seen are those designed to impress a mate – to indicate fitness for breeding. These find their best examples among the birds, whose males (which must compete for females) may evolve ever more extreme characteristics such as exotic colours, complex songs and extravagant displays to ward off other males, or impress females, of their own kind. Such characters may in some cases compromise survival – the Peacock's tail, which impedes its flight, is the best known example. It is thought that in the past the evolution of extreme characters by 'sexual selection' may even have led to extinctions – the enormous horns of the now-extinct Irish Elk, for example, would have made it extremely difficult for the animal to move through woodland or eat.

Perhaps more common in the world of animal colouration are various types of camouflage. This is not quite as simple as being the same colour as your background, although this must be part of it. Some insects, such as stick insects, actively mimic inanimate objects. In our own area there are dozens of small moth species whose patterning and shape are obviously meant to simulate bird droppings. That this is disgusting is of course why it works, although some, such as the little Chinese Character moth, look strangely beautiful to us.

Widespread among animal colouration is 'counter-shading'. You may have noticed how common it is for animals as diverse as sticklebacks, wading birds and deer to be paler coloured underneath and darker on top. Just as an artist will paint in shadows to give an indication of form and depth, countershading does the opposite – flattening out the effect of shadows to make the shape harder to see. Such animals have evolved to be darker on parts of the body which are best lit, and vice versa.

Even if it was the same colour, a plain animal against a plain background would be rather easy to see, as its outline would stand out, unless it was very flat indeed. By contrast, imagine a polka dot butterfly on a polka dot background – this would be much harder to see, because the edges of the dots would create a stronger signal than the edges of the butterfly.

This principle, of course, occurs in nature, where very few backgrounds or animals are completely plain, and is known as 'disruptive' patterning. There are limitless ways this may be effective, leading to the rich variety of extraordinary colour schemes in the natural world. Disruptive patterning can be described as patterning which 'creates the appearance of false edges and boundaries to hinder the detection or recognition of an object's true shape'. It is common for bold markings to meet the animal's margins, as this most effectively obscures its true outline. Sometimes patterns involving extreme contrast work very well, as *part* of the pattern is invisible at any one time, but the visible part does not correspond to the shape of the creature. Patterns involving false outlines or illusory, non-existent 'spaces', such as are found commonly in moths (such as in the pictured Buff Arches), are some of the most fascinating and beautiful to us.

In the human world, camouflaged military vehicles and uniforms generally include some sort of multi-coloured pattern. This is an example of humans learning from the disruptive patterning of animals.

Of course there are always exceptions and one-offs which make nature so interesting. The Comma butterfly, so common in our area, breaks up the stereotypical butterfly outline by having very convoluted edges to its wings. The larvae of Caddis Flies, which can be found in any of our local ditches, gather debris from their surroundings to create a tube in which to live, which also camouflages them very well, at least until they move.

Why humans should find many of nature's evolved patterns so aesthetically satisfying is beyond this column. We should just accept it as a happy occurrence and try to witness as many variations on this amazing richness as possible at first hand.

Disruptive colouration is common in moths, as in this Buff Arches.
Photo: Kurt Kulac CC BY-SA 3.0 Wikimedia Commons

Road Verges. By late June, Britain's waysides and grasslands are at their most colourful and inspiring. But across the country we are again seeing the now-familiar ritual of destructive and completely unnecessary mowing of wildlife-rich roadside verges.

Roadsides have become more important for wildlife as the countryside has changed. Farmed fields are no longer filled with poppies and cornflowers. Many of the countryside's wild, untended corners have been swept away by more intensive farming methods and larger machinery. Over 97% of all wildflower meadows have been lost – converted to other land uses.

Flowery grasslands, apart from containing diverse plant life, provide essential habitat for valuable and beautiful pollinating insects such as bees and butterflies. Tussock-forming grasses provide food and shelter for huge numbers of invertebrates, and nesting places for small mammals and bumblebees.

Nowadays, flowery grasslands are largely restricted to roadsides, as these are the last pieces of land more or less immune to the depredations of modern industrial farming. Roadsides are said to provide a home for 703 species of wild flower in Britain, including 21 of the nation's 25 favourites. Some of Britain's rarest wild flowers now occur only on roadsides. Roadsides are the habitat most frequently viewed by the public, and create a network of connections which allow existing larger areas of habitat to function as an integrated system.

Some 600,000 acres of grassy roadside come under the management of local authorities across the UK, giving councils a huge responsibility for the health of the nation's wildlife. The best way to manage meadow grasslands generally is a single cut in late summer or early autumn so that plants have a chance to flower and set seed first, or at other times if specific problems need to be contained. The period April to August/September should be avoided, and some verges could be left uncut altogether for the benefit of hibernating invertebrates.

Cuttings should always be removed, so that they don't sit on the surface like a nutrient-rich mulch. Verges which are too fertile tend to become swamped by nutrient-loving 'bully' species such as docks, nettles, cow parsley and coarse grasses, giving little scope for smaller and more colourful herbs to thrive.

Proper management ensures that road verges provide both a valuable resource for wildlife and a colourful and inspiring spectacle at the height of summer.

The reasons cited for cutting verges during summer include 'tidiness' and road safety. I have also heard it said that it 'stops weeds and invasive species from spreading into gardens and farmers' fields'.

Public safety is a *good* reason to cut verges – no-one would want roads to become dangerous by limiting visibility, say, around corners. But this is only a consideration in relatively few places. While 'tidiness' is generally a virtue, in the wild it is unnecessary and counter-productive. We could do with re-training our sensibilities to accept 'natural' looking roadsides, in the interest of halting biodiversity loss. Personally, I would much rather see flowers and butterflies in summer than cut grass.

If there is an occasional issue with the spread of invasive or pernicious weeds from roadsides into farmland and gardens, it should be remembered that wild verges also provide homes and breeding places for many of the important predators of crop and garden pests.

It is predicted that in the future, climate change caused by the burning of fossil fuels will cause significant biodiversity loss. Why would we hurry the process along by wasting diesel destroying it directly? To be fair, our own Council cuts road verges rather less often than it used to, but this is probably for economic reasons rather than specifically for wildlife.

There are, of course, examples around the town of patches of flowers being left or sown by roadsides for the benefit of bees and other wildlife. This is a great step forward, and shows how far understanding of the role of pollinating insects, and of 'wildness' on public health, has come on in recent years. These areas look fantastic and hopefully we will see more of the same.

Bats. If you go outside just as it's getting dark at this time of year you are quite likely to see a bat or two.

I have usually found that people are more enlightened about bats than is often suggested. As far as I know I have never, for example, met anybody who suffers from the purported misconceptions that bats can get tangled in your hair (they can't), eat through wires in your attic (they don't), or that vampire bats are on the loose in Britain (they're not). All of our species are beneficial insect-eaters. Although they will certainly, on occasions, occupy churches, the high, draughty tower is the last place to look for bats – during the summer months, like us, they require somewhere dry, sheltered and warm. They may be found in convenient cavities in even quite new buildings.

In the winter, bats seek out somewhere cold, undisturbed and stable-temperatured for hibernation. Amazingly, the vast majority of Britain's bats are unaccounted for in winter – we simply do not know where most of them go.

In summer, communal 'roosts' in houses, outbuildings and holes in trees contain mostly females and their offspring. Very unusually for such small mammals (and rather like humans), bats only give birth to a single young at a time, and lavish large amounts of parental care on their offspring to ensure survival. This means that when a colony is destroyed or damaged it may take a good many years to recover. This is one of the reasons that bat roosts enjoy such strict protection under the law.

In order to establish what is around them in the dark, bats are able to 'echolocate', (essentially 'shout' in sharp pulses), at frequencies much higher than humans can hear, and create an image based on the returning signal. As they approach a flying insect they increase the speed of the pulses in what is known as a 'feeding buzz'. Occasionally you may hear a high-pitched squeak from a passing bat – this is nothing to do with echolocation and is probably just a contact call to other bats. Bats' echolocation calls can be lowered to human-audible levels by inexpensive electronic bat detectors, and a few species can be identified by their calls using this basic equipment.

North East Lincolnshire's bats are relatively under-recorded but we can say for certain that five or six of Britain's seventeen breeding species live here, with probably a few more out there awaiting discovery. Small bats flying quickly and jerkily around houses are likely to be Common Pipistrelles, although they could conceivably be the slightly smaller Soprano Pipistrelles, which were only differentiated as a separate species in the 1990s.

If you are lucky you may encounter Britain's largest bat, the majestic Noctule, commuting high and straight between its roosting and feeding grounds while it is still relatively light. There is no special place to see this – you just need to be looking skywards at the right moment.

If you see bats coming out of a building or tree, and you think the roost is previously unrecorded, please contact me, or the Lincolnshire Bat Group.

Leaf Beetles. People's natural interest in wildlife may not always extend as far as beetles, although there are exceptions – Glow-worms for example, are part of this huge order. Stag Beetles are rather eyecatching for those in the south that have them. Woodworm and carpet beetles are well-known for the wrong reasons; Cockchafers, Cardinal Beetles and Burying Beetles perhaps may be known, and of course ladybirds.

The appeal of ladybirds is easy to understand – they are at once common, colourful and beneficial. A really high quality and burgeoning literature allowing the forty-something UK ladybirds to be identified fairly easily makes this a group many naturalists are happy to acquaint themselves with. However, there is another group of beetles whose most colourful members are even more jewel-like than ladybirds and sometimes just as common, although the family enjoys none of the other criteria that seem to confer popularity. These are the leaf beetles.

The leaf beetles, or Chrysomelidae, comprise one of the largest beetle families – indeed there are rather too many in the UK – nearly 300 species – to memorise easily. Although bright, metallic colouration is often a characteristic, others are small and relatively dull, and some cryptic species groups create an identification quagmire. And because they are all herbivores, many are also pests. For these reasons, leaf beetles enjoy nothing like the popularity of the ladybirds, although as a family they are fairly easily known and the most spectacular species are very beautiful creatures indeed.

A typical leaf beetle, if such a thing exists, is dumpy and domed like a ladybird, but may be larger. They are usually slow-moving, and may have rather flattened feet, looking a little like bi-lobed snowshoes. These flattened feet are a clue to the identification of the largest of our leaf beetles, the black, violet-tinged Bloody-nosed Beetle, which is famous for exuding a red fluid containing haemolymph and noxious chemicals from spaces in its carapace when disturbed. I have never seen one in North East Lincolnshire but they don't live far away – although they're not very mobile, this species could conceivably turn up.

Another very distinctive leaf beetle is the Green Tortoise Beetle, which is rounded and very flattened – not, it has to be said, much like a tortoise. Its wing cases and thoracic plate form a shield-like covering over the whole body so the head is invisible from above, which probably accounts for the tortoise reference. It may sit extremely flat to its foodplant – mints or some relative – for protection.

An exception to the 'round and dumpy' rule is provided by members of the genus *Donacia* – quite large, elongate insects which may be found quite commonly alongside water on emergent plants such as Reeds, Bur-reeds, pondweeds and bulrushes.

The intensely metallic green Mint Leaf Beetle is one of my all-time favourite insects, and may be found, as its name suggests, on mint, usually near water. It would be a good find in North East Lincolnshire, although I don't see why it shouldn't be here. Another nicely metallic species, the Green Dock Beetle, should be much easier to find, and look also for metallic leaf beetles on willowherbs and poplars, as well many other common plants.

A host of very small leaf beetles with enlarged back legs for jumping – the flea beetles – are enemies of farmers everywhere. Some are straw yellow and some a metallic blackish-blue, some with two distinctive yellow stripes on the wing cases. Brassicas such as Kale and Oilseed Rape may be ravaged by any of a number of species, including the very common Cabbage Stem Flea Beetle. Other crops such as cereals and Linseed also have their problem flea beetles.

Two especially good-looking leaf beetles are very well-known to gardeners. The first of these is the beautiful, enamel-red Lily Beetle. Both adults and larvae of Lily Beetle can reduce garden lilies to a skeleton in short order, so they are seldom popular, although it somehow seems wrong to try to eradicate such a good-looking animal. This is an Asian species, first discovered in Britain in 1839, but only really becoming common since the 1990s.

The second is the Asparagus Beetle, which can be a pest of commercial, as well as garden Asparagus. Its red thorax and yellow and black-patterned wing cases make this smart-looking beetle completely unmistakable.

Finally, one of the most dreaded, notifiable quarantine pests of potatoes and other crops is also a leaf beetle. Native to America, the Colorado Beetle was introduced accidentally to Europe in the nineteenth century, since when it has invaded Britain and been subsequently eradicated at least 163 times. The last invasion was in 1976 and it is not thought to be here currently, but it is wise to stay vigilant.

So if you see a domed yellow beetle just over a centimeter long with longitudinal black stripes, feeding on potato, tomato, peppers or their wild relatives, tell someone straight away. The plump larvae, also pests, are cherry red at first with a black head, becoming oranger with age.

Peaflowers. The 'legumes' or 'peaflowers' make up the third largest family of plants on Earth. Their flowers are instantly recognisable, usually comprising an upright 'standard', and boat-shaped keel. Many legumes are economically important, such as peas and beans, lentils, soya and peanuts. In our area the family ranges from large garden and street trees such as Laburnum and False Acacia, through shrubs like Gorse and Broom, down to the tiniest clovers in lawns.

Many legumes are common in our area, and I will try to pick out some of the special ones. On the sea wall at Humberston Fitties a fine, floriferous thicket of the introduced Spanish Broom is a handsome addition to the indigenous flora, with masses of large, yellow, scented flowers which only disappear completely in midwinter.

Also along the coast, the dunes and sea defences at Cleethorpes hold abundant creeping, pink-flowered Restharrow, with its glandular, acrid-smelling foliage. Both coastal and inland grasslands may turn yellow in midsummer with masses of flowering Bird's-foot Trefoil, identified by leaflets which appear to be in groups of five, although the basal two are technically stipules. The petals may have deep red colouration on the backs, giving an alternative name of 'Bacon and Eggs'. This species is the foodplant of the Common Blue Butterfly, and the flowers are important for all kinds of nectar-seeking insects.

On our drier saltmarsh look out for its much rarer relative, the Narrow-leaved Bird's-foot Trefoil. A third species, the much bushier Greater Bird's-foot Trefoil is usually found only near fresh water.

All the vetches and allies are included in this family, and are identified by their leaves with two opposite ranks of narrow leaflets, often with a tendril on the end. The blue-violet Tufted Vetch, and the magenta Common Vetch are the commonest species, although you may find the larger and more washed-out looking flowers of Bush Vetch here and there. Any vetch with very tiny flowers will be either Hairy Tare (if the flowers are white and in groups), or Smooth Tare (if blue and in pairs). The introduced, two-tone pink and white Crown Vetch occurs on waste ground at Armstrong Street in Grimsby and along the Humber wall, although I have never found it at Cleethorpes.

Bare and waste ground anywhere, especially on Grimsby Docks, may hold the two similar Melilots, with their tall spikes of small, golden yellow flowers and narrowly three-lobed leaves.

The little Black Medick is superficially like a tiny yellow-flowered clover, its seedheads, which look like a stack of plump-looking discs turning black when ripe, giving it away. Two true clovers, Lesser Trefoil and Hop Trefoil are very similar to the Medick, the latter with florets rather flattened from top to bottom, giving the overall impression of a small hop.

A number of special clovers may be found on our coastal dunes here at Cleethorpes. Both Red and White Clovers are of course common, although both have lookalikes. I have found the bi-coloured pink and white flowers of Alsike Clover in our dune slacks on one occasion. The deep pink Zigzag Clover, as far as I know, only occurs in one place locally, not on the coast, but on a roadside on Hewitt's Avenue close to Peaks Covert. On the upper saltmarsh and dunes look out for the uncommon Strawberry Clover, looking like a small White Clover, but with inflated fruits which look, I think, less like a strawberry than a hairy, pale pink raspberry. A clover growing on our coastal dunes with flowerheads elongated and densely grey-hairy will be Hares-foot Clover.

Three tiny, insignificant clovers growing among our trampled or close-cropped seaside turf are in fact quite uncommon. Rough Clover has white flowers, while those of Knotted Clover are pink. Rarest of all is the Clustered Clover. The populations of this plant occurring around Cleethorpes's Boating Lake lie many miles from the nearest other such record, and are by far the most northerly on the eastern side of England. With a close look, each minute purplish flower can be seen to protrude from a ruff of curled back sepals.

The last group to mention are the vetchlings. These are like vetches but with a leaf comprising only a single pair of leaflets, and include the garden Sweet Pea, the very common Meadow Vetchling, with its bright yellow, typical peaflowers, and the often-naturalised Broad-leaved Everlasting Pea, with its large pink blooms. There is a little of the latter on the banks of the canal near Tetney Lock.

Also in this genus is a really exquisite and special flower, and true botanists' favourite. The Grass Vetchling is an uncommon meadow species, the narrow, grass-like leaves being almost completely undetectable for most of the year. Then in midsummer, flowers of a unique and intense crimson-pink open up to give the plant's position away, borne singly or in pairs on longish, sometimes nodding stalks. Pasture grassland is

Grass Vetchling at Cleethorpes

briefly studded with dots of fabulous colour, before the plant again becomes cryptic for another year. In our area I know of just one place where it grows – a field in the western part of Cleethorpes Country Park, accessed from the end of Rosemary Way. I couldn't locate any flowers last week *[July 2016]* – the grazing looked a little tight this year – but there is still time for a final flourish.

Moth Trapping. For some reason, moths are a group of insects which many people don't seem to like. In this respect, the tiny handful of species whose caterpillars feed on people's clothes have a lot to answer for. Or maybe it's their night-time habits – their tendency to commit suicide in candle flames or spiral wildly around artificial lights – a characteristic which has lifted them to a prominent role in myth and superstition. An old Lincolnshire name for moths is 'souls'.

Many people will say that moths are just small and brown, and indeed many of them are. But equally, many are large, stunningly coloured; even garish. Unlike the butterflies to which they are extremely closely related, the appeal of moths' patterning and colouration tends to be more textural and rustic; often evolved for camouflage, at which they are extremely adept. In fact, a great many even common species are exquisitely beautiful – little miracles of natural design.

Almost as appealing are the English names we now use for moths, which for such an obscure group have remained remarkably constant over the years. This means that they are a group for which we don't really need to use Latin, which does nothing to harm their appeal. The names are nearly all very old – mostly early Georgian – and reflect the times in which they were named, with all manner of satins, carpets, brocades, footmen and tussocks, as well as names to spark the imagination, like Vapourer, Lackey, Flame, Gothic and Uncertain.

We are fortunate then, that moth-trapping is possibly the easiest and most instantly-rewarding kind of natural history there is. Simply put out a light and they will come – almost anywhere will do.

Some moths may be caught throughout the winter, although freezing nights will usually prove fruitless. Warm, muggy summer nights with no moon are best.

Simply leaving a bathroom window open and the light on will catch moths on a warm summer's evening. But lights with a high ultra-violet (UV) content are much better. Small commercial moth traps, which run on mains, car battery or generator, come in many designs, but all involve some sort of 'lobster pot' arrangement with a UV light poised over the hole. Egg boxes are placed inside to give the moths rough-textured nooks and crannies in which to hide until morning. Mercury vapour lamps catch the most moths but are very bright. Also quite effective are the blue actinic tubes like those you see in take-aways. On the best nights, thousands of moths may be caught in such a trap, and all you have to do is go to sleep, and the moths are there waiting for you in the morning. In places where a trap can't be left unattended, a UV light can be simply placed over a white sheet after dark, and moths can be intercepted as they arrive.

But there are some species which don't come readily to light, and for these, other methods need to be employed. It is possible to take advantage of many moths' liking for sweet things by 'sugaring', or providing 'wine-ropes'. Various mixtures of sugar, molasses and alcohol, not to mention one or two highly personal secret ingredients, may be painted onto tree trunks, or soaked into rope and left dangling from branches, from dusk onwards. Inspecting these by torchlight a couple of hours later should reveal several stupefied moths, feeding happily away. Similarly, inspecting flowers by torchlight can also be rewarding. Hardcore moth enthusiasts tend always to grow a little Nicotiana in their gardens in the hope of seeing the rare Convolvulus Hawkmoth, which has the largest wing-span of any British moth.

But there are some families of moth which are indifferent to all of these attractions. The day-flying 'clearwing' moths are a curious group, looking less like moths than soft, scaly flies or wasps. The Currant Clearwing may be a garden pest, but personally I would rather have the moth than the currants. Because they are so difficult to detect, all clearwings are chronically under-recorded, although we now have a new way of assessing their presence. This is by using pheromone lures, bought specifically for the purpose. These lures, simply hung in a small string bag from the branches of a tree, should attract clearwing moths in a few minutes on a sunny day, if they are around.

There are some moths which need nothing more than a bit of knowhow to locate. In July, go at dusk to anywhere there is rough grass – the Boating Lake or Cleethorpes Country Park for example, and look for the hypnotising 'lekking' flight of the male Ghost Moth. You should see many of these white moths doing their swaying 'dance' in the air just above the grass, to give off pheromones and attract nearby females.

Brown Butterflies. If someone asked you what you thought was our commonest British butterfly, what would you say? You might guess the Cabbage White, or the Small Tortoiseshell, or possibly the Peacock, because of their regular appearance in garden vegetable patches or at Buddleia.

Few would say the Meadow Brown, although in sheer number, this species far exceeds any other in these islands. It seems less common because its flight period does not begin until June and tails off by August. Its habitat is relatively fixed, being anywhere where tall grasses occur in sunny locations – roadsides, woodland rides, and as you would expect, meadows. Meadow Browns will stray into gardens, but mostly as an incidental consequence of their natural wanderings. But in large areas of grassland at the right time of year, they may be seen in their thousands.

The 'browns' are a large subfamily of butterflies which between them comprise fully a third of all European species. The caterpillars of every one, as far as is known, feed on grasses. If you're wondering why you've never seen the caterpillar of a brown butterfly if they are so common, it is because they feed at night, retreating into the sheltered bases of the vegetation during the day. They are much easier to find by torchlight after dark.

Here in North East Lincolnshire we have six species of brown. All except one inhabit open, sunny habitats – the exception is the buff-spotted Speckled Wood, which is almost always to be found in areas of dappled sunlight and shade. This butterfly has undergone dramatic fluctuations in its range over the years, and while it was almost completely absent from our area twenty-five years ago, it is now one of the very commonest butterflies here, with a flight season lasting from early spring until late into the autumn.

The Wall Brown is one of our more beautiful browns when seen well – especially the slightly larger female. The intricate orange wing pattern is slightly reminiscent of brickwork, but the name comes from this heat-loving species' tendency to seek out barish or stony grassland, or indeed walls, for their warmer microclimates. Populations have crashed recently across the country, but it has remained relatively common by the coast, and we have never been without it in these parts.

The Small Heath is another butterfly whose populations have dwindled almost without being noticed, so inconspicuous can the species be. It is the smallest of the browns, and always rests with its wings closed. It specialises in short grassland, where it always keeps low to the ground, its weak, erratic flight sometimes looking as though it is at the mercy of the wind.

The last of the browns to emerge is the Gatekeeper in mid-July. This middle-sized brown has large patches of orange on both fore- and hindwings, and should be especially looked for on the flowers of Bramble and Ragwort.

In rough grassland, the abundant Meadow Brown may easily be mistaken for the nearly-as-common Ringlet, completing the group of six. Both inhabit sunny grasslands, although the Ringlet is slightly less adventurous, seldom straying far from field edges or the heart of the colony.

Ringlet is a slightly darker butterfly on the whole. In flight the two are almost inseparable, but with a bit of practice, the slightest flash of orange will identify a Meadow Brown, while the merest glimpse of a thin white wing-edge marks a passing brown butterfly as a Ringlet.

Male and female browns may look quite different. In the Wall and the Gatekeeper especially, oblique scent glands on the forewings of the males impose themselves on the colour pattern, making sexing easy. These glands emit odours which can be detected by people whose sense of smell is relatively good – the male Wall is said to smell rich and sweet, like chocolate cream. The male Meadow Brown, which is smaller, darker and with less orange than the female, has a scent described as being like 'an old cigar box'.

For those willing to travel, Lincolnshire has three more browns to offer. The Grayling may be seen on the sandy heaths of the county's north-west, and the rare Large Heath occupies an isolated outpost on the peat of Crowle Moors. The beautiful Marbled White, a 'brown' which isn't brown, is a butterfly of chalk and sometimes other grasslands, and can be seen in good numbers at the Lincolnshire Wildlife Trust's reserve at Red Hill near Goulceby in the Wolds.

July

Volunteering. Despite various measures in recent decades to try to reverse the trend, wildlife in Britain is still on a downward spiral and needs our help as much as ever. It is no good expecting the government to help – the environment is not seen as a vote-winner, and as a consequence has a lamentably low profile in relation to its importance. One often gets the impression that the main political parties would only implement green measures at gunpoint.

Despite all this, behind the scenes there is a conservation 'mini-industry' battling against the odds to make things better for wildlife, before it is too late.

One of the most extraordinary things about this industry is that nearly all of the work is done by volunteers. Of course, at the head of the conservation organisations are professional scientists, land managers, administrators and spokespeople. But the work of this select group would be completely impossible without a vast army of unpaid helpers who chip in with a variety of skills. A single organisation alone, the British Trust for Ornithology, can call on 40,000 volunteers to collect its essential data, and our biggest conservation charity, the RSPB with more than a million members, apart from organising vast 'citizen science' projects, has at least nine full or part-time volunteers for every paid member of staff.

One of the most obvious uses for voluntary effort is in the submission of species records, so that ecologists know which species live where. The wildlife of the UK is better studied than that of any other country in the world, and 'dot maps' showing UK distributions now exist for pretty much every species that you can see without a microscope. Every dot on every map, or as near as makes no difference, was put there by an amateur recorder, or one acting in an unpaid capacity. Only when this information is collated does meaningful conservation become possible.

Another classic volunteering activity is habitat management. This may include such tasks as coppicing, scrub clearance, ragwort-pulling or the clearing up of waterways and beaches. The Conservation Volunteers, who organise this kind of work, have 2000 regional community groups and have been improving green spaces since 1959. Indeed, any conservation organisation owning land should welcome volunteer help for habitat management work.

Volunteers may also do almost anything else for which there is a need, whether it be acting as a guide, producing media content or manning stalls.

The reasons that people volunteer are many and varied. Some just do it for the exercise and the social contact. Others do it as a duty to put something back into the countryside which has given them so much pleasure.

It can also be a perfect way of taking essential first steps into a career in conservation, and many professionals have gained their first experience and training in this way. Just this week, a grant of £45,000 provided by the Heritage Lottery Fund has allowed facilities at the RSPB's Blacktoft Sands reserve at the head of the Humber to be substantially upgraded, so that now many more volunteers can be accommodated. More local people will now get a chance to enter the world of conservation 'proper', as well as contributing to the upkeep of this popular reedbed reserve, haunt of Marsh Harriers, Avocets and Bearded Tits.

Either way, volunteering offers the opportunity to work in some of the most beautiful and inspiring places in the country, surrounded by wildlife, and help to bring the same enjoyment to others.

If volunteering is too much of a commitment, there are still things that anyone can do to help wildlife. Whenever you see and identify a species, consider submitting the record. There are dedicated schemes for many common plant and animal groups, and the Lincolnshire Naturalists' Union has a system of county recorders who are happy to receive records, especially of anything unusual. Or you can tell me and I will pass it on.

Become a 'citizen scientist' – that is participate in one or more of the 'wide and shallow' schemes such as the RSPB's 'Big Garden Birdwatch', the Woodland Trust's 'Nature's Calendar' or the 'UK Ladybird Survey'.

Join conservation organisations, because every extra member increases their resources and lobbying power.

And importantly, quiz politicians on their parties' policies for wildlife and threaten to vote accordingly, even if you don't actually do it.

Burnets and Skippers. Most people would consider that they could tell a butterfly from a moth – but what, technically, is the difference? Actually there is none; both are members of the great order of the Lepidoptera – it's just that we have come to refer to a small handful of day-flying families, which have clubbed antennae and hold their wings flat above their backs at rest, as butterflies; the flat brown creatures of the night, in effect 'the rest', we differentiate as moths.

As you would expect, the situation is nothing like this simple, and there are many exceptions to the rule. A lot of moths are day-flying, and many are large and beautiful. Several species hold their wings folded together above their backs. Very many butterflies are small and brown, and the antennae of some are scarcely clubbed.

This means that certain families could have gone either way in the naming process. Representatives of two such enigmatic families are common in North East Lincolnshire grasslands round about now.

The first of these families is the 'skippers'. These are considered butterflies despite being the most primitive of the type. Their small wings and low, whirring flight makes them look rather like moths, and they hold their wings neither completely flat nor completely upright, at rest. The tips of their antennae are varied, but all have some sort of thickening at the tips. We have three species in our area, all coloured a rich tawny-orange. First to take the wing in June is the Large Skipper, followed slightly later by the Small and Essex Skippers, these two so similar that they constitute the most difficult identification challenge in the butterfly book.

The second family, often flying with the skippers but slightly more tied to grassland on lighter soils such as dunes, are the 'burnets'. These are colourful insects, which hold their wings folded flat or arched like a pitched roof over the body at rest. In contrast to the skippers, the burnets are grouped with the moths, despite their exotic appearance, thickened antennae, and the fact that they always fly by day. Our two local species, the Six-spot Burnet and the Narrow-bordered Five-spot Burnet are both a metallic blackish green with red spots and hindwings. This colouration is probably not for the benefit of other moths, but a warning to predators that burnets are distasteful if eaten.

Essex Skipper Butterfly

Wherever burnets are flying it is usually easy to find the papery cocoons from which they have emerged, attached like bulges to grass stalks. Telling the two species apart is as simple as counting the spots.

The low whirring of skippers and burnets in rank, sunny grasslands is an essential part of high summer in derelict fields, waysides, vegetated dunes and industrial edgelands. Look for them wherever grass grows tall, especially where there are flowering thistles, knapweed, vetches or trefoils.

In Praise of Grass. It may seem difficult to get excited about, but very few things on this planet are more important to humankind than grass. Almost all of the world's staple foodstuffs are grasses – wheat, barley, rye, oats, rice, maize, sorghum and millet – and grass is food for the animals producing the majority of our meat. Without grass we would have no beer, paper, football pitches, golf courses, lawns or thatched cottages.

What is the special property of grass which makes it so important? As a foodstuff it is ease of harvest. Grasses produce nutritious carbohydrate-rich seed close to the ground and all at the same height, making collecting in volume easier. Also, and very importantly, grasses grow from their bases, rather than from their tips like other plants. This means that they can be have their upper parts continually grazed down or cut, and still survive perfectly well. This is why lawns can be mown to within an inch of their lives, but flowerbeds can't.

Despite their lack of colourful blooms, grasses are not particularly difficult to identify, at least in flower, and July is the month to see the vast majority of our species at their best. Twenty-five or so species account for nearly all the grass you will see in an ordinary day, and most of these are quite distinctive in flower. North East Lincolnshire has about 65 species altogether, although this includes many habitat specialists. Among these are a suite of uncommon seaside specialities, such as the robust whitish-green Lyme Grass, as tough as packaging tape, which is so conspicuous on sand dunes from the Leisure Centre southwards. Even rarer is the Bulbous Meadow Grass, which after flowering briefly in April becomes an inconspicuous part of short turf around footpaths and car parks in the resort. Here in Cleethorpes it occurs at its northernmost British locality, some 45 miles away from its nearest other site.

The luxuriance of our common grasses creates the British countryside's celebrated 'greenness', and if allowed to flower our grasses can be extraordinarily beautiful. Britain has exported its grass flora to many less richly-vegetated parts the world, mostly for the purpose of grazing domestic animals. I have stood in a meadow near the top of a mountain in Costa Rica whose mixture of grasses was indistinguishable from those in an ordinary Lincolnshire field. The famous Kentucky 'blue grass' of the southern USA is nothing more than the imported British Smooth Meadow Grass, *Poa pratensis*, found commonly as a native along the roadsides and foreshore of Cleethorpes.

We have one rather less prepossessing species – the Wall Barley, *Hordeum murinum*, which used to be known as 'darts' by schoolchildren, at least in the days before smartphones. Celebrated for its flowerheads' ability to stick to, and crawl up underneath clothing, it favours spots where dogs have urinated – so you will see it beneath posts and fences, along public footpaths near houses, and around the edges of car parks by the beach. Despite its horrible habits, like most grasses it has a certain architectural elegance at its best.

Infauna. Here in Cleethorpes, we have an internationally important habitat whose creatures, while both diverse and abundant, are completely hidden from view. As a consequence these animals are almost completely unknown to the vast majority of people.

These are the myriad creatures which make their home beneath the surface of the mud on our beach – what marine ecologists call 'infauna'. Although out of sight, they are nevertheless there by the million, as indicated by the large numbers of wading birds we see feeding out there on the mud.

For animals, living in the intertidal sediment of an estuary is very tough. Not only are sediments unstable and subject to re-alignment by the sea, but the creatures living within them must tolerate huge variations in wetness, salinity, temperature and oxygen availability. There is no place to hide from predators except by burying within the mud itself.

Despite this, the estuarine habitat is vastly productive, helped by the inputs from rivers and the coming and going of the tides. Indeed, estuaries are one of the most productive environments on Earth – much more so than either the seas into which they drain, or the rivers which feed them.

The creatures beneath Cleethorpes's tidal mud come primarily from three groups – molluscs, crustaceans and worms. All three leave some signs of their presence to the passer-by.

Molluscs may leave their dead remains on the surface in the form of seashells.

Crustaceans are possibly the most varied group, from large crabs to shrimps, to woodlouse-like isopods, to tiny copepods and ostracods, and even the immoveable barnacle. Most are relatively cryptic, although they are diverse and very abundant in the intertidal zone.

The worms are also varied, from the little nematodes which inhabit every habitat on Earth, and are certainly abundant here, to some which more resemble earthworms. The multi-segmented 'polychaetes' are numerically and ecologically a very important group, comprising species which range in size from small to very large, and with a wide variety of life strategies. As a group they are extremely important in the diets of wading birds.

It is one of these, the Lugworm, whose casts leave the most visible sign on the surface of the mud. These casts often lie abundantly over large areas of the wet mud just beyond the main beach at Cleethorpes. The Lugworm lives in a 'U'-shaped burrow about 30cm deep, so generally out of reach of feeding birds. The cast is the extruded debris from its tunnel, and it is when the worm rises to excrete the cast that it become susceptible to being caught by birds. The other end of the burrow is a small round hollow in the mud, and can often be seen a few inches away from the cast.

Another large and common, but free-living polychaete worm, the Ragworm, is a predator or scavenger with a fringe of leg-like appendages along its sides, which changes colour from brown to green in the breeding season.

At Cleethorpes the highest concentration of mud-dwelling life occurs in the wet-but-stable mid-regions of the shore, where the substrate is neither too coarse and well-drained, nor too exposed to the violent action of the waves. In the vicinity of saltmarshes the fauna is particularly abundant, probably because of the shelter and high organic content of the mud here.

In fact, a large proportion of the animal biomass within the mud is accounted for by a relatively small number of very abundant species. First among these is the little mollusc known as the Laver Spire Shell *Hydrobia ulvae*, which despite being small (about 3mm) contributes well over half of all the animal life by weight beneath Cleethorpes's intertidal mud. This superabundant snail is an important food for birds, especially Shelduck. Young Cockles and the smoother Baltic Tellins, because of their bulk, are also important in terms of biomass. Birds such as Knot may eat these molluscs whole, and then crush the shells with muscles in their gut walls. In contrast, Oystercatchers may choose slightly larger molluscs, but go to the trouble of opening the shells and removing the contents.

The favoured food of Redshank are the little crustaceans in the genus *Corophium*, whose bizarre appearance, quite unfamiliar to most people, belies their abundance within the mud. Like other mud-dwelling animals, *Corophium* may leave their burrows when submerged by seawater, retreating back into the mud when the tide goes out. The very moment when they are uncovered gives wading birds their opportunity to pick them off, which is why you will see Redshank and other waders following the tideline.

Lacewings and Scorpion Flies. It is a shame that flying insects provoke such dislike in so many people. The vast majority are completely harmless, and many are beneficial, some to the point that we couldn't do without them. Their variety, life-histories and interactions are endlessly fascinating.

In fact, most of the multifarious clear-winged insects of the summer, the things to which we loosely add the suffix 'fly', fall into just a few major insect orders. A fly in the truest sense can be told by having only one, rather than two, pair of wings. Apart from bluebottles, hoverflies and the like, this group also includes the midges, craneflies and mosquitoes.

The water-loving dragonflies and damselflies should be known to everyone; also mayflies, with their long tail streamers and wings held aloft over their backs like a butterfly. The great order of bees, ants and wasps, including sawflies, constitutes a huge range of insects of all sizes, colours and life strategies, from the social bumblebees and hornets to the minutest parasitic wasps.

After that, we are just left with a handful of miscellaneous groups of ancient, delicate-looking insects with four clear wings, which do not fit into the other groups. Some of these are easily seen in our area.

Several such groups are closely connected with water, especially rivers, and so are unlikely to force themselves into our consciousness on a daily basis. The flattish stoneflies, with two horns or 'cerci' on their tails, and the dark brown or black alderflies, whose wings are held like a pitched roof over their bodies, are two of these.

Another group whose larvae are aquatic, but whose adults will readily turn up at lighted windows in our area are the caddis flies – those creature which anglers call 'sedges'. Also with wings held roof-like over the body, caddis flies may be quite large; they are usually brown with hairy wings – indeed the hairs emerging from the wing-membrane itself, and not just the supporting veins, seals the group's identify. The antennae are stout and held out in front of the head.

The charismatic snake flies have four equally-developed wings and a hugely extended thorax, giving them a long, almost snake-like neck. These outlandish-looking insects are commoner than you think, but seldom seen due to their habit of living mostly in the treetops.

This leaves two attractive groups of insects which you may see very easily in North East Lincolnshire, the lacewings and the scorpion flies. The delicate green lacewings will readily enter houses, often being found on the ceiling when a light has been left on and a window open. Any green lacewing found in winter will be *Chrysoperla carnea,* as this is the only species that overwinters as an adult. There are many similar species – some slightly yellower and some slightly bluer with dark markings. The eyes are always a beautiful reflective copper or gold colour, and repay a closer look with a lens or microscope.

In lacewings, a prerequisite to mating is a 'tremulation' duet, whereby each insect vibrates its abdomen, causing the leaf they are standing on also to vibrate. What was once thought to be a single species of green lacewing has now been shown to be several, which can be told apart buy their courtship 'songs'.

The eggs of lacewings are borne on distinctive stalks. Once hatched, lacewing larvae are highly beneficial to farmers and gardeners, being voracious predators on greenfly. Some species' larvae cover themselves with the dead remains of their prey to allow them to approach new victims more stealthily.

The brown lacewings are generally a less conspicuous group than their green relatives, and generally smaller. Another group of lacewings, the 'wax flies' are much smaller still, white or grey, and usually covered with a waxy powder. They could be superficially mistaken for whiteflies or other small bugs.

Finally, a search of lush vegetation in summer, especially where there are brambles or nettles, is likely to turn up the charismatic Scorpion Fly (pictured), with its black-patterned wings. The 'scorpion' in the name refers to the red genital capsule at the tip of the male's abdomen, which is held aloft and curved forwards over the body like a scorpion's sting. The front end of the insect looks no less fearsome, with a long downwardly-projected 'beak' with biting and chewing mouthparts on the tip – a feature not found in any other insect. In fact, scorpion flies are completely harmless, and not even good fliers. If disturbed they will simply close their wings and drop to the ground, so in order to catch one it is a good idea to hold something underneath it. Two almost identical species of scorpion fly are common here, with the difference discernible only by examining the red capsule of the male, or the ovipositor of the female.

There is no need, of course, to wait for any of these insects to fly in through the kitchen window – they may be sought in their wild homes. Even the scrappiest piece of wild land will harbour a fascinating ecosystem comprising very ancient creatures, which just needs the time and the interest to become acquainted with.

Scorpion Fly. Photo: Pavel Kirillov CC BY-SA 2.0 Wikimedia Commons

Poisonous Plants. The time when humans were forced to risk poisoning by experimenting with wild foods is long gone. In the twenty-first century, we are less likely than ever to risk putting dangerous wild leaves or fruit into our mouths, although I suppose we should still keep an eye on inquisitive toddlers when they're around vegetation. As a consequence, despite being constantly surrounded by a battery of natural plant toxins, cases of accidental poisoning these days are extremely rare.

In fact, they always were. Recorded deaths by poisoning from wild or ornamental plants would always have made national news. The problems, where such have arisen, have come from small children putting random things in their mouths; from 'food for free' foragers who have misidentified their target species, or from prolonged handling of the few most intensely toxic garden plants. Despite this, it probably pays to know which the dangerous species are – the knowledge doesn't hurt.

Berries are the obvious place to start, as their bright colours have evolved to say "come and eat me" to wild creatures. Many, of course, are edible, but the black berries of Privet and Buckthorn are worth avoiding, as are the spring-produced purple berries of Ivy, and the somewhat less common but extremely tempting orange and pink fruits of hedgerow Spindle. Eating the berries of Mistletoe would certainly ruin Christmas.

The clustered, bright orange-red berries of Lords and Ladies, borne commonly on low spikes in our local hedge-bottoms and woodlands, are highly dangerous if eaten. The red berries of those two unrelated hedgerow climbers, White Bryony and Black Bryony, are also poisonous.

Any of the wild nightshades, which in our area really means the Woody Nightshade and that weed of bare ground the Black Nightshade, should not be consumed, although their berries, with their changing colours, make them very conspicuous. The large black berries of Deadly Nightshade, or Belladonna are famously poisonous (the clue's in the name), although the plant is not at all common – the nearest I know to us is in Withcall Churchyard.

Some edible plants have poisonous parts – Tomato and Potato are examples where no other part of the plant except the obvious should ever be eaten. Cherry stones may contain cyanide, and Rhubarb leaves are also poisonous, although some would say the same about the stalks.

The pods of some leguminous plants could conceivably catch someone out because of their similarity to beans – Laburnum is extremely poisonous, as are Wisteria and that common street tree, False Acacia.

Daffodil bulbs, which, when in storage, have apparently been mistaken for onions, are also very poisonous. Conkers collected by children (although the custom gets less and less common) should never be put in mouths.

That family of wild plants the 'umbellifers' is an interesting group, and one in which errors are probably most likely to occur. The family is full of edible species such as Carrot, Parsnip, Fennel, Parsley, Dill, Celery and Coriander among others. However, superficially similar are poisons such as Fool's Parsley and Hemlock, the purple-spotted stems of the latter possibly growing to 2m or more tall. The plant famously used to kill Socrates was not actually this Hemlock at all, but one even more poisonous, the Hemlock Water-dropwort, a waterside plant which bears a superficial resemblance to Celery.

If one encounters the largest of all umbellifers, the huge Giant Hogweed, under no circumstances touch it – the sap will cause severe blistering of skin when it is exposed to sunlight, and the scars will take years to disappear. A similar but much milder reaction may come from its smaller, yellow-flowered relative, Wild Parsnip. The juice of buttercups, and the milky latex of spurges, should also be treated with respect.

Fifty or a hundred years ago, insect collectors used to make killing bottles out of chopped leaves of the common garden Laurel, which contain cyanide. So be careful if transporting large quantities of Laurel clippings in your car.

A group of very common garden plants should be mentioned for their extreme toxicity. Firstly the Foxglove or *Digitalis* is a common wild plant over most of Britain but rather less so with us, where it is usually an ornamental. Its tissues are the source of heart-stimulating drugs in tiny amounts, but are extremely poisonous in anything more. Monkshood, with its hooded blue flowers was implicated in the death of a gardener in 2014 after he had handled large amounts in his garden, presumably absorbing the toxin through his skin. The closely-related Delphinium is also poisonous, especially the seeds.

Cannabis is a species the effects of whose contained poisons are well-known, and this can occasionally be found growing where bird-seed has been spilled. Similarly, the Opium Poppy is an extremely popular and showy garden annual, and increasingly found in waste places in our area, growing from spilled seed. Its flowers are usually lilac with dark centres but may be white, red, variegated or doubled. Its foliage is always a distinctive pale green. This is the plant from which poppy seeds, used in baking, are taken, and also from which opium, and therefore its derivatives morphine, heroin and codeine, comes. In Lincolnshire one may occasionally see whole fields of Opium Poppies being legitimately grown for morphine production. The fields are very obvious in flower, but, no-one seems worried about this, as even if you had a desire to manufacture heroin, one of the world's most misery-spreading illegal narcotics, the process by which it is made from the plant is far too much like hard work.

Longhorn Beetles. Beetles are extremely numerous – in fact there are fifty times as many species of beetle on Earth as there are mammals, and the gap is widening all the time as more beetles are discovered. What's more, there are thought to be more 'unknown' species of beetle on Earth than 'known' ones.

Some British beetles are very well known – for example ladybirds,

Glow-worms, Cockchafers, Death Watch Beetles and Whirligigs. One of the most charismatic families of beetles, which includes a number of large, rare and colourful species, is the 'longhorns'. This is one of the first families the enthusiast will come to know. Not only does it contain some really large and spectacular insects, but almost all of the British species can be confidently identified in the field.

All of the longhorns are more or less elongate, and many have very long antennae, which give the family its name. One species, the Timberman, has antennae three or more times as long as its body. The larvae of most species bore tunnels through wood, which, unusually, they are able to digest. They are seen as beneficial in woodlands as they start off the process of decomposition and nutrient recycling. Just two species have larvae which do not burrow in wood, but instead 'mine' the stems of flowers of the carrot family, or 'umbellifers'.

Like all insects which feed within wood, longhorns are occasionally encountered emerging from beams, furniture and wooden packaging materials, and can be transported around the globe in exported wooden products. This means that almost any of the world's longhorn species could conceivably turn up in Britain. By hitching rides in this way, one or two species have become almost ubiquitous across the globe. Old timbers in houses would once have been subject to attack by longhorn beetles, but nowadays wood is treated, and such problems are rare.

One of the largest and most impressive of all Europe's beetles is a longhorn – the giant Capricorn Beetle. This monster insect once inhabited woodlands in the east of England – the wide and distinctive holes through which new adult beetles exit the wood have been found in sub-fossil trees. Although sadly now gone from Britain, this huge beetle still turns up occasionally as an import with foreign timber, providing a real shock for the finder. Lincolnshire must now be content with a similar but smaller longhorn – the Musk Beetle. This is still a large insect, with a metallic greenish-black colouration and very long antennae.

One of the best ways to catch up with longhorn beetles is to search suitable flowers, to which the adults are attracted, around the edges of our older woodlands. Umbellifers such as Hogweed, Bramble flowers, and shrubs with flattened heads of white flowers such as Dogwood, are particularly favoured. With a little practice, a longhorn beetle can easily be recognised as such at first sight, and a few of the commoner species easily learned.

180   **A Natural Selection** – *Wildlife Writings from the Cleethorpes Chronicle*

Last year Mick Binnion sent me photographs of two of our more distinctive longhorn beetles, both taken locally (below).

The first, the Wasp Beetle (left) is not only striped black and yellow for self-defence, but increases its chances of survival further by adopting the jerky movements and twitching antennae of a real wasp. These beetles can be seen almost anywhere in summer – I have now recorded two in my garden.

The second, the Golden-bloomed Grey Longhorn (right) with its dark-striped thorax and long, black-banded antennae, has become much commoner in our area in recent years. Always widespread through central and southern England, this species has now spread as far north as Teesside, probably as a result of global warming. This is one of the two species whose larva does not feed on wood, but burrows within the stems of the common wayside Hogweed.

Two local 'longhorns'. Photos: Mick Binnion

Flowers of the Saltmarsh. The saltmarsh at Cleethorpes, despite being rich in wildlife, is a relatively unfriendly habitat for people – it is the part of the beach holidaymakers are least likely to be seen wandering over. It is spiky, not just wet but unpredictably so, with hidden standing water and sinuous creeks, into which it is all too easy to step. It may be slippery, with each slip revealing smelly, black anoxic mud just beneath the surface. A simple walk back to shore is seldom straightforward across a saltmarsh. Even for a naturalist with an interest in such things, they can be quite hard work.

The suite of plants to be found on saltmarshes is small but specialised, with each species requiring its own way of coping with an occasional bath in salt water. Most of the special plants of saltmarshes have flowers which are inconspicuous or greenish – various grasses, rushes and sedges, Sea Arrowgrass, Sea Plantain, Marsh Samphire and Annual Sea-blite. Some have pale, mealy leaves, such as the abundant Sea Purslane whose little rounded bushes top the creek-sides right across our marsh, imparting a unique overall colour to this habitat.

But saltmarsh does have its bright colours – its special flowers – which repay the effort required to see them. Because of the hostile habitat in which they live, they tend to be flowers you can't see anywhere else.

The small, white, four-petalled flowers of English Scurvy-grass found in the drier marsh or on creek-sides give it away as one of the mustard family, or the 'crucifers'. As the name suggests, its wide, fleshy, slightly heart-shaped leaves are rich in vitamin C. Also, you may completely overlook the little Sea Milkwort until it comes into bloom, when its small pinkish-mauve flowers *en masse* give away its real abundance.

Also in the drier parts of the marsh, you may find stars of deep, clear pink, belonging to that little gentian-relative, the Lesser Centaury. It is much rarer than the Common Centaury of tracksides and barish places inland; shorter, and with more richly-coloured petals.

Also with five simple, pink or whitish petals are the two Sea Spurreys. Lesser Sea Spurrey is able to grow nearer to the sea than the larger-flowered Greater Sea Spurrey. If the gone-over flowerheads are rubbed between the hands the seeds will be revealed, which in Greater Sea Spurrey have little papery rings around their middles. While Lesser Sea Spurrey seeds may also have these rings, they are generally absent. Sea Spurrey flowers protect their important organs from immersion in salt water by closing and trapping a bubble of air within the folded petals.

Later in the summer, the common Sea Aster is much the tallest source of saltmarsh colour. This is the UK's native Michaelmas Daisy, the others (including one which can be seen on the dunes of the Humberston Fitties) all being American imports. Sea Aster has pale purple 'daisy' petals surrounding a yellow central disc, but also comes in a rayless form. The rayless Sea Aster seems to be able to grow much further down the shore than the rayed sort, and seems to be spreading at the expense of its showier conspecific. On the saltmarshes of the east coast, Sea Aster has its own species of bee – the Sea Aster Mining Bee (pictured). This is a rare insect with a very limited worldwide distribution, and our Sea Asters are of vital importance in its survival. The leaves of Sea Aster are edible, and increasingly being collected for the restaurant trade.

Of all the flowers of the saltmarsh there is a clear winner in terms of landscape impact – an iconic and almost habitat-defining flower. This is the Common Sea Lavender. From July through to early autumn the flowers of Sea Lavender may transform saltmarshes, turning them lilac-purple and creating a real spectacle. A mass of Sea Lavender flowering in a heat haze is one of the classic sights of our wilder 'soft' coastlines.

Sea Lavender at Cleethorpes

Sea Lavender is a 'statice' and as such has the ability to keep its shape and colour when dried, making it good in flower arrangements. Its leaves, which are not edible, can be told from those of the much more palatable Sea Aster by a fine hair-point at the tip.

The flowers of both Sea Aster and Sea Lavender are extremely attractive to insects, and in late summer they are worth checking for migrants fresh in from the sea, as well as native insects. In a good year, this may include abundant Painted Lady butterflies, and possibly Red Admirals and Silver Y moths, among others.

Saltmarshes may be no less colourful in autumn, as the foliage of many saltmarsh plants prepare to die back for winter. Reds and yellows are common from plants such as Samphire and Scurvy-grass, and Sea-blite may also contribute an exquisite bluish-purple.

The rare Sea Aster Mining Bee. Photo: Steven Falk

Bumblebee Nests. Any visitor to the Cleethorpes paddling pool at the moment will be greeted by two small signs on the stone benches around the sides reading 'caution – bee nest'.

Fortunately, most people are happy to sit next to the nests, even with small children. The comings and goings of a few bumblebees are unlikely to cause problems – they have no interest in stinging people unless they are seriously provoked.

Most bumblebees, including Britain's commonest, the Buff-tailed Bumblebee, nest in holes near or beneath the ground, often those made originally by small mammals such as mice and voles. Other species may weave a nest on the surface of the ground out of fine grasses and other materials, earning them the name of 'carder bees'. Only one species, the Tree Bumblebee, habitually nests above the ground – often in holes in trees, although it can also, on occasions, take over bird nestboxes or nest in the roofs of houses.

At the paddling pool, the higher of the two nests contains Tree Bumblebees, and the lower a colony of Buff-tailed Bumblebees.

Only queen bumblebees survive the winter. In the spring, they come out of hibernation and seek a place to start a new colony. When a suitable nest site is found, they will lay fertilised eggs which will become worker bees. These workers, which are smaller than the queen, will spend their lives collecting pollen and nectar to provision the growing larvae, essentially their own sisters, and tending the nest. The queen, meanwhile, stays at home and lays more eggs.

From about midsummer onwards, the queen starts to lay unfertilised eggs, which become male bees. Workers are physically unable to mate, although they are able to lay unfertilised eggs, which also produce males. At the end of the summer, these males will mate with new queens. All males, workers and old queens will die before the end of the year, leaving just fertilised new queens to sit out the winter.

The 'societies' of bumblebees and other colony-forming insects have gained a reputation as a model for altruism and order in the animal world, providing a lesson, many have said, for human civilisations. But things in the bumblebee's nest are not always as orderly as they seem.

Firstly, especially early in the season, queens may enter each other's nests and fight for control. This means that on occasions, the workers in a nest may be the offspring of more than one, or the wrong, queen.

Secondly, workers may sneakily lay unfertilised eggs in their own nest, as in terms of evolutionary 'fitness', they pass on more genes by raising sons than brothers. If the queen catches them doing this, she will try to destroy the workers' own eggs or larvae.

Some workers may take an even more radical approach, and lay their unfertilised eggs in a different nest altogether, thus passing on their genes without the burden of parental responsibility. This strategy is very profitable in 'fitness' terms if the risks can be negotiated, and is probably the first stage along the evolutionary pathway towards 'brood parasitism', or 'cuckoo' species.

Anyone watching the Cleethorpes paddling pool nests for a few minutes, can make the interesting observation that some of the bees going in and out don't look the same as the hosts. The usurpers are larger, and have slightly different patterning from the incumbent bees. In fact, the nests are being infiltrated by 'cuckoo bees' – completely different species which are entering with the aim of laying their own eggs in the host nests. By doing this, rather like the real Cuckoo, the cuckoo bees can put all their energy into laying eggs, and none into parenting.

Cuckoo bees only have this breeding strategy, and no other. They do not have workers or queens, but are simply either male or female. They are never seen collecting pollen as they have no need to provision young. Apart from that, cuckoo bees look very much like the 'true' bumblebees to which they are closely related.

So the web of intrigue being played out in the bumblebees' nest is far from being a perfect society for humans to aspire to. However, it does act as a fascinating insight into the workings of evolution.

Marine Conservation Zones. Politicians typically don't think much further ahead than the next election. In this respect, environmental protection is an irritation for them, being the most timeless and open-ended of all political imperatives. Despite its importance, politicians usually have to be dragged kicking and screaming into the environmental debate, from above by international commitments and from below by people pressure. This reluctance to act is based on a belief that immediate economic necessity is somehow at odds with environmental measures – a spurious notion that doesn't serve the future well.

This is nowhere better demonstrated than in the stewardship of Britain's seas. The heroic days of the fishing industry might have made Grimsby 'Great', but the North Sea ecosystem is still grotesquely damaged following many years of the kind of depredations which would never be tolerated on land. In the North Sea, it is estimated that 99% of fish biomass has been removed, and large parts of the sea floor have not been allowed to properly recover. Majestic creatures such as Blue-fin Tuna and Sturgeon, once widespread, are functionally extinct.

In these more enlightened times everyone, fishermen included, realise the need for sustainablility. But for the North Sea, recovery must come first. The bed of the North Sea has a varied terrain, with gorges, reefs, shifting banks, a variety of 'soil types' just like on land, and wildlife may be as colourful as you'll find anywhere in the world. But the parlous state of its fauna is generally not widely known, as it is out of sight beneath the waves.

In 2009, the Marine Act heralded a new era in marine protection, establishing a framework for the creation of a series of protected marine areas

Hornwrack

in UK waters. In 2012, 127 'Marine Conservation Zones' were suggested which would safeguard and protect a representative cross-section of habitats and species. Damaging operations would be forbidden in these areas, and a spectacular resurgence of life would result, boosting the fortunes of the fishing industry.

To widespread dismay, only 27 areas have actually been designated (only two in the North Sea and none around Lincolnshire or the Humber), and to this day, even this small group of sites receives no material protection whatsoever. One which was left out of the reckoning was our own 'Lincolnshire Belt', stretching out three nautical miles from the shore from just north of Donna Nook down beyond Mablethorpe. This shallow haven is a nursery for Sprat, Lesser Pipefish, Lemon Sole, Plaice and Herring. It has Bristleworms and abundant Brown Shrimps, and carpets of hydroids and bryozoans, including the lemon-scented Hornwrack (pictured) – looking like a light brown seaweed – which is so familiar to us when washed up on the Cleethorpes strandline. These are the waters in which our famous Donna Nook Grey Seal pups take their first swim.

It makes no sense to either conservationists or the long term interests of fishermen **not** to protect these special waters, and this is yet another example of decision-makers' short-sighted reluctance to put the environment first. The designation of all 127 Marine Conservation zones, including the Lincolnshire Belt, must surely come. Like all environmental matters, it can be forced up the agenda if we let politicians know that there are votes in it.

Another 23 Marine Conservation Zones were designated in 2016, including 'Holderness Inshore' which stretches down as far as the tip of Spurn Point, and more are planned in 2018. However, these are still effectively 'paper parks', with no material protection whatsoever.

Garden Snails. It is the sad lot of every gardener to have to do battle with that abundant and voracious herbivore the Garden Snail. But however many we remove, more always seem to appear.

Despite moving at a maximum speed of only 50 yards per hour, Garden Snails are born survivors. They can climb a needle-like plant stem, or pass over the edge of a razor blade without harm. They can walk up surfaces at any angle, including upside down, and stick to a surface with an adhesive strength many times their own weight.

They can survive very cold or very dry weather by sealing themselves inside their shells with a film of dried mucus. They have mechanisms which change the osmoregulatory properties of their cells and blood which prevent drying out in summer or taking on too much water or freezing in winter.

Garden Snails will eat a wide variety of wild and garden plants, leaving telltale mucus trails to identify the culprit and show where they've been. I find it quite impossible to grow Cucumbers or Hostas in my own garden without them being eaten by snails, and they will quickly move on to something else when those are gone.

If your garden is large and wild, especially if it has a pond, it could perhaps support creatures capable of keeping snails in check. They will be consumed, for example, by Hedgehogs, shrews and mice, amphibians, centipedes and large ground beetles. Also, many species of bird will eat them, especially the Song Thrush, which may leave the smashed shells on a tell-tale 'anvil' – perhaps a rock or paving stone.

In smaller and simpler gardens, snails may wreak havoc, and some method of control may be necessary. These days everyone should be aware of the undesirability of using the little blue metaldehyde slug pellets, which are extremely toxic to other garden wildlife, pets and small children. They have been implicated in the serious decline of Song Thrushes and Hedgehogs in Britain in recent times.

There are more harmless ways of discouraging snails. They have been shown, for example, to be put off by garlic or the caffeine in coffee grounds. Also, copper is said to deter them, as it gives them a slight electric shock when they move over it. So putting a complete ring of these substances around valued plants can sometimes keep snails at bay, although if leaves meet and touch above the barrier, snails will simply use them as a bridge and reach the plants anyway. Mulches of sharp material like broken eggshells have also been used, although you may sometimes see snails walking across them without a care.

Beer is extremely attractive to snails, and a sunken 'pitfall trap' containing beer may catch a certain number, although the trap needs to be refreshed regularly as the liquid evaporates quickly. Some people have planted sacrificial plants next to the ones they want to preserve, or soaked their unwanted garden weeds in beer to act as a tasty decoy.

The kindest method that I, and I suspect most people use, is simply to pick snails up bodily and chuck them away, in the hope that numbers will eventually be reduced. This is best done after dark, especially when it's damp, when the snails come more out into the open.

The problem with this, and indeed all methods of killing or removing snails, is that 'your' snails are actually part of a large and mobile population covering a wide area. This means that the snails you remove are quickly replaced by others moving in. You would need to remove the whole neighbourhood's snail population to make any difference, which is pretty much impossible. It is particularly illogical to throw them next door if everyone is doing the same.

To make it even harder, snails are known to display homing behaviour. How do they do this? They are more likely, apparently, to travel back along their own mucus trails, or those of other Garden Snails, than they are to simply move around at random. When trails are not present, it has been shown that they can still return to their garden of origin using smell.

Given that all methods of snail removal or control have the same problems, you might as well abandon the poisons and use more environmentally friendly and kinder methods instead. A recent study showed that despite their homing powers, snails very rarely come back if removed to a distance of more than 20 metres. So the very best solution to reducing the destructive effect of snails might be nothing more than perseverance and a good throwing arm.

Flying Ants. Sometimes, in hot, settled, summer weather like we've had this week, you may see a wheeling tower of gulls spiralling high upwards into a deep blue sky. Every now and then one will flutter to the side, as though to catch something.

The reason for this stack of circling gulls is almost always flying ants, on which they feed. When 'flying ant days' occur they can be a desperate nuisance to humans. On the ground, flying ants have ruined many a picnic and barbecue, and they may sometimes come indoors through open windows. In 2006 a Dorset cricket team even blamed losing a match and subsequent relegation on flying ants coming up from the wicket and temporarily stopping play.

Throughout the summer, most of the ants you see, the ones on the ground without wings, are workers – sexually undeveloped females. Their nests are made in soil, often under brickwork or in cracks in pavement, where they are easily found by following the trail of insects back. Inside houses, chemicals used to kill ants' nests often work by providing a tasty, but poisonous, bait, which the workers will faithfully cart back to the nest. The poison is usually slow-acting, to allow the ants to share it around before it has its deadly effect. This is a bit harsh on the ants – other deterrents which can be used to simply steer ants away from trouble include cucumber, cloves, mint, baby powder, lemon juice, coffee, chilli powder or cinnamon.

Each ants' nest contains a single queen, which may live for up to ten years. In the first part of the year, the queen lays eggs which will become worker ants. Workers go out to collect food for the colony – small invertebrates, nectar from flowers, or sometimes 'honeydew' from aphids. But at some point during the summer, using settled, warm weather as a cue, the queen, instead of producing workers, will begin to produce both males and new queens, both of which have wings. The reason for the wings is so that the reproductive ants can undergo massed 'nuptial flights', when mating take place. These are the swarms of flying ants we see on certain days in summer.

Synchronisation in swarming ants is desirable for several reasons. It makes a successful mating more likely, while also swamping the ability of predators to eat them all. If nuptial flights over a wide area all happen together, new queens may disperse and breed with males from other nests, preventing inbreeding. The new winged queens, with their strong powers of flight, benefit from being chased by as many males as possible, so they can sort out the fittest individuals for breeding.

You may hear people say that flying ants occur on the same day all over the country, but this is not really true. Such days may well correspond from place to place because the prompt is provided by the weather, but in fact they may be spread over some days or even weeks.

The males, which are the smaller and more numerous of the winged ants, do no work, existing only to mate with new queens, after which they die.

After mating, the new queen will fall to earth, lose her wings, and hopefully found a new colony, where she will embark on a lifetime of egg-laying. Large ants wandering apparently aimlessly over the ground after a flying ant day will be new queens searching for a nest site.

A sudden abundance of flying ants provides their predators with a temporary glut of food. As previously noted they are a particular favourite of gulls, and there are stories of gulls being 'drunk' on the formic acid produced by the ants in self-defence. Gulls which have gorged on flying ants, it is said, will flop around with no fear of traffic, or fly straight into moving vehicles. It is more likely that such gulls are just excited at such an easy feast, overly focused on eating, hot, or just full.

Plants in Pure Sand. If you start out somewhere behind Pleasure Island in Cleethorpes and walk towards the sea, somewhere on the outer sand dunes you will reach the very limit of where plants are able to grow. Mobile sand represent one of the harshest environments on Earth for wildlife generally – it is, in effect, a shifting, temperate desert.

A quick glance at the plants growing out on the furthest sand reveals that they are low in both density and species diversity, and that they are very specialised. They are not the same species as you see growing, say, as weeds in gardens.

Plants of mobile sand-dunes are classic 'stress-tolerators'. The problems of living here are obvious. Sand retains very little water, and hardly any nutrients. Because of the presence of particles of seashell, dune sands can also be very alkaline. The plants themselves suffer further drought by exposure – firstly by the action of relentless sea winds, but also by osmosis when the plants are sprayed by salt water, or occasionally inundated by the tide.

Also, sand dunes are extremely unstable. Sand is continually picked up and re-deposited by the wind, and in a storm whole dunes can be destroyed or transformed. Plants may be sand-blasted, buried, uprooted or washed away, depending on the spot where they grow.

Plant colonisation on mobile sand is usually made possible in the first place by organic matter deposited on the strandline. Debris carried by the tide will always contain a few viable seeds, and they take advantage of the enrichment from seaweed and the bodies of dead creatures washed up, to gain a toehold. Once established, growing plants will trap blowing sand and stabilise it with their roots, creating conditions for further colonisation.

Plants able to grow in almost pure sand tend to have certain characteristics. They often have a waxy outer cuticle to prevent water loss and resist sand-blasting, and this is why so many are a mealy, whitish-green colour. Sand dune plants may be fleshy, to store water, and may resist water-loss by osmosis by having very concentrated cell-sap. Many species have leaves with a reduced surface area, and dune grasses may have inrolled leaves and relatively few, sunken 'stomata' (air holes) to protect them from rapid dehydration.

Lastly, sand dune plants tend to grow very quickly, and some species have extremely extensive root-systems to hold them in place. Some can also spread sideways quickly by rhizomes, so stabilizing the dunes around them.

Eventually, such vegetation will add organic matter to the sand, which in turn creates better water-retention and nutrient status. After many years, a much more stable dune system may form, and the diversity of plant life will increase dramatically, as can usually be seen further back from the sea.

At Cleethorpes, the species most commonly responsible for trapping and stabilising mobile sand on the outer dunes is the Sand Couch grass, although it is joined in places by Red Fescue, and tall, bluish clumps of Lyme Grass. On the hostile seaward edge of the dunes you will find the rare Frosted Orache, with its silvery leaves, red stems and prostrate habit, and the Prickly Saltwort, looking like a tiny Gorse plant. The latter is both tough and fleshy in all its parts, and has such concentrated cell sap that it can suck in water by osmosis with the equivalent of 450lb per square inch.

The little Sea Sandwort, with its extremely regularly four-ranked rows of leaves, can also be seen poking through the most mobile sand here.

Many dune plants have insignificant green flowers, but there are exceptions. The Sea Rocket has beautiful pink, four-petalled flowers, and the rarer Sea Holly has rounded, spiny heads of blue flowers irresistible to bees. I have not seen Sea Holly at Cleethorpes this year *[2015]* – in recent years plants have been uprooted, possibly by gardeners, although they are unlikely to survive in normal soils.

Although not growing quite so close to the sea, do look for the imposing yellow spikes of Large-flowered Evening Primrose – possibly the most eyecatching of Cleethorpes's dune flowers in July.

Terns. The thing for which Cleethorpes is the most *internationally* important, more than sands, the pier, fish and chips, football or air shows, is the number and assemblage of protected waterbirds on the beach. Locals seem to take this extraordinary attribute almost entirely for granted, probably because the birds are usually distant and therefore mostly difficult to see.

Midsummer is the off-season for shorebirds. In June and early July the sandbanks are mostly birdless, save for a few desultory non-breeding Oystercatchers and gulls. But from late July onwards waders from the north, from sites relatively close-by to the remotest Arctic wildernesses, begin to return and build to a peak in numbers, often tens of thousands, by the autumn.

The species making up this extraordinary influx are largely the same ones which go on to stay, in varying numbers, throughout the winter. There is one group however, for which the late summer is the special time at Cleethorpes. These are the terns.

Terns are daintier and more dashing than gulls, with thin bills and forked tails. They feed by diving into the sea for fish.

Although I have seen six species of tern on Cleethorpes beach in the past, only three are common. A fourth, the Little Tern, has become much less frequent in recent years since the decline of its nearby breeding colony at Tetney. Of the three, the Sandwich Tern is the largest and whitest, with a black crest and bill. The other two, Common and Arctic Terns are both black-capped and red-billed, and provide a difficult identification challenge requiring a good view. Ecologically however they are quite distinct.

Common Tern breeds from the Arctic down the coasts of Europe and west Africa, and across to the Azores, Madeira and the Caribbean, with British birds wintering in west or southern Africa. In England, any tern breeding inland will be a Common Tern. In contrast, Arctic Terns are exclusively maritime breeders, which perform the most extraordinary migration of any animal on Earth. They are high latitude breeders, with Britain constituting the southern edge of their breeding range. Their incredible annual migration takes them across the whole globe to the food-rich areas around the Antarctic pack-ice and back, often crossing the Atlantic en route to take advantage of favourable winds. In its lifetime, an Arctic Tern may travel a distance equivalent to three round trips to the moon. An Arctic Tern experiences no winter, and more daylight in a year than any other living thing.

At high tide in late summer a quick scan of a sandbank may well reveal a mixture of adult and juvenile terns sitting among the waders and gulls. Adult Arctic Terns have no black tips to their red bills, and in flight, with good views and practice, their flight feathers which are translucent right to the outermost one, are also diagnostic. Catch them while you can – by early winter they will be very, very far away.

Leaf Miners. While in summer we are aware of a myriad specks and sprites living among us, the tinier end of the insect spectrum is usually considered too insubstantial and obscure to bother identifying, even by most naturalists. Little-known families of tiny flies, beetles, wasps and the like are seen to be the preserve of specialists, who may dedicate their lives to their microscopic differences.

In many ways this is a shame, as many of our tinier insects are just as colourful, beautiful, other-worldly and economically important as ever are butterflies or dragonflies.

There are times, however, when minute, almost completely unidentifiable insects may impose themselves on our consciousness by the consequences of their actions – parasites, thunderflies and garden pests are examples, as are gall-forming insects and leaf miners. With the latter two groups, although the insects themselves may go unnoticed, the various deformations and disfigurements they make on their foodplants do not. They are often disliked by gardeners and farmers for the damage they do to otherwise pristine plants, but for the naturalist they add layers of interest and provide clues to the existence of mini-ecosystems within ecosystems.

The study of leaf miners is a pursuit for the all-round naturalist, as it requires a good knowledge of both botany and at least four different orders of insect. This bringing together of disciplines is one of its attractions.

Anywhere there is abundant vegetation you will find leaf miners. The term encompasses all those insects whose larvae feed *inside* leaves – that is, between the upper and lower epidermis, where the flesh is softer and has lower concentrations of chemical defences and tannins. Larvae are also largely safe from predation in this protected environment. The results of their feeding are trails, galleries and blotches which are not only highly visible, interesting and sometime beautiful, but often unique to a single species and so readily identified.

So-called micro-moths are responsible for the greatest number of kinds of leaf mine. Their mines are usually visible on both sides of the leaf, and contain frass (or droppings) in a single line. In contrast, mines made by flies generally occupy either the upper or lower layers of the leaf (or a mixture of the two) and characteristically contain frass in two lines. Those made by sawflies are always blotches, and contain more copious, and darker, frass. A few weevils and leaf beetles may also make leaf mines.

If the larva is visible within the mine, those of moths, sawflies and beetles have chewing mouthparts, and often visible legs, although these may be much reduced. Fly larvae never have legs, looking like tiny maggots, and feed lying on their sides, using a piece of hardened headgear looking somewhat like a pickaxe to scrape away at their food.

Most helpful of all in the identification of leaf miners is the fact that most species are very choosy in the type of plant they feed on. Some are comparative generalists, but very many are specific to a single species of plant. This means that the first step in identifying a leaf-mining insect is to identify the plant on which it is feeding. This can sometimes even tell you the order of insect without further ado – for example, any mine on buttercups or Hogweed cannot be a moth as there is no leaf-mining moth which feeds on these species.

Most leaf-mining insects can be easily reared from infected leaves, although for some you will have to sit out the winter before the adult emerges. Occasionally, parasites of the larvae will emerge instead – about a hundred parasites of leaf miners have been identified although there are undoubtedly countless more waiting to be discovered.

Leaf Miner on Bramble

Some species of plants often have very obvious and well-known leaf miners – Lilac, for example, Holly and Bramble. Look for the silver, convoluted galleries of the moth *Stigmella aurella* on Bramble leaves (pictured). See how the width of the gallery increases as the larva grows. Sometimes the amber-coloured larva can still be found in its mine, munching away. The adult moth, when reared out, is a metallic coppery-purple with a shining cross-stripe, and an orange-tufted head. If it were not for the leaf mine, this species would doubtless go completely unnoticed.

There are over a thousand species of leaf-mining insect in Britain. There are several good keys on the internet for their identification – the most helpful ones are arranged so that you can look them up by foodplant.

Ditches. There are almost half a million kilometres of ditches in Britain. They are ubiquitous in the lowlands, and stretch surprisingly far up into the hills. Ditches are clearly not a natural habitat, with their long straight lines following geometric field boundaries and showing little relationship with natural landscape contours. They were created with practicality in mind – to drain fields and make them suitable for agriculture.

However, in the regions just behind our soft coastlines, such as here on the Lincolnshire outmarsh (where we often call them 'dykes'), they may represent the last remaining piece of watery continuity with the swamps of old – the flood-prone, summer-grazed wilderness of pre-reclamation times. The wildlife in our outmarsh ditches may be both rich and ancient.

Freshwater is always a magnet for wildlife, although the creatures of our agricultural ditches are subject to a variety of abuses. A neglected ditch will silt up and become terrestrial habitat within a few years. But ditches 'slubbed out' too vigorously – scoured both sides into steep-sided channels of bare soil or clay for huge stretches at a time – may take many years to recolonise fully.

A huge problem is the run-off from agricultural land, which can lead to blooms of algae or a smothering mat of duckweed, not to mention direct toxicity to animals. But when water quality is good and water levels maintained, ditches can contain a staggering assemblage of life. Because ditch networks are so extensive and lie mostly on private land, they tend to be undervalued, and very few have been subject to even superficial survey. Ditches crossing ancient, coastal grazing marshes tend to be the most valuable of all for wildlife, and nationally, several species occur in such ditches and nowhere else.

In winter, ditches may provide foraging habitat for Kingfisher, Snipe, Redshank and occasional Green Sandpiper. Water Rails may stalk the wider channels. The Water Vole – Britain's most declined mammal – is a creature of ditches as well as other fresh waters, and here on the Lincolnshire outmarsh we have a rare remaining stronghold. At night, wider channels may act as commuting routes for the water-loving Daubenton's Bat.

Amphibians, especially Common Frog and Smooth Newt, are ditch-dwellers, and ditches are rarely without one, or both, of our freshwater species of stickleback.

The presence of larger fish is usually disadvantageous to invertebrate life in ditches. Where large fish are absent, ditches may contain all manner of creatures: several types of water beetle including the impressive Great Diving Beetle; bugs such as Water-boatmen and Water Scorpion; larvae of dragonflies, damselflies and caddisflies; water slaters and water shrimps; fly larvae, various worms, giant Horse Leeches, flatworms and several species of water snail, should all be found. The water surface should have pond skaters and manic flotillas of Whirligig Beetles, each one with its two pairs of eyes, one looking up, the other down beneath the water. A closer look reveals smaller life still – water mites, water fleas and the little Cyclops, and the strange, tentacled Hydra which preys on them.

There have been moves recently to protect and even recreate some of the old Lincolnshire outmarsh pasture habitat, with its network of wildlife-rich ditches. Three main areas were targeted, although the furthest north of these was around Saltfleet. The last remaining fragments of outmarsh on the outskirts of our own town are seemingly abandoned to the needs of development. In my lifetime, some really exceptional dykes disappeared beneath the new housing of Cleethorpes's Country Park estate, sadly before their value was fully quantified. Only remnants of the old ditch system remain in the Park itself, and these are now invaded by stocked fish from the lake.

An additional modern problem for ditches is the presence of invasive alien plants. Rampant New Zealand Pygmyweed may clog ditches, and the deep crimson floating fronds of Water Fern may so comprehensively cover the water surface by late summer that it may look more like a red-coloured path than a ditch. More desirable plants can also, however, be found – in our area look out for the uncommon and distinctive Opposite-leaved Pondweed.

What ditches we have left should be managed sensitively, for each one is a potential wildlife gem. Wide buffer strips to prevent agricultural runoff, and rotational, little-and-often management should be the norm. Removed material should be piled up on the ditch side for a while before eventual removal, to allow contained creatures to return to the water.

Local Provenance. In recent years there has been a strong fashion for sowing native grasses and wild flowers into wild-looking places in the name of conservation. If done well, this is a good way of replacing the pollen and nectar sources so important to bees and other insects, lost over the last 70 years of ever-intensifying agriculture.

Because of sowing, roadsides (especially motorways) and all manner of municipal landscaping schemes now burst with colour from these newly-created 'wild' meadows. Among the signs of spring are the huge rafts of yellow Cowslips coming into flower along the sides of the A1 where they have been sown. Later in the summer and just as eyecatching, white masses of Ox-eye Daisy along some of our motorways almost certainly indicate the early stages of a wildflower restoration project.

Wildflower seed can be bought from garden centres for small-scale wild patches in gardens. Also, sowing so-called 'wildflower margins' on farmland is now an option in some of our agri-environment schemes, for which farmers receive payment.

But some have expressed concerns about the sowing of wild flower seed away from its place of origin. Wild flowers properly indigenous to the place where they grow have usually undergone natural selection so that they are well adapted to their environment. Flowers of the same species, which look identical but come from elsewhere, may be genetically slightly different, and not quite so well-adapted in that spot.

Sometimes different regional strains of the same species don't even look the same – the beautiful purple Knapweed of meadows, for example, tends to have large flowers with prominent 'rays' in the more southerly part of its distribution, while our northern ones have a tighter, more thistle-like flower. Some of the yellow Kidney Vetch or Bird's-foot Trefoil sown along the verges of our main roads are peculiarly robust, typical of continental forms – quite different from our own British plants.

Also, some native species such as Sainfoin, various Clovers and Salad Burnet have specially-bred fodder varieties which could be confused with the original wild plants.

All of this compromises the authenticity of our wayside flora. But does it really matter? Some say yes – that local forms of plants are part of a place's heritage, like regional accents or vernacular architecture. In fact they may be even more important than that, as plants and the genes they contain may have untold uses in the future, and to keep as much diversity as possible would seem the sensible precaution. Moving wild plants from one place to another can homogenise the natural world, in the same way that human cultures are also becoming homogenised.

So when it comes to transporting wildflower seed from place to place, how far is too far? This depends on how genetically different plants from different places actually are, and the truth is nobody knows. This leads some to invoke a precautionary approach and only take seed from localities extremely close by. For most people, British seed is good enough for British use, although sometimes seed from abroad is grown here, and *its* seed sold on as British, so the whole thing is more complicated than it sounds. Usually, at the end of the day, pragmatism is the guide.

There is actually another approach, sometimes suggested but rarely put into practice. This is to sow wildflower seed whose origin is not as local as possible, but as *genetically diverse* as possible. So seed from as many places as you could muster would be all mixed up, and sown together. This would give natural selection – 'survival of the fittest' – the widest possible genetic base on which to work its magic, with unsuitable characters quickly eliminated and plants produced which are perfectly adapted to the place in which they are put.

But these are subtle points. Although the best seed suppliers are sophisticated and conscientious in their approach, some so-called wild flower mixtures contain nothing of the sort, and the results can be quite comical. In fact, you might think that these mixes are better, because at least nobody would mistake them for the real thing.

Echolocation. I have made mention before in this column that bats 'see' in the dark by 'shouting'. In fact, they emit high-frequency clicks or bursts of sound, and pick up the echoes to formulate an image of their surroundings – a process known as echolocation.

To put bat sounds in perspective, human hearing is commonly stated to be in the range 20 Hz to 20 kHz (20,000 Hz). In fact, 20 kHz is very high pitched to a human and many people can't actually hear this frequency. The upper limit of human hearing also decreases, sometimes dramatically, with age. Humans are most comfortable at frequencies between 2 kHz and 5 kHz.

The sounds produced by bats when they echolocate range from about 20 kHz at the bottom end to over 100 kHz at the top end, so way above the hearing of any human. Our commonest bat, the Common Pipistrelle, produces its strongest echolocation calls at about 45 kHz.

All bats are strongly protected by law in the UK, and ecological surveyors need a reliable way of confirming the presence and identification of bats in a given location. Bats' night time habits make this difficult for humans, whose night vision is poor.

Luckily, there are various pieces of equipment available which can reduce the high-pitched echolocation calls of bats to audible levels, or even better, to plot them visually as a 'sonogram'.

A sonogram is a graph which plots frequency of sounds against time, and the patterns produced can not only confirm that bats are present, but can sometimes also be used to identify a bat with certainty.

Armed with such equipment, this summer I paid a visit to Cleethorpes Country Park at dusk. There are very few bat recorders in the northern part of Lincolnshire, and almost any record of bats, especially if they are identified reliably, are likely to be 'new'.

As it got dark, bats started appearing as soon as the swallows and swifts had left the sky. This is because bats fill the same insect-eating niche at night which is occupied by swallows and swifts in daytime.

I recorded three species of bat in the Country Park. Two of these were Britain's largest, and Britain's commonest bats, the Noctule and the Common Pipistrelle respectively. Both can be readily identified from their sonograms.

The last of the three is very difficult to identify from its sonogram as it produces a pattern very similar to other bats in the same genus. Luckily, its behavior identifies it immediately. This is the Daubenton's, or Water Bat. This bat can be seen in the last light of dusk or by torchlight, skimming back and forth low over the surface of water. This bat is well-known to anglers, and was common over the Country Park's main lake.

Bats are not the only creatures to produce ultrasonic sounds. Some insects such as bush crickets 'sing', or 'stridulate' at frequencies too high for humans to hear, and a bat detector can also be useful to locate and identify these during the daytime.

Some moths also emit loud, high-pitched ultrasound in flight, for reasons which were, for a long time, unknown. It is now thought that these sounds 'jam' the ultrasound of bats at the last second, to stop the moths from being captured.

Even some silent insects are sensitive to ultrasound to help them to avoid predation by bats. If you ever happen to see a green lacewing in flight, try rattling some keys close to it, as this produces strong ultrasound. Mistaking the sound for a foraging bat the lacewing will, as likely as not, close its wings and fall straight out of the sky.

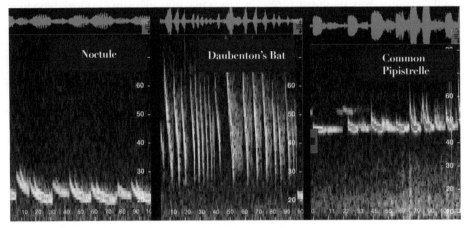

Three bat sonograms from Cleethorpes Country Park

Plants as Food. If you ever find yourself wondering what wildlife is 'for', it is worth remembering that all of the plants we use for food today started out as weeds growing in the wild. Some have been made unrecognisable by breeding, and the origins of some of today's foodstuffs are lost in time. For many others, the ancestors of the plants we eat are still alive and well, and growing wild around us in North East Lincolnshire.

Some wild foods remain unaltered by humankind and can still be gathered at will: Blackberry is a good example, along with Elder, Hazel, Rosehip and Sloe; all ubiquitous native plants, abundant in local hedgerows. Wild Cherry too is still easily recognisable as an ancestor of the sweet cherries we eat. Watercress, a so-called 'superfood', is the same wild plant which occurs for free anywhere there is flowing water, including many of our local ditches. Often growing with Watercress is the common Water Mint, whose hybrid with the non-native Spearmint gives us Peppermint.

Black Mustard, whose yellow flowers are so prominent on bare ground around Cleethorpes (try along Buck Beck or anywhere where there are roadworks) used to be the main ingredient for table mustard, but nowadays this is largely replaced by Indian Mustard.

Some species have been moderately altered by breeding and have escaped back into the wild – apples and pears fall into this category. Although these two fruits are now common in hedgerows around habitation, their wild progenitors, Crab Apple and Wild Pear, were probably always rare round these parts.

Many food species have their ancestral home in the Mediterranean or Asia, but have escaped from domestication and now become part of our local wild flora – Fennel and Chicory are two such plants, which can be seen growing together along the A180 out of Grimsby. Also in this category are all the plums and gages, which often go unnoticed until the fruits appear in hedgerows in late summer and give them away as interlopers. Horseradish, whose home is in the Eastern Mediterranean, is now very common along our roadsides, although it seems that nowadays nobody thinks to harvest its peppery roots to make horseradish sauce.

Some wild species have been more radically altered by humans. Three 'umbellifers' deserve a mention – look for the common Wild Carrot, whose white umbels sit above a distinctive ruff of forked bracts, in undisturbed and coastal grasslands. Less common are Wild Parsnip with its yellow umbels, and the greenish umbels of Wild Celery, the latter always restricted to the coast. All three are the wild ancestors of their namesake foods. The smell of Wild Celery when crushed gives its identity away immediately.

A walk along the sea wall at either Grimsby or Humberston will turn up the dark shiny leaves of Sea Beet, a fabulously versatile plant, which has been bred to produce, variously, Sugar Beet, Beetroot, Mangels and Chard.

Many wild plants are edible. Humankind uses only a very small fraction of the available species for food, and many more have the potential to be brought into cultivation. For this reason, among others, it is vital to conserve the functioning ecosystems in which these wild resources occur. Only that way will they remain available to us into the future.

August

Identification Skills. Any field or wayside in summer or autumn will contain yellow dandelion-like flowers. One is immediately aware that they are not all the same, and a number of species are probably involved. But what are they? Similarly with the yellow-flowered 'brassicas' – rapes, turnips and mustards. Similarly again with the white 'umbellifers' – parsleys, chervils etc.

Even within a small and colourful group like butterflies, it is not easy to tell a Small White from a Green-veined White from a female Orange Tip. To distinguish a Small Skipper from an Essex Skipper requires a very good view indeed. One needs to know what one should be looking for.

Without species ID skills, how can we decide which natural places need protection? How can we assess or quantify species' increases or declines? How do we gather important information on the effects of climate change? And how can we assess the fortunes of our pollinators, without which many of our crops would fail?

There is sometimes a perception that outside the charismatic groups such as mammals and birds, species identification is a job for an expert, possibly with a microscope. In fact, most species within any group are readily identifiable on sight, or at least with a hand lens. This even goes for the so-called difficult groups; grasses, mosses, beetles, bugs etc. Within each group however, there are always difficult pairs or small groups of species which pose more of a challenge. One big problem is that the rare ones often look very much like the common ones, so errors can really matter.

The literature which enables species identification is very variable – for birds it is unparalleled; for flowers it is pretty good (although alien lookalikes are often neglected), for beetles it either very expensive, piecemeal or out of date, and for mites it is pretty much non-existent.

The ability to identify all the members of at least one animal or plant group in the field has never been a common skill, but is getting even rarer. Nowadays, the low numbers of suitably qualified field surveyors is reaching something of a crisis point, at a time when such skills have never been more valuable, given the urgent need, and sometimes legal requirement, for environmental protection.

People these days tend to be less connected with the natural world. Also, changing educational emphasis from rote learning of facts to the development of cognitive skills – evaluating, reviewing and problem-solving – has led to natural history skills being neglected.

In fact, to distinguish between similar organisms is a highly complex task, requiring analytic processes of a high order. One must come to a conclusion based on a body of quantitative, qualitative and circumstantial information, based on balance of probability. Identification of species is very far from a mere memory test.

It bothers some that animals may have to be killed and dissected, or flowers picked, for the purpose of identification, although this substantially increases the chance of success. If organisms cannot be collected, one used to be taught to take notes in the field, and go back to identify the organism from the literature at home or in the lab. In fact, no good naturalist ever did this except in an emergency, and if they were to try it, they would fail much of the time. The information they collected would almost certainly lack the bit they turned out to really need.

Now we have camera phones and the help of the world community via the internet, this approach stands a much greater chance of success. The best way, however – the way it is done by the experts (when they don't want to kill things), – is to start small, with a manageable group, and learn what to look for *before* you go out. This way, precious moments spent in the company of the organism will not be wasted.

For the record, if you see an unmarked small skipper butterfly, look immediately at the tips of its antennae. Or a small white butterfly, look at the *underside* of the wing, especially the hindwing. For yellow brassicas and white umbellifers, forget the flowers and look closely at the pods or seeds.

Bindweeds. They are some of the largest and showiest of our wild flowers – the British equivalent of the tropical Morning Glories. Their flowers are at their best in full sun, and fold delicately after dark. But the bindweeds, with their seeming ability to smother all other vegetation in their path, seldom find themselves picked out for praise. In fact, by no means all species show such brutish behavior, and here in North East Lincolnshire we can boast a couple of special kinds.

When our bindweeds are in full bloom they are among the most noticeable of all wild flowers. The commonest species – the Field Bindweed – is the smallest-flowered, although large patches of its white, pink or candy-striped blooms are still a very prominent feature of late summer roadsides and the edges of arable fields. The flowers give off a pleasant smell in the sunshine, rather like almonds, and attract a variety of insects.

Field Bindweed is a born survivor. It produces very long-lived seeds, which may germinate in summer or autumn. It has sinuous roots which may descend to a depth of 20 feet, and produces extensive horizontal mats of rhizomes which can extend to cover a large area in a single season. Its winding aerial stems can quickly smother adjacent vegetation, and the plant can replicate itself from the smallest scrap of vegetative material. Damaged stems quickly produce a milky, antiseptic latex which seals the wound. But despite this array of survival skills, Field Bindweed cannot live without full sunlight or in closed vegetation – it needs at least some open, disturbed soil.

Perhaps the most noticeable of the bindweeds are those with the huge, pure white trumpet-flowers, which are so common everywhere that humans provide something for them to climb. There are actually two very similar species involved, both very common; one native and the other naturalised.

Hedge Bindweed is the native species, and can be identified by the pair of bracts at the base of the flower being more or less flat, and not properly enclosing the flower's green sepals. It is an aggressive climber able quickly to get the better of adjacent vegetation, even sometimes reaching the tops of small trees. In rich, damp, habitats disturbed by humans and then abandoned, this species may form extensive monocultures. If you ever find yourself at Chowder Ness on the Humber Bank at the west end of the Far Ings Nature reserve, look out for the beautiful pink subspecies *roseata* growing in its original reedbed habitat – it is the only place I've ever seen it.

The flowers of the very similar, introduced Large Bindweed have sepals almost completely enclosed by two large, rounded, slightly inflated, overlapping bracts. This is the easiest way to tell this species from the last, although occasionally hybrids may occur with intermediate characters. This tends to be the commoner of the two species around our town, and when it invades gardens can be a real nuisance. Like its relative, its aerial stems grow quickly, twining anticlockwise around any obstacle in their path, with stems sometimes winding round each other creating something a bit like rope. Removal by pulling at the twining stems can be very satisfying, although extreme persistence may be needed to eradicate it completely.

Growing on the landward side of the sea wall at Humberston Fitties is one

Sea Bindweed at Humberston

of our special bindweeds – the Sea Bindweed (pictured). The flowers are pink, often with white radial stripes, and the leaves are smallish and kidney-shaped – quite unlike those of other bindweeds. In the UK this species is exclusively coastal, growing only on sand dunes and the upper parts of sand or shingle beaches. Although quite resistant to trampling, it is suffering a national decline as its habitat comes under pressure from coastal works and human pressure.

Finally, there is a large, pink-flowered bindweed growing along Wendover Lane in Humberston not far from the Church, although it is much reduced in recent years as it has been removed from temporary fencing which it used for support. This unusual plant has been identified as *Calystegia x howittiorum,* or the natural hybrid between the white Large Bindweed and the pink Hairy Bindweed – the latter an alien of probably garden origin which no longer apparently grows in the area. This hybrid is a British endemic – that is to say it occurs nowhere else. One hopes the residents of that quiet cul-de-sac allow this special plant to retain its toehold in North East Lincolnshire.

Dragonflies. Dragonflies are among the most beautiful and spectacular of all insects, and our larger dragonflies are comfortably the biggest insects you will see in everyday life. The fact that their larvae are aquatic and therefore the breeding adults are tied to water, makes patrolling dragonflies an essential component of a hot summer's afternoon by lakes, rivers and ponds.

Dragonflies are engineering masterpieces displaying one of evolution's oldest and most successful designs. Insects closely resembling today's dragonflies were patrolling the Earth's waterbodies more than 300 million years ago, although some were considerably larger than they are now, with wingspans of 70cm. It is thought that this extreme size was possible due to a greater proportion of oxygen in the air at that time.

The beautiful network of veins in each of the dragonfly's four wings give both strength and elasticity, allowing aerial virtuosity almost unrivalled in the animal kingdom. In addition, dragonflies have extremely large eyes which they use to home in on their prey of flying insects. Like ours, their world is one primarily based on vision, and for this reason many species have attractive colour patterns which we can use to identify the species.

Extremely closely-related to the dragonflies are the damselflies. These much more insubstantial creatures have a much weaker flight and fold their wings over their backs at rest. Their low wing loading makes them much less agile, and their flight among waterside or floating vegetation is comparatively ponderous.

In conservation terms, dragonflies and damselflies pose an interesting dilemma. Generally, they are faring badly, as they are very sensitive to the destruction of wetland habitats, and deterioration in water quality in those that remain. But at the same time, many species are spreading dramatically northwards, turning up in places where they were previously unknown. This gives the misleading impression, especially in northern parts, that they are doing very well. Arguably, as many as seven species can be said to have colonised North East Lincolnshire and become regular during my lifetime, and the variety of dragonflies in our area has never been greater.

Here on the Lincolnshire coast we are also in a position to receive migrant dragonflies as they make landfall after sea crossings, although we do not seem to do so well in this respect as more southern coastal areas such as Kent and East Anglia.

Among the newcomers is Britain's bulkiest dragonfly, the Emperor, which can be seen restlessly quartering the golf course pond behind Humberston Fitties. Another is the Migrant Hawker. This is another large species with a dark abdomen spotted with blue, and any big dragonfly seen in gardens well away from water in late summer, or forming swarms at this time, is likely to be this species.

One of North East Lincolnshire's damselflies is a recent colonist to Britain. The Small Red-eyed Damselfly was first recorded in Britain in 1999, on the Essex coast. Since then it has undergone an explosive spread throughout southern and eastern Britain, although this has now slowed. There was a time not long ago when the Humberston Fitties ponds were probably the most northerly site for this species in the UK, although it has now crossed the Humber and can be seen as far north as North Yorkshire.

Small Red-eyed Damselflies are to be found resting on floating aquatic vegetation out in mid-water, and so are relatively difficult to see clearly from the bankside. With their blue-tipped abdomen and tomato-red eyes they are quite distinctive, although for a firm ID they must technically be separated from their relative, the Large Red-eyed Damselfly, a longer standing resident also expanding its range.

Another damselfly only recently arrived in Britain, the Willow Emerald Damselfly, also appears to be on its way north, having already *[2017]* reached South Lincolnshire.

If you can get a good, clear photograph of any dragonfly or damselfly in our area, I can almost certainly identify it for you. With so many species expanding their ranges both in Britain and Europe, there is always the chance of a rarity.

Ragwort. The common Ragwort, *Senecio jacobaea*, provides a wonderful example of how hysteria about an everyday environmental problem can get out of hand. The fabulous golden corymbs of Ragwort flowers are essential to the tapestry of a summer's day and buzz with life, attracting well over a hundred species of pollinating insect including many beautiful, rare and beneficial species. Thirty species of herbivore feed on nothing but Ragwort, and a third of these are scarce or rare. To lose Ragwort would be a catastrophe for wildlife.

The problem is, Ragwort is poisonous to horses. Horses tend to ignore the living plants, eating round them unless desperately short of alternative food. When baled as hay and eaten dry however, Ragwort is more palatable but remains just as poisonous, and can cause liver damage. As a consequence, horse owners don't like Ragwort and understandably so, but this dislike has spread to become an eradication mindset among councils and landowners generally, often furnished by astonishing levels of misinformation which can come right from the top.

To correct a few myths: Ragwort is a native plant, which is not increasing in the UK. It is no more poisonous than many other wild flowers; indeed 3% of the world's flora contains the same poisonous ingredient as Ragwort. It must be both digested and metabolised to cause poisoning, and it poses no threat to people or dogs because they do not eat it. Horses will not eat living Ragwort unless there is little else – this can be clearly seen in some heavily-grazed horsefields where flowering ragwort is the only standing plant. A horse would need to eat between 5% and 25% of its bodyweight in Ragwort to be poisoned; although one sick horse is one too many, poisoning is probably rare.

It is important to state that there is no legal obligation for anybody to pull up Ragwort – indeed, it is illegal to uproot any wild plant without the landowner's permission. It is simply not necessary to remove Ragwort unless it is likely to be baled for hay, or it is the only food available to confined animals. In all other situations the effects of Ragwort on wildlife and landscape are overwhelmingly positive.

Ironically, most of the traditional ways of removing Ragwort tend to result in failure. Pulling it up from the roots leaves a ring of root fragments in the soil, each of which grows into a new rosette, so potentially increasing the population several-fold. Mowing Ragwort while in flower, although visually satisfying, prolongs the life of the plants because it sets their life-cycle back a stage. Herbicides work, but kill all the other flowers in the field.

Because Ragwort is a biennial, the thing that kills it is *setting seed*. The seeds usually fall within a few metres of the parent plant, and need to land on bare soil to germinate. If a field is not overgrazed, so that the vegetation forms a closed cover – that is to say there are no hoofprints or gaps in which a Ragwort seed can find its way to the soil surface, the life-cycle should be broken after seeding and Ragwort should die out naturally.

Or, preferably, you could just leave it alone, crouch down by the flowers on a sunny day and take in the extravaganza of otherworldliness created by abundant insect life, and enjoy a brilliant yellow splash of sunshine.

Thunderflies. In Britain, the tiny, black, soft-bodied insects of the order Thysanoptera rarely exceed 2mm in length, and almost nobody looks at them closely. This may seem an obscure subject to tackle, but in fact we know these little creatures extremely well.

On the hottest, stillest, most humid days of late summer – the sorts of days that feel like they could easily end in thunder – a telltale itching will let you know that Thunderflies are swarming. For a day or so they seem to get absolutely everywhere. By the beach, ice creams are full of the little elongated black creatures. They may get in your eyes. They seem to be able to squeeze through impossibly small gaps, and can often ruin laptop screens and set off smoke detectors. A speciality is getting behind the glass of picture frames, where they die and sit there for ever more, as a distant reminder of summer.

Properly, these insects are known as Thrips. 'Thrips' is both the plural and the singular, so a single insect is known as a 'Thrips' (there is no such word as 'Thrip'). As insects go, they have many unusual characteristics. Insects generally can be divided into those undergoing complete metamorphosis, with a middle resting stage (pupa or chrysalis), and those like bugs and grasshoppers where growth is straightforward and the immature stages are just like small versions of the adults. Thrips are clearly one of the latter, but their life stages include a pre-pupal and pupal stage which cannot feed, and can move to only a limited extent. The winged adults are quite good fliers despite their wings being very narrow and with few or no cross-veins. Wide fringes of hairs on the wings increase their useful area considerably, and because of the small size of the insect, still help with flight.

The mouthparts are also highly unusual in that they are strongly asymmetric – the right mandible is lost during development, with only the left one developing fully. This left mandible is used as a piercing and scraping tool, with most species feeding on vegetable matter, although some eat fungi, and a few are predators.

In the UK we have a surprising 150 or so species of Thrips. A few of these are a problem to farmers and gardeners, and a few occur only indoors or in glasshouses. The Thrips you are most likely to notice when you see the insects themselves are those with stripy wings. These are a small family, the Banded Thrips, which are especially associated with flowering crops such as Oilseed Rape and Linseed, but which may occur anywhere. Second-stage nymphs of Banded Thrips are at least partly predatory.

Other species of Thrips are often quite host-specific. They may be found on flowers – Dandelions usually seem to contain a few. While many live on wild plants, almost every crop type has its problematic Thrips species. The usual visual damage occurs as mottling, blotchiness, discolouration or window-like patches on petals or leaves, although more serious damage such as non-development of flowers or seeds occurs in severe infestations. You may recognise the silvery marks on pods of peas and broad beans – the work of Pea Thrips, *Kakothrips pisivorus.*

The familiar Thunderfly is *Limothrips cerealium.* The adult females overwinter away from their breeding habitat, often under the bark of trees. They become active around the end of May, migrating to their foodplants of grasses and cereal crops, where they lay their eggs. The young develop within the folds of the developing flowerheads or leaf-sheaths. When the insects reach adulthood, mating takes place, and the short-lived males die.

The females use still, warm weather as a cue for huge migrating swarms, usually around harvest time, when they seek out winter quarters. This is when they become a nuisance and enter houses.

In no time at all the little creatures seem to disappear again, except those which have succumbed inside picture frames. These are doing no harm, and can be removed with a simple puff of air, making sure to seal the picture better next time.

Japanese Knotweed. Here in Cleethorpes we have a weed which has been called by the Environment Agency "indisputably the UK's most aggressive, destructive and invasive plant". To find it on your property is a big problem, and if you see it spreading towards your property from someone else's, you need to have a word with them quite quick. When it occurs in gardens it has made properties unmortgageable. It is the dreaded Japanese Knotweed.

The reason this plant is so reviled is that it both grows and spreads extremely quickly, making mincemeat of concrete and compromising the structure of buildings. It is extremely difficult to kill – the roots go very deep and it can regenerate from the tiniest scrap of vegetative material, which is how it spreads.

As a consequence, both the plant and the soil containing its roots are classified as controlled waste and must be removed and disposed of by a licensed waste control operator. If disposed of by burying, it must go many metres down, which is not practical for most people. Simply ripping it up and binning it could land you with a huge fine or even imprisonment. The astronomical expense of eradicating Japanese Knotweed from sites such as Wembley Stadium and the 2012 Olympic Village made the news at the time, the latter costing some £70 million.

Japanese Knotweed is native to Japan, northern China, Korea and Taiwan, where it is an early coloniser of volcanic lava. In this country, this habitat is mimicked by waste ground, demolition sites, neglected gardens, railway land, allotments, cemeteries, and road- and riversides. The reason it rampages unchecked in the UK is because we do not have any of its many herbivores or pathogens which keep it under control in its original home.

Japanese Knotweed was first introduced here in the nineteenth century as an exotic ornamental, and could still be found for sale in nurseries up into the 1960s. It can grow to well over the height of a person in a single season, dying back in the winter to leave bamboo-like dead stems. If these dead stems are removed in winter you might not even know the plant was there. In the spring it re-emerges, at first as small, red, asparagus-like spearlets, flourishing over several weeks into plants two or more metres high, the initial wine-red colour becoming red spotting on the stems. The leaves are large, and a distinctive heart- or spade-shape. The numerous creamy-white flowers in September are attractive to bees.

All Japanese Knotweed plants in the UK, and indeed in Europe, North America, Australia and New Zealand where it has also been introduced, are female. Although the flowers have anthers, they produce no pollen. Not only that, but all these plants are thought likely to belong to the same single clone, which means that together they may possibly constitute the largest female organism on Earth.

Worryingly, in this country, male parents for Japanese Knotweed *are* available, in the form of the male plants of two other closely-related alien species, Giant Knotweed and Russian Vine, with which Japanese Knotweed can hybridise. Any Japanese Knotweed appearing to have viable seeds must therefore be a hybrid – those with Giant Knotweed are commoner, as hybrids arising from a union between Japanese Knotweed and the more widespread Russian Vine are usually too weak to negotiate their first winter after germinating.

Japanese Knotweed at Cleethorpes

It is not illegal to have Japanese Knotweed growing on your land, but it is illegal to cause it to spread. As soon as your Japanese Knotweed encroaches on someone else's land, they can legally force you to deal with the problem. Complete removal has to be undertaken by a specialist and is very expensive, but it may turn out to be money well spent. Small infestations may be tackled over several years by weakening the plant with assiduous, repeated herbicide treatment. Some people will put the area down to grass and mow it gradually into oblivion, although the cuttings, of course, mustn't move from the spot.

Currently, research is ongoing into the introduction of Japanese Knotweed's natural enemies from its homeland. The problem, as you would imagine, is finding a creature that eats nothing but the target plant. A sap-sucking bug has been tried, but as of 2015, results are disappointing, and attention seems to be turning to other avenues, possibly a leaf-spot fungus. A solution seems nowhere close.

Japanese Knotweed occurs here and there in Cleethorpes, with some pockets no doubt lying undiscovered. It has recently been removed from the sea wall at the Fitties, but there is still a large patch between Pleasure Island and the sea. If you have it on, or near, your property, please try to solve the problem without falling out with your neighbours.

Returning Waders. It's August, and after a quiet summer our beach at Cleethorpes is again filling up with large numbers of wading birds returning from their breeding grounds to the north.

Here in North East Lincolnshire, estuary birds are the pick of our wildlife – our jewel in the crown. August through into the early autumn is the most rewarding time to catch up with our beach's waders. Firstly, conditions are congenial and good for viewing. Secondly, we have some nice high morning tides which concentrate the waders into places we can see them.

Also importantly, the returning birds are mostly in fine summer plumage, or various stages of moult. This makes them both more colourful and more varied. In the late summer, juveniles can often be distinguished from adults, and sometimes the sexes of adults can be told apart too. All of this makes looking at these birds a thoroughly enjoyable and educational experience at this time of year.

Waders start to return in late July, and from that time onwards there is a procession of waves of birds of different species, sub-populations, sexes and ages. The order which the different types of bird arrive depends on many things. The distance they have travelled, and where they have come from are important, but so is the breeding strategy of the particular species.

Birds are not like mammals. Because mammals must suckle their young, parental responsibility nearly always falls on the female. While only a female bird can lay eggs, once she has completed her clutch there is no reason why either parent shouldn't take the brunt of the responsibility for incubation and raising the growing chicks. Waders have a fascinating variety of breeding strategies, but unlike mammals, as a rule it is usually the male which does most of the parenting.

Some of our waders breed in the high Arctic, where the period of summer plenty is very short. For these species, there are advantages to leaving the breeding grounds as soon as possible. In most of Cleethorpes's common wader species, both parents look after the growing chicks until they are able to fend for themselves, then the young are abandoned. Since the males take on most of the parental responsibility, it is generally the females which leave the scene first. This behavior is particularly well-illustrated in the Knot, our most numerous wader, in which the female leaves very soon after the eggs are hatched, leaving the male to do the remaining parenting alone.

One of our high Arctic waders, the Sanderling, can do something called 'double clutching'. This is where the female lays the first clutch of eggs and leaves it entirely to the male to look after, then immediately lays another clutch which she looks after herself. This way, she can double her reproductive output with little penalty in terms of time, but food has to be very plentiful to make it work.

All of this means that there tends to be a specific order in which birds from any given species arrive back on the Humber and other wintering grounds. First to arrive, often in July, are adults of both sexes which have failed to breed. These will often be in stunning summer plumage, and are exemplified by the handsome black-bellied Grey Plovers, which start to appear on our beach at the height of summer.

Next to arrive are adults which have bred successfully, starting with the females, which tend to evacuate the breeding areas first. Males follow slightly

Bar-tailed Godwit, Dunlin and Knot gather on Cleethorpes beach

Grey Plovers in summer plumage. Photo: Colin Smale www.fotolincs.com

later, although there is much overlap. Lastly, often in late August or September, are waves of juvenile birds, usually with quite distinctive plumages, which have migrated last without their parents.

As always, the problem for us humans is getting close enough to these birds to see them properly, and the birds on the beach remains one of our area's most under-appreciated natural spectacles. If you have binoculars or a telescope, in August look for adult Knot and Bar-tailed Godwit in their stunning deep red summer plumage, and Grey Plovers with their black faces and underparts. Other species to look for are Dunlin, Redshank, Curlew, Turnstone, and the ever-present Oystercatchers. Sanderling and Ringed Plovers can be seen on drier sand. Also look for non-waders such as Shelduck, Little Egrets, Cormorants, terns and gulls, including the Great Black-backed – the largest gull in the world.

Our Ailing Horse Chestnuts. England's conker trees are in a terrible state of health. These days Horse Chestnuts can be expected to turn brown and shed their leaves from as early as mid-July, spoiling North East Lincolnshire's leafier suburban and parkland landscapes during summer. Anyone driving down Humberston Avenue at the moment could be forgiven for thinking that autumn had come extremely early.

Horse Chestnut was introduced to Britain in the sixteenth century, but didn't start to be widely-planted until the early 1800s, quickly becoming one of the country's commonest and best-loved ornamental trees. In 1985 a small and destructive moth, the Horse Chestnut Leaf-miner, was described new to science as an infestation charged across Europe from east to west. The first sighting of this moth in Britain was in 2002 in Wimbledon, south-west London, and since then the moth has become ubiquitous throughout England wherever Horse Chestnuts occur.

The caterpillar of the Horse Chestnut Leaf-miner burrows between the upper and lower surfaces of the Horse Chestnut leaf, causing characteristic translucent blotches with brown centres. These blotches eventually coalesce and cause the leaf to die and fall. Although infestations are vast and unsightly, the trees always come back into leaf again the following spring.

Ironically for such a destructive pest, this little insect is very beautiful when seen under a microscope, being an exquisite iridescent bronze colour, banded with smart black and white pinstripes. If you want to see one, put an infected leaf in a sealed container for a week or two and adult moths are sure to emerge.

But often that is not all that emerges from infected leaves; you may also see tiny wasps, some metallic bright green. These are parasites on the Horse Chestnut Leaf-miner caterpillars. The adult wasp lays an egg inside the caterpillar, and the emerging grub goes on to eat the caterpillar alive from the inside. Occasionally more than one wasp species will emerge, as parasites are themselves parasitised by other wasps still smaller, known as hyperparasites. Sometimes different species of parasite compete for food within the same caterpillar host, and emerge together. Several species can sometimes emerge from a single leaf.

Parasitism by wasps seems to have little impact on the next year's infestation of moths, so the problem of prematurely-browning Horse Chestnuts would seem to be with us to stay. The life cycle of the moth *could* be broken, if every last fallen Horse Chestnut leaf was gathered up and destroyed during winter. This would, however, require superhuman effort, and co-ordination on a grand scale.

Samphire. Among the many little-appreciated riches of our coastline here in Cleethorpes is a flowering plant of real character. If not actually nameable, it will be immediately recognised by almost everyone, as the last and toughest piece of greenery to be found out on the flats before you reach actual seawater. It is a pioneer of the barest, slimiest and most wave-splashed mud, intolerant of competition, and looking like a small, upright bunch of green, beaded pipe-cleaners, or a miniature cactus, like those from the westerns. It is, the Marsh Samphire (pronounced 'samfer'), also sometimes known as Glasswort.

Samphire is edible, and a bit of a delicacy in the posher restaurants, where its maritime origins set it apart from ordinary vegetables. It is often used as a garnish for fish, with which it goes extremely well. It is rich in iodine, and packed with phytochemicals which may protect the heart and cellular DNA. Charles and Diana famously included wild Samphire, fresh from the Sandringham estate, in their wedding breakfast in 1981. It is expensive, which makes the fact that our own Cleethorpes Samphire goes almost completely unharvested, slightly strange.

As kids we would occasionally pickle it, but most authorities suggest quickly boiling it or steaming it, and then coating with it butter or oil. The range of potential recipes is huge, and scope for experimentation endless. If you prefer, it can simply be eaten raw. Once picked, it should be kept dry, or it will soon wilt.

Above each 'joint', small, insignificant flowers occur in groups of three, set into, and flush with, the fleshy stem. The stem itself actually consists of fused pairs of leaves tightly gripping a hidden central spine. When eaten, the convention is to hold the plant by the base and pull the flesh away from the spine through the teeth.

Samphire's fleshiness is one of the keys to its ability to survive regular inundation in salt water. The plant contains a high concentration of salts to resist the osmotic pressure from surrounding sea. Salts may accumulate in the flesh close to the tips of the plants' branches, and if internal concentrations become excessive, the last segment or two may be shed. This high salt concentration led at one time to the plant being used in the production of glass and soap, hence 'Glasswort'.

For the botanist, identifying the different kinds of Samphire is very difficult indeed, and there is no real consensus on what constitutes a 'good' species. Indeed, rather than species, 'sorts' is perhaps the best word to use. In fact, two of these sorts are quite distinctive, although I have seen neither (so far) at Cleethorpes. These are the Perennial Glasswort – as its name suggests, the only perennial of the group, which spreads by a mat of underground rhizomes and always contains some sterile (flowerless) shoots. The second is One-flowered Glasswort, which, also as its name suggests, does not have its flowers in the usual groups of three, but borne singly.

All the rest, indeed all of ours here, are superficially similar, at least until the early autumn when they change to a rich variety of colours from yellow, through orange, to deep red and purple. Although these autumn riches make identification scarcely any easier, Samphires may still be separated into two basic camps – the *Salicornia europaea* group, with a distinctly 'beaded' outline, and the *Salicornia procumbens* group, whose stems are more cylindrical. Beyond that, regional variations make taxonomy almost impossible, and we just have to appreciate them in a more generic way.

The location of stands of Samphire on our beach will change from year to year, as the positions of suitable marine sediments shift. Although Samphire is very common, we probably don't have enough here for it to be gathered commercially. This wouldn't be desirable in any case, as the multiple wildlife designations of the estuary create a presumption against its removal, and besides, the uprooting of any plant is illegal without the permission of the landowner.

Despite this, it is illogical and counter-productive to deny the public the occasional taste of wild-picked food, and in many ways, it defeats the point of conservation to do so. But the environment in which Samphire grows is filthy and slippery, and prone to being cut off by the tide, and picking it is back-breaking. So both determination and care are required.

If you really want to collect Samphire from our beach, please only take enough for personal use, and snip the tops with scissors, leaving the root in the ground to regenerate. Although the sea is a lot cleaner than it used to be, I would also give the plants a really good scrub.

Samphire

Eye-spots and Other Confusion. Have you ever looked at the butterflies in your garden and wondered why there is such an astonishing variety, colour and complexity of their patterned wings? How can such extravagance be explained? How have they evolved?

Even the plainest butterflies have no trouble finding and identifying their own kind, so it is not that. 'Sexual selection', where extravagant colours can be used to advertise an individual's general fitness and therefore its suitability as a mate, is a possibility, although this does not explain the precise nature of the patterns.

Other reasons for distinctive colouration are more concerned with the need to avoid being preyed upon. Camouflage is an obvious form of predator avoidance by colour, and indeed many butterflies are beautifully camouflaged, especially on their undersides. As most butterflies sit with their wings folded above their backs, such camouflage can afford excellent protection at rest. But when many species open their wings they are extremely bright and conspicuous, and such patterning is obviously not meant to be cryptic.

Many insects are distasteful or poisonous, and have evolved to protect themselves from attack with so-called warning colouration, often yellow and black stripes, but sometimes also incorporating red (think of hornets and bees). It is advantageous for both predator and prey that the same well-recognised colour scheme is universally understood, and indeed for more harmless and palatable species to copy it. Mimicry of warning colouration would also be of use to butterflies.

But even this still does not account for the sheer variety of patterns we see. The answer probably lies in understanding that butterflies' predators, primarily birds, do not perceive shapes and colours as we do. Birds have only their instinct and a little learning to guide them, and rather than rationalising what they see as 'a butterfly' as we would do, they are more tuned in to certain individual cues and illusions which they associate with danger.

Firstly and most obviously, these signals include 'eye-spots', which are commonly seen on butterflies' wings. Some eye-spots are particularly lifelike, complete with white 'catchlights'. Eye-spots can both give the illusion that the butterfly is a much larger creature than it is, and also deflect any pecks (which are often directed at eyes), away from the butterfly's body. Butterflies can often be seen with telltale peck marks on their eye-spots.

So now we must explain why butterflies have not evolved to look more *exactly* like any specific threat. The answer is believed to be that illogical signals may be even more effective at disconcerting a predator than straightforward mimicry. By both startling and confusing a predator simultaneously, a butterfly can give itself the extra second or two it needs to escape.

The common Peacock butterfly is camouflaged at rest. On opening its wings, two large eyes are revealed, and spreading them further reveals another two, making four – a confusing illusion. Both Peacock and the Small Tortoiseshell sport the black and yellow stripes of warning colouration along the leading edges of their wings, with the Small Tortoiseshell also including the fake white tail-tip of an imaginary bumblebee. The Peacock's eye-spot lies next to a tooth in the wing, which, alongside the eye, could create an illusion of the head of a bird. Indeed, each eye-spot need not represent an eye at all, but, with some imagination, the head of a large insect, perhaps a bee, complete with tiny white eyes and giant mandibles. The blue, segmented borders to the Small Tortoiseshell's wings are thought to mimic the caterpillar of the common Lackey Moth, one of the world's ten most toxic caterpillars. Butterflies with short 'tails' on their hindwings such as hairstreaks and swallowtails very often have small eye-spots next to the tails, to give the overall impression of a bird with an open bill – an aggressive posture.

Spot the warning signals– Peacock and Small Tortoiseshell Butterflies

With these patterns, the more you look the more you see. There are undoubtedly many more such illusions waiting to be revealed, and perhaps some we will never comprehend.

Hornets. Over the years I have frequently received reports of Hornets in the north-east part of Lincolnshire. While Hornets do occur here, as often as not the reported creature has turned out to be nothing more than a rather large queen wasp.

Misidentifications became somewhat more likely during the 1990s, when an invasive species newly arrived in the UK, the Median Wasp, colonised our area. On arrival, this species immediately became Britain's second largest wasp, queens being larger than anything previously seen over most of Lincolnshire.

Hornets, however, are bigger still. Once a real Hornet is seen, you can be in no doubt as to its identity, based on size alone. Other technical details which immediately identify a Hornet include extensive chestnut brown colouration on its foreparts, and an absence of yellow markings on the thorax. Unlike other wasps, the familiar stripes are dark, but not completely black.

Hornets have always been familiar insects in the south of England, where they inhabit woodlands and larger gardens, especially those containing mature trees. Familiarity has led to southerners largely losing their fear of Hornets, despite their huge size. When face to face with a Hornet, the same rules apply as to any wasp – don't make sudden movements (like striking out in fear), or interfere with a nest. Hornets prefer to avoid confrontation unless directly threatened.

Wasps of all kinds are carnivorous, and use their stings to subdue and kill their prey. It is not unusual to see Hornets attack victims as large as the biggest dragonflies. Unlike the stings of honeybees, those of wasps are not intended primarily for use against large vertebrates (like us), so a Hornet's sting, although more painful than that of a honeybee, is less potent in terms of both content and volume of poison. A Hornet's sting is probably no more dangerous than the sting of an ordinary wasp, and only those unlucky people likely to suffer an extreme allergic reaction need really worry.

In North East Lincolnshire, Hornet sightings are sufficiently infrequent that they cause great excitement, or panic, depending on your viewpoint. Genuine records in recent years have come from Bradley/Dixon Wood, Irby Dales, Waltham, Tetney Blow Wells and Scartho. In 2014 Mick Binnion photographed a Hornets' nest in Bradley Woods, and on May 31st this year,

Chronicle reader Colin Julier found one trapped in his shed in Healing. In North East Lincolnshire we are right at the northern edge of the species' range, but Hornets are undoubtedly becoming commoner here. This could be because of tree planting schemes, and also probably as a result of global warming.

Because of the Hornet's large size and sting, there is good reason for other, more harmless insects to have evolved to look like Hornets for protection. Two similar moths, for example, the Hornet Moth and Lunar Hornet Moth are large (but rather poor) Hornet mimics, and completely harmless.

Britain's largest hoverfly, *Volucella zonaria,* is another Hornet mimic, currently spreading northwards because of global warming. I have seen it several times now in our area, one of which was at Peaks Covert last month. Its larvae live within the nests of real wasps and Hornets, and no doubt the mimicry helps the female fly to enter the nest. Its large eyes and single pair of wings should always give it away as a fly.

Two large sawflies deserve a mention. Despite their name, sawflies are not true flies, but more closely related to the Hornets themselves. They are told from other bees and wasps by the absence of a narrow 'waist'. The first, the Giant Wood Wasp is even larger than a Hornet, but lighter and slighter in build. The ovipositor, or egg-laying organ of the female may look like a giant sting, but the insect is completely harmless to humans.

Perhaps the very best Hornet mimic is the very rare Large Alder Sawfly, which is turning up much more frequently in Britain these days. Because of its rarity, it is arguably more interesting than the Hornet itself. It can be separated by its thick 'waist' and clubbed antennae.

Wader Spectacular. For the next month or so you can see one of the greatest sights in the whole of natural history here at Cleethorpes, albeit slightly distantly, as numbers of wading birds on the estuary reach an impressive peak.

At the end of the short Arctic summer, large numbers of waders evacuate their remote northern breeding grounds and migrate southwards, congregating on the estuaries of western Europe, including the Humber. While many will stay here for the winter, others are merely stopping off on their way further south or west. Birds from Canada, Greenland, northern Scandinavia and Arctic Russia mingle with British birds at this time, with most still sporting their smart breeding plumage.

At low tide the birds distribute themselves widely over the extensive mudflats of the estuary where they can find their invertebrate food. They cannot stay on the flats all the time however, and must find somewhere to 'sit out' the high tide safe from predators. Such places are called 'roosts'. The offshore sandbank due east of Cleethorpes Leisure Centre is one of the largest wader roosts on the whole of the Humber, and on the highest tides tens of thousands of birds may gather here.

At first sight there may seem to be nothing happening out on the sandbank when birds are roosting, but sooner or later something will cause the birds to take flight. This may be the appearance of a predator, or may merely be natural movements as birds are pushed into the air by a rising or falling tide. On the best tides, with a bit of patience we can witness the phenomenal spectacle of thousands of birds twisting and turning in the air together. The flocks will often seem to change colour from dark to light and back, as birds turn one way and the other.

The most spectacular movements occur when a flock is trying to avoid an aerial predator. Anyone witnessing this must surely ask themselves: 'how do the birds co-ordinate their movements with such speed?'

Research has shown that each bird is actually trying to stick within the flock for protection, while also keeping an optimum distance from its neighbours so as not to collide. Each bird is only paying attention to a handful of birds

A flock of Knot at high tide at Humberston

around it, copying their movements. In this way, changes of direction spread through the flock like a very fast 'wave'.

There is no really high water for the rest of August, but you might want to try the 9th to the 13th September when some really big early morning tides should cause a great aerial display. The best views will probably be had somewhere between the meridian line and the pumping station, or distantly from Cleethorpes Leisure Centre.

Greenfly. If you've ever parked your car under a Sycamore or Lime tree on a hot summer's day, you will know that you can sometimes return to find it covered in a sticky substance, devilishly hard to remove, which has obviously dripped from the tree above. Indeed the very leaves of the trees themselves may appear shiny with the same substance.

Naturalists of the past also knew this sugary liquid, noting that it often contained aphids, and concluded that they must be eating it. In fact, the opposite is true – the aphids are producing the sticky honeydew.

Aphids are prolific breeders, and at the height of the season a middle-sized Sycamore tree may hold up to 2 million aphids. Aphids feed by inserting their sucking mouthparts into the plant's foliage to locate the phloem, or sugar-conducting tissue. When they have done so, they need to do no more, as the sugary solution forces itself under pressure up the feeding tube and into the aphid's body. The problem is that although the solution is rich in sugars, it is low in protein, and the aphid must take very much more liquid on board than it needs, in order to get enough. The excess sugar is excreted through the back end, falling as globules of sticky honeydew.

When it coats leaves, excess honeydew may be taken by a variety of other creatures as a substitute for nectar. Wasps, flies, butterflies and moths can all sometimes be seen imbibing honeydew from the surfaces of leaves. This may be the reason that hairstreak butterflies can exist exclusively in the treetops where flowers don't occur.

The production of honeydew is the basis of the celebrated relationship between aphids and ants, whereby the ants 'farm' the aphids for their sweet honeydew, in return for offering the aphids some protection against predators. Among the many creatures from which aphids need to be protected are lacewing and hoverfly larvae, and both the larval and adult stages of ladybirds. Aphids numbers may also be reduced by a host of tiny parasitic braconid and chalcid wasps.

Honey made by bees which have fed on honeydew rather than pollen and nectar is rich, very strong, and particularly high in antioxidants and complex sugars. We don't get much 'honeydew honey' in Britain, but it is a speciality of the Black Forest of Germany, and is now also produced in New Zealand. The absence of pollen for food means that these bees must be fed a protein supplement.

It is a good job that so many common predators eat aphids, as the speed at which they breed would soon cause problems. The key to their fecundity is an ability to breed without sex, with females producing clones of themselves by live birth – sometimes several times per day. What's more, the newborns already have the embryos of their own offspring inside them like Russian dolls, so generation times are very short, and a single individual can become thousands very quickly.

Some mid-season generations of aphids may be produced with wings, especially if the health of the foodplant is starting to suffer. These winged forms are responsible for dispersal – carrying the infestation from one plant to the next. With some aphid species, the type of host plant may change in predictable ways through the season. As the autumn approaches another strategy arises -probably brought on by shortening day-length or falling temperature – with both males and females starting to be produced. After these mate, the females will lay eggs, which will overwinter on the host plant, ready to start next year's explosion of clones.

If the weather remains clement, sometimes aphids may simply continue breeding through the winter. At Barton I have known insect-eating warblers which should have migrated to Africa subsisting on Giant Willow Aphids, which were showing no sign of a winter shutdown.

We probably know aphids best as garden greenfly, particularly those which infest the flower buds and young green shoots of roses. In fact there are hundreds of species, including blackfly on beans, the small green Cabbage Aphid, the white Woolly Aphid of apple trees, and many others, including some serious agricultural pests. For garden infestations, the use of insecticides is not recommended for obvious environmental reasons. Heavy rain will simply wash greenfly off foliage, but can't be relied upon for control. A regular artificial hose down however, could keep numbers below a critical threshold. An additional way is to encourage their predators, by maintaining a bit of judicious neglect in the garden's wilder corners, by providing overwintering habitat such as wood piles or insect hotels, and by creating plenty of flowers in succession throughout the season.

Species-richness. Places with high 'species-richness' – those that are teeming with a variety of life – are assumed to be more valuable in conservation terms than others. Diverse sites are more likely to be in ecological balance; they are both loved by people, and good at safeguarding our wildlife for the future. Species-rich sites are more likely to contain rarities.

But actually, any attempt to count the total number of species in a place is doomed to failure. Even within a simple, highly visible group like butterflies or birds, the number of species counted is partly a function of the time spent looking, with new species still being added after many years. Most groups are so obscure that very few people have the skills to identify them. And to that we must add the huge variety of protists, diatoms and other microbes which can be found anywhere (but whose species composition certainly differ from place to place), which are studied by almost nobody. The total number of species recorded is so dependent on the amount of effort put in, especially the availability of experts, that the result is almost meaningless.

In fact, counting every species in a single place has almost never been tried. The best attempt is probably the work of Jenny Owen, who spent three decades trying to identify every living thing in her ordinary Leicester garden. She had to enlist the help of countless specialists over the years, and eventually came to a total of 2,673 species, a number which is almost certainly a considerable underestimate.

This would make her garden among the best places for wildlife in Britain, and as valuable as rainforest. But of course there is nothing special about her garden; the total is just a function of the time put into recording.

The way around this is to realise that diversity isn't everything, and that all species are not equal. Some of our most valuable habitats – saltmarshes, heaths and bogs, for example – are quite species-poor, but the species they do contain cannot live anywhere else, and are dependent upon that habitat's continued good condition. Almost any sort of damage inflicted upon habitats like these will result in diversity going *up* (as common species move in), but value going down.

Luckily, we have a priority system for species and habitats. Some of this is set out in our domestic legislation, some laid down by the EU, and some by international consensus. If a site contains species or habitats which are judged to be valuable or at risk, it automatically qualifies for special treatment under the planning system. Also, the presence of such species helps conservationists to know which sites to protect.

*

On 8th August just gone, a fine Pectoral Sandpiper dropped into the lagoons at the Humber Mouth Yacht Club, found by James Smith. This is a rarity, and a fascinating one. It breeds across most of the Arctic, but not in Europe. Odd birds arriving in Britain are suspected to have been brought across the Atlantic accidentally by the jet stream, having possibly first travelled to North America from Siberia via Alaska, on their way (had they not gone wrong) to South America. But nobody can be sure whether some of our east coast birds don't actually come the other way, originating directly from the east. This is an enigma yet to be resolved.

This bird was particularly special for me, as it became the 200th species of bird I have seen within a 2 mile radius of my house. This is a very high total, which was only made possible by my house's position close to good coastal habitat. Given the small travelling distances and therefore low fuel use, I am claiming this as a 'green' birding achievement!

But actually the number means relatively little – it is simply a result of many years of accumulated recording effort. It's greatest purpose was to get me out of the house, scrutinising and learning to understand the ecology of my local area, and in this it succeeded. I found out a huge amount about my own patch, finding many rarities from other groups as I went along, and enjoyed it all immensely.

The message from my '2 mile 200', and the work of Jenny Owen in her Leicester garden, is that you don't have to go very far at all to discover an unbelievable wealth of wildlife. The secret is simply to look, look harder, then look harder for longer.

Mosquitoes. More urban lifestyles, cleaner living conditions and better drainage of the land have made the dreaded mosquito less of a problem for us than in the past. Cold, run-down houses, animal shelters and outside toilets, which once provided mosquitoes with perfect resting and hibernating places, are now much less important parts of our daily lives. In addition, the mosquitoes themselves, like all insects, are much less abundant than they were in the recent past. To illustrate this, just think what a car number plate used to look like after a long summer journey forty years ago, and look at one after the same journey now.

But we may still occasionally suffer that most irritating experience of hearing a 'mozzie' in the dark when we're trying to go to sleep, then not being able to find it when the light is turned on. Similarly, anybody standing outside in a natural habitat at dusk on a warm, still summer's evening, especially near water, would be in no doubt that there are still plenty around. In fact, the UK has about 33 species of mosquito.

In other parts of the world, mosquitoes are much more of a problem, carrying many serious diseases – malaria, yellow fever, dengue fever, West Nile virus, Zika virus and more. In Britain we suffer none of these, but we did have malaria here up until the late 1900s, although in a fairly mild form. Known as the 'ague' it was commonest in the marshier parts of southern and eastern Britain, such as the Fens of East Anglia, the Thames estuary and parts of the south coast. In the Fens, people would grow Opium Poppies in their gardens so that relief was readily to hand. Quinine was another anti-malarial drug, which could be taken, happily for some, in the form of a gin and tonic. Despite some limited re-occurrences among soldiers returning from the two world wars convalescing by the sea, the disease is now long gone.

In Britain, mosquitoes are really no more than an irritation, although their bites can cause quite serious swelling, and itch horribly. A mosquito attack is not really a 'bite' in any real sense, their mouthparts being more realistically likened to an extremely fine hypodermic needle.

The insertion of the mouthparts actually does no harm at all – it is the mosquito's habit of regurgitating waste into the wound before it flies off which does the damage, and in other parts of the world, spreads the diseases.

It is only the female mosquito which takes a blood meal, which it requires to mature its eggs. It generally homes in on its target by following the trail of carbon dioxide from its breath. Male mosquitoes use their mouthparts solely for taking nectar from flowers, and are completely harmless. Males can be told from females by their extravagantly plumed antennae.

In Britain, mosquitoes fall into two groups. The five or six species in the genus *Anopheles* are those which sit with their bodies at a steep, head-down angle, tail, and sometimes back legs, in the air. These are the species which would be capable of transmitting malaria, if we still had it here. All the other species rest with their bodies parallel to the surface on which they are sitting. Although not malaria-carriers, several of these are still a nuisance.

Mosquitoes lay their eggs in still, or very slow-flowing water. Some species do so in clean, natural habitats, and some are exclusively coastal. Others may use any old bit of standing water, from rot holes in trees to water butts, blocked drains, animal troughs and bird baths; even water which has collected in buckets, old tyres and the like. The air-breathing larvae can often be seen 'hanging' down from the water surface, swimming off with jerky movements when disturbed.

It is by no means a foregone conclusion that we will never have mosquito-borne diseases in Britain again, with malaria probably the prime candidate for a return. More international travel, and global warming allowing more warmth-loving species to colonise Britain, will probably be the process by which this occurs. The species of mosquito which causes much of the trouble in the tropics can sometimes arrive here on planes, so while we would never want to get rid of standing water altogether, we should perhaps dispense with unnecessary puddles in the immediate vicinity of airports. Mosquitoes which can transmit malaria are already here – it is the disease which is not, but that could change.

When not biting people, mosquitoes are a valuable source of food for Swallows, martins, Swifts and bats, and their larvae are prey for many aquatic predators. Mosquitoes are a group about which there is still much to learn, even in the UK, and with a bit of effort, there is still room for the layperson to uncover information important for humanity.

Siskins. Cleethorpes Chronicle reader Chris Johnson recently sent me a picture of a handsome Siskin, which appeared with two others on his garden feeders in early August *[2014]*. In fact, this unusual sighting marks an anniversary – it is exactly fifty years since the species was first recorded at an artificial food source in a British garden, in Surrey.

In Britain Siskins are strongly associated with the north and west where they breed in extensive conifer plantations in upland areas. They are much less common as breeders in the south and east, with the coniferous woodlands of the Breckland of East Anglia and the New Forest providing noteworthy outliers. In recent decades Siskin populations have strongly increased in the UK, partly, it is thought, as a result of a wealth of maturing conifer plantations, and partly because of Siskins' new-found tendency to visit garden feeders.

As well as occurring in Britain, Siskins are extremely common as breeding birds across Scandinavia, the Baltic states and Russia. The seeds of trees on which they feed are a notoriously unreliable resource, and outside the breeding season local movements or larger migrations are necessary to find food or escape the cold. After breeding, Siskins from both Britain and further afield spread out from their summering grounds, distributing themselves thinly but widely across Europe; they may sometimes occur as far south as the Mediterranean or the Middle East. Troupes of incoming Siskins on the Lincolnshire coast during easterlies in October and November are a regular and evocative sign of autumn. Their thin, monosyllabic calls as they fly overhead may not attract the attention of the casual by-stander but are distinctive once learned. In North East Lincolnshire, small flocks may occasionally stick around for the winter where there are Alder or Birch trees. A very small number will visit gardens for an easy meal, especially in lean times towards the end of the winter. Birds appearing here in late summer are among the earliest evacuees from their breeding grounds and are certainly of British origin.

It would be possible to pass over a Siskin as the much commoner garden Greenfinch – they share the same basic green colouration and distinctive yellow sides to the base of the tail. Siskins, however, are usually specklier, and also have much darker wings sporting distinctive transverse pale yellow or white wing-bars. The smart black cap of Chris's bird indicates a male.

Wasps. We are entering that quarter of the year when our advanced, social wasps – that is to say, the common old black and yellow 'jaspers' which seem to terrify us so much – finally find themselves with a bit of leisure time. Worker wasps, having spent the summer busily constructing and maintaining the nest and provisioning the colony's larvae with mashed insect food, now find themselves at maximum abundance and with their colonies winding down. They are able to spend the retirement of their lives pottering, and seeking out sweet foods such as those abundantly provided by ourselves.

Picnics, beer gardens, orchards and anywhere where refuse is disposed of will be magnets for wasps from now on, all of which bring them uncomfortably close to humans.

Wasp stings are painful, and for an unlucky few, dangerous. Needless to say, panicking and flapping wildly at wasps is not the best way to avoid being stung. A wasp won't go out of its way to sting you unless you interfere with a nest, but a wasp batted around by someone with their eyes closed may be tempted to try to defend itself. Keep your eyes on where a wasp goes (so you don't sit on it), and stay calm.

Wasps' nests are amazing structures. They are built of a kind of wafer-like papier-mache, created by scraping wood from trees, buildings or fenceposts and mixing it with saliva. The structure starts off like a kind of umbrella suspended by a stalk from above, inside which are downward-facing cells in which the larvae are reared. When a layer is complete, a series of narrow struts are constructed which hold the next, lower umbrella, in place. Eventually there may be between about six and ten tiers, forming an overall ball-like structure, all enclosed within an outer covering. The entrance is always at the bottom.

Any particularly large wasps seen now will not be workers, but new queens and the males with which they must mate. These are raised towards the end of a colony's life, in special large brood cells. You may still see wasps on warm days right up until early winter, but eventually the cold will kill off all but the new queens, which must find somewhere to hibernate.

Most people would be hard-pressed to tell one species of common old wasp from another, with the exception of the Hornet, which is a very much larger creature, still rather uncommon here. In fact we could possibly find as many as eight of the normal-sized species in North East Lincolnshire, two of which – the Saxon Wasp and the not-so-small Median Wasp – are relatively new arrivals in Britain.

Most wasps' nests are located not in people's roofs, but in holes and burrows in the ground, attached to woody vegetation somewhere deep and sheltered, or in tree holes or other natural cavities. A single species, the Cuckoo Wasp, is a brood parasite of another, the Red Wasp. The Cuckoo Wasp makes no nest and has no need for workers – only queens and males occur.

Only four or five of our social wasp species would ever build nests in the roof spaces of houses or other buildings. Of these species, two are very much commoner than the others, the Common Wasp and the German Wasp. In fact, both of these species would rather nest in holes in the ground than in our roofs, with the tunnel leading to that of the Common Wasp generally very much longer than that of the German Wasp. Both will excavate earth below their subterranean nests to make space for falling waste, including dead wasps, from their nests. The need to accommodate waste is the burden of all colony dwelling animals, ourselves included.

The German Wasp tends to collect well-weathered wood fibres to make the pulp for its nest – so its nest is a definite grey colour. The Common Wasp's nest, which may also be larger (exceptionally a metre across), is yellower or browner. An average mature colony of Common Wasps may have about 7,500 small, and 2,300 large, cells, from which about 10,000 workers, 1,000 queens and 1,000 males may be produced.

This level of production can make wasps extremely abundant in late summer and autumn. Wishing them gone or small-scale extermination attempts are probably a waste of time. The number of queens starting new colonies each spring is probably always about the same, although wasps of all species, like insects generally, are declining.

Some flowers are particularly good at attracting wasps in the autumn, and foremost among these must be Ivy. I know of at least three places locally where very fine clumps of mature Ivy and their supporting trees have been completely removed from streetside locations, I suspect because they attracted literally thousands of wasps in autumn. Along with the Ivy flowers went all the other beautiful and useful nectar-feeding insects for which the species is so valuable. Indeed, even the reviled 'jasper' may remove thousands, if not millions, of greenfly and other pest insects from gardens in the course of raising its colony's young.

September

'**Sea grass**'. As we know, Natural England have now agreed to let us remove the sea grass from the beach north of the Leisure Centre. This has taken much of the heat out of the subject as far as Cleethorpes locals are concerned, although there are signs that it is beginning to spread back again. It may be time, therefore, to have an objective and considered look at this unpopular plant and get to know it a little better.

The first thing to say is that 'sea grass' is not its real name. Its proper English name is Common Cord-grass, or scientifically, *Spartina anglica*. You will hear most naturalists and botanists simply referring to it as 'Spartina'. In fact, it is not the only villain in this story, as racing towards the holiday beach alongside it is another 'pioneer' species, the succulent, edible Samphire.

While we usually talk about a species having been around for thousands or millions of years, Spartina is unusual in that its origins are extremely recent, the species being less than two hundred years old. Its origins have become a classic and much-cited example of 'evolution in action'.

At first there was just a single species of Spartina in the UK, the Small Cord-grass *Spartina maritima*. This is a less robust species than our own plant, and not very common, although it occurs as far north as the mudflats of south Lincolnshire. In 1816 or just a little earlier, a second, American species, Smooth Cord-grass, was accidentally introduced to Southampton Water in the ballast water of ships. The two species hybridised, creating a new, sterile cross, which spread vegetatively along the south coast for a while, but then went into decline.

At some point, one of these hybrids underwent a spontaneous doubling of its chromosome number – something which happens occasionally in the plant world, and which has given rise to many successful new species. The result was a fertile, invasive new grass, unique to England, which is the Common Cord-grass we see abundantly today.

Although perfectly able to spread on its own, this new grass was also widely transplanted, both around the UK and indeed the world. The purpose was usually to firm up and stabilise coastal mud, sometimes with a view to the reclamation of the land. A little Spartina was originally introduced to the area around Buck Beck outfall, and the supply was considerably bolstered by seed from similar introductions on the Humber's north shore.

Spartina cannot get a foothold where wave action is too rough. At the other extreme, if left undisturbed long enough, eventually Spartina may raise the level of the mud on which it grows to the extent that it develops into different vegetation types, or even toxifies the mud. Our own Spartina is already becoming outcompeted by another finer-leaved grass, Common Saltmarsh Grass, over large parts of the marsh.

The benefits of Spartina to estuary animals are mostly a result of the increased shelter it creates, and dead organic matter it contributes to the adjacent mud. Just a glance at the saltmarsh off Cleethorpes will reveal that some birds such as Shelduck, Little Egret and Redshank prefer this environment to open sand, with the marsh also full of 'little brown' seed-eating passerines such as Skylarks, Meadow Pipits and Linnets in autumn and winter. The saltmarsh mud is also packed with invertebrate life, comprising a slightly different assemblage to that of the adjacent open mud. Saltmarsh creeks are a valuable nursery area for many species of sea fish.

Saltmarsh can also protect the low-lying parts of our town from flooding by dissipating wave energy before the sea wall is reached.

Common Cord-grass (Spartina anglica) at Cleethorpes

Saltmarsh is a declining habitat, and we are obliged by international agreement to protect it, indeed to increase the area of this vegetation type in the UK. This is why we get such a hard time when we ask to remove it.

The future northward spread of the saltmarsh at Cleethorpes is dependent upon the sheltering effect of the large 'whaleback' dune which sits to its seaward side. If this dune continues to lengthen northwards over time, the shelter it confers will also allow Spartina to extend its range northwards along the beach. The situation at the moment seems broadly stable, although maritime sediments are notoriously dynamic, and we await developments with interest.

Here in Cleethorpes, nobody would begrudge us keeping our short stretch of beach clear for tourism, and I believe the decision to keep it as golden sand is right. But we must guard against the kind of thinking that prioritises the economy over nature every single time. In the end, the economy cannot function without the services provided by a healthy environment, and there is a point at which the constant nibbling at the natural world has to stop.

Grasshoppers and Bush Crickets. Unless you count buzzing, the insects are not a very noisy group of animals. Some moths and beetles can apparently squeak, although I have never heard it; nor have I ever heard the tapping of Death Watch Beetle, now very uncommon in the timbers of houses.

A notable exception to this rule is provided by the grasshoppers and crickets. Although the soundscape they create in the UK is subdued compared with that in the Mediterranean or tropics, still nothing evokes the essence of a hot, rank grassy wayside or sunny summer meadow like the chirping of these insects.

Grasshoppers and the closely-related bush crickets are particularly characteristic of the second half of the summer, which is when they become fully adult. It is the males which 'sing', for the same reasons as do male birds – to attract females and ward off other males. Grasshoppers may be extremely abundant in coarse, undisturbed grassland, with numerous insects leaping away from every footfall in the right habitat at this time of year.

Grasshoppers are herbivores, and bush crickets omnivorous. They do not have a full metamorphosis, and they are often green or brown, although striking pink forms of some grasshoppers do occur. They are food for many other animals, and are relatively easy to catch. Conveniently, the sounds they produce make them identifiable without even being seen.

A grasshopper can be told from a bush cricket by its short antennae. The antennae of bush crickets are characteristically long and slender, often very much longer than the body of the animal itself. Grasshoppers sing, or 'stridulate', by rubbing a kind of comb on their back legs along a ridge on the wings, while bush crickets sing by rubbing their wings together.

The sounds made by grasshoppers and bush crickets span a wide range of frequencies, often within, but also well beyond, the range of human hearing. The three common species of grasshopper in our area, the Field, Meadow, and Lesser Marsh Grasshoppers, all make easily audible sounds. A fourth species not so widespread here but which could occur, the Common Green Grasshopper, has a more constant and relentless song, also heard easily with the 'naked ear'.

Bush crickets are the insects which the Americans call 'katydids'. They tend, as a general rule, to produce louder and higher-pitched sounds than grasshoppers. All bush crickets are warmth-loving, and as a consequence the south of England has a more cacophonous summer soundscape than the north. Only one species of bush cricket, the Short-winged Conehead, has so far colonised North East Lincolnshire, but several species are moving northwards with global warming, and now occur not very far away at all. These species would seem poised to add themselves to our local summer soundscape in the not too distant future, and we should listen out for them.

The Short-winged Conehead stridulates at a frequency towards the high end of human hearing, but with the help of a bat detector the racket it produces, comprising alternate 'chuffing' and 'whirring' sounds, can be all too clearly heard. A walk along the grassy sea wall at the Humberston Fitties, among other places, should reveal a singing male every few feet, although they can be amazingly hard to see.

Its close relative, the Long-winged Conehead, with a similar but more uniform and unchanging song, is now half way up Lincolnshire on its northward march, and could well be with us soon. The Dark Bush Cricket makes a hard, easily-audible 'chip' sound from dense vegetation right through the autumn, while the Speckled Bush Cricket has a similar short sound, but much weaker, challenging the ability of the human ear. Both species occur not far away and are spreading.

One of the most likely bush crickets to colonise our area next is the large and handsome Roesel's Bush Cricket, which makes a loud, continuous high-pitched sound like crackling, or buzzing, electricity wires. This sound can even be heard from a moving car if the windows are open. Lastly, the Oak Bush Cricket does not stridulate at all, but 'drums' with a hind leg on a leaf. This is the species most likely to be attracted indoors at night by household lights.

Scented Plants. Botany is the field of natural history where the sense of smell really comes into its own. Many flowers, of course, are perfumed – these aromas are generally pleasant to people and insects alike, and designed to attract pollinators. However, the volatile chemicals produced by the leaves or other parts of the plant are much more varied and interesting, and can of course be sampled when the plant is not in flower.

Plants have evolved these chemicals mostly to deter herbivores – even smells and tastes which are pleasant to us may be intolerable to insects or grazing mammals. Many plants with scented or flavoured foliage are non-natives, utilised as culinary or garden herbs – lavender, rosemary, rocket, parsley, coriander, sweet basil and lemon balm are all examples. Many more are used in various drugs and medicines.

In the wild, 'volatiles' given off when a plant is crushed can sometimes be useful in identification. Various similar-looking 'umbellifers' can be told apart by the smell of their leaves, as can mints and other 'labiates'. Hedge Woundwort and Black Horehound for example, which look superficially like mint, smell extremely unpleasant, making misidentification impossible. Elder, Wild Celery and Wall Rocket are three more of North East Lincolnshire's wild plants whose smell distinguishes them immediately from similar relatives.

Plants smells can be evocative of certain habitats, for example the double hit of Wild Thyme and Salad Burnet (which smells of cucumber) when walking over close-grazed chalk turf. When the drier dunes at Cleethorpes are mown at the back end of the year the strong smell of Wild Onion accompanies the smell of coumarin (the chemical in grasses which makes the scent of new mown hay), as millions of stems of this mostly cryptic plant are simultaneously sliced through.

Three of North East Lincolnshire's scented plants deserve a special mention. Firstly Ramsons, whose intense garlic scent is hugely evocative of damp, dappled ancient woodlands in spring. The oval leaves and starry white flowers can form extensive carpets in these special places. Locally try Dixon Wood or Town's Holt; April and May are best – the leaves are gone by June.

Secondly, Sea Wormwood – a rare plant of sea walls, docks and drier saltmarshes, whose foliage has an intensely sweet smell similar to absinthe, although it is not this, but a close relative, also growing locally, which is the actual source of absinthe oil. Sea Wormwood provides us with one of Britain's most extraordinary wild smells – the plant can be recognised visually by its finely-dissected, whitish-green sprays growing low to the ground. Very small quantities grow at Humberston and Grimsby docks; please don't take too much!

My own personal favourite is nothing more exotic than the ubiquitous wayside Hogweed. It is not the flowers or the foliage which produce the smell, but the seeds. On close inspection these rounded, flat discs, held aloft throughout the late summer and autumn, contain reddish scent glands, looking like drawn-out teardrops. Pick a few, orientate them in the same alignment, and break across the line of the red glands for a special scent that has been described as 'an old barn full of apples'. This aroma is a wonderful secret, and a fitting reminder of the end of summer.

Sparrowhawks. If you watch any patch of sky in our area for long enough, a Sparrowhawk is bound to cross your line of vision. Its general small size, short neck and long tail, and flight pattern of a few, rather deep wingbeats followed by a soaring glide on horizontal wings, should identify a Sparrowhawk at pretty much any distance. A female can be a quarter as big again as a male, and twice as heavy. When the two sexes are seen together the size difference may seem very marked, although the same identification criteria apply.

Unusually, both sexes may engage in breeding display flights, choosing mainly warm days from early spring onwards. Horizontal flight with deep, slow, deliberate wingbeats may turn into a shallow dive, followed by an upward swoop with closed wings, the bird seemingly carried vertically by its momentum alone. Breeding may occur anywhere where there are trees – any decent-sized woodland will have them, as well as being common in wooded farmland and the leafy suburbs of cities and towns.

In fact, soaring in an open sky is only one situation in which you are likely to see a Sparrowhawk. This is an aerial hunter, almost exclusively of other birds, which it chases down in low level, dashing forays, often along linear features. In this way, it takes prey items by surprise as they break from cover. On many a drive down an enclosed country lane you may be accompanied by a Sparrowhawk methodically skimming the base of a hedge close to the ground, sometimes keeping perfectly ahead of your car for many hundreds of yards. On other occasions you may be aware of a sudden commotion and flash of feathers as one of these low, speculative flights passes through your garden, sending the bird table regulars scrabbling for cover. The final stages of a successful pursuit may be almost recklessly acrobatic.

The familiar sad-looking pile of feathers you occasionally find on your back lawn is the work of a Sparrowhawk. Occasionally, the hawk will still be there, standing on top of its kill, casually plucking away. This is the third situation you are likely to see this bird, and the one which will usually afford the best view. While the female can be identified by its essentially brown tone with a finely barred breast, the small male is a glorious combination of reddish front and glossy, slaty-blue back. Both have piercing yellow eyes.

Don't mistake a Sparrowhawk for any of the small falcons, of which Kestrel is easily the commonest here. Only a Sparrowhawk will come right into your garden – a Kestrel's longer, narrower wings are not designed for manoeuvrability, and the bird will not enter confined spaces anything like as readily. Conversely, a Sparrowhawk will never be seen hovering stationary in the air over grassland, as a Kestrel does.

Because of their choice of prey – i.e. garden and game birds – Sparrowhawks often find themselves rather unpopular. This is in stark contrast to other common birds of prey – Kestrels, owls and the like – which tend to seek out small mammals. It seems we are not as ready to leap to the defence of mice and voles as we are Song Thrushes and pheasant chicks. Although you will often hear people say that Sparrowhawks are responsible for local declines in small bird populations, the evidence consistently fails to back this up – several favoured prey species have increased as Sparrowhawks have also increased.

A natural experiment by which this could be tested has occurred in the last 60 years. In the late 1950s and 1960s, the use of organochlorine pesticides on cereal crops all but wiped out the Sparrowhawk from large swathes of England, and at this time it became functionally extinct in Lincolnshire. Poor breeding success caused by thinning of the birds' eggshells was a problem, and some of the more toxic products would kill adults outright.

Consequently, when I was a child, we never had Sparrowhawks here in Lincolnshire. However, successive restrictions on the use of organochlorines from 1962 onwards led to a progressive recovery of numbers, and Sparrowhawks started to reappear regularly in our area in the 1980s. Recovery thereafter was fairly rapid, and nowadays they are back to, or exceeding, former numbers.

We wouldn't want to be without these engaging predators again, so the loss of the occasional garden bird would seem to be the price we have to pay. We must console ourselves that niches made vacant by Sparrowhawk predation are quickly re-filled.

Silver Y and Other Insect Travellers. When one thinks of animal migration, one immediately thinks of birds – Swallows, Swifts, warblers or waders maybe, or Cuckoos – or perhaps in other countries, mammals such as Wildebeest, Caribou or the great whales. In fact, the insect world also contains many long-distance migrants, including some of North East Lincolnshire's commonest garden creatures.

Migration is a risky business, and for animals which move from place to place the benefits must outweigh the risks. With insects, as with birds, migration is always a way of taking advantage of abundant unoccupied territory occurring in a place where the creature could not survive the whole year round. At our latitude, summer is usually the time for insect invasions, because it is inability to cope with frost which is nearly always the problem.

Not so common but very noticeable are some of our large migrant Hawkmoths, such as the enormous Convolvulus Hawkmoth, which a lucky few will see hovering at *Nicotiana* or other tubular flowers in their gardens at dusk. It occasionally occurs here in Cleethorpes.

When southerly winds predominate in spring and summer, the migrant Painted Lady butterfly can become the commonest species at garden Buddleia, with some years' invasions very much bigger than others. In open spaces sometimes these butterflies can be seen powering strongly northwards just above the ground, in the process of migration.

The abundant little hoverfly known as the Marmalade Fly, with its distinctive yellow body with paired black bands, is another species which can invade in enormous numbers. Occasionally, stories arise of holidaymakers fleeing south and east coast beaches under 'attack' from swarms of these entirely harmless, flower-visiting creatures.

Two more moths deserve a mention. In June 2016, reports came in of 'biblical' numbers of the tiny Diamond-backed Moth invading the country, set, it was said, to devastate crops of brassicas when they got down to breeding. Indeed even here in Lincolnshire, these moths caught in headlights could seem like driving through rain, and our own Cleethorpes 'bioblitz' event in June recorded many thousands at their moth trapping sessions.

Lastly, a moth so common that I can guarantee that it has occurred in your garden or at your lighted window every single summer. This is the common Silver Y moth, a classic migrant insect. The Silver Y is one of the great family of noctuid moths – fat-bodied and slim-winged – with more than 400 species in the UK. Most are some combination of grey or brown, often with rustic, or camouflaged patterning. The Silver Y, although basically brown, is surprisingly beautiful on close inspection, with a forewing pattern like glossy inlaid wood, and a striking metallic golden 'y' on its forewing. In hovering flight, its two-tone brown hindwings help to identify it.

Silver Ys invade Britain each year in immense numbers, with precise abundance varying between years. Moths on migration are picked up in large numbers on oil platforms out at sea, and have been known die in such numbers as to make 'slicks' on the water. On making landfall they may be abundant on coastal flowers such as Sea Lavender. On some warm summer nights, going out in the garden with a torch may reveal dozens or even hundreds of these moths feeding hummingbird-style at garden flowers such as lavender and Buddleia.

Recent research has shown that these moths' migrations are much more sophisticated than was ever believed. Not only will moths wait for the wind to go round to the right direction before setting off, but they will then move to the height at which the wind is most helpful, allowing them to travel at speeds in excess of those of migrating birds, and covering up to 400km a night. When the wind changes, they will come to earth and wait for it to change back.

It was believed for many years that northwards migration of insects was a speculative, one-way journey, and such insects were eventually just killed off by the frost. It has now been shown that Painted Lady butterflies will make the return journey in the autumn, and this indeed may be the rule with other migrant insects too. Silver Y moths have also been shown to migrate southwards in autumn – in some years it is thought that 200-240 million Silver Ys will enter the UK, breed here, and then up to a billion of their offspring will return to Africa in the autumn. The mechanisms by which they achieve this feat of navigation are largely unknown, made even more amazing by the fact that the returning moths are not the same ones which made the outward journey.

You may remember the Euro football final between France and Portugal in 2016 was plagued by many thousands of moths. These were Silver Ys, many very possibly on their way to Britain.

Black Stork. Although rare birds can turn up literally anywhere, most are found along Britain's coastlines. Unsurprisingly, the west coast of Britain and Ireland is the place to see rarities from America, while the east coast tends to receive rare birds from Scandinavia, northern Europe and Siberia. Birds overshooting from the south tend to be more evenly distributed across the country.

The Lincolnshire coast is therefore a great place to see rare birds, and outings here in spring and autumn are considerably spiced up by the possibility of the unexpected, much more so than in most landlocked places.

Coasts facing the open sea are more likely to receive tired migrants than those in the shelter of estuaries, and the position of Cleethorpes within the Humber Mouth is a slight problem for us, although we still get our fair share of unusual species during the migration seasons.

Spurn Point, just across the water, is one of the very best places on mainland Britain for seeing rare birds. A look at its position on the map immediately reveals why this is so – not only is it the first landfall for many birds crossing the North Sea, but birds traveling southwards along the east coast are progressively funneled along the Spurn peninsula until they are concentrated in an extremely tiny area, where rarity-hunters are ready and waiting to see them.

Early September is only the beginning of the autumn migration season, but already Spurn has racked up an astonishing list of rarities this late summer and autumn *[2015]*. One of the massive frustrations for Lincolnshire's birders is that once birds have left Spurn and headed southwards, they seem to fan out over a huge area and simply disappear.

So rarity-hunting in Lincolnshire is a harder work than it is just across the water at Spurn. The smooth curve of the Lincolnshire coast provides abundant, under-watched habitat with few obvious bottlenecks in which migrant birds can become concentrated, except perhaps for Gibraltar Point. It should be no surprise then that this is one of the Lincolnshire coast's prime spots for migrant birds, but even here the coast of Norfolk is clearly visible across the water, and many birds will simply cut straight across the 'corner'. Indeed it is thought that some birds make the jump straight from Yorkshire to Norfolk, and miss out Lincolnshire altogether.

Very large soaring birds such as eagles and storks, which don't much like travelling over water, provide something of an exception. Such birds are not only easy to see, but can probably be trusted to cling fairly closely to the coast. This means they are less likely to 'go missing', wherever they roam.

The very rare Black Stork is such a bird, and this year (2015) has seen an exceptional influx into the UK, with some people even suggesting an unprecedented six different birds in the country together. Dark, huge-winged and prehistoric-looking, Black Storks are both very distinctive, and difficult birds to miss.

On 3 August, Black Storks were seen at Spurn, Alkborough, and by a lucky observer at the Humber Mouth Yacht Club, Tetney. The next day, 4ᵗʰ August, what was probably the Tetney bird made a flypast along the coast of Lincolnshire, where many locals were waiting to catch up with it. One was also seen at Read's Island, up the Humber, the same day. The next day, one was at Gibraltar Point, where it stayed until 8ᵗʰ August.

The bird at Spurn wore a distinctive numbered ring, fitted as a nestling, indicating that it was a first-year bird originating from a forest in the Ardennes. It stayed put until 10ᵗʰ August, but the next day had crossed the river into Lincolnshire, and was seen by numerous observers in the north-eastern part of the county, close to the coast. What were possibly different birds were reported on the same day from Gibraltar Point and Europarc, Grimsby.

Finally, when we thought the excitement was over, a Black Stork was seen by Dave Bradbeer over private allotments in Cleethorpes on 1ˢᵗ September, eventually flying over Sidney Park and away to the north. Was this our last chance to see this large and majestic rarity?

Indeed it was – for that year at least.

Hummingbird Hawkmoth. At least once every summer someone tells me they have seen what they think is a hummingbird in their garden. Hummingbirds are of course an exclusively New World family of birds, and what people are actually seeing is the charismatic Hummingbird Hawkmoth. 2014 has been a good year for these special insects, with many sightings from North East Lincolnshire.

The Hummingbird Hawkmoth does indeed look and behave like a hummingbird. With a wingspan of slightly more than two inches it can be seen darting from flower to flower on sunny days, hovering and probing flowers for nectar with its long, uncoiled proboscis. The greyish-brown wings move so fast that they appear as a blur, and make an audible humming or throbbing sound. The moth has a stout, white-spotted body and distinctive orange underwings, which identify it immediately. It is strongly attracted to flowers with long corolla tubes holding plenty of nectar, such as Honeysuckle,

Buddleia, Escallonia, Phlox, Lavender, Petunia, Nicotiana, Red Valerian and Fuchsia, or in the wild, Viper's Bugloss. They have the remarkable ability to never visit the same flower twice, although the cues needed to make this behavior possible are still unknown.

Hummingbird Hawkmoths are recorded in Britain every year, but in wildly fluctuating numbers. They are very common residents across southern Europe and central Asia, and migrate northwards during the warmer summer months, breeding as they go. The caterpillar is up to 6cm long and can be either green or brown, always with white and yellow stripes and a prominent and colourful horn at the rear end. The caterpillars can be found fairly regularly in the UK, feeding on various bedstraws or madder. Locally-bred moths are probably the reason for the late-summer peak in sightings.

There is still time to see Hummingbird Hawkmoths this year before the onset of bad weather, when the adult moths will die off or undergo a limited reverse migration. Hummingbird Hawkmoths have great difficulty surviving our winters, which means that the continued presence of this moth in Britain is dependent upon annual recolonisation from the south. Occasionally an adult will try to hibernate in Britain, and if they find a warm enough spot they may survive for a while, and sometimes one may be disturbed from its resting place in winter.

Over-tidiness in the countryside is the enemy of the Hummingbird Hawkmoth. as well as much other wildlife. The phenomenal numbers seen in the summer of 1946 were said to be a result of the relaxation of cutting of waysides and meadows during World War II. The last really 'big' year for these moths in Britain was 2003.

Hummingbird Hawkmoth. Photo: J-E Nystrom CC BY-SA 2.5 Wikimedia Commons

Spiders' Webs. Spider silk is an amazing substance, exhibiting a unique combination of strength and stretchiness. Spiders have multiple uses for the silk they produce – they may use it to make their egg sacs, or wrap up, and immobilise a struggling prey item. Sometimes large numbers of spiders – new hatchlings or adults of the smaller species – will take to the air *en masse* when conditions are right, 'ballooning' in the wind, each on single strands of their own silk – an effective method of dispersal. Although the odd one will travel hundreds of miles in this way, the vast majority come to earth close by, leading to massed sheets of gossamer covering grassland or draped from shrubs. This phenomenon is made particularly visible by the dew of an autumn morning.

The best-known use for spider silk is, of course, to produce webs to catch their prey. Not all spiders make the well-known 'orb' webs, with some species' constructions more resembling sheets or tunnels. A spider may be coaxed out of a tunnel web by touching the outer rim with a vibrating tuning fork, which the spider will mistake for a struggling insect.

The large, traditional orb webs which adorn your garden in autumn are most often made by the common Garden, or Cross Spider. Autumn is when these spiders reach maturity, and dewy mornings make their webs much more visible.

This fairly large spider (the females are much larger than the males, especially when laden with eggs) can be readily identified by the white marks forming a cross on the abdomen. You may also see a closely-related species – the Four-spotted Orb-weaver – which can be larger still; indeed a gravid female may be the heaviest of all British spiders. It is very variable in colour, but four white spots should be clearly visible on the abdomen, especially on browner individuals.

When one sees a particularly impressive Garden Spider web glistening on an autumn morning, one can only wonder at how this feat of engineering has been achieved by such a small animal working from instinct alone. In fact, the early stages of web construction may be fairly haphazard – a kind of trial and error.

The spider always starts by spanning the gap between two supports with a single 'bridging' thread. It may achieve this by attaching the thread, dropping down and walking round from one support to another, spinning silk as it goes, and later tightening up the line. But if there is a breeze, the spider is more likely to stand on one support and let the wind carry a line of silk until it becomes entangled on the other side, and then walk across it to fix it securely in place.

Subsequent threads may be randomly created then destroyed again, with the spider sometimes taking long rests. But certain rules are broadly followed, and eventually a 'proto hub' – a central point with a few radiating threads – emerges, with the spider generally starting in the middle, and reaching the surrounding supporting structures by either walking, dropping down or swinging, Tarzan-style.

With the proto-hub in place, the stages of web-building are now much more predictable, and mostly carried out without rests. The radii proper and the threads which form the frame (including an all-important supporting one across the top), are next, and the position of the central hub may be subtly changed at this time. Many of the original radii are replaced.

When all the radii are in place, a loose spiral is first created outwards from the centre, followed shortly afterwards by the familiar, closely-spaced, sticky 'capture spiral', created tirelessly and with amazing dexterity, with each whorl kept equidistant from its neighbour. When the spider is finished, it sits motionless in the centre and waits for its prey to stumble or buzz in.

Amazingly, spiders may rebuild their webs every night, recycling the old web by eating it. If they build again in the same place, the anchor and frame threads may be retained, but the radii and capture spiral are always created afresh.

Plant Galls. I have noted in this column before that many of our tinier species gain our attention not by their actual presence, but by the disfigurements they leave on their host plants. First among these must be the gall-formers. Indeed, one may need never to see the actual creatures to build up a respectable species list during a walk anywhere well-vegetated in summer or autumn.

It is a neat trick – the tiny organisms involved attack specific plant cells to irritate or stimulate them into cancer-like growths, inside which they, or their larvae, feed happily away, protected from predators and surrounded by abundant food. The resulting growths are very varied but consistent within a type, and may be anything from very cryptic to very colourful and obvious. Although only a few types of gall are familiar to us, there are in fact over 1000 gall-forming organism in Britain. Because almost all are specific in terms of their host plant, a bit of cross-discipline natural history is required in their study, which is technically known as 'cecidology'. A gall is defined not as a species in itself, but as a relationship between the attacker and its plant host.

In fact, a gall may contain more than just the original instigator. Some species called 'inquilines' may lay eggs in plant galls, their larvae living inside the gall without harming the rightful occupant except by competition for food. Others – parasitoids – will also lay eggs in the gall, but the larvae will actively seek out and prey on the hosts or inquilines. Parasitoids may in turn have hyperparasitoids. So one must not assume that an insect emerging from a gall is the one that caused it. In a gall such as a good-sized oak-apple, a whole mini-community of species may be living inside.

Galls may be originally induced by viruses, bacteria, nematode worms and eelworms, but most are created by fungi, mites or insects.

Most of the fungal gall-formers are smuts or rusts. The latter, with up to five different spore-producing stages, have some of the most complex life-cycles of any organism. Also formed by a fungus is ergot – that elongated black gall seen so often protruding from the flowerheads of grasses. Ergot is very poisonous, and has been responsible for a great many human deaths when inadvertently ground up and eaten in cereal products, and not without a fair bit of hallucinogenic delirium along the way.

Gall mites have elongated bodies unlike more familiar mites, and four legs at the front end. They produce very miscellaneous galls, including many 'felt galls' and 'leaf rolls'.

Among the insects, galls may be formed by bugs, flies, sawflies and gall wasps. Gall midges, as their name suggests, are a family of flies whose members often produce galls, as are the Tephritid fruit flies. Those familiar hard swellings on the stems of the abundant Creeping Thistle are galls caused by a Tephritid – a little picture-winged fly, *Urophora cardui*. Zone down to the micro scale, and you may be lucky enough to see the charming display of this little red-eyed fly, as it waves its black-and-white patterned wings, one then the other, on its thistle host.

Perhaps the most commonly-noticed gall of all is the Robin's pincushion, found on the stems of wild roses. This gall's hard central core is surrounded by a chaotic reddish mass of fibrous, branched 'hairs'. The core usually contains many chambers, each occupied by a larva of the wasp *Diplolepis rosae*. The new gall wasps emerge in the spring, just in time to re-infect developing buds. Interestingly, males of this wasp are extremely rare, and the females can produce fertile eggs without mating.

Galls may be found on a huge variety of herbaceous and woody plants, but the 'host with the most' is undoubtedly Oak, with over 50 different associated galls. Oak apples and marble galls should be known to everybody who frequents places where oaks grow. The wasp which forms oak-apples, *Biorhiza pallida*, has two generations, a sexual one and a non-sexual one. Each 'apple' contains a number of larvae which complete their metamorphosis within the gall, the sexual adults chewing their way out in summer. Each oak apple produces either exclusively male or exclusively female wasps. After mating, the females crawl down to the ground, and lay their eggs among the tiny rootlets of the oak. The resulting larvae form small, spherical galls, inside which they stay for about 18 months. At the end of the second winter, an army of asexual, wingless females emerges and climbs the tree, oblivious to the cold, and lays eggs on the new buds, occasionally in sub-zero temperatures, and the cycle starts again. The insect's two year life cycle means that two completely independent, 'even-year' and 'odd-year' populations may co-exist on the same tree.

The creator of marble galls is another wasp with alternating generations – *Andricus kollari,* with the asexual generation laying its eggs on a completely different tree – the non-native Turkey Oak – on which much less conspicuous galls are formed. This wasp itself is not native to Britain, having been introduced in the early 19th century, the gall being valued as a source of tannin for dyeing and ink-making. The hard 'marble' with its characteristic exit hole may persist on an oak twig for years, and is particularly noticeable in winter.

Several species of Oak gall wasps have been extending their European ranges westwards recently, and some and have colonised Britain. This is thought not to be a result of global warming, but increased personal travel and movement of produce, facilitating transport of these tiny insects. One such is *Andricus quercuscalicis*, which causes the distinctive, knobbly 'knopper gall' on acorns. This species caused alarm when it arrived in the 1960s, but half a century later there remain plenty of unaffected acorns to perpetuate the species. Look for a heavily infested tree along the passage down the side of Humberston C of E School.

Cecidology is one of those satisfying kinds of natural history which traverses the taxonomic disciplines, in which there is an unending source of interest extremely close to home, and in which anybody can make valuable discoveries. Even when too tired and jaded to chase birds, butterflies and the rest, there is another lifetime's work to embark upon, right there.

Birds and Berries. From midsummer onwards, long before the leaves start to turn, considerable colour is added to the waysides, hedgerows and gardens of Lincolnshire by the ripening of berries.

Berries are part of an age-old and beautifully co-evolved system involving fruit-eating birds. The plant uses some of its resources to provide its seeds with a coloured, fleshy coating attractive to birds, and in return the bird consumes the fruit and ejects the seed, still viable and ready-manured, well away from the parent – a dispersal distance which couldn't be achieved any other way.

To an extent, plants are in competition with each other for birds, and birds with each other for food. This has driven the evolution of an optimised system where plants and birds are conveniently matched, and mutually beneficial.

The classic berry-consumers are our five species of thrush. In addition, Starlings, Woodpigeons, Robins, warblers such as Blackcap, Garden Warbler and Lesser Whitethroat, and even Spotted Flycatchers will also eat berries where they are accessible and plentiful. Some birds, such as finches and tits, may remove the berry's flesh and eat the seeds within. This behavior is disadvantageous to the plant, and as a consequence some berries have evolved seeds which are very hard or even poisonous, but which are fine to be swallowed whole.

Some forty or so native British plants produce berries. Some are herbs, like Lords and Ladies, and Stinking Iris. Others are climbers like Honeysuckle and Black Bryony. But the most important species for sheer volume of berries tend to be shrubs and small trees. Most abundant in our area are the ubiquitous hedgerow Hawthorn and to a lesser extent Elder and Sloe, so often draped with their attendant scrambling, and berry-bearing, Dog Roses and Brambles. Rowan, Dogwood and Guelder Rose have become more important since their inclusion in housing estate and roadside landscaping schemes.

Many additional berry-bearing plants are grown in gardens, notably Cotoneaster and Pyracantha, although we might also mention Amelanchier, Berberis and Laurel.

Red and black are by far the commonest colours for wild berries because of their 'noticeability' to birds, although other colours occur. It is thought that some berries with a 'bloom', such as Juniper and Sloe, reflect strongly in the ultra-violet, which unlike us, birds can see. Red is a more noticeable colour than black, to birds as well as humans, and sometimes black berries are borne on red stems or pedicels, presumably to make them more visible, as in Elder and Dogwood. Blackberries, too, pass through an unripe red stage on their way to turning black, and a single species, Wayfaring Tree, may have berries of both scarlet and black in the same bunch.

Patterns of berry consumption by birds are mostly dictated by the availability of a few common species. Abundant plants with soft, watery fruit, such as Elder and Blackberry, are very much in demand, but tend to 'go over' rather quickly. Elder produces almost the perfect berry – popular with all potential fruit-eaters, and especially popular with Starlings. A flock of Starlings will quickly strip an Elder bush of its berries, always from the top down.

Hawthorn is also a very important source of food for Blackbirds and other thrushes. Apart from being small and palatable, 'haws' are both extremely abundant and tend to persist longer on the tree than more succulent berries.

During the common species' peak fruiting time, other berries tend to be ignored. Some species find their niche by having berries which ripen earlier in the summer, such as Rowan, currants and cherries. By contrast, some, such as Holly, have very long-lasting berries which remain available long after others have either been eaten or have withered on the tree. Ivy berries are the last to ripen, often after New Year and sometimes well into the following spring.

Different bird species have their preferences, although their diets show considerable overlap. Song Thrushes, for example, have a known liking for the red fruits of Yew. Small birds can't swallow large berries but can peck at the flesh. Even when berries are smaller, sometimes large birds like Mistle Thrushes will vigorously defend a profusely berry-laden tree against other birds.

Here in North East Lincolnshire we have an additional berry-bearing bush, the Sea Buckthorn. The orange berries of this beautiful coastal shrub often provide a valuable first meal for immigrant thrushes arriving in from the sea in autumn.

Daddy Longlegs. Autumn is the time to see one of the largest of Britain's flies – that ponderous, gangly creature of dewy lawns and lighted bathrooms, the Daddy Longlegs. In fact there are over 300 species of Daddy Longlegs in Britain, but our abundant autumn species is *Tipula paludosa*.

Although huge and related to mosquitoes, these clumsy, bouncing creatures do not tend to strike fear into people like that other leggy group, the spiders. Although the female has a sharp point on the tip of her abdomen, there is nothing at either end of a Daddy Longlegs which can hurt anybody – the point is simply an ovipositor, or egg-laying tube. The tip of the abdomen of the male is much more blunt-ended. As all country children know, when grabbed, the legs of a Daddy Longlegs tend to come away – a possible defence against being caught by birds.

The larvae of Daddy Longlegs are known as leatherjackets, and can be found in large numbers in grassland soils – sometimes millions per hectare. Despite being a potential pest in grassland and crops, they constitute an important food source for small mammals and many grassland birds, notably Rooks and Starlings.

These leggy flies are not to be confused (as they often are in popular articles) with the North American Daddy Longlegs – a completely unrelated group which we in the UK call harvestmen. Harvestmen also have long, very spindly legs, but are technically arachnids. They are commonly found on the ground among litter, or on trees or walls. They are not particularly closely-related to spiders and are unlike them in many ways. They are generally slower moving, and their body parts are apparently fused so there is no 'waist'. Unlike spiders, harvestmen have only two eyes; they do not make nests or spin webs, and although they prey on other small creatures, they may also eat carrion or decaying vegetable matter. Several species are very common here in North East Lincolnshire, and as their name suggests, they become particularly visible in late summer and autumn.

There is a myth in America that harvestmen (or, as they say, Daddy Longlegs) possess the most virulent venom on Earth if only they could pierce human skin. This is nonsense – in fact they have no venom at all.

There is only one other source of confusion, and this is the Daddy Longlegs Spider (*Pholcus phalangioides*). These are the familiar slow-moving, spindly spiders that make untidy webs in the corners of rooms in every house. This species has a huge world range, but has a generally southern bias in the UK. However, it is spreading northwards, probably because of a combination of global warming and an ability to colonise centrally-heated buildings. In places where the average annual temperature throughout the year drops below about 10 degrees Celsius, this species is mainly confined to cellars, where the temperature is more stable. Despite this it has still been recorded as far north as Shetland.

A Daddy Longlegs Spider disturbed in its web may suddenly start to gyrate wildly, becoming a blur. This behaviour is designed to distract and confuse predators, so that they cannot pick a moment, or a spot, to attack. Despite seeming somewhat lightweight, this spider can tackle prey much heavier than itself, using its long legs to hold prey at a distance while it wraps it in silk. Indeed, it may take the large hairy house spiders which run across carpets at this time of year, as well as mosquitoes that wander into the house. For this reason, these spiders would be very beneficial, if we could bring ourselves to leave them alone. Unfortunately there is no chance of this happening – it is joked that this spider's natural habitat is pub toilets, and that it is the most hoovered-up spider on Earth.

So why do all these unrelated creatures have such long, spindly legs? Although the reasons certainly vary from one to the other, in all cases the long legs act as, or contain, sense organs. In the 'real' Daddy Longlegs, there is probably also a balancing role during flight and egg-laying.

Leatherjackets may cause problems for farmers and gardeners. In 1935 an infestation of leatherjackets at the Lord's Cricket Ground caused bald patches on the wicket, causing, it is said, unaccustomed spin for much of the season.

Apart from this, one thing all these creatures have in common is that they are utterly harmless to humans, so please respect their short lives.

Rare Breeding Birds. Round these parts anybody daring to stick up for wildlife in the face of the onslaught of business interests tends to get labelled, derogatorily, as a 'twitcher'. Of course only a tiny proportion of the environmentally-minded public can be described as such, and in any case I have never really understood why such a thoroughly harmless pastime as twitching should attract such bile; or indeed, any bile at all.

'Twitchers' are naturalists, and share many or all of their sensibilities, values and concerns with naturalists everywhere. Indeed they tend to be among the most knowledgable of the tribe. Identification skills underpin the whole of ecology and conservation, and these can only be fully developed by seeking out the rarer species and getting to know their idiosyncrasies in the field. This involves hard work, but also moments of transcendent pleasure in thoroughly beautiful places.

Modern internet-based information systems have made it easier than ever to find out where rarities have turned up at any one time. When I was a teenager in the 1970s, all the information on where rare birds could be seen was kept in a big scruffy paper diary, by the phone, in a tiny café on the Norfolk coast called 'Nancy's'. When you rang Nancy's (usually from a rural call box), whoever was sitting by 'the book' would read you the news. By the time you had acted on the information you were often too late and the bird had flown.

That sense of frontier, adventure and sub-culture has long gone in the face of the information age. However there is one type of rarity information which is still suppressed completely – simply not spoken – and that is when rare birds make a breeding attempt. This is of course to deter the last few of those anachronistic ne'er-do-wells, egg collectors. It is understood by everybody with an interest in wildlife that the news blackout is a small price to pay for the safety of the birds.

When breeding is over, however, the news comes out, and there are often surprises. Back in the days of Nancy's, for example, there were only two species of heron breeding in Britain – now there are, arguably, eight.

The news of the 2014 season has now emerged, and apparently rare breeding attempts have occurred at either end of the county of Lincolnshire this year. Down south, a pair of Glossy Ibises, dark, iridescent wading birds from southern Europe with long downcurved bills, have built a nest at Frampton Marsh on The Wash. Although they raised no young, this was the first ever breeding attempt by this species in the UK.

Up on the Humber, fractionally over the border into East Yorkshire, a pair of Montagu's Harriers had more success, raising a single chick. This youngster was one of only twenty, from seven pairs of birds, in Britain this year. This is the rarest of all Britain's breeding birds of prey, looking somewhat like the Hen Harriers we occasionally see on the coast here in winter, but slenderer and more buoyant in flight. RSPB Humber Sites Manager Pete Short had plenty of 4am starts guarding the nest, but said "it has been worth every minute to ensure that this fantastic bird breeds successfully".

Barnacles. A glance at our beach's many wooden breakwaters, rocks on the foreshore, or the metal legs of the Pier itself, will reveal a grey crust of barnacles. It is usually barnacles which make any hard surface at the seaside so painful to walk on in bare feet.

Barnacles are roughly the same conical shape as limpets, and attach to hard surfaces in a similar way. Indeed many people would have no hesitation in describing both as kinds of shellfish. However, barnacles are not even remotely related to limpets, or indeed any mollusc. They are in fact, rather amazingly, crustaceans, which makes them more closely allied to lobsters, crabs and shrimps.

The connection between barnacles and other crustaceans only became apparent when the young stages were observed. A barnacle's eggs are carried on the underside of the shell, or 'mantle'. After hatching, the young are released into the sea as tiny, free swimming larvae. It was only by noticing the similarity between these swimming stages and those of other crustaceans that the barnacles' true ancestry was realised.

There are two larval stages, the first of which is called the 'Nauplius' – a swimming animal with three pairs of legs, a single eye and a rudimentary shell. After several moults, the next stage, the 'Cypris', is reached, which has two eyes, six pairs of swimming legs and two shells. The Cypris however is short-lived and does not feed, but instead attaches itself to a hard surface, using cement exuded from special glands. It is now that the legs which will become the feeding organs grow longer, and the hard mantle is formed around the creature. The eyes, limbs, tail, antennae and original armour are all subsequently lost, and the creature is now fixed in place by its head, lying on its back, legs in the air, within a shell.

The shell has an opening at the tip, with a moveable lid in four sections. When exposed by the retreating tide, this lid is closed, retaining the seawater environment inside that the barnacle needs to stay alive. When re-submerged, the lid opens and the creature's six pairs of curved, double legs are extruded. Their pulsating, fan-like movement sifting their food, mainly plankton, from the water column above, and transporting it down inside the mantle and towards the mouth, with its three pairs of jaws.

You may read in many places that the common and widespread barnacle of North Sea coasts is the Acorn Barnacle (*Semibalanus balanoides*). Although I have found this species here and there on our foreshore, our barnacles at Cleethorpes are overwhelmingly a different species – an alien import from Australia or New Zealand, *Elminius modestus*. This species first appeared in Britain in Chichester Harbour in 1945, probably introduced on the hulls of ships or from ballast water. It took just 38 years for the species to spread as far north as Shetland and it is now found all around the coasts of the southern North Sea. This species can tolerate a wider range of temperatures and salinity than the Common Acorn Barnacle, is faster-growing, and can produce more broods of young in a year.

Barnacles will attach to moving objects as well as rocks and breakwaters. They often foul the hulls of ships, from which they must be periodically removed. When attached to whales, their exact configuration can be used to identify individual animals for research purposes.

Mussels will eat barnacle larvae, and adult Barnacles have many predators including whelks and starfish. Whelks can grind through the barnacle's mantle, to get to the softer parts inside.

Harlequin Ladybirds. If you're old enough you may remember the ladybird plague in the hot, dry summer of 1976. This was caused by ideal conditions for breeding of their aphid prey in that warm year. I can remember walking down Weelsby Road crunching thousands of ladybirds underfoot; vegetation took on a kind of purplish look, and the flying adults were so abundant in the air that if you weren't careful they would fly into your mouth.

Exactly 30 years later, North East Lincolnshire received another ladybird invasion, this time more subtle. This was colonisation by the most invasive non-native insect ever to enter Britain, the Harlequin Ladybird.

The Harlequin Ladybird is originally an Asian species. In 1916 it was introduced to the USA to control crop pests, and although it took a while to get going, it is now North America's most widespread ladybird. It has recently entered South America.

From the early 1980s, introductions were made into Belgium, France, Germany, the Netherlands, Greece, Czech Republic, Italy, Spain, Portugal and Switzerland. It quickly became established in all of those countries except Portugal and Spain. Inevitably it spread to surrounding countries, and the first record from Britain was in 2004, in Essex. It reached North East Lincolnshire in 2006, and also Austria, Wales, Denmark and Norway in the same year. By 2007 it had reached Sweden, Scotland and Northern Ireland. It has now entered the continent of Africa. No other species has ever been known to conquer so great an area in such a short time.

In Britain, Harlequins pose a threat to our native ladybirds. They are larger, and their larvae are better defended, than our common native species. They breed quickly, and are active much later into the autumn and early winter than our own ladybirds. Even when their usual food of aphids and scale insects are abundant they will still consume many other small invertebrates including the larvae of other ladybirds. Under pressure they will even become cannibalistic. At difficult times of year they can sustain themselves on soft fruit, pollen and spores. In winter, large aggregations of hibernating adults can be a nuisance to humans in buildings.

Harlequins do have natural enemies, including several parasitoids, fungi and bacteria. However, Harlequins are thought to have 'out-spread' their enemies, and an ecological balance has not been reached over much of their new territory.

The Harlequin is now one of our commonest ladybirds here in Cleethorpes. Worryingly, studies have highlighted declines in seven out of eight common native ladybird species, corresponding with the spread of the Harlequin. But there is no point in trying to control Harlequins now – the best we can do is try to understand the dynamics of their invasion and their interactions with other species. One hopes that they may eventually reach an equilibrium with our indigenous fauna such that they can all co-exist, or that pathogens already here will adapt to this new host.

Although they are extremely variable, it shouldn't be too hard to identify a Harlequin Ladybird. They are slightly larger than the very common 7-spot Ladybird, with legs almost always brown. Although their basic ground colour can be yellow, orange, red or black, the commonest patterns are orangeish-red with 15-21 black spots, or black with two or four red spots. The thorax may have broad white sides, or may be white with spots forming an 'M'.

The UK Ladybird Survey would like to hear about *any* ladybird you see. There is a superb smartphone app (iRecord Ladybird) which includes help with identification as well as allowing you to submit a record from your phone. You can also submit records through the UK Ladybird Survey website. Only with help from the public can the plight of ladybirds be followed, studied and analysed in detail.

House Spiders. Now is the time of year when that dreaded group known as the house spiders becomes particularly visible, as they race across living room carpets and get trapped in baths and sinks. For most of the year these large spiders (the genus *Tegenaria*) are happy to keep out of the way of danger, lying in wait for their prey undisturbed in their 'funnel' webs in the corners of sheds, outhouses and log piles, or behind long-standing furniture. In August and September however, newly-mature males break away from their webs and strike out in search of females. This is when they often come indoors, and can be spotted charging about in the open.

Males can be told by the presence of enlarged 'palps', looking like boxing gloves, at the front end, although they also tend to have longer legs than females. Males do not live as long as females, seldom lasting beyond about eighteen months. After breeding, males die off and are often consumed by the females. In this way the males indirectly contribute valuable nutrients to their offspring.

Spiders in this genus were actually a rare sight in the north-eastern part of Lincolnshire until the mid 1960s, when they underwent a sudden northwards expansion, for reasons still unknown. The really big house spiders here could belong to one of two species – *Tegenaria gigantea* or *T. saeva* (like many spiders they have no English names). North East Lincolnshire lies outside the traditional core area for either species, and it is possible that most or all of our large house spiders may now be hybrids between the two, a situation now pertaining over most of the north of England. More research is needed, but strangely there seem to be few volunteers.

If these species could be tolerated in houses (which of course they never are), they would provide a valuable service, ridding the house of small insects such as clothes moths, carpet beetles, houseflies and mosquitoes. Although they look menacing and move quickly, they are completely harmless to people. If handled roughly they could give a tiny nip, but their fangs and venom are too insubstantial to adversely affect a human.

Fear of spiders is one of the very commonest phobias. It may be a hang-over from our distant evolutionary past (when venomous, ground-living spiders would certainly have been a problem), but it is much more likely to be picked up from others in childhood. For this reason it is important never to display fear of spiders in front of children. If house spiders stay still for long enough, they can be easily and harmlessly removed in the traditional way, using a glass and card. Drop them a long way from the house though, or they could come straight back in.

October

Ivy. October, and it's that time of year when one of our most important plants for wildlife is bursting forth into unseasonal flower.

Our common Ivy has a number of unique characteristics which make it an essential wildlife resource in woodlands, and along hedgerows and waysides. Firstly, it is our only evergreen climber, and so affords excellent year-round shelter for invertebrates and spiders, as well as habitat for hibernating butterflies, roosting bats and of course roosting and breeding birds. Many species of bird will nest in Ivy, especially if it is thick, including thrushes, Wrens, Robins, finches, Spotted Flycatchers and even Woodpigeons. Ivy is essential for the summer generation of the Holly Blue Butterfly, whose caterpillars feed on the unripe flower buds into the early autumn, before descending the plant to pupate.

Unusually, Ivy has two very different forms. The first is a vegetative state which although technically immature, may last indefinitely – this is the form which has the well-known three-lobed leaves. This form can thrive in deep shade, producing ground cover in woodlands, or climbing trees, fences and buildings. Eventually the leading shoots will reach the light, and when growing in sunnier conditions, the mature, reproductive form of Ivy may start to be produced. This form has dense, shiny, oval leaves, and produces the plant's flowers and fruit.

One of Ivy's most important benefits to wildlife comes from the fact that its flowers and fruits come in the 'wrong order' from most other woody plants, with flowers blooming late into the autumn, and berries being formed in late winter and persisting through the spring. In this way, Ivy fills something of a 'hungry gap' for both insects and birds.

A glance at the flowers of Ivy on a sunny day between September and November will reveal a wealth of insect life. Worker wasps are usually present, and worker bumblebees may also be seen. These insects are soon to die off, leaving just the overwintering queens, for which Ivy is an essential source of late-season fuel. Some of the hoverflies seen at Ivy will be black and yellow wasp mimics, among them no doubt *Myathropa* and *Helophilus*, which are both beautifully-marked and completely harmless. Honeybees are often present at

Ivy flowers, as are their hoverfly mimics from the genus *Eristalis*. The larvae of these mostly brown flies are the 'rat-tailed maggots' of smelly puddles and other wet, decomposing matter. Other flies at Ivy may include the black 'Noon Fly', with its distinctive orange wing bases.

The butterflies of autumn may frequently be seen at Ivy flowers – Red Admiral is the classic, but Comma, Peacock and Small Tortoiseshell may also be seen. Hibernating Brimstone butterflies are beautifully camouflaged among the mature leaves.

In the spring, Ivy berries provide food for birds just when other supplies are running short. Woodpigeon and even Blackcap may be looked for among the usual thrushes.

Some people seem to have a dislike of Ivy, believing it to harm trees. In fact it is not a parasite in any way, being rooted in the ground like any other plant, and using the tree only for support. To say it does *no* harm is probably an overstatement – a tree completely laden with Ivy is more susceptible to being blown over by the wind, and if a tree is already in poor health it may be further compromised by competition for moisture below ground, and life-giving light above it. When specimen trees in very public places are becoming swamped in Ivy, removal might be advised on grounds of aesthetics or even safety, as Ivy can cover weaknesses and decay in the branches. But in all other situations it is preferable to leave it in place – the wildlife value far outweighs other considerations.

Red Admiral at Ivy blossom, Humberston

Even aesthetically, a dressing of Ivy can impart a dark, gothic charm to otherwise bare winter hedgerows and woodland fringes, which we should certainly miss.

'Citizen Science'. Wildlife conservation in Britain cannot function without knowledge of where species live, how common they are, and whether they're increasing or decreasing. Keeping abreast of this gigantic and never-ending task is well beyond the capabilities of the small band of professional ecologists working in Britain today. So the job falls to a dedicated army of volunteers who submit wildlife records to various recording schemes in their spare time. This huge body of unpaid data-gatherers is only really found in the natural sciences, and the phenomenon has come to be known as 'citizen science'.

Although a term only recently-coined, citizen science is not a new concept; the vast majority of advances in natural history have always come from enthusiastic amateurs. Some projects, such as the bird ringing scheme of the British Trust for Ornithology, require the long-term dedication of trained experts, who give their time and skills both for their own enjoyment and in exchange for a personal stake in a worthwhile cause. These days, however, there are recording projects to suit all levels of effort and skill, and easy data input via the internet has made scientist-led mass participation events all the rage.

This approach is particularly well-suited to groups of animals with 'few but common', easily-identified species, such as butterflies. Over the years, information on the fortunes of British butterflies has mostly come from the UK Butterfly Monitoring Scheme. In this scheme, experienced butterfly counters walk the same 'patch' every week between spring and autumn, recording butterflies as they go. The scheme started with 34 sites in 1976, but now has more than 1000. This scheme has the disadvantages that it is very labour-intensive and naturally geared towards the best places for butterflies. So to complement this project, the charity Butterfly Conservation has introduced a number of simpler and more wide-ranging recording schemes designed to involve and enthuse much large numbers of people, with each giving easily-manageable amounts of time.

Two such participants this year were Cleethorpes Chronicle reader Chris Johnson and son Sam, who, with nearly 45,000 others, took part in Butterfly Conservation's 'Big Butterfly Count', recording mostly in their Laceby Acres garden. This scheme, in which all participants together made a total of 43,500 individual fifteen minute butterfly counts in 2014, set out to create a comprehensive snapshot of the status of Britain's commoner butterflies at the height of summer. What this scheme lacked in fine detail, it made up for in volume – having only started in 2010, this is already the biggest butterfly survey in the world.

The news coming out of 2014's Big Butterfly Count is that despite a fine and warm July, 15 out of 21 target species were less abundant in 2014 than in the previous year, with the 'whites' faring particularly badly. The Small Tortoiseshell continued its comeback however following years of decline, and Red Admiral and Speckled Wood were also more numerous this year. It wasn't a great year for migrants from the south such as the Painted Lady and the day-flying Silver Y Moth, possibly owing more to conditions in the areas of origin than anything happening at home. Despite a decline in numbers from 2013, the spectacular Peacock butterfly topped the rankings for the very first time.

For more examples of 'citizen science', also check out the RSPB's 'Big Garden Birdwatch'; BTO's 'Garden Birdwatch', the 'UK Ladybird Survey', the Woodland Trust's 'Nature's Calendar,' the 'National Plant Monitoring Scheme' or the BSBI's 'New Year Plant Hunt'.

Brent Geese. At Cleethorpes it's around now that we start to see the return of one of our most charismatic estuary birds, the Brent Goose. These geese breed in the high Arctic of central Russia, mostly on the Taimyr Peninsula. They leave their breeding grounds in August, flying westwards to their wintering areas in Britain and France, via the Baltic. Although the first birds usually arrive at Cleethorpes before the end of September, numbers in Lincolnshire tend to finally peak a little after Christmas, with birds from the Waddensee of Holland and Germany moving further west to reinforce numbers here on British estuaries.

This smallest and darkest of our geese may be seen all the way up to Cleethorpes Leisure Centre feeding among the saltmarsh creeks, but the largest numbers are to be seen at Humberston and Tetney, where a flock of hundreds can be seen each year, regularly commuting between the tidal marsh and the fields behind the sea wall. The birds will often take to the air, compact flocks stretching out into long, untidy strings on longer flights. Their collective low-pitched flight calls constitute one of the estuary's most evocative natural winter sounds.

The favourite food of Brent Geese is Eelgrass, although this is not a common plant in our parts. They will also feed on that green slimy alga known as *Enteromorpha* which lies commonly about our tidal sands and tangled up in saltmarsh, and grasses and other succulent plants of the marsh itself, especially later in the winter. More recently they have taken to popping back over the sea defences to feed on grassy fields, winter cereals or young oilseed rape. They are particularly fond of grass leys containing White Clover. This can bring them into conflict with farmers, although ours seem to be tolerated well enough.

Because their summering grounds are so far north, breeding success for Dark-bellied Brent Geese is very variable from year to year. The weather in summer may be very unpredictable in the Arctic. Also, the three-year cycles in Lemming abundance are strongly correlated with breeding success – when Lemmings are scarce, Arctic Foxes tend to prey on Brent Geese and their goslings instead. Interestingly, a measure of breeding success can be gained when the geese arrive back on the Humber, as juvenile and first winter birds can be recognised by thin white stripes on their wings, which can be seen either on the ground or in flight (pictured). When no juveniles arrive back with the adult birds in the autumn, you know the breeding season has been a poor one.

There are other reasons to scrutinise Brent Geese in our beach's flocks, as sometimes birds from other races may get caught up with our 'Dark-bellied' birds. The most regular of these is the Pale-bellied Brent Goose, which breeds in a completely different part of the Arctic – in this case Greenland and northern Canada. This race usually winters in Ireland, although there is a small outlying wintering ground at Lindisfarne in Northumberland. Pale-bellied Brent Goose undertakes the longest migration of any goose, including a stretch of more than 1800 miles without stopping, and a negotiation of the 10,000 feet high Greenland icecap. Visually it is not very different from our own race, but can usually be picked out by its paler flanks.

Much rarer still is the North American and far east Asian race of Brent Goose, known as the 'Black Brant'. This is a very dark goose with distinctly two-tone flanks and a wider neck-ring. Unfortunately, Black Brants can hybridise with our own dark-bellied birds, leading to some confusing intermediates.

Brent Geese.
Photo: Colin Smale
www.fotolincs.com

Brent Goose numbers in the UK fluctuate, but are much higher now than half a century ago. Increased protection from shooting and a change of feeding habits are probably the main reasons. Our birds are relatively easy to see, and constitute one of the estuary's characteristic winter sights and sounds. It remains to be seen what the effect of the now under-construction Bishopthorpe Windfarm will be, sited as it is so close to the arable fields in which our own birds often feed.

Counting Birds in Flocks. During the last two weeks we have seen some of the highest tides in recent years, and this has created some great wader spectacles over the beach towards the south end of the resort.

Part of my day job as an ecologist and naturalist involves counting flocks of waterbirds. The commonest question I get asked while doing this is 'how do you count the birds accurately when they're so far away and they won't stop moving?' This picture shows the problem; how many Knot would *you* say are in this photograph, taken on Cleethorpes beach?

How many Knot?

It is very important to estimate numbers as accurately as possible. Only this way can information be gained about movements of birds, and population increases or declines. Added to this, any site containing more than 1% of the north-west European population of any species of wildfowl, or more than 1% of the east

Atlantic flyway population of any species of wader, is automatically considered for protection under EU law. Any site with more than 20,000 birds altogether is also considered. Finally, a wetland in Britain counts as nationally important if it regularly holds 1% of the British population of any bird. The Humber Estuary exceeds these levels for a number of species, and of course this could not be assessed without accurate counts.

Human beings are extremely bad at coping with large numbers – that is to say as numbers rise, we have less and less ability to comprehend and conceptualise them. Accurately assessing numbers in the thousands is difficult for us, and as a consequence there is a natural tendency to strongly underestimate large numbers of 'things', including birds in flocks.

A couple of winters ago I watched, with a friend, a flock of Starlings flying around Cleethorpes Pier before going to roost under the structure, on a windy afternoon. After watching the flock for a full quarter of an hour, my friend came to the conclusion that there were about a thousand birds in the flock. To test this I photographed the flock and counted them later from the picture; in fact there were over 2,700 – my friend's guess was a little over a third of the actual total.

As bird counters, we are taught various techniques for counting flocks of birds. When numbers are smallish, and individual birds are static and can be seen well, they can be counted simply, one by one. When the numbers get above a few hundred, the usual method is to start by counting say 50, or 100, to see what such a number looks like in the context of the flock, then count the rest in 'blocks'. This is of course less accurate, but at least makes an estimate possible.

After a good deal of practice, a hundred, and a thousand, have a 'look' about them, and this makes the job of counting even huge, swirling flocks slightly less onerous than if coming to it fresh. Under these circumstances, as in any scientific situation, uncertainty must be acknowledged, and even then there are occasions when one has to admit defeat.

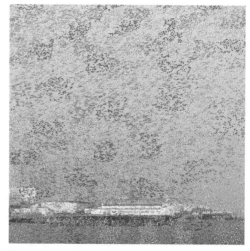

In groups of 100

There is a relatively easy way to 'calibrate' one's judgment of flock size. This is to photograph a flock, then afterwards place a coloured dot on each bird in the picture, in groups of, say 100 (as I have done here). This task has become much easier since the advent of computers and photo editing software. Using this method we can see how accurate our assessments actually are.

Did you have a guess how many Knot there were in the photo? In fact, there are 16,047. This means that there are between three and four times as many Knot in this single photograph as are needed to designate Cleethorpes beach as being of International importance for this species.

Street Lighting. With the nights now drawing in everybody should by now have had a flavour of North East Lincolnshire's new LED street lighting. My impression is that the reaction has been mostly favourable – the new lights certainly constitute a massive saving in electricity (and therefore cost and carbon footprint), which is a huge environmental step forward. They're more directional too, reducing unwanted 'light trespass' to gardens and windows, and reducing 'skyglow'.

Of course there is an extent to which any street lighting is bad for wildlife. For the whole of evolutionary history animals and plants have adapted to the daily cycle of light and dark. As a day-living species, we tend to think of activity during the lighter hours as being the norm, but in fact fully 30% of invertebrates and 60% of vertebrates are nocturnal, requiring the cover of darkness to evade predators, breed and find food. Street lighting disrupts natural patterns in a number of ways – from birds singing at night to clouds of hypnotised moths unable to break away from lamps and falling easy prey to bats. Both plants and animals judge seasons by the relative lengths of day and night, and the moon and stars are used by many animals for local movements or longer migrations. One can safely assume that street lighting makes these tasks much harder.

We should clearly be attempting to reduce the impacts of artificial light on natural systems. Different animals have very different modes of colour vision, and are sensitive to different wavelengths of light. Red light is invisible to most creatures, so if street lights glowed a warm red, most creatures would effectively be in total darkness. As long as humans found this acceptable, this would be the friendliest compromise between the needs of people and those of animals. Even red light, however, could be disruptive to migrating birds (which *can* see red), or plants, which use red light in photosynthesis.

Other colours are more problematic, and the broader the spectrum of light emitted, the more likely the light is to be disruptive to wildlife. Light emitted in the ultraviolet part of the spectrum could be particularly troublesome – it is invisible and therefore useless to us, but not so to the great majority of organisms.

Our new LED lights produce a hard white light with peaks in the blue and green parts of the spectrum, allowing pretty good colour rendition in humans. From the point of view of aesthetics and perceived security, I much prefer them to the old sodium ones, although the range of wavelengths of the new lights is disconcertingly wide compared with the more limited, orange glow of the old sort.

This is a problem which cannot be satisfactorily solved. There may be an argument for dimming street lighting in the mostly-deserted early hours, or the judicious turning off of individual lights or whole sections at various times, to allow hypnotised insects to escape. Happily, there is already an intention to consider deflectors when streetlamps are needed adjacent to known wildlife sites.

Some areas, both on a small and large scale, should remain forever dark. Such places should form a network – a kind of dark infrastructure – allowing creatures of the night to move around without hindrance. Domestic house and garden lights too, of course, should be used sparingly, and with wildlife in mind.

Aquatic Invaders. It is a sad fact that many of the world's fresh waters now contain invasive alien species. The number of such interlopers seems set to increase as more and more creatures are moved away from their native ranges by humans, and established aliens spread. Let's meet three aquatic alien animals living among us in North East Lincolnshire.

The first is a reptile. If you sneak up to the water of Cleethorpes Country Park's wildlife area very slowly on a warm day, you may see what look like turtles basking out in the sun. If disturbed they will soon dive quietly back beneath the waterweed. These are Red-eared Terrapins – natives of southern USA.

Britain has no native turtles, terrapins or tortoises to confuse them with, but separation from other alien species is easy because of the red stripe behind the animal's eye. Terrapins in the wild in the UK all result from releases – they are quite commonly kept as pets, but may be set free when owners realise they are not particularly easy to keep, and can live for up to 40 years.

Red-eared Terrapins are opportunist omnivores. They can feed on vegetation, but they may also take fish, amphibians, small waterbirds and invertebrates. They may also interfere with breeding birds such as Moorhen by basking in their nests. During the winter they hibernate at the bottom of the water, entering a state of torpor.

No Red-eared Terrapin has ever been known to breed in the wild in the UK – it is simply too cold here. However, a couple of degrees of global warming could change all that. I first saw terrapins in Cleethorpes Country Park in 2008, and they are still there, alive and well, in 2016.

The second alien water creature is a crustacean. Gaze down into the water of the Freshney in top town, the Lud at Hubbard's Hills, or fresh waters elsewhere, and you may catch a glimpse of the American Signal Crayfish. The 'signals' are pale patches on the claws, which identify the species. This crayfish, first introduced to Britain in 1976, is considered a pest as it has wiped out our only native crayfish, the White-clawed Crayfish, from many of its former haunts, including some of our Lincolnshire rivers. It has done this both by competition for food and shelter, and by direct predation. Most seriously, the American species carries a disease known as 'crayfish plague', actually a fungus *Aphanomyces astaci,* to which it is resistant unless extremely stressed, but which quickly kills the native species.

American Signal Crayfish is another opportunist omnivore – it will eat plants, but will also take fish, amphibians, invertebrates or other crayfish, including its own species. The native range is north-western USA and south-western Canada.

The last of the trio is also a crustacean – the large, vigorously-burrowing, highly predatory, Chinese Mitten Crab. The species first appeared in Europe in Germany in 1912, having been introduced in ships' ballast water. By 1935 it had reached the Thames and by 1949 it had been recorded in Yorkshire, although the main population explosion in Britain occurred in the 1990s. It is now widespread in many British estuaries and inland waterways – the Humber was thought to be one of the original points of entry.

Chinese Mitten Crabs occupy the saline/fresh water transition zone, where they have no real competitors. They can only breed in the sea, but prefer to moult in fresh water, and so will readily migrate between the two. Records from other European countries have shown they can move far enough upstream to easily penetrate the whole interior of the British mainland, although in reality they may be hampered in their progress by sluices and locks.

Chinese Mitten Crabs are thought to be fairly well-established in

Lincolnshire, where most records have been maritime. Although occasionally encountered upriver, they are not yet frequent enough to be considered a nuisance here. In other parts of Europe, however, they have done huge amounts of damage by burrowing into banks and jeopardising the integrity of flood defences. Even in our area, that possibility still remains a threat.

Chinese Mitten Crabs can easily be identified by their pincers which are covered by a mat of hair, giving the appearance of mittens.

It has long been accepted that invasive alien species are a bad thing – the second biggest threat to biodiversity on the planet, it is said, after habitat destruction. When particular alien species start to become a nuisance to humans, the problems they cause can cost eye-watering amounts of money to put right. Freshwater habitats seem particularly susceptible to successful colonisation by invasive, non-native species – stressed, artificial waterbodies especially so. This makes keeping our aquatic ecosystems as natural and healthy as possible doubly important.

Having said this, even in places where humans have introduced new species, extinctions among indigenous wildlife are surprisingly rare. As a consequence, introduced species almost always make a place *more* biodiverse. They can sometimes create new relationships with existing wildlife, and provide evolution by natural selection with new drivers. In a world already profoundly altered by humans, some believe that the introduction of species to new places by people just adds a new dynamic to an already dynamic system, and we shouldn't automatically resist change. There will be losers, but also winners.

I'm not sure I agree with this entirely, and invaders of freshwaters can be particularly problematic. But we might as well try to enjoy the creatures ineradicably naturalised here. None of this degradation – if you agree that's what it is – diminishes our responsibility to provide special places; unpolluted and of sufficient size and connectedness, where wildlife of whatever origin or in whatever combination can continue to support itself.

Red-eared Terrapin in Cleethorpes Country Park

Autumn Leaves. The vibrant and glorious hues of autumn are one of the delights of living at a temperate latitude, and provide some compensation for the dreary winter to come. This is the time of year when ornamental and native trees complement each other beautifully in a transformative explosion of colour.

All leaves contain a number of pigments. First among these, and most abundant, is chlorophyll – the green substance which makes photosynthesis possible. So dominant is this pigment that it makes leaves in summer simply appear green. Chlorophyll is degraded by light (just like ink fades on paper when left in the sun), and must be constantly replaced.

But also present in leaves are carotenoids and flavonoids. The purpose of these pigments is to help the leaf to absorb additional frequencies of light, and to stabilise the process of photosynthesis. Flavonoids are yellow, and carotenoids yellow, orange or red. These pigments are normally hidden by the abundance of chlorophyll.

As the days become shorter and cooler in autumn, trees start to re-absorb valuable nutrients from the leaves back into stems and roots. Also, at this time, a corky substance starts to form at the base of leaves (which eventually makes them fall), which starts to cut off supplies to the leaf. Chlorophyll is the first pigment in the leaves to break down, 'unmasking' the colours of the other, mostly yellow pigments beneath.

But the very deepest reds and purples are caused by another set of compounds, which are not present throughout the year – these are the anthocyanins. These pigments are created afresh by the leaf in autumn, in response to a build-up of sugars in combination with bright sunlight. The creation of anthocyanins in the light is why one side of an apple, but not the other, is often deep red.

The reasons for anthocyanin production are unknown – some say that the red colour discourages late-season insect damage, while others say that anthocyanins protect the leaves during the last days of photosynthetic activity, stopping them from falling until as many nutrients have been re-absorbed as possible. Interestingly, when tree sap is more acid, redder colours are produced, with more alkaline sap creating purples.

Many of our native trees show consistent colour changes in autumn. Beech will turn a brilliant translucent golden orange, with Oak a more opaque russet. Ash, our commonest wild tree, flushes a smoky yellow before the leaves fall. Alder does not change at all, the leaves falling while they are still green. Our roadside Limes turn a fine yellow which contrasts with its dark twigs, while wild cherries may show simultaneous yellow and vivid red.

The maples are a genus famed for their autumn colours. We only have one native species, the Field Maple, which turns a rich butter-yellow. Sycamore, a common wild tree and 'honorary' native maple, also turns yellow in autumn. Some fine exotic maples line the highways of Cleethorpes including cultivars chosen for rich autumn colours. Now is the time of year to see them at their striking and varied best.

Indeed it is around the edges of towns – in parks, cemeteries and the older, leafier suburbs – where the variety of planted species makes autumn colours the most extravagant. Here, dark, unchanging evergreens and purple-leaved varieties of beech and cherry contrast with native trees, street plantings and exotics celebrated for their autumn colours, such as non-native maples and False Acacia. In gardens, Virginia Creeper (though not a tree) and Stag's-horn Sumach provide some of the deepest and richest reds of all.

In terms of the display of colours in autumn, not every year is the same. Colour tends to be most intense when hot, bright autumn days are coupled with cold, clear, but not freezing nights. During fine days sugar is produced in the leaves, but cold nights stop it from being re-absorbed so readily, facilitating the development of red anthocyanins.

If strong winds or frosts come too early, a disappointingly short display can be the result. If the autumn remains calm and bright throughout, a colourful, prolonged and ever-changing spectacle may last well into December.

Collared Doves. The advent of satellite television has provided an unexpected benefit to one of North East Lincolnshire's commonest garden birds.

In the 1930s the Collared Dove was restricted as a European bird to the Balkans, where it had probably previously been introduced from India. From there it underwent an unprecedented spread westwards across Europe, probably as a result of a change in the dispersal behavior of young birds.

The first sighting of a Collared Dove in Britain was in Lincolnshire in 1952. In 1955, one or two pairs bred at West Runton near Cromer in Norfolk, but the event remained a secret until it was broadcast on national radio by the famous ornithologist James Fisher in the late 1950s. By the mid-1960s, Collared Doves had spread over most of Britain and were a relatively familiar sight. Exponential growth followed, eventually levelling out, and even declining slightly in recent years. Even so, Collared Dove is now one of Britain's commonest and most familiar garden birds.

The range and abundance of the Collared Dove generally mirrors that of human habitation, although they are not really birds of the centres of big cities where they are replaced by Feral Pigeons. Collared Doves generally prefer leafy suburbs, small towns and villages and agricultural settings where they can find both nest sites and food, comprising weed seeds, and spilt grain or stock feed. They may congregate in large numbers where food is abundant, although the sight of flocks of Collared Doves in newly-harvested late summer fields seems now to be a thing of the past.

Collared Dove is one of very few species whose nest can be found in any month of the year. Although nests in mid-winter are uncommon, I have seen a newly-fledged chick surviving perfectly well after a fortnight of snow so deep that it brought the north of England to a standstill.

The nest is a flimsy affair made of twigs and lined with grasses. The nest site is often given away by piles of twigs on the ground below, which the birds have accidentally dropped. Collared Doves will nest in most above-ground situations, showing a slight preference for conifers, and they are one of the species which can be found nesting in Leylandii hedges. Where no trees are available, such as on many of North East Lincolnshire's newer housing estates, Collared Doves have taken to nesting on the brackets of satellite dishes. At a pinch they will also use outside security lights and other high man-made structures.

The pair nesting on the satellite dish bracket of my own Chartdale house have brought off two broods this year, rearing first one chick then two. The second of these broods did not fledge until mid-October, and knowing this species they may even try for another breeding attempt this year. Several other houses on the same estate also have Collared Dove nests behind their satellite dishes, and similar choice of nest site has also been reported in many other, widely separated parts of Britain. Unfortunately predation by Magpies, crows and sometimes even squirrels is rife in this situation, and unfortunately many chicks do not survive very long. This is partly a consequence of the lack of vegetation cover to be found among much modern housing, making it easy for predators to locate their prey.

Seawatching. There is a suite of perfectly valid Lincolnshire birds which is familiar to almost no-one except those who bother to look for them. These are the ocean-wandering seabirds which pass our shores out at sea – navigate using our coastline – but which almost never venture over the land.

The pursuit of these birds is called seawatching, and is the reason for little clusters of people on headlands and open coasts, peering seemingly aimlessly out over the waves. The classic seawatchers' targets are the shearwaters, skuas, petrels and the rarer gulls, but also include Gannets, auks, divers and sea ducks. Many of these species' lives are tied to the oceans, and they may live perfectly well far out at sea – but they must come ashore to breed. Few such species have any need to make landfall in Lincolnshire, with our gently-shelving coastlines unsuitable for cliff- or burrow-nesting birds. So to see them we must choose a suitable spot, stare out to sea, and wait for them to pass by offshore.

Migration seasons – especially autumn – are generally best. In settled weather birds may spread out over a wide front, fly very high, or stay far out at sea, and as a consequence, seawatching on some of the nicer days can be very unrewarding. But when the wind is strong and from the right direction, watchers can be treated to the spectacle of a constant, varied passage of species which there is no other way of seeing here.

Birdwatchers cannot always precisely describe which are the best kinds of weather for seawatching. Strong onshore winds in autumn are a safe bet, pushing birds close in where you can see them. Seabirds may also come close in bad weather, poor visibility, or ahead of squalls. Sometimes winds from other directions also produce good results, for reasons which are more obscure. North-westerly gales, for instance, may lead birds from north of the UK to enter the North Sea for shelter, and appear unexpectedly off our coasts. The best weather for birds is, unfortunately, often the most hostile for the watcher, so wrapping up extremely well is often advised on the best passage days.

Here in Cleethorpes, our position within the mouth of the estuary is a disadvantage – we miss out on birds which simply follow the east coast straight up and down. But certain winds will lead seabirds to enter the shelter of the Humber, and there are days in autumn where we may see a passage of Gannets or Fulmars offshore at Cleethorpes. The auks – Guillemot, Razorbill and conceivably Puffin – are also possible; grebes may be seen, as may Great and Arctic Skuas, and almost anything else at a pinch. Some ducks which never come ashore in Lincolnshire will enter the waters of the estuary too, notably flocks of Common Scoter, whose all-black males are distinctive, and occasionally its rarer relative the Velvet Scoter, with its diagnostic white wing-patch. Divers, those most primitive of all Britain's birds, may also fly past Cleethorpes, or be seen swimming out on the sea.

There is no doubt that to maximise results from seawatching, coastal watchpoints facing the open sea are best. From North East Lincolnshire one may travel northwards to Spurn or Flamborough Head, which are celebrated seawatching hotspots. Southwards, Trusthorpe near Mablethorpe has handy brick shelters from which watchers may view the open sea. At Huttoft car terrace, one may watch the birds from the comfort of a vehicle.

Because birds may be fairly distant, seawatching may be a serious test of one's identification skills. Nobody can identify everything that passes, and where there is doubt, a second opinion can help. Distant auks may be all but unidentifiable. Three of the skuas – Arctic, Pomarine and Long-tailed – require experience to separate, as do the three divers – Red-throated, Black-throated and Great Northern. The black-and white Manx Shearwater has a similar relative, the Balearic Shearwater, although the all-dark Sooty Shearwater should be identifiable given a good enough view. The latter is one of the great ocean travellers – appearing off Lincolnshire but breeding no closer than the south Atlantic. The Fulmar, although coloured like a gull, is given away as a petrel-relative by its stiff-winged, shearing flight.

All of these species may be accompanied by flocks of the more usual gulls, waders and ducks. A sighting of a dark petrel – maybe Storm Petrel or Leach's Petrel – in the North Sea makes for a very special day, although they are known to come inshore at night. Every seawatcher dreams of seeing an albatross or a tropicbird, although these would be once in a lifetime events, even for seasoned seawatchers.

Seawatchers may also see mammals at sea – seals are a common sight, as sometimes also is that little cetacean the Harbour Porpoise, whose dorsal fin will sometimes be seen rolling periodically above the waves.

Jays and Acorns. Autumn is the time of year when that most colourful and arboreal of our native crows, the Jay, becomes much more conspicuous. When seen well the Jay is an exotic-looking bird – greyish pink, with a black speckled cap and black moustachial stripe, black and white wings, a black tail and a brilliant white rump. Its most striking visual feature is a small group of covert feathers at the bend of the wing, which are a stunning bright blue, barred with black.

Jays are usually very sedentary, and mostly secretive for large parts of the year. In dense woodland they may only be given away by their harsh, screeching calls. However, in autumn Jays are much more likely to be seen out and about in the open, often undertaking short, laboured, bouncing flights between trees.

In fact, Jays have a very special relationship with Oak trees. Jays are omnivorous, opportunistic and adaptable in their diet, but are very fond of acorns, and may be dependent on them for survival for large parts of the year. So important is the relationship between Jays and acorns that the specific epithet of the Jay's scientific name, *glandarius,* is derived from the Latin word for Oak.

The nature of the acorn crop is that it is superabundant for a short time in autumn, but after that, it's gone. This is the reason for the tireless and conspicuous activity of Jays at this time of year, as they busily harvest and cache their food for consumption during the lean days of winter. They must manage to put their collected food out of the reach of other animals, but also remember where they put it.

In autumn, a Jay may spend up to ten hours a day caching acorns. Carrying two or three (exceptionally up to nine) acorns in its gullet and usually one in its bill, a Jay will take acorns well away from the parent tree. It will place them in secret hiding places including natural hollows, crevices in tree bark and in holes which it makes in soil with its bill, usually underneath leaf litter. In the course of a season, a single Jay may hide thousands of acorns in this way. Jays have an amazing talent for remembering where they have cached acorns, using mostly visual cues to re-find their food.

However, inevitably some are missed, and these may germinate and grow – in fact, this is the chief dispersal mechanism for Oak trees. A germinating acorn needs light, and if acorns were simply to drop from their parent tree, conditions would almost always be too shaded for the seedlings to survive, and in any case they would not conquer much territory.

By caching acorns, Jays can act as the engineers of new woodland. If open ground surrounded by existing woodland is allowed to undergo natural succession, tree seedlings of species such as Ash and Field Maple which have heavy, winged seeds, will gradually creep in from the edges, reaching the middle last. Because of the caching behavior of Jays, Oak will, in contrast, appear more or less equally across the area, indeed having a slight tendency to start from the centre and spread outwards.

In some years there is another reason why Jays are more conspicuous in autumn – this is when the acorn crop fails right across northern Europe and Scandinavia, and Jays must travel to find food. In such years we in the UK can receive large numbers of Jays from the Continent, despite their general aversion to travelling over open water. Our own Jays may also move westwards, as the acorn crop tends to do badly in the same years here as abroad. In these years, Jays may be seen flying in off the sea, or moving along the coast in flocks.

In our area, any Jay seen on the coast away from older woodland could be a migrant. Otherwise you may see them in any of our larger woodlands, or anywhere else Oak trees occur such as cemeteries, large gardens or more well-wooded farmland. Or at this time of year they may simply fly over your car where there are abundant roadside trees.

Living Fossils. Some species of plant growing among us in North East Lincolnshire today can be described as 'living fossils'. This is not a technical term of course, but has been applied to plants which have few or no living relatives, and whose lineage can be traced far back into geological time, so that they appear to be 'from the past'. To qualify as a living fossil, a species must have lookalikes which extend back beyond any of the Earth's great mass extinction events, the last of which eliminated the dinosaurs 65 million years ago.

No species of plant from so long ago has come down to the modern day completely unchanged – that is asking too much. However, some have clear ancestors which go back a very long way. For example, long before the evolution of flowering plants about 160 million years ago, the Earth's lush green forests and swamps contained plants we would clearly recognise from today's North East Lincolnshire flora as ferns, horsetails, and conifers, some of the latter possibly similar to our garden Monkey Puzzles.

One of the best and most fascinating examples of a 'living fossil' growing in this area today is the Ginkgo tree, *Ginkgo biloba*. Trees bearing a resemblance to Ginkgo first arose about 270 million years ago (older even than the mass extinction *before* the one that killed off the dinosaurs), with plants certainly attributable to this genus first arising during the Jurassic period. The dinosaurs walked among many species of Ginkgo, but diversity quickly waned, and by the time these giant reptiles died out there were only one or two species of Ginkgo in the northern hemisphere, and another one in the southern hemisphere. By 2.5 million years ago, only the modern *Ginkgo biloba* survived, and this was restricted to a single area of what is now central China.

Ginkgo has no close relatives, although it is thought to be distantly allied to the cycads, which are sometimes grown in British houses and frost-free gardens. Ginkgo has very distinctive fan-shaped leaves, and female trees produce unusual fruit-like seeds on stalks. When they fall and rot, the smell of the fruits has been likened to rancid butter or vomit, and for this reason usually only male trees are cultivated.

Ginkgo is widely consumed as a herbal supplement for conditions caused by poor blood flow, especially to the brain, such as dementia, memory loss, vertigo, defective colour vision and tinnitus. Advice should be sought before taking Ginkgo however, as there are several well-documented side-effects and contra-indications.

Ginkgo leaves turn golden yellow in the autumn. In our area, examples of this fascinating and ancient tree can be seen near the entrance to Grimsby Cemetery (near the derelict house), in People's Park (opposite the statue), and a small specimen also grows in the churchyard at Humberston. At Humberston it can be seen growing close to a handsome Dawn Redwood, *Metasequoia glyptostroboides,* itself another living fossil, this genus also going back well beyond the last mass extinction.

We should not mention mass extinction events without reminding ourselves that we are in the middle of another one as we speak – this time caused by the unsustainable use of the planet by humankind. For some reason, it is ridiculously difficult to get decision-makers to give this ongoing catastrophe any attention at all.

Sea Fish. One might assume that the brown, swirling waters of the Humber straight out from Cleethorpes are relatively lifeless, but in fact they contain a very diverse assemblage of sea fish. Eighty-six species had been recorded in the Humber estuary at the last count, although the number present is probably higher. These include resident species, winter visitors, marine species which may move into the estuary at certain times of year, and some which use the estuary shallows as nursery grounds.

In addition, there are some species which occupy both fresh and salt water at different times in their life cycles, such as Eel and Salmon. These must pass through the estuary on their way from one to the other.

Sea anglers at Cleethorpes may catch Flounder, Dab, Saithe (aka Coley or

Pollock) and Sea Bass, among others. At low tide in summer they may take that sociable, bottom-dwelling shark known as the Smooth Hound, and Thornback Ray in late summer or early autumn. Cod follow Whiting into the river around about now (end of October), and are the main winter quarry.

A recent survey of the estuary's sea fish also found both Long- and Short-spined Sea Scorpions (the latter also known as Bull Rout), as well as Pogge, Pouting (or Bib), Sea Snail, Five- and Four-bearded Rockling and Smelt; also that closely-related pair of flatfish, Turbot and Brill, Grey Gurnard, the eel-like Butterfish, Lesser Pipefish, an unidentified Dragonet or two, and the venomous Lesser Weever.

When the tide goes out, some fish are left in the pools, creeks and runnels of the beach and saltmarsh. These are the fish most likely to be encountered by holidaymakers and walkers on the foreshore.

Needless to say, most of these fish are small, often juveniles, indicating the importance of the beach and saltmarsh habitat as a nursery – indeed fish eggs can also sometimes be found. But if you were to paddle in some of the larger, sandier creeks (not always a sensible thing to do!) you may occasionally disturb a decent-sized flatfish, perfectly camouflaged against the sand.

Of the flatfish, the Flounder is by far the commonest here. It is a classic fish of estuaries, capable of tolerating water which is quite fresh, only really going out into the open sea to breed.

You might also encounter the young stages of two more flatfish, Plaice and Sole. Plaice breed in the open sea to the north of the Humber in spring, with juvenile fish entering the estuary especially in the late summer or autumn. Sole may breed more locally or even in the estuary itself, again contributing a few juvenile fish to our creeks.

Other common inshore fish whose young stages can be found in our beach pools include Sea Bass and Herring, and there are many more which could potentially occur.

But the fish which most people associate with creeks and pools are the resident tiddlers – the classic little fish netted by children in summer.

Shoals of the small, silver Lesser Sand Eel may be seen in the shallower parts of the sea, and runnels and creeks crossing bare sand. These fish are long and thin, allowing them to both swim and bury easily in the sand, which they do to escape predation by a whole host of birds and other fish.

Pools within the saltmarsh may contain fish which are visibly browner than Sand Eels. Some of these may be common old sticklebacks, which, although essentially freshwater species, are also quite common in nearshore marine environments. But most of these fish, the ones looking markedly wider at the head end, will be gobies. Gobies form shoals on or near the surface of the sand, against which they are extremely well camouflaged – indeed, like the flatfish, they may only be seen when they move. They are easily disturbed, but harder to catch than you might think.

Gobies feed mainly on small crustaceans. A goby's pelvic fins are fused to form a sucker, which prevents the fish being swept away by waves when the tide washes over them. Gobies breed in estuaries, their eggs being laid under stones or sometimes in the hollow sides of seashells, where they're defended vigorously by the male until they hatch.

Two of Britain's seventeen or so species of goby are relatively common on our beach, the Common Goby and the Sand Goby. The Common Goby is frequent all around the coasts of Britain, sometimes reaching high densities on estuaries due to multiple spawning during the warmer months, and rapid growth. The often slightly larger Sand Goby is more likely to be found further down the shore where the water is more reliably saline.

Netting in creeks and pools will inevitably turn up crustaceans as well as fish. Shore Crabs are very common on our beach, as are Brown Shrimps, and all manner of other smaller, other-worldly-looking armoured creatures.

Common Goby. Photo: Ove Glenjen CC BY-SA 3.0 Wikimedia Commons

Hedgehogs. When I was a child, Hedgehogs were a common sight in my Humberston garden. They were unusual among wild mammals in that they seemed to show very little fear of humans, possibly something to do with being so well-defended. We used to feed them milk and bread, which was entirely wrong – it is now known to give them indigestion and diarrhoea – water and cat food is recommended for Hedgehogs these days.

Dead Hedgehogs were once such a common sight on the roads that people would sometimes make tasteless jokes about their misfortune. This was humour that would scarcely be understood by today's youth, so unusual is it to see such things now. Hedgehogs' strategy of curling up in a ball when in danger does not serve them well on roads, and there was a theory that natural selection has led Hedgehog populations to acquire the running habit, rather than curling up, leading to far fewer dead animals being seen. In fact, evolution cannot act this quickly, and a dramatic fall in numbers is the real cause.

In the 1950s there were an estimated 36 million Hedgehogs in Britain. By the 1990s this had fallen to about 1.5 million. In the last ten years about 40% of Hedgehogs are thought to have disappeared. Some have predicted the Hedgehog's total demise as a British wild creature by 2025, although this is unlikely – there will always be some hanging on somewhere. Nevertheless, I have met people well into their twenties in Humberston, where I grew up, who have never seen a Hedgehog in the wild, knowing them only from children's stories.

The reasons for this decline are many and varied, but first among them is thought to be that biggest of all problems for biodiversity generally, habitat loss. The removal and poor management of hedgerows and loss of permanent pasture and wild corners on farmland, and the carving up of the suburban landscape by Hedgehog-unfriendly roads, are probably among the major specific causes.

Actually, lines of old suburban gardens lying adjacently can make a respectable patch of habitat for Hedgehogs. Old gardens tend to be both different from each other and internally varied, with good vegetation structure and hiding places, and plenty of food. Indeed Hedgehogs are very beneficial to gardeners, as they eat slugs and snails. But of course, adjacent gardens tend to be sealed off from each other by fences and walls, so that the animal cannot utilise the habitat as a whole. As a consequence they often do not have the size of feeding range they need to survive. Modern gardens, of course, tend to be much too small.

There is always a pronounced peak in Hedgehog deaths around Bonfire Night. This is because it is exactly the time of year when they are looking for somewhere to hibernate, and piles of old wood make the perfect spot to create their winter nest. When this happens, needless to say, many are burned to death or horribly injured.

There are some simple things you can do to help the few Hedgehogs that remain among us. Firstly, link your garden with your neighbour's by making a small gap at ground level. Five inches by five inches is all that's required – this is too small for most domestic pets. Encourage others to do the same.

Leave some long grass, and avoid pesticides, especially slug pellets.

Always construct bonfires on the day they are to be burnt. Even if the material is collected beforehand, only move it into its final position on the last day. If this really can't be done, protect the fire with a circle of outward-leaning chicken wire a metre tall, staked firmly in place, to stop Hedgehogs from entering during the night. Before lighting the fire, shine a torch into the pile, and listen for the hissing alarm call of a Hedgehog.

If you find a Hedgehog in a bonfire soon to be lit, place it, with as much of its nest as you can and some newspaper or towelling in a secured, high sided cardboard box with air holes, cat food and water. Put it in a quiet, safe place until after the festivities are finished, then let it go somewhere sensible.

'Pinkfeet'. Sometimes, our resident population of feral Boating Lake Greylag Geese will take to the air and have a fly around the town, their raucous honking providing an alarm call on many a morning. However, at this time of year, if you see much larger flocks of grey geese flying much higher in characteristic 'V' formations, this is an altogether different phenomenon – the spectacular annual migration of wild Pink-footed Geese to their British wintering areas. If you look skywards for long enough you are bound to see this fabulous sight, which is the very essence of wildness, at least once or twice in an average autumn. If flocks are low enough, the relatively high-pitched, melodic chorus of their combined calls can be heard; far removed from the grating utterances of the local Greylags.

Pink-footed Goose has a very limited world population, with the great majority of birds breeding in Greenland and Iceland. At the end of the Arctic summer the Greenland birds join up with the Icelandic birds and this whole population 'ups sticks' to Britain. Once here they congregate strongly at certain traditional sites – eastern and southern Scotland are strongholds, as are the estuaries of Lancashire in the west, and the North Norfolk coast in the east. The upper Humber estuary provides another, lesser gathering point.

There is much movement of geese between UK wintering sites, depending on weather conditions and availability of food. Pink-footed Geese used to be saltmarsh feeders, but nowadays they prefer farmland where they will feed on spilt grain, sugar beet tops, improved grassland and then winter cereals as the winter progresses. In autumn the general direction of travel among North East Lincolnshire birds is southwards towards Norfolk, but 'skeins' (as their strung-out travelling formations are called) can sometimes be seen taking up rather random directions as they wander between feeding areas.

Flying in 'V' formations greatly assists heavier birds in undertaking long distance migrations. Each bird flies in the 'upwash' from the wingtip vortices of the bird in front, reducing drag, and therefore migratory range, by 60-70%. The leaders, who cannot benefit from this uplift, change over from time to time, so that fatigue is spread among the flock.

The British population of Pink-footed Goose has risen dramatically in recent decades, possibly as a result of better winter feeding. But there is still concern that the whole breeding population of Greenland and Iceland is aggregated in such a small number of wintering sites, giving the species an ongoing conservation priority. Counts of British birds are usually undertaken in early November.

The sight of migrating 'pinkfeet' is a highly evocative sign of autumn, which can be experienced anywhere in our region. Don't mistake flocks of gulls going to roost at dusk, which also fly in 'V' formations, for these long-distance travellers.

November

Waders in Fields. Interesting birdlife can be found everywhere. But it has to be said, here in North East Lincolnshire our generally flat, intensively farmed countryside and urban sprawl, with its shortage of woodland, dry climate and mostly clay soils, has no real claim to specialness. It is made special, however, by proximity to the sea.

Here on the coast we tend to be able to identify strong waves of bird migration more easily than folks inland, and we may even see birds flying in directly from the sea. This is particularly impressive in easterlies in autumn, when flocks of incoming thrushes and Starlings may call excitedly as they finally achieve dry land, diving down into our food-laden gardens, hedgerows and pastures. They may be joined by Woodcock, Long-eared Owl, Bramblings, and others. Daybreak after a night-time 'fall' of migrants may see coastal bushes alive with Robins, Blackbirds and Goldcrests, resting and refueling before dispersing further inland. Rarities and other migrants may cling closely to the coast for navigation, and so be easier to locate here than elsewhere.

The Humber estuary is internationally-designated for its huge flocks of waders and other waterbirds which overwinter here, or stop off here on their way to other wetlands on the so-called 'east-Atlantic flyway'. Indeed, the sheer numbers of waterbirds make the Humber one of the six most important wetland sites in the UK.

As habitats go, estuaries are very dynamic – they are completely transformed by the tide twice a day, and both the amount of prey and the number of birds consuming it are highly variable. Freezing conditions can sometimes make food completely unavailable to feeding birds out on the mudflats. This means that fields on the landward side of the seawall may be used at high tide or when food becomes difficult to find. This makes inland fields within a mile or so of the sea effectively an extension of the protected estuary habitat. This cannot be said of the vast majority of similar 'ordinary' farmed countryside further inland.

Not all wading birds are equally inclined to move inland onto fields. During the very highest tides – those that cover every last bit of mud and marsh –. some Arctic-breeding waders such as Knot, Bar-tailed Godwit and Grey

Plover will merely circle aimlessly overhead until the tide goes down a little, or otherwise be displaced much further down the coast.

Some species breeding closer to home are quite happy in grassland habitats and will readily move onto fields. The black-and-white Oystercatcher tends to do so when its food becomes scarce out on the mud-flats, such as during freezing weather or at the end of winter. At such times, Oystercatchers may turn up in all sorts of places – I once saw one on the Hewitt's Circus roundabout in midwinter.

Redshanks will feed happily around shallow puddles on any sort of short, open grassland, and are occasionally joined by Dunlin in fields. Fields immediately behind the coast along the Humber bank west of Grimsby may hold internationally-important numbers of Icelandic-breeding Black-tailed Godwits at high tide, as well as flocks of Lapwing and Golden Plover, the latter two species seeming equally at home on either side of the sea wall.

But it is the largest of all our beach waders, the stately Curlew, which, although superficially shy, probably comes most closely among us, feeding on our paddocks, playing fields and the last remnants of outmarsh pasture among the houses and factories of the town. In spring, the plaintive upslurred wail and broken trills of the Curlew are an essential and much-celebrated sound of its upland breeding grounds. But we also hear this sound on the Humber at other times, or when they pass over our gardens en route to their feeding fields.

Curlews can survive well on fields and may actually use the habitats the 'other way round' – habitually occurring inland but moving onto the estuary to roost. Their long, curved bills allow them to probe deeply for worms and other invertebrates; the very longest-billed birds are females. Numbers of Curlews are boosted in winter by birds from the continent and Scandinavia escaping the cold, and many of our North East Lincolnshire Curlews originate from there. Where Curlews occur, sometimes Starlings will mimic their trilling calls from our suburban rooftops.

In our town, a revival of house-building threatens to destroy many of the Curlew's inland feeding fields, these being exactly the sort of neglected green edgelands which are most ripe for development. By rights, estuary birds should carry their protected status with them inland over the sea wall, but sadly, numbers of Curlews and other waders are rarely high enough in our grassy inland fields to sway the planners. Maybe new houses will create new grasslands around their edges – or so we hope – so that protected estuary waders will get to keep their 'plan B'.

Foraging. Autumn is a time of plenty in the countryside, and there is a huge variety of plants and fungi out there which we as humans could technically eat.

Foraging for wild food was a historical necessity for the very poor, but has been out of fashion for many years due to the abundant availability of cheap food in the shops. Nowadays, foraging is again becoming more popular, both with chefs and foodies, and those seeking to reconnect with nature. TV foragers such as Ray Mears have popularised the eating of wild food, and seem to be encouraging us to do the same.

Blackberries are the one wild food still habitually taken by people wherever they occur in quantity. One occasionally encounters mushroom pickers, and the odd person collecting sloes or elderberries. But nowadays it is more commonplace to see wild fruit falling and rotting on the ground, often while the same thing, or similar, is being paid for in the supermarket nearby. The culinary uses to which the many green herbs of meadows and waysides can be put is hardly known by people today.

You may be expecting me to encourage you to get out there and gather the free food growing all around us. In fact, there are many reasons why this may not be a good idea.

Foraging for wild food was last commonplace in times when the countryside was more resilient and bountiful. Nowadays we have a burgeoning population and the countryside has never had so little to offer. While nobody will miss a bit of wild food picked responsibly, if everyone foraged, the countryside would be a trampled mess with damaged ecosystems and much of our wild animals' essential food removed. The key is to take wild foods sustainably and in moderation – but who is to judge what that means? It remains up to each individual to not go over the top, although it must be all too easy to get carried away. In some places the problem has become acute – Epping Forest is now closed to foragers and patrolled by guards in autumn, and the New Forest is going the same way.

Then there is the problem of misidentification of plants and fungi, and unknown reactions to previously unencountered chemical compounds. The situation with mushrooms is well known – although there are not many poisonous ones, mistakes can be catastrophic. Some very palatable herbs are extremely like some very poisonous ones – Chervil and Hemlock, for example. Some herbs may cause adverse medical reactions in certain people, and trying anything new when you are pregnant, for example, is not advised.

Anything foraged from too low down risks having been in contact, or worse, with dogs, rats or other animals. These can be the source of parasites which can infect humans. Thorough washing of plants, at the very least, is advised, unless they are taken from a good height, and possibly even then.

Plants from cities or alongside roads could have absorbed pollutants from the air or soil. Of course you may point out that modern foods from the supermarket also contain all manner of natural or unnatural compounds whose harmfulness is simply a matter of dosage. One must decide upon the risks of consuming the chemicals present in all foods, wild or bought, for oneself. But do consider the historic use of the land from which you pick wild food – it may not be as natural as you think, and it is not labelled.

Lastly and leastly, there are few indications of how best to cook with wild plants, and foraging could simply be a recipe for some very uninspiring food.

These days it is common to see fruit such as plums, apples and pears going unpicked in people's gardens. This is one case, at least, when it is a pity to waste such an abundant supply of free food. You could offer to pick someone's fruit for them in return for giving them some of the resulting produce. There are already organised schemes like this in some cities.

Five thousand years of agriculture has resulted in a reliable and abundant supply of good food. Buy organic, or from farm shops and other small producers by all means – growing your own is even better. But there is simply no need to deplete natural ecosystems to eat these days. Guidelines for sustainable foraging are being drawn up as we speak, and in the meantime, please take wild food responsibly.

Ridge and Furrow. The tapestry of hedged fields that forms Lincolnshire's countryside today is a result of a series of Enclosure Acts which came into effect, parish by parish, over many years, between 1720 and 1850. This finally put what was previously communally-worked land into private ownership, where it has stayed ever since. Prior to that, for probably half a millennium, the so-called 'open field system' was the norm.

In the medieval open field system, a parish typically contained a village or hamlet and two or three huge fields. Hedgerows were rather uncommon, and did not form complete circuits around fields like they do now. The fields would contain a few thousand individual strips of farmland or 'selions', a (very rough) average of 220 yards long and 11 yards wide. Selions would be grouped into 'furlongs'. Ownership of individual selions was complex. Few people farmed their own strips; they may be owned by the lord of the manor or freeholders, and farmed according to a hierarchy of agents, tenants and subtenants. An individual's strips may be spread around, or belong to more than one owner, which acted to share out the good and bad land. All strips in a furlong grew the same crop in the same year, and each year some land would be set aside for fallow or the communal grazing of animals.

The system had numerous advantages – it provided adequate food for everybody; almost everybody had at least a small stake in the process, and the villagers could work together as a community, sharing equipment, labour and expertise.

In the early days, a plough would be pulled by animals – teams of oxen, later horses. It would have had only a single ploughshare and moldboard which generally turned soil over to the right. This meant that a strip had to be ploughed in a kind of clockwise pattern, with the plough passing one way up one side of the strip, and the other way down the other side, so soil was always thrown towards the middle.

Over very many years this would lead to a pronounced ridge along the middle of the strip, with the troughs, or furrows, between the ridges marking the boundaries of ownership. The building up of these ridges was by no means strictly necessary, but was in most places encouraged as it promoted drainage, especially when the furrows were aligned down a slope.

A team of several oxen and a plough are quite long, and need to describe quite a wide arc at the end of the strip in order to turn round. In order that the plough didn't have to be pulled out of the soil too soon, the ploughman would aim slightly away from the direction of turning before swinging. This leads to ridges which, rather than being absolutely straight, describe a characteristic shallow, reversed 'S' shape. When horses took over, ridges tended to be slightly straighter.

In places, the creation of ridge and furrow actually carried on after enclosure, although later ridge and furrow tends to be in longer, narrower and in straighter runs. Similarly, features such as cart ruts and irrigation systems can sometimes be mistaken for ridge and furrow. Where enclosure hedges cut straight across an old pattern of ridge and furrow, this helps to verify a feature's true age.

Ridge and furrow is visible in many places today as a series of characteristic parallel wave-like undulations, almost always in a grassy field. Although not necessarily of itself good for wildlife, ridge and furrow does tend to indicate continuity of habitat over many years. Also, the drier ridges and wetter troughs tend to create a more diverse mix of grassland plants than a more uniformly flat field.

Ridge and furrow is the last obvious remnant of medieval farming we have left. It can still be seen in numerous places around the edges of our town, and indeed around many of the villages of the Lincolnshire coastal marsh. Ridge and furrow is destroyed by modern farming methods, and such fields' position around villages means that they tend gradually to get nibbled into by housing developments.

Thrushes. This is the time of year when Britain's thrushes are on the move. Of North East Lincolnshire's five common species of thrush, the largest, the Mistle Thrush, is the most sedentary, with most birds remaining near their breeding areas all year round. Nevertheless, a few will still arrive on the east coast in autumn, with a similar low-key movement of our own birds pushing southwards, sometimes to France and beyond.

In easterlies in autumn it is possible to witness 'falls' of Song Thrushes freshly in from the sea, although the scale of migration is smaller than for our other migrant thrushes. A modest south-westerly movement in autumn and back again in spring is the norm in Europe, with the additional birds complementing our own resident population.

Anyone spending time out of doors at this time of year couldn't fail to notice the large influx of Blackbirds. Already one of Britain's commonest breeding birds, Blackbird numbers are hugely augmented in Autumn by birds escaping cold weather and food shortages on the near continent, in Scandinavia and the countries of the Baltic. Blackbirds can often be seen flying in from the sea in favourable winds, and on the right mornings tired immigrant Blackbirds can litter coastal bushes and trees. Last year I saw a Blackbird flying up the beach at Cleethorpes, having come straight in off the sea, pursued mercilessly by a hungry Peregrine. On this occasion, despite its long journey it mustered enough energy to avoid becoming the falcon's next meal. Many Blackbirds are merely passing through on much longer journeys; interestingly the birds from the furthest north may finish up furthest south. Northern Blackbirds can push south as far as Spain and Portugal in winter, but may get there via our own gardens.

The two remaining thrush species are winter visitors only – they do not breed here. The handsome and colourful Fieldfare breeds across

Fennoscandia, with the whole population moving southwards and westwards in winter, into the milder parts of Europe. Many flocks spend the winter in British orchards, hedgerows and fields, although as with the other species, some are just passing through.

The greatest migrant of the five is our smallest thrush, the Redwing. This handsomely-marked thrush, with its bold white eyestripe and red underwing patch, breeds in Scandinavia and Russia, with some Redwings undertaking the longest migrations of any of the European thrushes. How they distribute themselves in winter depends a lot on weather patterns and food availability, and Redwings do not necessarily take the same route in subsequent winters – a bird wintering in North East Lincolnshire this winter could spend next winter as far away as Iran. There are always good numbers of Redwings in Britain, and flocks can be seen feeding on berries in hedgerows or on earthworms and other invertebrates in fields. Their thin, high-pitched calls as they pass overhead in autumn are well-known to birdwatchers, and contribute one of autumn's essential, often subconscious, background sounds. These calls can often be heard from migrating birds at night – if you hear them in the daytime, look upwards and you are sure to see parties of these delicate thrushes, which are similar in size to Starlings, passing overhead.

Predator Control. As an ecologist for a living, I have lost count of the times I have heard landowners or country folk assert that such-and-such an animal (usually some sort of predator) should be 'controlled' because there are 'too many of them'. It is usually because that species is perceived to be suppressing numbers of some other form of life we value for pleasure or profit. The situation is, however, almost always much more complex than first imagined.

From memory, I have heard this assertion applied to seals (fish stocks), Cormorants and Otters (fishing lakes), Foxes (game, and wild ground-nesting birds), Badgers (bumblebee nests, ground-nesting birds and TB-free dairy cattle), Woodpigeons (arable crops), Magpies and crows (garden-, farmland and gamebirds), Herons (ornamental fish), deer (ancient woodland flowers), Buzzards, Sparrowhawks and Kites (garden birds and Pheasant chicks), wild geese in winter (cereal crops), Peregrines (racing pigeons), and just once, Oystercatchers (cockles and mussels).

On the subject of predator control (which people assume I will be 'against'), more than one person has said to me "what ecologists don't seem to understand is the need to keep a balance". In fact, as I always respond, the study of 'the balance' is what ecology *is*. It is really *all* we do. Having said that, I accept their premise that in today's profoundly human-altered landscapes, the notion of a 'balance of nature' – an idealised stable endpoint – is a bit of a myth. In fact, we manage habitats so as to keep species assemblages within parameters deemed appropriate for the various conservation priorities, or more often, to protect rural incomes. Such management leads to successional change being mostly held in various kinds of suspended animation. Many believe direct intervention by predator control to be an acceptable tool in the management toolkit, but because cruelty and killing are involved it can be very controversial, and opinions are deeply divided.

With a little digging, a 'balance' turns out, very often, to be the last thing the person seeking to control something actually wants. They just want less of the thing to which they have a culturally-determined dislike; an unnaturally high number of some prey species they enjoy seeing, or a flabby surplus of something which can be harvested or shot, which must spend its life blissfully un-worried by anything except, eventually, humans.

There was a time when Bears, Wolves and Lynx roamed our countryside, but they were completely eradicated by humans because they threatened or were perceived to compete with our interests. In the sixteenth century, there was a bounty on the head of almost anything, from rats and mice to sparrows, Bullfinches, Herons and Kingfishers, to woodpeckers, squirrels and Moles. This is not to mention more obvious predators such as Foxes, Polecats, Buzzards, Ravens and the like.

The Victorians killed Skylarks and Corn Buntings in vast numbers, believing them to be pests of cereal crops, as well as mercilessly slaughtering any other predator or competitor for our food, including blasting whole rookeries out of trees. Some quite appalling practices went on right into my childhood in the early 1970s.

We've come a long way since then, with landowners coming to an accommodation with the vast majority of creatures which they used to kill routinely. However, legal quarry is still taken, and one-off licences to control other predators are still granted in some distinctly odd circumstances, giving the impression that a little slaughter is sometimes allowed just to quieten down some strong opinions.

There is one thing about predation which is strongly counter-intuitive, and it is this: even when predation levels are manifestly high, it is still extremely difficult to prove that predation is causing a reduction in prey numbers. "But if they're not lowering prey numbers", you will hear landowners ask, "then what are they eating?"

This is a good question. Predators may simply be removing a surplus of prey before it is killed by something else – starvation, disease, overcrowding, or some other limiting factor. The removal of a prey item may make others of its kind more likely to survive by freeing up resources. Birds whose eggs are taken may quickly re-lay, and productivity remain unchanged.

Some prey species are well able to survive high levels of predation; after all, they have been doing so, and co-existing with the same predators, for millennia. There is a 'tipping point', of course, where predation exacerbates, rather than replacing, other forms of mortality, but until this point is reached, a predator may feed without limiting its prey at all.

Also, genuine declines due to predation very often have their roots in habitat degradation or land management issues, especially ones that favour predators over their prey. An extreme example to make a point: if a large, farmed estate contains only one bush, it is easy for the Magpie to find the Blackbird's nest. So – is the problem too many Magpies, or too few bushes?

And we should point out, of course, that predators and prey must necessarily regulate *each other*. There must always be fewer predators than prey, and a predator will either starve to death or move on well before the last prey item is eaten. When alternative prey is available, the situation becomes more complex, and the food web may require more working out, and more cunning manipulation.

But predators certainly *can* depress numbers of prey, and it would be disingenuous to deny that there are situations – including in nature conservation – when they can be a real nuisance. The uphill struggle of trying to protect certain kinds of rare ground-nesting birds springs immediately to mind.

Such situations give us difficult decisions to make, and sensibilities may differ. A long, slow transformation in attitudes to predator control is underway, but is not yet stable and resolved. But at least we should be thankful that the days when anything with sharp teeth or a hooked bill would be removed as a matter of course over vast areas, are behind us; at least in most of lowland Britain. Nowadays it is mostly understood that a few predators are the price we pay for a diverse countryside and avoidance of unacceptable cruelty. Predators are still often disliked, but mostly seen as an occupational hazard of rural ways of making a living. Indeed, in nature conservation situations, some of our rarer and more charismatic predators may now have a considerably higher conservation priority than their prey.

If, in an individual case, predation turns out to be such a problem that intervention is absolutely necessary, surely everything else should be tried first before one resorts to lethal control. Maybe this could be by more effectively preventing access to prey; scaring off, or diverting predators where possible; or in exceptional circumstances sacrificing areas of land to the animals, for which compensation is made available.

The very best way of all must be to enhance the extent and quality of habitat for wildlife generally, so that prey numbers can build to a level beyond which predation is incapable of tipping them into catastrophic decline.

Yew. When we view the myriad shades of green in our English landscape, the darkest tone of all does not, as you might expect, belong to an exotic conifer, but a British native tree whose cultural and landscape significance would be difficult to overstate. It is that densest, sombrest, longest-lived and most characterful of evergreens, the Yew.

Yew has always been present in British woodlands, growing on all but the most acid soils. Birds deposit the seeds in their droppings, and Yew will germinate readily on well-drained chalk or limestone hillsides, where it may occasionally form dense thickets. When allowed to grow without competition, a Yew tree will not reach any great height, but it may be very wide, its outer branches sometimes reaching down to the ground enclosing a dark, bare, inner 'room' around its convoluted, iron-hard trunk.

Some Yew trees are believed to be thousands of years old. Beyond 400 years of age the heartwood of a Yew tree dies and the tree becomes hollow, making specimens any older than this impossible to age accurately. New shoots may arise from the base of the trunk, appearing at first as buttresses or fluting, and eventually coalescing with the existing trunk. The tree may send out roots into its own rotting heartwood, or produce new plants where its branches touch the ground.

This can make old Yew trees into extraordinarily characterful structures. Although seldom elegant, their convoluted shapes, along with the longevity and dense, evergreen foliage, may lead to Yew trees acquiring a venerable, gothic presence. This has given Yew trees an obvious natural role as important cultural landmarks and places of spiritual significance.

The most obvious thing about Yews nowadays is their strong association with churchyards. Many reasons have been put forward for this. A tree which is both extremely long-lived and evergreen is an obvious symbol for immortality. Yew sprays may also be used as 'palm' in church. Less popular are the theories that Yew was placed within enclosed churchyards to keep it away from livestock, or to provide decoration or shelter for churchgoers.

In fact, in many places the Yew trees are plainly considerably older than the churches themselves, probably indicating that Christianity has taken over sites that were already sacred, and already marked by Yews in pagan times. One could go further, and say that some of the original pagan sites may have been deliberately created in locations where Yew trees already existed. The association between Yews and sacred places may go back well into prehistory.

In Lincolnshire and eastern England generally, churchyard Yews tend not to be of any great antiquity. You can see some attractive Yews which are by their own standards rather young, in the churchyards at Humberston, Waltham and Old Clee, although unusually, St Peter's in Cleethorpes, with its rudimentary churchyard, has none. Grimsby cemetery has some statuesque Yews, and there is an obvious group of Yews along the roadside at the front of Weelsby Woods, and more along the way at Weelsby Hall.

Yew trees in places like these are often not the original wild type, but a 'fastigiate' variety, sometimes called Irish Yew, which forms a more compact shape with upwardly-swept branches. This variety, originating from two small trees found growing on a limestone crag in Fermanagh in the 1760s, is considered to be a better tree for landscaping, more like the funereal cypresses of the Mediterranean. It is also more amenable to shaping – indeed Yew lends itself extremely well to topiary. If you are in the south of the county, do go and look at the shaped Yews in the gardens of Ayscoughfee Hall near Spalding, or the Clipsham Yew Avenue in old county of Rutland. One of the two original Irish Yew seedlings can still be seen growing at Florencecourt in Fermanagh.

Yew is usually dioecious, which is to say that the male and female parts grow on different trees. In fact, they may occasionally occur on the same plant, or a plant may switch from one to the other over time. Male trees produce toxic, allergy-inducing pollen in the spring, although mercifully most of the 'Irish Yews' are female. The red fruit of the female tree forms a kind of cup around the seed, technically knows as an 'aril'. The red, fleshy part of the fruit is the only part of the plant which is not poisonous, but don't try it. A bird will cope by eating the fruit whole, passing the contained, poisonous seed undigested, along with a dollop of fertiliser.

Water Voles. Within my own lifetime, Water Voles were so common that seeing one scarcely warranted a mention. A walk along any ditch, drain, lake or slow-flowing river with firm enough, vegetated banks, as well as reedbeds or other more extensive wetlands, would yield Water Vole sightings, or at least signs that the animals were present.

Evidence of Water Voles includes holes in the banks, both above and below the waterline. Holes link up to groups of underground chambers at differing heights, to cope with fluctuating water levels. Where there are large populations, holes can sometimes be so extensive that riverbanks can become unstable and collapse.

Holes above the water level are often accompanied by flat feeding 'lawns', often containing the remains of half-eaten food. Water Voles' latrines, containing small piles of shiny, lozenge-shaped green or black droppings, are used by the animals to mark their territories, and can be used by surveyors to assess Water Vole population size.

The animals themselves will swim across the surface of any still or slow-moving open water in full view, although they are also excellent divers. On or near the banks, they feed in a characteristic hunched sitting position, so long as they are undisturbed. But the most evocative sign of Water Voles is the distinctive 'plop' as they dive into the water for safety ahead of the walker.

Sadly, this sound is seldom heard nowadays as the Water Vole is the most threatened of all British mammals, with an approximate 97% decline in the UK since 1960. Part of this decline can be put down to long-term changes in the management of waterways and their vegetation, pollution, and other deterioration in water quality. Recently, however, the decline has been much accelerated by the spread in the UK of the escaped, non-native American Mink since the 1950s and 60s. The Mink preys directly on Water Voles and shares its waterside habitat, with female and juvenile Mink often being small enough to enter the voles' burrows. By the year 2000, the problem seemed intractable, and conservationists were predicting the imminent extinction of the Water Vole in Britain.

Nowadays, although water Voles are still uncommon, the situation doesn't look anything like as bleak. One lifeline for the Water Vole lies in the return to its old haunts of the Otter. A 'mustelid' like the Mink, the much larger Otter will outcompete its smaller relative in the same habitat, such that an increase in Otter usually leads to a decrease in Mink. Also, methods of trapping Mink have made great strides forward, and now concerted eradication effort in the Mink's strongholds can substantially depress Mink numbers.

Mink is thought to occur on most major and minor watercourses in Lincolnshire, and there are numerous sightings in our area. Lindsey Marsh Drainage Board (stretching from Grimsby to beyond Skegness) has an ongoing programme of Mink trapping for the specific purpose of helping Water Voles. Otter, as noted by this column before, has also now returned to our area, being present in the Freshney, Louth Navigation Canal and Waithe Beck. The effect on the balance between these three mammals remains to be seen.

The 'dykes' of the Lincolnshire outmarsh have always been something of a stronghold for Water Voles, including the old fields on which the Cleethorpes Country Park housing was built. There are still a few Water Voles to be seen in the last remnants of this habitat around Buck Beck and the Country Park itself, but don't confuse them with rats, which are also present there. They also survive tenuously on waterways at the Fitties, and in Grimsby they persist in Gooseman's Drain and at points along the Freshney.

Sea Buckthorn. In 2002, the plant conservation charity Plantlife had an idea to raise the profile of plant conservation in the UK. They invited people all over Britain to vote for a special plant to represent their county – a so-called 'county flower'. Twenty-five thousand votes later, it became clear that the project had hit a major snag, with almost every county choosing the same plant: Bluebell. In something of a panic, the charity hastily declared Bluebell to be the 'national flower of Britain', and removed it from the voting. Every county was asked to poll again, this time making a simple binary choice between their top two 'non-Bluebell' choices.

Lincolnshire, rather oddly, chose the Dog Violet. Dog Violets are nice enough flowers, accompanying many other late spring blooms along undisturbed waysides and ancient woodland rides. They do not have a scent like the earlier-flowering and richer-coloured Sweet Violet, and they are not really one of the first harbingers of spring, like the equally common Early Dog Violet. What is more, they have no particular association with Lincolnshire.

What makes this choice even more puzzling is that in terms of a county plant, Lincolnshire has a *clear* winner, and that is the Sea Buckthorn *Hippophae rhamnoides*. Here in North East Lincolnshire we take this thorny but colourful shrub completely for granted. Indeed we consider it an 'invasive' on our sand dunes, removing it by the lorryload to prevent it from smothering a less-competitive dune flora, and improving access to the beach.

Nationally, Sea Buckthorn is rare, as of course is any plant which can only grow by the sea. While it occurs as a native in every east coast county from Northumberland down to Kent, Lincolnshire has far and away the largest indigenous populations of Sea Buckthorn of any British county. Its unique combination of black twigs, silver-green foliage and orange-red berries provides the essential colour palette for many of the Lincolnshire coast's remoter dunescapes.

Sea Buckthorn provides the first shelter, and the red berries the first food, for exhausted migrant birds fresh in from the sea in autumn. The berries are also edible to humans (they are rich in antioxidants and other minerals), although they

are as sour as lemons and devilishly difficult to gather. I have seen bottled Sea Buckthorn juice on sale on the Baltic and on the Russian side of the Gulf of Finland, where it is no doubt a commoner plant than it is here. Although 'bletted' and sweetened before consumption, this fruit is still an acquired taste.

The abundant berries long outlast the leaves on the plant, and in the low sunlight of a midwinter afternoon they can make the dunes at the south end of Cleethorpes appear aflame. By the spring when the leaves reappear, what berries remain are mostly bleached to pink or white.

Sea Buckthorn

Wildlife Photography. Wildlife photography is a challenging pastime requiring a great deal of knowledge, technique, dedication and skill to do well. Yet this column is furnished every week with wildlife photographs of the highest order, in many cases courtesy of a group of skillful local photographers, taking pictures around us here in North East Lincolnshire.

So what are their secrets? What equipment do they use? What techniques and tricks do they employ to get such good results? I asked them, and this is a whistle-stop tour of their responses.

As you might imagine, the subject of equipment was one on which they all had something to say. Wildlife photography is about taking your chances, and the best camera, one said, "is the one you've got with you". While there's no doubt that it's possible to get good wildlife photographs with a point-and-shoot or a modern smartphone, our best wildlife photographers all use fast SLRs allowing manual control of aperture, shutter speed and sensitivity (ISO), with a small selection of lenses. And they all emphasise the need to know how to use them.

A standard, multi-purpose lens may do for many things – subjects you can approach easily and which stay still – trees, flowers, tame animals, for example. For smaller subjects, insects and the like, a macro lens is required.

A smaller aperture (i.e. a higher f-number) gives a greater depth of field (area in focus, front to back), and so is generally desirable, although with flowers, a cluttered background can sometimes be softened by judiciously easing up on this rule. For insects, the depth of field needs to be a great as humanly possible to get the whole creature, legs, wings and all, in focus. Depth of field can be extended a little further if necessary by moving slightly further away from a very close subject, and cropping the picture later.

When photographing birds in flight or other fast-moving animals, a fast shutter speed is more important than aperture size if you want to keep everything sharp. A camera which can manage very high shutter speeds and a very high number of frames per second in a burst, is a huge advantage. Long lenses – say 200mm up to 600mm – provide the necessary magnification for animals which it is impossible to approach closely, and relatively inexpensive converters can increase the zoom still further. If an animal is close, some cameras have a silent shutter which can help not to scare the subject. Other equipment may include a tripod or bean bag for stability, and any number of home-made gizmos for specific uses. A car may act as a hide.

When it comes to fieldcraft, all respondents stressed subject knowledge and patience. If you're not properly in place at the right moment, you can't press the button. If you're in for a long wait, take supplies, and whatever is needed for comfort.

The first hour of daylight probably provides the best light, as well as maximum animal activity and relative lack of disturbance from passing people. Providing food or water nearby, and natural landing materials, may attract animals into photogenic areas.

One of the best pieces of advice is always to plan a picture beforehand – to photograph the subject in the mind's eye first. Opportunities to get the perfect picture may come and go so quickly that failure to have everything already set – aperture, shutter speed, composition – will as likely as not result in a missed opportunity.

Nowadays, it is straightforward to manipulate pictures afterwards using computer software such as Photoshop – cropping, brightness, etc. Sharp focus, if not present on the original, cannot be re-created. If you have to choose, make sure an animal's eye is in focus. Composition, too, is a bit of an art – if the subject is not centrally placed (it usually looks best on about a third, as a rule), it should be facing *into* the frame. Uncluttered backgrounds often work extremely well.

And finally, the absolute golden rule: *the welfare of the animal always comes first.* A good photographer understands, studies and anticipates the behavior of the subject, without affecting its normal behavior. No animal should be flushed, cajoled or kept from its nest. Insects should be on their correct foodplant. Photographs of creatures moving away from the camera – of animals obviously flushed or fleeing – should be looked on with special suspicion!

When one takes full manual control of the camera and the subject's habits are intimately understood, there may be are no limits to artistic creativity in wildlife photography, and rules are there to be broken. Exceptionally, a really unique wildlife photo may find itself in high demand.

Very many thanks to Don Davis, Colin Smale, Mike Pickwell, Carole Crawford and Malcolm Crawford for sharing their knowledge.

Autumn Migration, 2015. Rare birds can appear at any time of year, but are much more frequent in spring and autumn when migrants are naturally on the move.

The classic rarities of spring tend to be birds from further south overshooting on their northward journey. Birds at this time tend to be adults in breeding plumage, making the lengthening and often warm days of spring an exciting time to be out looking for birds. Southerly winds are best for rarity-hunters in spring.

But autumn tends to produce more, and on average better, rarities. There are more birds out there in autumn when the breeding season has just ended. All the inexperienced juveniles of the year are dispersing away from their breeding areas, but have not yet experienced the high mortality of their first winter.

Many young birds set out on their first migration in completely the wrong direction and get caught up in weather systems which take them even further off track, and they sometimes turn up on our shores. As you might imagine, the east coast is a good place to pick up grounded rarities from Scandinavia, continental Europe and Siberia. Easterly winds and poor visibility are the conditions that get birdwatchers excited at this time of year.

October is the peak month for rarities, but the autumn season proper may last from late August through to early November. The Lincolnshire coast always receives its share of rarities in autumn, although there are generally rather fewer where we are, inside the mouth of the estuary. Nevertheless we in North East Lincolnshire always get a few noteworthy rare birds.

Although tempting fate, we are probably now in a position to review autumn 2015 in terms of rare birds here in North East Lincolnshire.

The wasteland behind Blundell Park was the place to be for those small to medium-sized predators the shrikes this year. At the end of August a Red-backed Shrike popped up, to be replaced towards the end of October by its relative the Great Grey Shrike, both birds being found by John Nelson. These birds' generic name *Lanius* comes from the Latin for 'butcher', alluding to shrikes' habit of impaling their prey on thorns.

A Wryneck, a small, camouflaged woodpecker-relative, was found by Dave Bradbeer in private allotments in Cleethorpes at the end of August, with a fly-by Spoonbill in the same place a couple of days later.

A Red Kite, which may have been a wandering bird from reintroduction sites in Yorkshire or Northamptonshire, floated over Cleethorpes on 9th October.

Meanwhile, a steady trickle of commoner migrant birds provided background interest. These may have been birds of the British uplands dispersing to lower latitudes post-breeding, or birds from points north stopping en route to their wintering grounds in Africa. Redstart, Whinchat, Pied Flycatcher, Wheatear, Grey Wagtail, Siskin and Stonechat all made appearances in Cleethorpes during the autumn. Buzzards passed overhead, and in tidal waters, passage waders such as Spotted Redshank, Greenshank and Curlew Sandpiper joined our usual estuary species. Skeins of Pink-footed Geese passed regularly overhead on their way to wintering grounds, probably on the North Norfolk Coast.

Nationally, this year's autumn rarity season was noteworthy for an exceptional influx of the tiny but prettily-marked Yellow-browed Warbler.

Breeding from the Ural mountains eastwards, these tiny warblers would normally winter in south and south-east Asia, but a few always turn up in the UK in autumn. Sightings have become more frequent in recent years – range expansion by the species is a possible reason, but each year a proportion of migrants are thought to set off on the right line, but in the wrong direction along it, subjecting themselves to weather systems in northern Europe or over the North Sea, which land them on our own east coast. In our area this year there were two Yellow-browed Warblers at Grimsby Cemetery and another at Europarc, although undoubtedly others were missed.

Thanks go to Dave Bradbeer, Ian Shepherd, Chris Atkin, Chris Heaton, John Nelson, Dave Wright, Josh Forrester, Terry Whalin and James Smith for their autumn records.

Seal Time. It's seal time again at Donna Nook! Now is our opportunity to see one of Britain's most breathtaking and accessible wildlife spectacles practically on our doorstep. Grey Seal is the largest carnivore to be seen on land in the UK, males sometimes approaching three metres in length and weighing up to six hundredweight. A total of 1,676 pups were born at Donna Nook in 2013, and numbers are again high this year despite the events of 5 December last, when a devastating high tide scattered seals far and wide, separating mothers from their pups and bringing the visitor season to an abrupt close. On that night, heroic seal wardens battled in the darkness to remove obstructing visitor fencing and bring stranded pups back to their mothers on the marsh. Luckily, by that stage of the season the pups were mostly of an age to be able to cope with this trauma, and mortality was kept to a minimum.

Seals first started to breed at Donna Nook in the 1970s, but at that time they were mostly confined to the outer sandbanks. By the 1980s a few were starting to occur further up the marsh, sometimes right up to the foot of the dunes. Nowadays numbers have dramatically increased and this behaviour is the norm.

Grey seals spend most of the year at sea, where they feed on fish, or hauled out on distant sandbanks. They start to arrive back at Donna Nook to breed in late October, and the first white pups are born shortly after this. Seal numbers build to a maximum in the second half of November, after which departing animals exceed new arrivals. By the second week in January only a few moulting seals remain.

These days there is a well-organised visitor system, allowing all the drama of the seals' breeding season, from bloody fights between huge rival bulls to females giving birth and nursing pups, to be witnessed at close range and in safety without disturbing the animals. Huge numbers of people now make the pilgrimage from all over Europe, and visitors may have to stand two or three-deep at the fence at weekends at the height of the season. For this reason, weekday visiting is strongly recommended. Also, the new car park at 'Stonebridge' is quite poorly-designed and very tight when full, and on peak visitor days it is advised to take the right turn to the overflow car park before the very end of the road is reached.

Wardens, of which there are up to eight on a busy weekend, are available to guide visitors and dispense information. The wardens' biggest challenge in recent years has been to stop determined photographers from marching out across the marsh to the tideline, where they can harass and scatter breeding seals, causing pup mortality several times the background level. This, of course, breaks the golden rule of wildlife photography, which is always to put the welfare of the animal first. The problem seems to be diminishing these

days, but constant vigilance, including dawn patrols by wardens, is still needed to combat this problem.

There is no need to upset breeding seals. One can enjoy a world class 'big game' experience at incredibly close quarters by simply sticking within the appointed areas.

Grey Seals, Donna Nook

Waxwings. As winter approaches, birdwatchers all along the east coast and further afield begin to wonder whether this will be a 'Waxwing year'. Waxwings are one of those birds you can't get tired of seeing. Not only are they exotic looking, tame and with a propensity for turning up in easily accessible places, but the irregular nature of their mass appearances, or 'irruptions', gives them an added, almost mystical quality.

Waxwings are visitors from the far north. The closest breeding grounds to Britain are in northern Scandinavia, but they inhabit the vast Arctic and sub-Arctic taiga forests right across Russia and into America. In the winter they must evacuate all but the southernmost fringe of this habitat, with birds usually reaching as far south as the Low Countries and the Balkans in Europe, across to central China and Japan in the east.

Waxwings are superbly adapted to cope with the cold, and unlike some of the thrushes and other northern 'passerines' which visit us in winter, have no pressing need to seek out Britain's milder climate. However, they are very dependent upon supplies of berries for food, and it is the depletion or failure of the Scandinavian Rowan crop that usually triggers large movements across the North Sea.

In irruption years, the first appearances of Waxwings, and the largest flocks, tend to be seen in the east of the UK, and we here in Lincolnshire are well-placed to receive them. After landfall they will quickly move to wherever there is an abundant supply of berries, which often means garden or amenity plantings in cities and towns. While they still favour their traditional food of Rowan berries in Britain, they will settle on any abundant source of fruit, with a particular liking for Cotoneasters, Pyracantha, cherries and Viburnums.

Birdwatchers understand well what is required to locate Waxwings. Once settled, Waxwings can be so tame, and occur in such well-populated urban places, that flocks often present themselves with no difficulty. However, when they first arrive here in the autumn or winter, silhouetted small groups of what are apparently Starlings or Redwings in roadside and coastal treetops should be given a second look for the telltale crest.

When Waxwings have been reported in an urban location, the first thing on arrival is to find the most likely berry-laden trees – often municipal plantings – and wait. Waxwing flocks tend to alternate frenzied communal berry-guzzling sessions with local reconnaissance flights and will often disappear for a while, but come back to the same source of food again and again if the viewer is patient. However it is also understood that a Waxwing can eat its weight in berries in a few hours, and depletion of a berry crop by a decent-sized flock is usually rapid, and so there is usually only a time slot of a few days at most in which to see them before they move on.

It is perfectly possible to see a lone Waxwing, but most of the time they occur in flocks of varying size. On 9 November 1965, about a thousand birds were reported in Louth, but this was an exceptional count. I have seen flocks of a few dozen in many parts of our own town during good winters.

Waxwings will usually allow the watcher to come fairly close, one assumes because they have no fear of humans across most of their breeding range. Although essentially a pinkish-grey colour, their plumage includes a host of subtle and not-so-subtle features and colour splashes, including a beautiful curved black mask and matching chin patch, a black-and-yellow-tipped, grey-blue tail, and tiny red tips to some of the secondary feathers looking like sealing wax, from which they get their name. Just as distinctive is the call – a fairly quiet ringing trill with a mild bell-like quality. At close quarters the audible fluttering of the wings when taking off or alighting is also unlike most other birds of similar size.

Most arrivals of Waxwings occur in autumn and early winter, and exceptionally they can stay around until May. Waxwing irruption years seem to have become more frequent in recent times, although it remains to be seen whether this trend will continue. In some years there are very few or none, and to find a Waxwing at all in such years is a great challenge. But don't miss them if it is an irruption year – seeing Waxwings at close range in the heart of the town is one of the great wildlife experiences of the British winter.

Small Mammals. Although you may occasionally see a little mouse–like animal dashing across a country road in front of your car, our smaller mammals are generally quite good at keeping out of sight. They are actually surprisingly abundant, but keep hidden because they are preyed on by a whole host of wild predators. We have several sorts here in North East Lincolnshire, and perhaps more that are under-recorded.

When you know what to look for, there are several clues as to just how common these creatures actually are. One is their tendency to be brought into houses by cats. Another is the fact that owl pellets, which may themselves be found in large accumulated piles, are substantially composed of their remains. Lastly, the litter layer of rank, unmanaged grasslands may, at least to the trained eye, be so riddled with runs and tunnels as to dictate the very structure of the vegetation itself.

There may be other clues – droppings or nibbled cardboard in houses, caches of food in winter birds' nests, chewed grass stems, or wild foodstuffs with characteristic holes or toothmarks. If you're lucky you may find the small, spherical nest of the Harvest Mouse in reeds or other dense vegetation. In summer the high-pitched shrieks of fighting shrews in dense undergrowth may be audible many metres away.

Two kinds of mice may commonly be found in houses and outbuildings. The rather plain, greyish House Mouse is the one most likely to form colonies indoors, struggling to survive for long away from human habitation. The richer yellow-brown and more two-tone Wood Mouse is ubiquitous in lowland habitats in Britain, and may sometimes enter houses. Wood Mice are extremely common and adaptable creatures, with a varied, omnivorous diet. The extremely similar but slightly larger Yellow-necked Mouse is very much rarer, and can usually be told by a yellow patch right across the chest, although very rarely I have also seen this feature on Wood Mice.

The nest of the tiny, gingery Harvest Mouse is seen more often than the animal itself – it is a tennis-ball-sized sphere of woven grasses, built above the ground in reeds or other herbage. It is only occupied during the breeding cycle, during which time the mouse pushes into the nest through the outer wall at random points; if an exit hole is apparent, the nest is certainly deserted. Harvest Mice have prehensile tails, making them adept at foraging above the ground. While other mice may struggle and give you a nip when handled, Harvest Mice are fairly docile creatures whose tiny size and warm colouration makes them especially appealing when seen up close

Voles can be told from mice by their blunter noses, smaller eyes and ears, and shorter tails. These vegetarians generally inhabit long grass and hedgebanks, making a network of runs. A rather plain brown vole with a short tail will be a Field (or Short-tailed) Vole. This species undergoes regular cycles in abundance whose peaks are often given away by visible local increases in its predators. The slightly smaller Bank Vole is a warmer colour, especially along the centre of the back, and has a slightly longer tail.

The shrews, although a similar size, are entirely unrelated to all the foregoing animals. They are voracious carnivores identified by their pointed noses, tiny ears and sharp, red-tipped teeth. Shrews live life at high speed – they are short-lived, neurotic and often aggressive, and must consume the best part of their bodyweight in food each day. They may starve to death after even short periods without food, and as a consequence a licence is required to trap them.

We have three sorts of shrew – the Common Shrew is the most abundant. Of the trio, it is the middle one in size, and has a stripe of subtly warmer colouring along the flanks between the brown upperside and the paler underside. The more two-tone Pygmy Shrew is the tiniest of all Britain's mammals – it weighs less than a 2p piece and has one of the highest metabolic rates of any animal. It has a slightly longer, hairier tail, a more domed head and proportionally larger feet than a Common Shrew. Any very small, wild-caught shrew must be this species as shrews are full-size when they leave the nest.

Much the largest shrew is the Water Shrew. It is much blacker than the others, with a whiter underside, and often white patches on the ears and eyes. It is quite capable of giving an unpleasant nip if badly handled, made more so by the injection of venom via grooves in the teeth. They may be found away from water, but are usually associated with ditches, streams and other waterbodies, in which they regularly take the plunge in search of prey. Adaptations for swimming include stiff bristle on hind feet and a keel along the underside of the tail.

We have Water Shrews in Laceby Beck, and I'm sure elsewhere. Harvest Mice are not common in our area, but there may well be some awaiting discovery. In the unlikely event that you find a Yellow-necked Mouse, do tell me straight away – it will be a 'first' for the northern half of Lincolnshire.

Vice Counties. The conservation of wildlife is only possible when you have information about what species live where. Compiling this data requires a veritable army of people to submit location information on the plants and animals they see, so that distribution maps can be plotted. Sending in records takes effort and time, and one has to be bothered – but thankfully, many people are.

When submitting a record of a sighting, simple names of places, like 'Cleethorpes Beach', are not particularly helpful. The unit that the compiler has to work with is usually a square on the Ordnance Survey (OS) national grid, whether it be a 1km square, 2km square or 10km square. Only with records in this format can the compiler put a 'dot on a map'. Many sites inconveniently lie across boundaries of squares, especially, as you would imagine, when you least want them to.

So recorders will usually ask that a wildlife record is accompanied by an OS grid reference. This is much easier than it used to be. In the not too distant past, you would have had to spread the OS map out on the table, find the position of the organism to be recorded, and read off the grid reference like 'battleships', remembering (and people frequently didn't) that you go 'along' first and 'up' second.

Nowadays there are several mapping websites where you can just hover the cursor over an aerial photograph and read off the exact grid reference from the bottom of the screen. Hand-held GPS devices are also available which can tell you the grid reference of the spot you're standing in, so you can record it at the time. Now, even smartphones have a GPS facility which may be accurate to 5 metres, and there are apps available for making biological recording simplicity itself. So there is no longer any excuse for not providing information on an organism's precise location.

For most plants and animals, Britain as a whole is too big a unit for summarising information on species' distributions. Counties, on the other hand, are of a manageable size for collecting records, and hence the first port of call for records of any kind are 'county recorders'. These are usually well-qualified volunteers who receive records from individuals and feed them into the national system, acting both as a helpful expert and quality-controller for doubtful records as they go.

The problem with counties, of course, is that their boundaries tend to change. This can quickly make a farce of biological recording, as, for example, plants which are literally rooted to the spot, appear to move from one county to another. Changing county boundaries can make it impossible to track the fortunes of species or populations over the long term.

For this reason, recorders in nearly all groups use what are known as the Watsonian vice counties. These were devised by Hewett Cottrell Watson in 1852, and are permanent entities based on the ancient counties of Britain. The larger counties (like Lincolnshire) were subdivided, so that all vice counties are of a more similar size. On the vice county map shown, how many can you name?

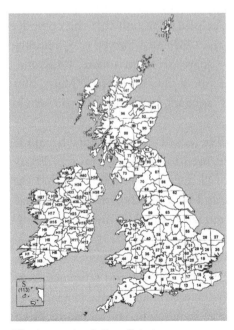

The vice-counties of Great Britain.
Courtesy of BSBI/Ordnance Survey

For the purposes of biological recording, we in Cleethorpes are squarely in vc54, 'North Lincolnshire'. Vice county boundaries are absolutely and ineradicably fixed. So a plant on Cleethorpes beach is forever in Lincolnshire, whatever funny ideas politicians might have.

One of the irritations of biological recording is the reluctance of most of the birdwatching fraternity to use the same vice county system as everybody else (there are honourable exceptions). The very problems that the system was designed to eliminate are alive and well in bird-recording.

The very best way to record any organism is with an Ordnance Survey grid reference. This short code will identify a location with absolute accuracy. For example, go and check out the rare native subspecies of Black Poplar growing at Cleethorpes Boating Lake. It is at TA 31841 07275, in vc54.

Snow Buntings. Every winter for several years now the beach at Humberston has played host to some special visitors from the far north, and happily they have returned again this year *[November 2014]*.

Snow Buntings are the most northerly breeding songbirds on Earth. In summer they inhabit the desolate boulder fields, rocky coasts and frozen treeless plains of the tundra fringing the Arctic Ocean, from Alaska through Canada, Greenland, Iceland and Scandinavia and around to Siberia, seldom occuring anywhere where the summer temperature exceeds 10 degrees Celsius. They can be very common in places so remote that competition with other birds is eliminated, and in some Inuit villages they may nest in buildings, becoming the high Arctic equivalent of the sparrow.

There is a very small outlying breeding population in Scotland, perhaps only 70 pairs, occupying the bare tops of the highest mountains in the Cairngorms and some of the most elevated western peaks. Amazingly, they attempt to remain in this inhospitable environment through the winter, only descending below 1000m when deep snow makes life any higher impossible.

Snow Buntings from the Arctic must retreat to lower latitudes in winter, usually settling in the steppes of central and eastern Europe and the expansive wildernesses of the Baltic and North Sea coasts. British birds are believed to derive mainly from the Icelandic breeding population, but birds from other parts of the Arctic have also been recovered here. Flocks are to an extent nomadic, but will sometimes remain faithful to areas where the feeding is good. 'Tinkling' flocks of Snow Buntings are a wonderful addition to the British east coast's wilder expanses of shingle, sand and marsh.

Where tides provide a strandline or uncover patches of buried seed, Snow Buntings form tight, restless flocks which creep along the ground in a characteristic 'rolling' motion, the birds from the rear constantly leapfrogging to the front of the flock. With a good view these are beautifully-patterned birds showing great individual variation, their russet, black and white markings reflecting their bare, rocky or sandy, and often snowy natural habitat. They show more white than any similar passerine bird, with males having much whiter wings than females, especially noticeable in flight. When disturbed, Snow Buntings take to the air like a blizzard of snowflakes, accompanied by soft rippling contact calls. The flock characteristically wheels round and fragments, before reconvening to settle again, beautifully camouflaged, to feed.

Like many creatures already living at climatic extremes, Snow Buntings are one of the species most at risk from global warming. It is thought that an ameliorating climate could be responsible for pushing many species' ranges to higher latitudes, and in mountain areas, uphill. This could put paid to Scotland's small mountain-top population of Snow Buntings, and also give Arctic breeding birds nowhere to go.

Look for these attractive Arctic visitors along the outer dunes anywhere between Cleethorpes and Humberston. A number of other songbird species can be seen on the saltmarsh, including Skylarks, Meadow Pipits, and other buntings and finches. The only other small birds forming tight flocks like Snow Buntings should be Linnets or possibly Twite, which don't show nearly so much white, and do not usually frequent the open beach.

Snow Buntings on the beach in winter. Photo: Don Davis

December

Technology for Revealing Nature. Our basic five senses are enough to allow us to appreciate a fair amount of the wildlife around us, but even so there is still so much that we miss. So many of our plants and animals are too small, too distant or too inaccessible to give up their secrets. To reveal such delights, technology can help, or may indeed be the only way.

The first two problems – to reveal organisms which are too small or too distant – are long solved. Although invented many years earlier, it was during the Victorian era that microscopes became inexpensive enough to be widely-used. This led to huge advances in the identification of smaller invertebrates, fungi and plants, as well as revealing a myriad more organisms too small to have been previously seen.

The original technology for studying birds – which, of course, it can be very difficult to approach closely – was the gun. Shooting would be used to acquire specimens and skins, leading to the first competent and rigorous classification of our birdlife. Again, it was during Victorian times that this approach was gradually replaced by the use of field optics – telescopes and binoculars – for the more conservation-minded study of birds. Nowadays technology has moved on again, and we can fit tiny transmitters to our migratory birds to send back previously unknown information about where they go when they leave our shores.

Creatures of the night have always posed a problem for humans, as our night vision is so poor. The age-old use of trapping and field signs is these days being partly replaced by the use of inexpensive digital trail cameras which can be set up to record all night, and the results simply examined on screen in the morning. Surprise sightings captured by carefully-placed trail-cams have recently advanced the knowledge of the distributions of some of our rarest mammals – recently a Pine Marten, for example, was captured on camera in the North York Moors, despite there having been no other sightings there since 1982.

Bats, those classic creatures of the night, can be identified by their ultrasonic echolocation calls, and the use of dedicated technology is the only way of making these calls accessible to humans. Older, simpler bat detectors can bring the calls into the range of human hearing in real time, creating a variety of clicking, plopping and warbling sounds in what for us is the comfortable mid-range. To the trained ear these are perfectly good enough to identify a fair proportion of our British bats to species level. Nowadays there are gadgets one can attach to a smartphone or tablet which create visual representations – sonograms – of the calls which persist as a permanent record for perusal at one's leisure. Some programs will even attempt to 'auto-identify' the species. It has long been a common survey technique to leave dedicated digital bat recorders out all night unaccompanied, and study the sonograms at the comfort of one's desk the next day after a good night's sleep.

A similar technique is now adopted by the UK bird fraternity, having already been used successfully for ten years or more in America. This time it is straightforward, 'actual-frequency' sound recording which is involved, rather than the interpretation of ultrasonic sounds. At migration times, microphones are attached to low-cost digital recording devices and placed in sheltered locations facing the night sky, to record the calls of overflying birds. Again, the results of many hours' recording can be condensed into a collection of key moments the next day on a computer, and the results can be a revelation. At the right times of year the night sky may be filled with the sounds of overflying migrants – often species completely incongruous with the habitat over which they are flying. Utterances of thrushes, waders, terns and many others are readily identifiable, and there is an ever-growing online community ready to help with the more difficult bird calls. Where calls are *very* similar, again visual sonograms are a help. Although some species are mostly silent on migration and therefore under-represented in this soundscape, some more vocal rarities have proved to be much more regular than sightings on the ground would ever suggest.

Technology then, from all of the above to moth traps and submersibles, from infra-red photography to electro-fishing to electron microscopes, has brought so much of the cryptic natural world into our consciousness. But plants, animals, fungi and unseen creatures still have to be identified.

Identification is a huge part of what a naturalist's time is spent doing, and becoming proficient, even in one group, can be the work of a lifetime. Failure to gain correct identifications for difficult and cryptic taxa is a constant source of frustration in an otherwise immensely satisfying pursuit, and for the professional can be the stuff of nightmares. Intractable identification problems can obstruct both conservation efforts and scientific research, as well as dampening enthusiasm for seeking out nature generally.

Ultimately, there is only so much one can do – not only must many organisms go down as 'don't knows', but people are often put off studying whole groups of otherwise beautiful and rewarding animals and plants because of a few persistent and tedious identification problems.

This is where the greatest technological revolution of our time is currently unfolding, with the use of so-called 'DNA bar-coding'. Recent advances mean that only a small fragment of animal or plant tissue is needed to extract and multiply up the DNA, decode it, and 'label' the species with a high degree of accuracy. Indeed it may do even more than this – this technique has already highlighted several instances where what was thought to be a single species was in fact several similar ones, and conversely, where apparently separate species were just different 'morphs', or in some instances male and female, of one and the same. To create a reference library of 'bar-codes' for all species will be a long haul, but a start has been made.

Amazingly, using this technique one needs only to analyse a sample of soil or water to identify the creatures that live in it. Sampling pondwater for its 'environmental DNA' is already becoming an accepted way for ecological consultants to confirm the presence of that scourge of British developers, the Great Crested Newt.

So will DNA bar-coding eventually make naturalists redundant? No, it will not. It may well take some of the more mechanical data collection activities away from the experienced naturalist's realm and make them achievable by anybody, and for many naturalists this may mark the beginning of a much happier and more carefree era. Naturalists with identification skills will always be needed to assess abundance (including change), work out life histories and clarify ecological relationships, and interpret the wonders we perceive around us for others.

My personal hope is that it will merely take away one of the major causes of stress in what is otherwise one of the most rewarding pursuits imaginable.

Some Common Mosses. The natural world is full of amazing and wondrous organisms which escape general attention because they are so small. If one can learn to look more closely and 'tune down' to a completely different spatial scale, there are whole other worlds to explore, and the smaller you go, often the more extraordinary the creatures become. A hand lens, or even a microscope, are handy aids, the expense of which is abundantly repaid.

In this column I have mentioned insects in this regard on numerous occasions. In the plant world, a step down from the familiar 'higher plants' are the more primitive mosses and liverworts. These are the oldest of all land plants, whose relatives date back some 450 million years. As a group, mosses are known to everyone, but in terms of study, they are often neglected. This is a shame, because with a closer look they can be exquisitely, sometimes primaevally beautiful, and many common sorts are readily identified.

Mosses and liverworts can be found almost anywhere, and are a familiar sight on walls, roofs, tree trunks, lawns, rocks and soil, often in great profusion. Unlike higher plants they have no conducting tissue – tubes or vessels for transporting water or nutrients – and so the plants need to be small and at most only a few cells thick. This can make them wonderfully delicate and translucent, and they are sometimes quite colourful. They are especially attractive when wet.

Mosses don't produce flowers or seeds, but they do have fruiting bodies. In fact, their reproductive system constitutes a reversal of the normal order. The main body of a moss – the green, leafy shoot – is not the equivalent of leafy stems on a higher plant. In fact, it is equivalent to the tiny sexual parts of a conventional flower. Organs carried by the leafy parts of a moss produce the eggs and sperm. Splashes of rain or other moisture are needed to bring these together (hence the liking for damp places), and the product of successful fertilisation is the fruiting part of the moss – the 'sporophyte' – often comprising a fine stem with a capsule at its tip.

Mosses are unusual in that these two generations never physically separate. Instead, one lives upon the other, so the two look like different organs of the same plant. The hair stalk is called a 'seta', and the capsule at the tip contains the radial structures which we may loosely equate to the petals of a conventional flower. In fact, these tooth-like structures, collectively known as the 'peristome', are designed to open or close depending on the amount of moisture, to regulate the dispersal of spores.

Mosses may also reproduce vegetatively, and some produce little buds or detachable hairs – bulbils or gemmae – which can grow into whole new plants when broken off. The presence or position of these can often be used to identify the species.

For the botanist, studying mosses has advantages over other groups. Firstly, because most mosses thrive on moisture, winter can be when they are at their best.

Secondly, a moss picked and allowed to dry out does not lose its integrity, but may be brought miraculously back to its plump best when it is re-wetted. I have known a completely dried moss specimen from the 17th century brought back in this way, and identified perfectly well.

Thirdly, we in Britain have a much higher proportion of the world's mosses than we do of other plants. One reason for this is that the spores are so light and easily carried by air currents that there are few barriers to dispersal, and many mosses' distributions are limited only by available habitat. At most latitudes, only places which are extremely dry are notably poor in mosses. Needless to say, the wet west of Britain has more species than the east – indeed, Britain's Atlantic fringe is one of the best places for mosses in the world.

Mosses have been used as packaging material and for decoration and moisture retention in hanging baskets. Most importantly, peat, that resource so invaluable for both people and wildlife, is made primarily from moss – the sponge-like *Sphagnum* of moors and wet heaths.

In our area, look for the bright green carpets of Sandhill Screw-moss *Syntrichia ruralis* subsp. *ruraliformis* (pictured) on our sand dunes – it is at its most obvious in winter, and best after rain. A mass of Springy Turf-moss *Rhytidiadelphus squarrosus* grows through the grass on the frontage of

Humberston Church, and in many lawns. Mosses on the walls and roofs of our homes will no doubt include the frosted-looking Grey-cushioned Grimmia *Grimmia pulvinata*, the only slightly less hoary Wall Screw-moss *Tortula muralis*, or the neat, glossy, deep green cushions of Capillary Thread-moss *Bryum capillare*, among others. In garden plant pots or on earth made bare by fire, look for the exquisite swan-necked setae of Bonfire Moss *Funaria hygrometrica*. A little dark moss growing in cracks in pavement with tiny white tips, can only be the Silver Moss *Bryum argenteum*.

Sandhill Screw-moss (Syntrichia ruralis subsp. ruraliformis)

Colour Ringing. These days it is possible to attach relatively small satellite transmitters to birds to find out where they go. This has been most famously done with Cuckoos, and much of what is known about the routes they take on migration has been discovered this way.

Before such transmitters became small enough for the purpose, everything we knew about bird migration was from bird ringing – the attaching of lightweight rings to birds' legs. In fact ringing tells us much more than simply where birds end up. Nowadays, ringing is more often used to work out survival rates – how many young birds leave the nest and survive to become adults, and how many adults survive the pressures of breeding and migration. This is particularly important for species which are declining, as it tells us which stage of the life cycle is causing the problem.

If we, say, see Swallows in both the UK and South Africa, this tells us nothing except that Swallows live in both places. If we can ascertain that they are the same Swallow, this tells us very much more. This is what ringing achieves, although it is necessary to pick the bird up dead, or at least to re-trap it, in order to gain this information.

A better way of following a bird's progress is to give it a clear marking which can be seen in the field. This way multiple data points can be gathered without either trapping or disturbing the bird, or having to find it dead. You may occasionally see swans with neck rings, Red Kites with wing tags, or gulls daubed with dye, for this purpose. These relatively inelegant methods are unusual – the commonest way is by colour-ringing. This is when rings are placed on the legs of birds in unique colour combinations, or with letters/numbers which can be easily read from a distance.

It is obviously important that colour-ringing schemes communicate with each other to avoid duplication – the whole point about ring combinations is that they are unique. Luckily there is a central point where schemes are listed, which also allows field observers to find the appropriate project for the colour-ringed birds they have seen. It can be found at www.cr-birding.org.

There are literally hundreds of colour-ringing schemes in Europe, covering birds from the smallest to the largest. There are thirty or so schemes for Avocet alone. This means that colour-ringed birds are encountered relatively frequently in the wild. Nowadays, binoculars, telescopes and cameras have become so high quality that there is often no problem in recording the colour rings of wild birds. Sometimes the birds are so tame that their rings or numbers can be read with the naked eye.

It was colour-ringing which told us that a Black Stork (ring reading F05R) which died on migration near Madrid on 20 October 2015, was the same bird seen in Lincolnshire earlier in the year, featured and photographed in this very column.

One of the most famous colour-ringing schemes is that involving Icelandic-breeding Black-tailed Godwits — rare and elegant birds which inhabit the Humber Estuary, from Pyewipe westwards, in winter. In any decent flock, some birds will have coloured leg-rings which are quite easily recorded.

Nearly all gull species, especially the larger ones, have been the subject of colour-ringing schemes at some time, and gulls can be great travellers. This can make hunting through gull flocks for colour-ringed birds quite productive, and extremely useful to those running the schemes.

Our most familiar colour-ringed bird at the moment is Black-headed Gull J6N8 (pictured), which was ringed at a lake south-east of Oslo, Norway, in

June 2011. It is currently spending its third consecutive winter with us here in North East Lincolnshire, and can be seen regularly around the car park near the Buck Beck outfall, where it is relatively tame.

Recording colour-ringed birds is a rewarding way of making your birdwatching really count, and extremely valuable in helping discover vital information about our birdlife. Also, if you find a dead bird, remember to check it for a standard metal ring, and if present, please return it to the address stamped on it. Every record is important.

Black-headed Gull J6N8 has returned to Humberston several winters in a row. Photo: Chris Atkin

November 2017 update: J6N8 is now in its 5th consecutive winter at Cleethorpes, having been back to Norway in the meantime.

Fairy Rings. After rain in autumn and early winter is the time when fungi become most apparent. Of course fungi are always there – what we know as mushrooms and toadstools are merely the visible fruiting bodies of a much larger and far-reaching organism which lies beneath the substrate out of sight. This unseen body takes the form of a cotton wool-like 'mycelium', or mould. This mycelium is responsible for the essential task of breaking down dead or dying organic matter and recycling nutrients, with a little help from bacteria.

Fungi important to humankind include yeast, penicillin, mildew, dry rot, ringworm and of course, edible mushrooms. Fungi are so ubiquitous that it is said that if every trace of matter were removed from a woodland except its fungi, every detail of the wood would still be perfectly visible, like a grey mycelial ghost.

Anybody with a lawn knows that fungi can grow in rings. Even when the toadstools themselves are not present, these rings are given away by circles of lusher green grass. Sometimes the ring is doubled, with the inner one looking distinctly unhealthy or trampled, and in classic cases there is a third ring even within this, composed again of lush green grass.

For many years the reason for the formation of these rings was not known, and an extraordinary wealth of explanations developed. Moles, ants and lightning were all put forward as possible causes. Much more varied and interesting are the supernatural explanations and their accompanying superstitions, some of which are still observed by modern day children. Commonly, the 'trampled' part of the ring was attributed to the circular dances of fairies or other nocturnal sprites, giving them the common name of 'fairy rings'. This explanation has also given its name to the species of toadstool most likely to be seen growing in rings: *Marasmius oreades*, or the Fairy Ring Champignon.

It has long been known that the soil beneath the trampled part of the circle is 'mouldy', and herein lies a clue to the real answer. Like all fungi starting from a central point in a homogenous medium, the infection will spread out in a circle, dying off behind so a ring is formed. At its leading edge, the action of the growing fungus breaks down organic matter in the soil to produce ammonia, which is then converted into nitrates, fertilising the grass and causing the lush green outer ring. The unhealthy, 'trampled' ring within this is caused by the choking, toxic and water-repellent effect of the fungal mycelium at the peak of its passage. If there is an inner fertile strip, this is also caused by released nitrogen compounds, this time from bacterial decomposition of the newly killed-off grass.

Generally speaking, larger rings are older, and some very large ones in ancient grassland may be hundreds or even thousands of years old. Fairy rings are very hard indeed to remove from lawns, although why anyone should want to eliminate these fascinating natural occurrences is anybody's guess.

Lapwings. An iconic bird of open spaces which has been part of life in our area since time immemorial, is not doing very well.

The Lapwing draws attention to itself both in winter, by its huge flocks which seem to 'glitter' in flight, and in spring by its charismatic, noisy territorial displays. In the past, both adults and eggs were taken in huge numbers for food, although thankfully this is now a thing of the past. Despite these historical depredations, the Lapwing retained its status as a common bird until advances in the scale and efficiency of modern farming in the second half of the twentieth century forced it into decline. Today there are only a third of the Lapwings there were in 1975.

The Lapwing is still the commonest breeding wader in Britain, and one of very few wading birds with rounded wings, giving it a more languid-looking, 'flappier' flight than its relatives. At a distance it appears black and white, although with a close view its upperside glints with beautiful iridescent green, navy and magenta. The long, thin black crest is unique among British birds.

With so many cereal fields now autumn-sown, any large field still bare by the spring is almost guaranteed to invite the attention of breeding Lapwings. The display flights of the males, in which they bank steeply from side to side, tower and swoop until they almost brush the ground, are accompanied by loud, evocative calls – a spring sound known to everyone, at least subconsciously. Their nests, placed on open ground and defended vigorously, are easy to find, making their eggs simplicity itself to steal or prey upon. Farmers in the past, and even sometimes today, will stop the tractor, get out and remove a clutch of eggs from the vehicle's path to save them from being crushed, although the scale and technology of farming nowadays makes this impractical most of the time.

Lapwings need to lead their chicks into short, old, preferably wet grassland soon after hatching, and they will also breed directly in this habitat. An absence of this kind of grassland near to fields with enough bare soil in spring – and it is a juxtaposition getting harder and harder to find – can result in breeding failure. Sometimes Lapwings will improvise by nesting on man-made shallow wetlands, natural shingle, mineral workings or saltmarshes.

As early as late May, small post-breeding flocks of Lapwings will start to gather. Later in the year Lapwings, which dislike extreme cold, will disperse in large numbers ahead of bad weather. Nearly all of Europe's Lapwings move to the continent's milder fringes in winter, with fully half to three quarters of them wintering in Britain. Continental Lapwings join our own birds to form the huge gatherings we see on farmland and along our 'soft' coasts in winter. Typically, Lapwings will join together with their more streamlined relative the Golden Plover, to form some truly impressive flocks.

Being so closely associated with humans, the Lapwing has accumulated a long list of common, vernacular, or country names. 'Green Plover' is one, and also 'Pyewipe', a name very familiar to all of us in these parts. Evidently these birds must once have occurred in some numbers, and no doubt bred, on that short piece of once-wild coastline west of Grimsby Docks which bears its name. Large numbers in winter can still be seen on coastal fields further west along the Humber bank, as well as to the south of us at Tetney and North Cotes.

Another vernacular name was 'Peewit', sometimes 'Pewit', 'Pewet' or 'Puet'. There was a 'Pewet Inn', now long lost, by the shore to the west of Grimsby – its location now subsumed beneath Humber bank concrete.

As an aside, there is an old Grimsby saying: "eggin' back o' Doig's", which, in answer to an inquiry about someone's whereabouts, means something like "mind your own business". "Eggin", of course, literally means collecting wild birds' eggs, and Doig's was a shipyard on the west side of the Royal Dock. Some will tell you that this saying was meant to be deliberately nonsensical and evasive, there being obviously no birds to "egg" behind Doig's. This theory might well be true but seems strange, especially with that area being named after a bird. Even today with Pyewipe's smothering of industry there are internationally important numbers of birds on the flats there. Another theory is that the "eggin'" referred to the easy-to-find eggs of the charismatic wader which gave that area its name.

Fin Whale. On the morning of Thursday 26th November 2015, we in Cleethorpes were visited by a very special creature, although not under the best of circumstances. At about 9am the coastguards were alerted to a dead whale that had washed ashore straight out from the resort. Although the best part of a kilometre from the sea wall, it could be discerned from the land as a white strip lying on the sand, on the far side of the distant ridge.

This animal was initially identified as an adult Minke Whale, the commonest whale species in the North Sea. However, it was plainly bigger than the couple of Minkes washed up at Horseshoe Point a few years back, and at ten metres long, this creature would have been a real whopper for that species.

In fact, it was only a baby – a juvenile Fin Whale. When fully grown, the Fin Whale is the second largest mammal on Earth, exceeded only by the giant Blue Whale, the largest animal ever to have lived. Fin Whales are faster swimmers than Blue Whales, sometimes achieving in the region of 25 mph, and they can dive to about 200m. Fin Whale calves are born at nearly seven metres long.

Fin Whales are distributed throughout the world's oceans, from sub-tropical to sub-polar regions. They are said to prefer coastal and shelf waters, where they feed on small fish and crustaceans. They have no teeth, but a sieve of 'baleen', protruding from the upper jaw. Large quantities of water and prey are taken in at a gulp, and then the mouth closed and water excluded through the baleen plates, leaving the food within the mouth of the whale.

Fin Whales are migratory, and although the routes and timings are complex, they can be broadly described as travelling from warmer areas in winter (where they breed) to colder, polar regions in summer (where they feed). They are seen relatively frequently in British waters on migration, although almost always to Britain's north and west, broadly from Shetland round to south-west Ireland.

Fin Whales communicate by a range of low, far-carrying vocalisations. While our ears are very poorly equipped to hear underwater, sound actually travels extremely well in water, and whales may hear each other from great distances. Unfortunately, all of the sounds made at sea by humans, such as ships' engines, military sonar and pile-driving for offshore rigs and turbines, are also extremely loud to a whale, and may disrupt their normal behavior. Large whales are also susceptible to the accumulation of man-made toxins in their tissues, and these may be passed from mother to calf through milk. Other threats include collisions with boats and entanglement in fishing gear.

Because of their large size, Fin Whales were also a target for commercial whaling, with huge numbers being killed up until the middle of the twentieth century. Whaling was banned in 1986, although Iceland is still to this day permitted a small, and controversial, quota. Numbers are recovering a little, but no-one knows if complete recovery is even possible.

This was the third Fin Whale to be washed up on North Sea coasts in 2015, the other two being at Harwich in Essex, and Thanet in Kent. Nevertheless, a Fin Whale in the North Sea is still a very unusual occurrence. Fin Whale calves wean from their mothers at high latitudes during the summer, and it is likely that the youngster on its southward migration entered the North Sea by accident and was 'funneled' into unsuitable waters – a fate which has befallen many whales entering the North Sea over the years. The North Sea is generally not deep enough for Fin Whales, and does not contain enough food for them to survive. Indeed, our young whale did look extremely thin, and was almost certainly very undernourished.

Young Fin Whale washed up on Cleethorpes Beach

Dead whales are technically the property of the crown, although disposal is the responsibility of the owner of the beach, in this case the Council. Disposal of such large decomposing animals can be an expensive and complicated business, so it must have been a big relief when the whale was carried away on the next high tide.

Otters. Otters have returned to North East Lincolnshire after nearly facing extinction in England only 35 years ago.

Otters have been in Britain for a very long time, with fossilised bones going back about three million years. From the twelfth century until the second half of the twentieth, Otters were common enough to be hunted, in what was widely considered as the cruelest of all blood sports. Hunting was finally outlawed in 1978, despite the hunting lobby fighting ferociously to resist the ban.

Hunting was only part of the reason for the Otter's catastrophic decline in the twentieth century, with most of the blame laid at the door of water pollution from pesticides such as organochlorines and PCBs. Habitat loss also played a part, as rivers were straightened and riverside habitats simplified. When I was a child in the 1970s, there was no chance at all of seeing an Otter in Lincolnshire, their range by then having become restricted to south-west

England, Wales, north-west Scotland and the Isle of Man. In the latter two places they are as much an animal of the seaside as of rivers, and despite many trips to the Scottish coast to see them, I failed to locate them there either.

Otters are perfectly designed aquatic hunters, with their flat, graceful bodies, webbed feet and strong tail for steering. Their nostrils, eyes and ears are all aligned so they can be held out of the water together, and a full set of carnivore's teeth ensure successful hunting. Although they prefer fish, they are the most omnivorous of all Britain's mammals. Breeding can occur at any time, and litters are usually of two or three, but up to five, pups.

Otters have a long history of domestication, never more perfectly described than in Gavin Maxwell's *Ring of Bright Water*. Henry Williamson's *Tarka the Otter* also went a long way to popularising these fascinating creatures.

By the turn of the millennium, bans on harmful pesticides, cleaner rivers and full protection under the law meant that the Otter's revival was well underway. By 2011 the Otter had returned to every British county, with Kent being the last to be recolonised.

In our part of the world, Otters have now been seen in all of our local watercourses, including Waithe Beck, the Louth Navigation Canal and the River Freshney, including its outfall in Grimsby's Alexandra Dock and Riverhead. Otters are still, however, extremely difficult to see as they are few in number and extremely shy. Their trails and signs, which are much easier to locate, include large, five-toed footprints, and distinctive droppings, or 'spraints'. These are black and tarry at first, drying grey and crumbly. Fish bones and scales can usually be seen, and their smell, sweet and oily, is not particularly unpleasant and completely diagnostic.

In more than four decades spent tracking down Britain's animals and plants, Otter spraints are the nearest I have come to the actual animal, and Otter remains by far the commonest species I have never seen.

Holly. For the rural communities of the past, midwinter would have been a bleak time, and it is no surprise that successive cultures have created festivals to give people some cheer around, or just after, the shortest day. Our modern Christmas celebrations have merely added new cultural layers to older, pre-existing midwinter festivals.

Essential to all these festivals is the custom of bringing evergreens into the house. The decorated Christmas tree is a relatively modern idea, the custom spreading here from Germany just a couple of hundred years ago. The type of tree used, always a conifer and most commonly a spruce of some kind, is invariably an introduced species, which may be a clue to the custom's lack of antiquity.

Much more ancient is the habit of bringing sprigs of native evergreens such as Mistletoe, Ivy and Holly indoors, to act as symbols of eternal life and fertility at this darkest time of the year. Further south in Europe, people would have replaced these species with plants such as Bay or Rosemary.

Very few people these days would bring Ivy into the house, although I'm not sure why the custom has faded. The other two species are still commonly used however, and sold, for the purpose of decorating houses at Christmas. Compared with the abundant mythology surrounding Mistletoe, the use of Holly is much more uncomplicated and seems to be based simply around its decorative properties, although the leaves and berries have been used to symbolise Jesus's crown of thorns, and blood, respectively.

Holly is a dioecious plant, meaning that the male and female parts occur on separate trees. Only female trees produce berries, and to do so they must occur not too far from a male tree so that insect pollination can take place in spring. So please don't be tempted to cut a Holly tree down because it doesn't bear fruit!

Both male and female Holly flowers are four-petalled and white, although the males may possibly be slightly yellowish and the females sometimes pinkish. Pollination is chiefly carried out by bees, although other small insects will also be seen at the flowers. The sex of a Holly plant cannot be ascertained until it starts flowering, usually at between four and twelve years old.

Among the numerous modern garden cultivars of Holly are several prickle-less, as well as many variegated forms. Because each is propagated vegetatively, an individual cultivar is either always male or always female. So remember, if garden varieties are your thing and you have no other Holly nearby, that you need more than one sort, including one of each sex, if you want berries. Confusingly, the cultivar 'Golden King' is a female, whereas 'Silver Queen' and 'Golden Queen' are both male. 'Golden Milkboy' is male as you might expect, while 'Silver Milkboy' is given different genders in different literature. Most are named more sensibly, and a very few varieties, even more helpfully, are self-fertile.

The prickles along the edge of a Holly's leaf point alternately upwards and downwards for maximum protection, although leaves near the top of a mature tree may be less well defended. Despite this, and quite surprisingly, most domestic animals and wild deer will readily eat Holly, especially the younger shoots which sprout back after the tree is cut. Holly leaves are relatively nutrient-rich and available when other leaves have fallen – indeed, consumption by domestic animals is the traditional fate of Christmas Holly discarded after twelfth night.

Holly is a very common British native species, occurring in hedgerows and woodlands. It tolerates shade, and often forms thickets which give good protection to birds and other animals. It readily pops up from bird-dispersed seed. Conspicuous Holly trees may be used as landmarks and sightlines by farmers and landowners, often being retained for this purpose when surrounding vegetation is cut or removed. The berries are an important resource for winter birds, and the foliage is the foodplant of the Holly Blue butterfly caterpillar's first of two annual generations.

So go out and collect some Holly this Christmas, and reclaim the connection between the festival and the lull in the year's natural rhythm which it is designed to alleviate. When it's all over, a New Year's resolution may be to spend more time outside among trees and other wildlife, especially in winter when the temptation to go out is weakest.

Robins. The Robin is the undisputed bird of Christmas. The association became firmly fixed in the 1860s when the habit of sending Christmas cards became commonplace. In Victorian times, anyone in an occupation whose uniform was bright red might acquire the nickname 'Robin', especially in the armed forces. Postal workers were among those public servants who wore red, and the earliest Christmas cards would often depict a Robin carrying an envelope, to indicate the connection with the postal service.

However, the Robin's association with midwinter and Yuletide far pre-dates the Victorians. There are many reasons why this might be so.

Firstly, the Robin provides a splash of colour at the darkest time of year. Its breast is not so much red as dark orange, and both male and female share this feature. The Robin's round head and upright stance, as well as its large, dark eye, make the species intuitively likeable to humans.

This is helped considerably by the fact that Robins are so tame. Before people came along, Robins were birds of woodland, where they would follow around large herbivores such as Wild Boar, picking up the invertebrates they turned up by their digging. On the Continent Robins are still, to this day, relatively shy woodland birds, and continue to glean their food in this timeless way. In modern Britain most of our woodland megafauna has now gone, and instead the Robin will attend closely as people turn over soil in their gardens. In doing this they may become extremely tame, and they can be coaxed relatively easily to feed from a gardener's hand.

The most obvious winter association comes in the fact that the Robin is the only bird which sings all year round. In fact there is a very short period in midsummer when Robins may fall silent, while they undergo the energetically-expensive process of moult. But as we move into autumn, Robins, and unusually it is both males and females who sing, will strike up again, remaining vocal on and off throughout the winter. The Robin's song is thin and wistful, with complex, fluid, tapering phrases. It is a song known, even if only subconsciously, by everyone.

Not only can the Robin's song be heard throughout the winter, but they may also sing at night, especially so since the advent of street lighting. Some believe that the Nightingale which supposedly sang in Berkeley Square was most probably a Robin.

The reason for the Robin's year-round singing is its propensity for extreme territorial aggression. You will hardly ever see two Robins together, and if you do, they will probably be male and female. Two males forced together, or disputing ownership of a piece of ground, will fight viciously. Robins have been known to kill members of their own and other species in territorial disputes.

In the spring and summer the Robin's song is somewhat richer than in winter, although it is more easily lost among the other birdsong. Robins will famously nest in any sort of cavity, including in man-made objects. They will readily take to open-fronted nestboxes, and Robin is one of only three species of bird to have nested in my tiny Chartdale garden (the other two are Blackbird and Collared Dove).

The Robin has always been unofficially Britain's favourite bird. This position was formalised in 2015 when nearly a quarter of a million people voted for a national bird for Britain, with voting finishing on the day of the general election. Robin scored a massive victory, gaining nearly three times as many votes as either second or third placed Barn Owl and Blackbird.

This popularity is probably partly based on a notion that our Robins are sedentary birds. In fact, many of our breeding Robins move south when it turns cold, while many of the birds we see here in winter may be immigrants from Germany, Poland or Scandinavia. Evidence for this immigration can be easily witnessed at dawn during easterly winds and rain in autumn, when coastal bushes may be littered with exhausted Robins, fresh in from the sea.

Godwits. Of all the migratory wading birds to be seen on the beaches and mud flats of the Humber estuary, the most elegant are the godwits. We have two species here – the Bar tailed Godwit and the Black-tailed Godwit, although they are sufficiently different that you should never have to resort to looking at the tails to separate the two.

Godwits are tall, graceful birds with long legs and bills. The straightness of the bill quickly separates a godwit from the larger Curlew or its relative the Whimbrel. Similarly, the long legs separate godwits from equally long-billed Snipe, which in addition does not usually occupy the same open beach habitats.

By far the commonest godwit on the beach at Cleethorpes is the Bar-tailed Godwit, which can be seen in good numbers at all times of year except midsummer. On the highest tides, impressive flocks of many hundred Bar-tailed Godwits may congregate at Cleethorpes, on the sandy ridge opposite the Leisure Centre. Just after their arrival back from their northern breeding grounds at the end of the summer many male Bar-tailed Godwits will still be sporting their rich red breeding plumage, making flocks of this species a very handsome sight. Our birds will have flown here from breeding grounds in Arctic Scandinavia and western Russia.

Our other godwit species, the Black-tailed Godwit, is an even more striking bird, longer-legged still, with bold black-and-white patterning on its wings in flight. Although this is technically a British breeding species, 'our' handful of Black-tailed Godwits all migrate to southern Europe or north Africa in the winter. However, at the same time, much of the Icelandic-breeding population of this species decamp to Britain, where they are faithful to a relatively small number of wintering sites, one of which is the south bank of the Humber.

Black-tailed Godwits are much less common on the sand at Cleethorpes than their slightly smaller relatives. However, every year from late summer onwards a couple of thousand of these handsome birds occupy the extensive, muddy flats, coastal fields and lagoons between Pyewipe and Killingholme. This number may as much as double at autumn migration time, with birds heading further afield passing through. Unfortunately, this internationally important population currently finds itself 'in the way' of the proposed Able Marine Energy Park at Killingholme. For this reason, there is a plan to create new habitat for these birds on the Yorkshire side of the river – what is known in the jargon as 'mitigation'.

One understands that the Yorkshire farmer involved isn't happy, but one suspects that little will stop the project now. Mitigation is generally a hit-and miss process, which nobody is ever sure will work. If it does not, this wintering population will lose a big slab of essential habitat, and the consequences of this are unknown. If it does work, the birds will be ok but Lincolnshire will lose part of a rare and special wildlife spectacle to the 'other side'.

The next time someone tells you that the needs of nature and the needs of people have to 'find a balance', do bear in mind how readily these birds were brushed aside when jobs were at stake.

The Twelve Days of Christmas. Our own English, or Grey, Partridge will never be found in a pear, or any other, tree. Nevertheless, this remains one of many enduring images of our British wildlife to be found in the Christmas tradition. Indeed, it might be noted that in the song 'The Twelve Days of Christmas', the gifts 'my true love gave to me' on each of the first seven days are all birds, except for "five gold rings", and even that, some think, may refer to Goldfinches, an old name for which is 'Goldspink'.

The species given as gifts on the first and second days of Christmas are two of the most severely declined birds in the whole of Europe, although so divorced from nature are we these days that even at Christmas, this irony seems seldom even to register.

Agricultural intensification is the reason for the decline of the lovely Grey Partridge. All schemes to bring numbers back up have so far failed. They can still be seen in our area, especially on the coastal fields south of the town, although they are very much less common than they were.

The commoner, introduced Red-legged Partridge is only slightly more likely to sit in a tree, but would look quite ill-at-ease there. In fact, the 'pear tree' reference can be explained by the fact that The Twelve Days of Christmas originates from a group of older French songs, whose verses accumulate in the same way as ours, and in which the gift on the first day is also a Partridge. The French for partridge is 'perdrix', whose similarity (using one's best French accent), to 'pear tree' cannot, surely, be a coincidence.

At Christmas, two Turtle Doves should be far away in West Africa, unless something has gone wrong. For the first time, tiny transmitters have been fitted to Turtle Doves to plot their migration routes, in at attempt to get to the bottom of their catastrophic decline in the UK – 96% since 1970. This rate of decline, also mirrored elsewhere in Europe, puts the Turtle Dove in serious danger of global extinction. A shortage of weed seeds on farmland in the breeding season and hunting pressure on migration are thought to be two of the main reasons for the losses, although there could be others. This year, 2016, was the first year ever that I didn't see a single one in Lincolnshire, although I understand a few were around.

Hens, French or otherwise, are too delicious ever to be allowed to go extinct, although the conditions in which they're kept aren't always as great as they could be. Modern hens are descendants of the Red Jungle Fowl of Asia.

'Calling birds', of which the song contains four, is thought actually to be a modern mis-hearing of 'colly birds', 'colly' being an old word for 'black'. It is true that Blackbirds are at their most abundant with us in midwinter, with numbers considerably swelled by birds from the continent escaping the cold.

Geese are, of course, not a-laying in December, but numbers generally are on the up, both in the wild and in non-migratory, feral populations such as that around our own Boating Lake.

Now is also the time to see our rarer swans, which a-swim on day seven of the song. Our common resident swan is the Mute Swan – one of our most familiar, as well as largest and heaviest flying birds. But there are two other sorts to look out for in winter, which can be told by their straight-edged yellow, not knobbed orange bills. Of the two, the Whooper Swan (pronounced 'hooper') is the most regular here. Breeding in Iceland, Whooper Swans migrate to traditional wintering grounds across the UK, arriving usually in October and November. A few individuals will however break away and spend time in other places – the middle of open fields anywhere along the coast are a good place to see them in our area, so be sure to check swans in fields or flying over the coast for the telltale yellow bills. At one point this autumn, four Whoopers, sadly not seven, swam in a creek on Humberston beach. The smaller Bewick's Swan has less yellow on its bill and is a much less regular visitor, but occurs here from time to time.

Latin Names. Every species of living thing has a scientific, usually Latin, name. While birdwatchers, butterfly and moth enthusiasts can probably get away without ever using them, every other type of naturalist should least have a stab at them if they want to make themselves understood.

I have heard many people say that the scientific names put them off – they are unpronounceable and difficult to learn. I can't agree with this; if you can cope with '*Tyrannosaurus*' and '*Chrysanthemum*', you can cope with anything. Don't worry about pronouncing Latin names correctly; nobody does, even the experts. You can gain some credibility though, by remembering that an 'e' at the end is usually enunciated, like 'Penelope'. Sometimes the Latin and English are the same, like 'Dahlia', and 'Rhododendron'.

English names, while superficially easier to learn, are often confusing, can vary greatly from place to place, and are incomprehensible to foreigners. The common *Arum maculatum* of North East Lincolnshire woodlands has more than 150 recorded English names; you may know it as Lords and Ladies, Jack-in-the-Pulpit, or Cuckoo Pint. By contrast, scientific names are unique, internationally consistent, and form a system based on a hierarchy of relationships with other species. This means that the more names are learned, the more the system comes 'into focus', and the easier additional species become to remember – a kind of virtuous circle. It is often easy to place an unknown species into its Latin family or genus straight away, without having a clue as to its English name.

Although Latin is the commonest language for scientific names, a very high proportion are actually Greek (like '*Anemone*', or '*Daphne*'), or from other languages. *Cortaderia*, the giant Pampas Grass of garden lawns and municipal beds, is from Portugese. *Coffea* (Coffee) is Arabic, *Jasminum* (Jasmine) Persian and 'mays' (*Zea mays*: Maize) is American Indian. I only know of one 'Latin' name which is from our own language – the rare resin-scented Bog Myrtle, *Myrica gale*. 'Gale' is straight from English – 'Sweet Gale' is an old name for the plant.

This lovely aromatic shrub has never been officially recorded from North East Lincolnshire, but I like to think it may once have occurred in its natural habitat amongst the wet, scented, peaty riches of the original Freshney Bog, before it was sadly drained nearly a hundred years ago.

If you discover a species new to science you get to give it your own scientific name, and this is every naturalist's dream. Unfortunately it is extremely bad form to name a new species after yourself. It is far better that your best friend discovers it; they are then free to name it after you.

Mistletoe. Wild plants associated with Christmas include Holly and Ivy, and of course the various non-native conifers used as Christmas trees. But up there among the botanical icons of Christmas is that unusual plant, Mistletoe.

Mistletoe is easiest to see in winter. It is partly parasitic, photosynthesising for itself but also taking water and minerals from its host tree. This allows it to have the apparently supernatural properties of being able to live a healthy life without roots, way above the ground, and remain green throughout the year.

For this reason Mistletoe has been revered by herbalists for hundreds of years, and has a prominent role in European mythology, legends and customs. Although somewhat poisonous, these days there is some evidence that Mistletoe, taken as a herb, may have sedative and anti-tumour properties. Like other evergreens it is traditionally brought inside the house in midwinter, although superstition meant that it was banned from some churches. The white berries held between splayed leaves make it an obvious fertility symbol, and in old Scandinavian folk tales, Mistletoe has been used to represent peace and love. These properties in combination have led Mistletoe to its role in the Christmas tradition today.

Mistletoe is spread primarily by birds, including two in particular, the Blackcap and the Mistle Thrush, the latter almost certainly named after it. The berries of Mistletoe are extremely sticky, and in the process of wiping excess fruit off their bills, these two birds can inadvertently glue the contained seed into crevices in the soft bark of trees. Here it may start to grow by putting out a sort of shallow root called a 'hastorium', which penetrates the wood of the host tree. Sometimes the seeds will pass through the gut of a Mistle Thrush, still sticky, and cling to twigs after being ejected, with the same result. Mistle Thrushes have always been common, but there is a suggestion that the huge increase in numbers of wintering Blackcaps in the UK is promoting a general increase in Mistletoe in the wild.

It is just as easy for humans to propagate Mistletoe, simply by squashing the seed-containing berries into crevices in the branches of suitable trees. In Britain, Mistletoe is recorded growing on hundreds of different host tree species. However, it has clear preferences, with Apple the commonest host, probably followed by Lime and Poplar.

The centre of the British distribution of Mistletoe is in south-west England and the Welsh borders. Mistletoe likes low altitudes, warm, damp summers and cold winters, and no-one is really sure whether climatic conditions or a liking for that area's abundant apple orchards is responsible for this pronounced regional stronghold.

Although in its core areas local Mistletoe may be sold in markets at Christmas, most of the material we buy in Britain is harvested in northern

France – from the Poplars of Picardy and the apple orchards of Normandy and Brittany.

The small green flowers of Mistletoe, produced early in the year, are pollinated by small flying insects. Very few creatures are to be found on the foliage itself – in fact only six are known to use it: one moth (the Mistletoe Marble Moth), a weevil and four bugs. Two of these species were only discovered since the year 2000, and two of the bugs are intimately connected, with one living by feeding on the other.

In our area, Mistletoe is not particularly common, although it does occur here and there. I know of only two places in Cleethorpes where it can be found, in gardens on Bradford Avenue and Trinity Road. Waltham and Scartho (especially Waltham Road) are comparative strongholds, although one prominent Mistletoe-containing tree on Barnoldby Road, Waltham was cut down in recent years. A good clump, easy to find, occurs on False Acacia in Waltham churchyard.

If you find Mistletoe, remember to record the species of host tree, and possibly look for its associated herbivores. If you have an apple, or any other tree in your garden, you could try to start off a Mistletoe plant from seed.

A Changing Countryside. It is possible to teach yourself quite a lot about natural history in a fairly short time if you put your mind to it. Getting a feel for the finer points of habitat, and understanding patterns of abundance so you can apply balance of probability to identification problems, takes a little longer.

But one thing which only a lifetime spent watching nature can make you appreciate, and possibly not even then, is the amount and speed that things change. What was once grassland is now woodland, and wasteland, housing. Species come and go. We now have many species in North East Lincolnshire which we never had when I was a child – birds of prey such as Buzzard, Sparrowhawk and Hobby, and Little Egrets at the coast. The insect fauna is richer now, as a warming climate has resulted in the northward expansion of many charismatic southern species.

But there have been losses too – nowadays people can scarcely believe that the extremely rare Red-backed Shrike nested in Weelsby Woods as recently as 1978, alongside Grasshopper Warbler and Lesser Spotted Woodpecker, now also gone. Willow Tit, Turtle Dove and Spotted Flycatcher, once very common, are now special birds.

On balance, and very depressingly, the clear tendency among our wildlife is still inexorably downwards. Of course the baseline, to which each person refers, is their own youth. But more change took place before we were born than ever did after, and we must consider the possibility that things are even worse than they look. This has been called 'shifting baseline syndrome'.

Within my lifetime, the types of problem have changed. In the 1970s it was direct habitat destruction – hedgerow removal, pond infilling and the ploughing-out of old grassland. Some fairly unpleasant chemicals were thrown onto farmland, which caused extinctions along the food chain. People talked a lot about 'acid rain'.

Nowadays we have a more enlightened attitude to existing habitats of value, and tend to try to protect them from direct harm. They still, however, tend to exist only as 'islands' within farmland which is increasingly sterile. A high proportion of our more valued wild species now exist only as relicts, effectively trapped in small patches of habitat, unable to go anywhere, just waiting for a chance event to wipe them out. It may take a year, maybe ten, maybe a hundred, but it can only go one way. It is a process we see all the time.

Ironically, our lowland landscape now comprises farmland habitats which are managed too intensively, and semi-natural ones that aren't managed intensively enough. Farming is now a large-scale, clean, efficient industry, while our old woodlands are no longer coppiced, or flower-rich grasslands grazed or cut for hay.

One of the very biggest problems in today's countryside is excessive fertility. Find somewhere high where you can get a good view of the landscape – all those fresh greens are caused by fertility, mostly from artificial nitrogen and phosphorus-based inputs. Phosphorus, especially, causes enrichment – eutrophication – of waterbodies. This fertility has spread into the hedge bottoms and roadsides, where it favours a few aggressive weeds – you can name them: Nettle, Bramble, Cow Parsley, Hogweed, Bracken, Cleavers and a suite of coarse, aggressive grasses – at the expense of a richer, more diminutive, more stress-tolerant flora. Indeed, any habitat nowadays not dominated by these few 'bullies' is almost automatically given a conservation priority.

Incredibly, even these places are not safe from excess fertility, as nitrogen deposition, from agriculture, transport and industrial emissions, descends out of the very air itself.

Pesticides on farmland have ensured that the number and biomass of insects is now drastically reduced from former times. This has effects across habitat boundaries, and may have contributed, for example, to decreased numbers of Swallows and martins, Swifts and bats, among many others.

The spread of alien species is another concern, as introduced animals and plants affect the functioning of natural ecosystems. In our area, Harlequin Ladybird, Muntjac deer and the dreaded Japanese Knotweed are three which spring immediately to mind.

And lastly, global warming is already causing distributional changes in our wildlife. This might not have been such a problem if species could simply move northwards (or uphill) in accordance with the climate, but because of the fragmentation of semi-natural habitats, mostly they cannot.

To reverse the downward trend will need even more effort than we're putting in now. A rigidly protected, clean, joined-up green infrastructure is a prerequisite for any recovery. That is, if we can get anyone interested enough to create such a thing. Unfortunately, we tend to become locked into the vicious circle that the less wildlife there is, the less opportunity for inspiration there is, so the less we bother protecting the wildlife.

Bitterns. In the days when the lowlands of England contained thousands of square miles of inaccessible glittering morass only inhabited by birds and fish, that shy brown heron-relative the Bittern was relatively common. In such places it was often taken by locals for the table or killed in numbers and sent to market. When its eerie 'booming' call was heard from the unseen depths of the marshes, local people generally took this as an omen of bad luck.

Eventually, a protracted decline through extensive wetland drainage and persecution led to the last British breeding attempt in 1886, and from that date the Bittern was absent as a breeding bird until 1911. After something of a renaissance in the 1950s, it again declined, and in the 1980s and 1990s the Bittern was again confined to only a handful of sites.

The Bittern was now perfectly placed to act as a flagship for the whole of bird conservation in Britain. It had all the attributes – it was large, subtly beautiful and very rare. It was the shyest of all British birds, making any sort of sighting into a real occasion. When threatened, Bitterns tend to adopt extravagant poses, umbrella-like with wings half spread, or with bill pointing directly skywards, making the patterned plumage blend perfectly with the surrounding reeds. The amazing booming of males in spring is one of the strangest, most far-carrying and lowest-pitched sounds made by any bird.

Lastly, Bitterns are strongly faithful to an extremely valuable habitat, such that the conservation of Bitterns also helps other wetland wildlife. The Bittern became a one-bird fundraising machine for the RSPB, and much good conservation work has rested on the popularity of this species.

In 1979, the EU Birds Directive stipulated that Britain must do what it could to restore its Bittern populations. This it did by designating 'Special Protection Areas' for the species, one of which is the Humber Estuary.

The Bittern's habitat is extensive mosaic of reedbed and open water, containing good populations of fish on which it can feed. The expansive wetlands of the East Anglian coasts and Broads are strongholds, as are the Somerset Levels, parts of south Wales, the Humber and Leighton Moss in Lancashire. In recent years, huge inland wetlands in Suffolk and Cambridgeshire have also been created which, it is hoped, will provide refugia for Bitterns in the event that their coastal reedbed homes are degraded by sea level rise.

All this good work has led to 2014 being a record year for breeding Bitterns in the UK, with 140 booming males. This is more than in any other year in recent times.

Bittern numbers are augmented in winter by migration from the near continent. Immigrant Bitterns tend to be slightly less tied to huge reedbeds and may be seen in more modest wetland areas, and on occasions they have even been flushed from the reedier parts of Cleethorpes Country Park. Their local stronghold, however, remains the reedbeds of the old clay pits at Barton upon Humber, where they now breed again.

Seeing a Bittern involves a great deal of patience. By watching large reedbeds, especially in winter, one can sometimes see Bitterns making short flights, especially to their roosting places towards dusk. All sightings of Bitterns on the ground are a matter of good fortune. For the best chance, try the Far Ings Nature Reserve, just west of the Humber Bridge at Barton.

Environment and Politics. I have heard it said by developers who are prevented from doing whatever they want by environmental legislation, that such restrictions constitute an unnecessary burden on 'progress'. I have even heard people, when they get really frustrated, ask what wildlife is even 'for'.

It is an easy question to answer. Everything we eat, most drugs and fuels, and many materials and fertilisers started off as wildlife. Wildlife is responsible for soil formation, nutrient cycling, the pollination of our crops, carbon sequestration, the purification of water, pest and disease control, and the very oxygen we breathe.

And none of this is to even mention the spiritual and health benefits of wildlife. It has been shown with very little doubt that proximity to nature aids recovery from illness, improves mental health, and reduces crime in cities. As a naturalist of 45 years, I do not know why these things would come as a surprise to anybody.

In fact, we have scarcely scratched the surface in the possible uses for the resources which abound in the natural world, especially now we have the technology to transfer genes from one organism to another. This means that many of the raw materials we will need for the *entire* future of the human race are living among us now, *as wildlife*.

So isn't the extent to which we neglect and degrade the natural world incredibly short-sighted?

In one of ecology's classic quotes, Aldo Leopold argued as early as 1949 that "to keep every cog and wheel is the first precaution of intelligent tinkering". We seem not to have learned this lesson in the 66 years since this was written, as wildlife has been declining ever since, and continues to suffer neglect and destruction at the hands of the economy's need to continually grow.

One of the biggest problems has been that in traditional economic models, services provided for free by the environment are given a value of zero – they are completely taken for granted, as though they were an endless and indestructible bounty which the business of economics can plunder without consequence. This, of course, is abundantly disproved.

Some ecologists have tried to combat this by attempting to calculate a monetary value for various 'ecosystem services'. They say that if we had to pay for them, the processes provided by the natural world would cost more each year than the value of all the rest of the world economy put together. Factoring in the destruction of our 'natural capital', they say, tells us the *true* cost of goods and services.

But this approach is fraught with danger. Firstly, the numbers are often guesses, and therefore readily manipulated. And anyway, how do you put a valuation on 'wonder'?

Furthermore, valuations encourage trade, such that, for example, ancient landscapes with their history, folklore and millennia of co-evolved species could be traded for larger quantities of meaningless and depauperate new habitat elsewhere. Such trade-offs are almost always hypothetical and spurious. The natural world simply has to be placed outside the system of trade – it is too important.

There have always been arguments about the relationship between economic growth and sustainability. Some think that 'ecosystems', as such, don't even exist. Such arguments have a bearing on how we treat the environment. Sadly, the environment cannot afford to become temporarily unfashionable – it will not be in the same state when we decide we need it after all.

Much of our environmental legislation comes from Europe, which seems to increase hostility towards it even further. Of course, nature knows no national boundaries, and priorities have to be set in an international context. So we should accept these rulings as being made in good faith, with a well-informed overview.

The purpose of most environmental legislation is actually not to impede economic progress, but to encourage it, but without damaging the life support system that holds it up. The logic is surely inarguable.

So to have more respect for the environment should really be on everybody's list of New Year's resolutions.

Big Cats. Each year there are literally thousands of reports of 'ABCs' – or 'alien big cats' – roaming the British countryside – far more, indeed, than there can possibly *be* such animals, given the paucity of other evidence. A stereotypical sighting would involve something like a panther or a puma, the size of a Labrador, with a long tail. They are often, but not always, said to be black.

That wild populations of some large species of feline should persist as some sort of relic from our ice-age fauna is implausible. So if any of these sighting are real, they must refer to released or escaped animals. People do keep big cats in captivity of course, and it would be amazing if the odd one didn't find its way, accidentally or deliberately, into the wild once in a while. Indeed, there are tales of people releasing pet 'big cats' when they become unmanageable, or after the Dangerous Wild Animals Act in 1976 made keeping such creatures abruptly illegal without a licence.

Some wild-roaming big cats have apparently been killed or captured, and so we are sure, or fairly sure, they were real. A Canadian Lynx was shot in Devon in 1903, its worn teeth indicating a long period of pre-captivity. A wild Puma was captured in Scotland in 1980 and placed in a zoo, where it appeared tame and was given the name 'Felicity'. A car hit and killed a Jungle Cat in Shropshire in 1989, and in 1991 a Eurasian Lynx apparently killed 15 sheep in Norfolk before being shot. Elsewhere, either an Ocelot or a Serval on the Isle of Wight, another Scottish Puma near Aviemore, a Caracal in Northern Ireland and another Eurasian Lynx, this time in Cricklewood, London all, we hear, had their bodies recovered, one way or another. In 2017, a Lynx named Lillith was disgracefully shot dead by Ceredigion Council after two weeks roaming wild, having previously escaped from a zoo in mid-Wales. Interestingly, not one of these cats was black.

Black, contrarily, seems to be the commonest colour of big cats whose identity remains enigmatic or disputed, including the now most famous of them all, the 'Beast of Bodmin'.

As for reports of big cats in our own area, the day in March 1991 when four Lions escaped from the Circus and roamed down Grimsby's Victoria Street chased by a clown, probably doesn't count. A mystery big cat known as the 'Grimsby Growler' captured the imagination for a while, although there is an unconfirmed report that it turned out to be a black greyhound, now taken in and living happily as a house pet in Wybers Wood. Similarly, in 2014, a temporarily liberated black dog called Dora, which could be seen on the coast between Cleethorpes and North Cotes any day of the week, was described as looking like a 'big cat' by many observers, which just goes to show that the identification of wild animals at a distance can be much harder than you think.

In 2017, a big cat sighting at Obthorpe, South Lincolnshire made the headlines, and included an accompanying very blurred photograph. Quotes by the observer such as "it can't be a horse, because horses can't climb logs, it can't be a cow because they can't either, so it doesn't leave many options other than a big cat", strangely didn't help the sighting's credentials, and also show how hard animals can be to describe. Similarly, and closer to home, the 'Brigsley Beast' in 2014 was said, rather vaguely, to be "walking in an unhurried way with ears on the side of its head". Of course these descriptions do not exclude the possibility of big cats – indeed the observers seemed pretty sure that that's what they were. But somehow they do not help to alleviate scepticism.

Expert analysis of footprints or DNA at the carcasses of livestock supposedly killed by well-observed big cats rarely turn up anything other than evidence of dogs or Foxes. But thousands of sightings continue to flood in, and some – just one or two – may be real.

There is a small army of people who claim to have seen a big cat here in Lincolnshire. In 2010, the introduction of the subject on Rod Collins's fascinating Lincolnshire-themed website unleashed a torrent of responses, with tales of big black cats coming in from Tattershall (x2), the A180 at Grimsby (x2), Humberside Airport, Immingham/Stallingborough, Cadwell Park, Osgodby, Burwell Church, Blyton, Tetney (x2), Holton-le-Clay, Caistor, North Scarle, Barrow upon Humber, Worlaby, Brandy Wharf (x2), Lincoln, Scopwick/Blankney, North Kelsey, Bigby, Mablethorpe, Misterton and Horncastle.

Reports of brown or pale 'big cats', or similar animals whose colour wasn't specified, came from the Yarborough Estate, North Ormsby/Wold Newton, Laceby, Saltfleetby, Hubbard's Hills, Nocton, Welbourn, Weelsby Woods, Bradley, Cherry Willingham, Laughton, North Somercotes, Grasby, Fulstow, North Thoresby, Grainthorpe, Humberston Fitties, Swallow and Alford. A creature described as a Lynx was commonly reported from the Laceby/Wybers Wood/Great Coates area of Grimsby, for a time.

I know professional ecologists for whom the identification of wildlife is part of their training, who swear to have seen a big cat in the wild in Britain. So what is the truth?

Some such records may just be mischief-making. Many more must be straightforward misidentifications, and surely refer to domestic cats or dogs. Such erroneous reports may create a ripple of hysteria, leading to multiple apparent sightings in the same general area.

Whatever one may privately believe, it is probably intellectual bad practice to discount every single one out of hand. Although undoubtedly rare, such animals are known to have occurred. Although genuine sightings are likely to be straightforward escapes or releases, can anyone say with absolute certainty that big cats have *never* bred in the wild in Britain? Probably not, although it is instructive that Christopher Lever's definitive, popular work on the UK's naturalised animals (a work which includes such obscure escapees as Mongolian Gerbil, Black-tailed Prairie Dog and Himalayan Porcupine), mentions big cats not once.

More interesting, I think, is what these sightings say about *us*. We know that our observers have seen *something,* and occasionally that will be a real escaped big cat. But it is worth noting that supernatural tales of large black animals are common in European cultures, where they have arisen multiple times. Black cat sightings seem now to be a modern version of – and to have supplanted –

formerly widespread tales of ghostly black dogs, especially common in the folklore of rural Britain and indeed Lincolnshire. Such dark, enigmatic animal apparitions seem to be something in which we still have a deep-seated need to believe.

We – that is, humankind – have lived alongside dangerous big cats in the wild for most of our evolution. It is today's cosseted existence, in which the thing we fear most from nature is the odd wasp, which is the more unusual state of affairs. The biggest big cats can be deadly, and so the fact that we find their potential proximity such cause for excitement is probably something etched into our deepest survival instinct. Our big cat sightings are no doubt a mixture of reality, mistakes, excitability and hoaxes in unknown proportions, the last three (if not all four) involving a deep and fascinating adventure into human psychology. This makes them, if anything, even more interesting than just any old sighting of a rare creature in the wild.

When we try to turn a black shape in a Lincolnshire field into an (unlikely) big cat, rather than a (likely) large domestic moggy, black dog or something else, we are re-igniting part of our deep subconscious long made redundant by modern life. Which is, after all, what we are doing when we have an emotional response to *any* aspect of nature, whether that be a big cat, a snake or a spider; or for that matter a sunlit woodland, a butterfly, a flower meadow, or anything else mentioned in this book. Nature is not just a luxury; it is part of us, and we are part of it. It is something we need in order to be complete human beings.

Bibliography

The newspaper column format did not require me to provide references at the time, and regrettably I did not have the foresight to record my sources as I went along. Thankfully, however, additional factual material for this book tended to come from relatively few places, and I can remember most of these.

I list here all those that I can recall or recover, as well as a few key publications to which I tended to return again and again. The three 'Britannicas', for example, provided a particularly rich seam.

In addition, I have used this bibliography to recommend some of the best ID field guides and a few publications of local interest, as well a good solid cross-section of classic natural history writing, trying to include 'a bit of everything'. Of course this aspect of the list is highly arbitrary and reflects my own personal leanings. I think it's fair to say, however, that there is a core of essential reading here which would constitute a fine start to anyone's British natural history library.

ACKROYD, C. (2009). *Natures Power and Spells: Landscape Change John Clare and Me*. Langford Press.

ALLEN, D.E. (1994). *The Naturalist in Britain*. Princeton University Press.

ASHER, J., WARREN, M., FOX, R., HARDING, P., JEFFCOATE, G., JEFFCOATE, S. (2001). *The Millennium Atlas of Butterflies in Britain and Ireland*. Oxford University Press.

ATHERTON, I., BOSANQUET, S., LAWLEY, M. (2010). *Mosses and Liverworts of Britain and Ireland – a field guide*. British Bryological Society.

BALMER, D., GILLINGS, S., CAFFREY, B., SWANN, B., DOWNIE, I., FULLER, R. (2013). *Bird Atlas 2007–11*. BTO Books.

BARNARD, P.C. (2011). *British Insects*. Royal Entomological Society.

BARNES, S. (2004). *How to be a Bad Birdwatcher*. Short Books.

BEE, L., OXFORD, G., SMITH, H. (2017). *Britain's Spiders*. WILDGuides.

BRITISH TRUST FOR ORNITHOLOGY *Bird Trends*. https://www.bto.org/about-birds/birdtrends/[insert year]

BRITISH WILDLIFE. Bi-monthly magazine (essential reading!) Part of NHBS Ltd, Totnes 01803 467166.

BROWN, A., GRICE, P. (2005). *Birds in England.* T & AD Poyser. (The Poyser mark is a badge of quality in ornithology).

BSBI HANDBOOKS http://bsbi.org/handbooks. (Essential ID for botanists).

CHAPMAN, J.L., REISS, M.J., (2003). *Ecology – Principles and Applications.* Cambridge University Press.

CHINERY, M. (1993). *Insects of Britain and Northern Europe (3rd ed.).* Collins.

CLEGG, J. (1967, 1986, 1992). *The Observer's Book of Pond Life.* Warne/Penguin. (Everyone should own at least one Observer!)

COCKER, M., MABEY, R. (2005). *Birds Britannica.* Chatto & Windus.

COLINVAUX, P. (1978). *Why Big, Fierce Animals are Rare.* Princeton Science Library.

COLLINS NEW NATURALIST SERIES http://www.newnaturalists.com/index.html. (All wonderful – and collectable. Take your pick. My recent favourites are *Alien Plants* by Clive Stace and Michael Crawley, and *Farming and Birds* by Ian Newton).

DARWIN, Charles (1st ed. 1859, facsimile 1964). *On The Origin of Species.*

DAVIES, N. (2015). *Cuckoo – Cheating by Nature.* Bloomsbury.

DICKSON, B., PINNEGAR, J.K. (2010) *Skipper Newson of Grimsby – the Sturgeon Hunter.* British Wildlife 21:6 416–9.

DUNSTAN, D.J., HODGSON, D.J. (2014) *Snails Home.* Physica Scripta 89:068002.

ELKINS, N. (1988). *Weather and Bird Behaviour.* T & AD Poyser.

FALK, S., LEWINGTON, R. (2015). *Field Guide to the Bees of Great Britain and Ireland.* Bloomsbury.

FIELD STUDIES COUNCIL. http://www.field-studies-council.org/publications.aspx. 'Aidgap' Guides, fold-out charts; wildlife packs; Royal Entomological Society Handbooks; some Biological Records Centre Atlases. (All invaluable stuff).

FISH, J.D., FISH, S. (2011). *A Student's Guide to the Seashore.* Cambridge University Press.

GIBBONS, E.J. (1975). *The Flora of Lincolnshire.* Lincolnshire Naturalists' Union.

GOOLEY, T. (2011). *The Natural Navigator.* Virgin Books.

GRIME, J.P. (1979). *Plant Strategies and Vegetation Processes.* John Wiley & Sons.

HARRIS, S., YALDEN, D.W., TROUGHTON, G. (2008). *Mammals of the British Isles: Handbook, 4th edition.* The Mammal Society.

HEMELRIJK, C.K., HILDENBRANDT, H. (2011) *Some Causes of the Variable Shape of Flocks of Birds.* PLoS ONE 6(8): e22479

LOVINS, L.H., LOVINS, A., HAWKEN, P. (1999). *Natural Capitalism.* Little,

Brown and Company.

HAYWARD, P.J., RYLAND, J.S. (2011). *Handbook of the Marine Fauna of North-West Europe.* Oxford University Press.

HOWSE, P. (2014). *Seeing Butterflies – New perspectives on colour, patterns and mimicry.* Papadakis.

INNS, H. (2011). *Britain's Reptiles and Amphibians.* WILDGuides.

JOHNSON, O., MORE, D. (2004). *Collins Tree Guide.* Collins.

JONES, N.V. (1988). *A Dynamic Estuary: Man, Nature and the Humber.* Hull University Press.

JUNIPER, T. (2013). *What Has Nature Ever Done for Us?* Synergetic Press.

KAM, J van de., ENS, B., PIERSMA, T., ZWARTS, L. (2004). *Shorebirds – an Illustrated Behavioural Ecology.* KNNV.

LEAHY, K. (1986) *A Dated Stone Axe-hammer from Cleethorpes, South Humberside.* Proc. Prehistoric Society 52:143–152.

De LEEUW, J., (2005) *Diving into the Icebox.* In: Drent, R., Tinbergen, J., Bakker, J., Piersma, T (2005) 'Seeking Nature's Limits'. KNNV.

LEOPOLD, Aldo (1949). *A Sand County Almanac.* Oxford University Press.

LEVER, C. (2009). *The Naturalized Animals of Britain and Ireland.* New Holland Publishers.

LEWINGTON, R. (2015). *Pocket Guide to the Butterflies of Great Britain and Ireland.* Bloomsbury.

LINCOLNSHIRE WILDLIFE TRUST. 'Find a reserve'. http://www.lincstrust.org.uk/wildlife/reserves

MABEY, R. (1996). *Flora Britannica.* Sinclair-Stevenson.

MABEY, R. (2005). *Nature Cure.* Chatto & Windus.

MANNING, C.J. (2016). *Atlas of the Terrestrial and Semi-aquatic mammals of Lincolnshire.* https://drive.google.com/file/d/0B_46EQMp4TyISEx1dGdqQnZMM2s/view

MARREN, P., MABEY, R. (2010). *Bugs Britannica.* Chatto & Windus.

MCCLINTOCK, D. (1966). *Companion to Flowers.* G. Bell & Sons.

MAXWELL, G., (1960). *Ring of Bright Water.* Penguin.

MEAD, C. (1997) *Pathetic bundles of feathers – birds and roads.* British Wildlife 8:4 229–32.

MEEK, W.R., BURMAN, P.J., NOWAKOWSKI, M., SPARKS, T.H., HILL, R.A., SWETNAM, R.D., BURMAN, N.J. (2009) *Habitat does not influence breeding performance in a long-term Barn Owl* (Tyto alba) *study.* Bird Study 56:369–380.

NATURAL HISTORY MUSEUM (Annually since 1992). *Wildlife Photographer of the Year.*

NATURALISTS' HANDBOOKS. Currently standing at 34 volumes. https://pelagicpublishing.com/collections/naturalists-handbooks?page=2. (All marvellous).

NEWTON, I. (2007). *The Migration Ecology of Birds.* Elsevier.

NOWAKOWSKI, M., PYWELL, R.F. (2016). *Habitat Creation and Management for Pollinators.* CEH Wallingford.

OGILVIE, M., WINTER, S. (1989) *Best Days with British Birds.* British Birds Ltd.

OLSEN, L-H. (2013). *Tracks and Signs.* Princeton University Press.

O'REILLY, C., ROSE, F. (2006). *The Wild Flower Key.* Frederick Warne.

OWEN, D. (1985). *What's in a Name - A look at the origins of plant and animal names.* BBC.

OWEN, J. (2010). *Wildlife of a Garden – a thirty-year stu*dy. Royal Horticultural Society.

OXFORD, G. (2011) *Large House Spiders in the British Isles, past present and future.* British Wildlife 23:1 34–41.

POLAND, J., CLEMENT, E. (2009). *The Vegetative Key to the British Flora.* BSBI.

PRESTON, C.D., PEARMAN, D.A., DINES, T.D. (2002). *New Atlas of the British and Irish Flora.* Oxford University Press.

RACKHAM, O. (1986). *The History of the Countryside.* J.M. Dent.

RATCLIFFE, D. (1977) *A Nature Conservation Review.* Cambridge University Press.

ROBINSON, D.N. (1989). *The Book of the Lincolnshire Seaside.* Baron Books.

ROSE, C. (2005). *In a Natural Light.* Langford.

ROSE, F. (1989). *Colour Identification Guide to the Grasses, Sedges, Rushes and Ferns of the British Isles and North-western Europe.* Viking.

ROY, H.E., BROWN, P.M.J. (illustrations by Richard Lewington) (in press) *Field Guide to Ladybirds of Britain and Ireland.* Bloomsbury.

RUSS, J. (2012). *British Bat Calls.* Pelagic Publishing.

SIMPSON, S.D., BLANCHARD, J., GENNER, M. (2013) *Impacts of climate change on fish.* MCCIP Science Review 2013:113–124.

SMALLSHIRE, D., SWASH, A. (2004). *Britain's Dragonflies.* WILDGuides.

SPARKS, T.H., ATKINSON, K., LEWTHWAITE, K. (2015) *Centenaries, masting and Speed.* British Wildlife 26:4 267–70.

SPARKS, T.H., ATKINSON, K., LEWTHWAITE, K. (2016) *The Speed of Spring, 2015.* British Wildlife 27:4 265–8.

SPARKS, T.H., JEFFREE, E.P., JEFFREE, C.E. (2000) *An examination of the relationship between flowering times and temperature at the national scale using long-term phenological records from the UK.* Int J.Biometeorol 44:85-7.

STACE, C.A. (2010). *New Flora of the British Isles.* Cambridge University Press.

STREETER, D., HART-DAVIES, C., HARDCASTLE, A., COLE, F., HARPER L. (2009). *Collins Flower Guide*. HarperCollins.

SUTHERLAND, W.J. (ed.) (2006) *Ecological Census Techniques*. Cambridge University Press.

SVENSSON, L., MULLARNEY, K., ZETTERSTROM, D. (2009). *Collins Bird Guide*. HarperCollins.

SWINNERTON, H.H., KENT, P.E. (1976). *The Geology of Lincolnshire*. Lincolnshire Naturalists' Union.

TARAYRE, M., SCHERMANN-LEGIONNET, A., BARAT, M., ATLAN, A. (2007) *Flowering phenology of Ulex europaeus: Ecological consequences of variation within and among populations*. Evol. Ecol. 21:395–409.

THOMAS, C.D. (2017). *Inheritors of the Earth: How Nature Is Thriving in an Age of Extinction*. Penguin.

TINBERGEN, N. (1958). *Curious Naturalists*. Basic Books.

VAUGHAN, J.G., GEISSLER, C.A. (1997). *The New Oxford Book of Food Plants*. Oxford University Press.

WALKER, K. J., SPARKS, T. H., SWETNAM, R. D. (2000) *The colonisation of tree and shrub species within a self-sown woodland: the Monks Wood Wilderness*. Aspects of Applied Biology 58:337–344.

WARING, P., TOWNSEND, M., LEWINGTON, R. (2017). *A Field Guide to the Moths of Great Britain and Ireland*. Bloomsbury.

WERNHAM, C., TOMS, M., MARCHANT, J., CLARK, J., SIRIWARDENA, G., BAILLIE, S. (2002). *The Migration Atlas*. T & AD Poyser/BTO.

WHITE, Gilbert (1789). *The Natural History of Selborne*. Now in 300+ editions.

WILSON, E.O. (1992). *The Diversity of Life*. QS.

WRIGHT, J. (2014). *The Naming of the Shrew: a curious history of Latin names*. Bloomsbury.

WRIGHT, S.L., ROWE, D., THOMPSON, R.C., GALLOWAY, T.S. (2013) *Microplastic ingestion decreases energy reserves in marine worms*. Current Biology 23:23 R1031–3.

XENO-CANTO. http://www.xeno-canto.org. Online library of bird songs and calls.

Index

Lightning Source UK Ltd.
Milton Keynes UK
UKHW02f0106140418
R1677000001B/R16770PG320851UKX1B/1/P

9 781911 589457